Adoption by Lesbians and Gay Men

To Jerli —

10/12/12

Adoption by Lesbians
and Gay Men

A New Dimension in Family Diversity

EDITED BY DAVID M. BRODZINSKY

ADAM PERTMAN

With best wishes —

[signature]

OXFORD
UNIVERSITY PRESS

OXFORD
UNIVERSITY PRESS

Oxford University Press, Inc., publishes works that further
Oxford University's objective of excellence
in research, scholarship, and education.

Oxford   New York
Auckland   Cape Town   Dar es Salaam   Hong Kong   Karachi
Kuala Lumpur   Madrid   Melbourne   Mexico City   Nairobi
New Delhi   Shanghai   Taipei   Toronto

With offices in
Argentina   Austria   Brazil   Chile   Czech Republic   France   Greece
Guatemala   Hungary   Italy   Japan   Poland   Portugal   Singapore
South Korea   Switzerland   Thailand   Turkey   Ukraine   Vietnam

Copyright © 2012 by Oxford University Press, Inc.

Published by Oxford University Press, Inc.
198 Madison Avenue, New York, New York 10016

Oxford is a registered trademark of Oxford University Press
Oxford University Press is a registered trademark of Oxford University Press, Inc.

Library of Congress Cataloging-in-Publication Data

Adoption by lesbians and gay men : a new dimension in family diversity /
edited by David M. Brodzinsky [and] Adam Pertman.
p. cm.
Includes bibliographical references and index.
ISBN 978-0-19-532260-6   1. Gay adoption—United States. 2. Gay parents—United States.
3. Lesbian mothers—United States. I. Brodzinsky, David. II. Pertman, Adam. III. Title.

HV875.72.U6A36 2012
362.734086'64—dc23   2011017400

9 8 7 6 5 4 3 2

Printed in the United States of America
on acid-free paper

This is a remarkable book, not just on one count but on four.

First, it is remarkable that it exists at all given that little more than three decades ago, even the idea of lesbian mothers raising their own biological children was viewed as an outrage or, at best, as something that should be prevented to save the children from lifelong psychological harm. As one prominent member of the British Parliament put it in 1978, "This evil must stop for the sake of the potential children and society, which both have enough problems without the extension of this horrific practice. Children have a right to be born into a natural family with a father and a mother. Anything less will cause lifelong deprivation of the most acute kind for the child." At that time, lesbians who fought to keep their children when they divorced lost their custody battle almost without exception—and, knowing the inevitable outcome, most did not even try.

Second, this book is remarkable because it talks not only about lesbian mothers raising children but also about gay fathers—and not just about raising their own children but about raising children whom they have adopted. Just a few years ago, the idea of gay men adopting children was unthinkable not only to the general public or adoption agencies, but also to gay men themselves—and still remains so to many people. Yet this serious, confident, and rigorous book discusses lesbian and gay adoption just as its precursors discussed adoption by heterosexual parents, and leaves the reader wondering, "Why all the fuss?"

Third, this book is remarkable because of the breadth and depth of knowledge it brings to its subject, and because of the quality of each and every one of the chapters. The topic of adoption by lesbians and gay men appeared to be one about which very little was known. Yet the editors, two of the most eminent figures in adoption in the world, have brought together key academics and practitioners in the field to produce a book showing that, in fact, rather a lot is already known about lesbian and gay adoption. As the authors themselves point out, there is much more to be learned about this new route to parenthood, not least about the experiences and outcomes for the children of lesbian and gay adopters. This book provides a solid foundation from which to progress and maps the areas in which more information is required. The authors are all experts in their different fields and, together, have created a state-of-the-art collection of chapters ranging from historical and legal aspects, to social and psychological considerations, to practice issues including the assessment of prospective adopters and postadoption support. Everything you might want to know about lesbian and gay adoption, and which it is possible to know at the present time, is to be found in this important book.

Finally, this book is remarkable because it demonstrates just how much scholarly thinking about the family, and, in particular, about the processes through which the family influences child development, has changed in recent decades. We have moved from a view of the family in which structure is what matters—the presence of a mom, a dad, and their biological children—to a greater understanding of the importance of the quality of family relationships for children's psychological well-being. Research on lesbian families, which shows no differences in psychological adjustment or gender development between children in lesbian and heterosexual families, demonstrates that parental sexual orientation does not have a direct effect on child development. It also suggests that the benefit of fathers to their children's development is not so much because of their maleness, but, instead, derives from their role as another parent in their children's lives—providing, of course, that their relationship with their children is a positive one. Moreover, research on adoption and, more recently, on children born through assisted reproduction—who, like adopted children, lack a genetic link to one or both parents—shows that genetic relatedness to parents is less important for children's psychological well-being than are positive family relationships. Adoption by gay men is breaking new ground in terms of family structures and, over time, will increase our understanding of the role of fathers in child development and address the more fundamental question, "Do children need mothers?"

This groundbreaking book is a testament to the importance of systematic study and empirical research and is essential reading for anyone connected to lesbian and gay adoption in any way.

Susan Golombok, Ph.D.
Centre for Family Research,
University of Cambridge.
7th January 2011.

Modern adoption practice in the United States, regulated by state law and carried out by professionally trained social workers, emerged in the first half of the twentieth century (Brodzinsky, Smith, & Brodzinsky, 1998; Esposito & Biafora, 2007; Pertman, 2011). During this period, adoption was viewed primarily as a means of finding a "suitable" family for children who would not be raised by their birth parents because of the stigma of out-of-wedlock pregnancy. What constituted a suitable family, however, often was quite narrowly defined by child welfare professionals. Guided more by personal values and stereotypes than by empirical data, social workers typically included primarily individuals who were white, married, younger than their mid-40s, infertile, free of disabilities, and with at least middle-class income.

The practice of "screening out" unsuitable adoption applicants continued unabated for decades. In fact, this practice began to change in earnest only in the early 1980s, when the number of children in foster care grew dramatically, with many who had been freed for adoption continuing to linger in care because of insufficient numbers of potential parents. Faced with this dilemma, child welfare professionals began to rethink their notions of what constituted acceptable mothers and fathers for waiting children. They were abetted in their task by two important trends: (1) the significant growth of nontraditional families in the second half of the twentieth century (e.g., children being raised by single parents, divorced parents, stepparents, grandparents, and parents of different ethnicities) and (2) the availability of developmental and family-based research showing that children can grow up emotionally healthy in a wide range of family types. In short, both demographic trends in the second half of the twentieth century and emerging social science data suggested that the concept of "suitable family" should be expanded.

In response to this new information, as well as to the burgeoning numbers of children lingering in foster care, adoption agency policy and practice reversed course, moving in the direction of "screening in" as many different varieties of parental applicants as possible (Brodzinsky et al., 1998). For example, public agencies eliminated income criteria for adoptive parents, thereby allowing working-class and lower-income families to adopt children. In many cases, these adoptions were (and continue to be) supported by financial and medical subsidies because of the children's special health, psychological, and educational needs. In addition, foster parents, once precluded from adopting, gradually began to be viewed as an invaluable resource for children needing permanency. Today, in fact, children adopted from the child welfare system are more likely to be adopted by their foster parents—often minority group members—than by another group of individuals (U.S. Children's Bureau, 2008). Other changes in policy and practice have led to increases in adoptions by single adults, unmarried couples, fertile individuals and couples, older adults, people with disabilities–and, in arguably the most remarkable evolution (or revolution) over the past few decades, they have resulted in a fast-growing number of adoptions by lesbian and gay individuals, both in the public agency sector and through private agencies (Gates, Badgett, Macomber, & Chambers, 2007; Pertman, 2011).

Adoption by lesbians and gays has not been uncontroversial, however. Indeed, many agencies, caseworkers, and judges remain opposed to placing children with sexual minority individuals, despite a growing body of research indicating positive outcomes for children raised by lesbians and gay men (Stacey & Biblarz, 2001), and despite support for this type of adoption by most relevant professional organizations in medicine, psychology, sociology, social welfare, and law (Howard & Freundlich, 2008; Mallon, 2006). In fact, the Child Welfare League of America, which serves as the primary professional organization setting standards for excellence for adoption practice in the United States, has stated that adoption applicants "should be assessed on the basis of their abilities to successfully parent a child needing family membership and not on their ... sexual orientation" (Child Welfare League of America, 2000).

The debate about adoption by lesbians and gay men, as well as the development of best practice standards in this area, requires sound empirical data and a thorough understanding of the parameters influencing such placements. Unfortunately, to date, the scholarly and social casework literature regarding adoption by sexual minority individuals and couples has been approached in a piecemeal fashion, with each relevant discipline (e.g., law, social welfare, psychology, and sociology) providing its own unique contribution to the topic, but in relative isolation from the influence of other disciplines. As a consequence, progress in developing best practice standards and understanding the unique needs of lesbian and gay adoptive parents and their children has been impeded.

This book was conceived with the goal of integrating information across disciplines—and thereby expanding our knowledge about adoption by sexual minority individuals. It brings together an outstanding, interdisciplinary group of professionals who are working on issues related to adoption by lesbians and gay men. The idea for the book grew out of a small conference on lesbian and gay adoption held in the Spring of 2005 and co-sponsored by the Center for Adoption Policy, the Evan B. Donaldson Adoption Institute, and the Justice Action Center at New York Law School. Several of the individuals who presented at the conference were invited to contribute to the book, as were a number of scholars, researchers, and practitioners who were unable to be at the conference but who are recognized experts on the topic in their respective fields. The work on this book by its editors was also supported by grants to the Evan B. Donaldson Adoption Institute from the Bohnett Foundation and the Arcus Foundation.

Our intent is to paint a clearer picture of a rapidly growing new family form in America and, in fact, in many Western European countries as well. Families headed by single and coupled lesbians and gays are not only altering the dynamics among the parents and children directly involved—as well as those within the communities in which they live—but they also are helping to reconstruct fundamental social attitudes about lesbian, gay, bisexual, and transgender (LGBT) people and family life in general.

To accomplish this admittedly ambitious goal, we asked our contributors to examine adoption by lesbians and gays from multiple perspectives. In Chapter 1, Cynthia Russett provides a historical overview of the emergence of adoption in the United States, both as a social service and as a family arrangement. Her analysis tracks the changing views of how dependent children were treated by authorities, from colonial times to the present, and situates adoption by gays and lesbians in the context of emerging family diversity. In Chapter 2, Adam Pertman and Jeanne Howard introduce the reader to adoption by sexual minority individuals in relation to changes in relevant policy, practice, and law. In the context of the thousands of children lingering in foster care who need permanent adoptive homes, they make a strong rational and empirical case for the need to expand the eligible pool of parental applicants by suggesting that all agencies reach out to the gay and lesbian community as a resource for these waiting children. This is followed, in Chapter 3, by Annette Appell's discussion of the changing nature of adoption law in the United States that has encouraged, and at times, undermined, the placement of children with lesbians and gay men.[1] Her analysis calls for greater advocacy in passing legislation that supports adoption by sexual minority individuals, including laws that allow for joint and second-parent adoptions. In Chapter 4, David Brodzinsky presents data from a nationwide survey of adoption agencies regarding their policies and practices related to adoption by lesbians and gays. Information from the study suggests that there is greater interest and support among adoption agencies in working with sexual minority individuals than is commonly believed. Next, Chapter 5, by Charlotte Patterson and Jennifer Wainright, and Chapter 6, by Nanette Gartrell, Heidi Peyser, and Henny Bos, present overviews of the researchers' respective longitudinal studies on outcomes for children raised by sexual minority individuals. Both studies, as well as other research reviewed by the authors, provide strong empirical backing for the belief that children raised by lesbians and gay men are as emotionally, psychologically, and socially healthy as their peers raised by heterosexual parents. In Chapter 7, Gerald Mallon describes agency practices in working with lesbians and gays who are interested in adopting children. Specifically, he explores different approaches that agencies often take in their homestudies of sexual minority individuals and couples, and discusses the pros and cons of various strategies. Then, in Chapter 8, Devon Brooks, Hansung Kim, and Leslie Wind present survey data on the supports and services needed and utilized by lesbian and gay adoptive parents compared to heterosexual adoptive parents, both before and after child placement.

Although their findings suggest that the majority of services needed and used by the two groups of parents are mostly similar, they also identify services that lesbian and gay adopters are more likely to require and utilize. The stressors encountered by sexual minority adoptive parents, and the strengths they manifest in coping with these stressors, are the themes of Chapter 9, by Scott Ryan and Suzanne Brown. These authors present data showing that even in the face of moderately stressful family circumstances, lesbian and gay adoptive parents display a high level of parenting competence, resulting in strong parent–child relationships. Of course, all parents and families will, at times, be challenged by the stressors in their lives; when this happens, psychological counseling is often useful. In Chapter 10, Abbie Goldberg and Mark Gianino explore various assessment and clinical issues in working with adoptive parents who are lesbian or gay. They argue that successful clinical work with this group of individuals requires specialized training for professionals, both in the area of adoption and in the issues unique to LGBT individuals and couples. Finally, in Chapter 11, David Brodzinsky, Robert-Jay Green, and Katie Katuzny summarize what we know about adoption and parenting by sexual minority families, as well as what we know about social service practices and clinical work with this population. They also highlight areas of research, social service practice, and legal advocacy that require further exploration by the professional community and end their chapter with guidelines for supporting "best practices" in this area of adoption.

Although no book can cover all the topics relevant to its subject area—and this book is no exception—we believe that our contributors have successfully pulled together a vast body of knowledge associated with adoption by lesbians and gays. In so doing, it is our hope, as editors, that this book will not only pave the way for additional research on the topic, but—most important—will present a clearer picture than there has been to date of what constitutes best practice in working with this group of individuals and their children.

David M. Brodzinsky
Adam Pertman

Notes

1 Most of the authors in the book make reference to the 2008 Arkansas voter referendum that banned adoption by lesbians and gay men, as well as a 2010 Arkansas court ruling that declared the law unconstitutional and the state's subsequent appeal of this ruling. On April 7, 2011, after the book was in production, the Arkansas Supreme Court rejected the appeal and upheld the lower court's ruling declaring the ban on gay/lesbian adoption to be unconstitutional.

References

Brodzinsky, D., Smith, D., & Brodzinsky, A. (1998). *Children's adjustment to adoption: Developmental and clinical issues.* Thousand Oaks, CA: Sage Publications.

Child Welfare League of America. (2000). *Standards for excellence in adoption.* Washington, D.C.: Child Welfare League of America.

Esposito, D., & Biafora, F. A. (2007). Toward a sociology of adoption: Historical deconstruction. In R. A. Javier, A. L. Baden, F. A. Biafora, & A. Camacho-Gingerich (Eds.), *Handbook of adoption: Implications for researchers, practitioners, and families* (pp. 17–31). Thousand Oaks, CA: Sage Publications.

Gates, G., Badgett, M. V. L., Macomber, J. E., & Chambers, K. (2007). *Adoption and foster care by gay and lesbian parents in the United States.* Technical report issued jointly by the Williams Institute (Los Angeles) and the Urban Institute (Washington, D.C.).

Howard, J., & Freundlich, M. (2008). *Expanding resources for waiting children II: Eliminating legal and practice barriers to gay and lesbian adoption from foster care.* New York: Evan B. Donaldson Adoption Institute. Available at www.adoptioninstitute.org.

Mallon, G. (2006). *Lesbian and gay foster and adoptive parents: Recruiting, assessing and supporting an untapped resource for children and youth.* Washington, D.C.: Child Welfare League of America.

Pertman, A. (2011). *Adoption nation.* How the adoption revolution is transforming our families - and America. Boston: Harvard Common Press.

Stacey, J., & Biblarz, T. J. (2001). (How) does the sexual orientation of parents matter? *American Sociological Review, 66,* 159–183.

U.S. Children's Bureau. (2008). *Trends in foster care and adoption FY 2002–FY 2006.* Retrieved from www.acf.hhs.gov/programs/cb/state_research/afcars/trends.html June 1, 2008.

ACKNOWLEDGMENTS

This book was supported, in part, by funding from the Evan B. Donaldson Adoption Institute, which is grateful to the following organizations for their support of its work on LGBT issues: David Bohnett Foundation, Arcus Foundation, Gill Foundation, Human Rights Campaign, and Rainbow Foundation. We also would like to thank the Center for Adoption Policy and its Executive Director, Diane Kunz, as well as the Justice Action Center at New York Law School, for their co-sponsorship of a conference on gay and lesbian adoption; the idea for this book derived from that conference. Finally, we want to thank Leslie Lorquet for her help with the indexing for the book.

To the thousands upon thousands of children who still need nurturing and permanent families, and to the men and women — including LGBT individuals and couples — who are willing and able to adopt them.

CONTENTS

Annette R. Appell, J.D.
Professor of Law and
Associate Dean of Clinical Affairs
Washington University

Henny Bos, Ph.D.
Assistant Professor of Childhood
    Education and Family Support
University of Amsterdam

David M. Brodzinsky, Ph.D.
Research and Project Director
Evan B. Donaldson Adoption
    Institute and
Professor Emeritus of Clinical
    and Developmental Psychology
Rutgers University

Devon Brooks, Ph.D.
Associate Professor of Social Work
University of Southern California

Suzanne Brown, LCSW
Doctoral candidate
Mandel School of Applied Social
    Sciences, Case Western Reserve
    University

Nanette Gartrell, M.D.
Associate Clinical Professor
    of Psychiatry
University of California,
    San Francisco and
Distinguished Scholar
Williams Institute, UCLA
    School of Law

Mark Gianino, Ph.D.
Clinical Assistant Professor
    of Social Work
Boston University

Abbie E. Goldberg, Ph.D.
Associate Professor of Psychology
Clark University

Robert-Jay Green, Ph.D.
Executive Director
Rockway Institute and
Distinguished Professor
California School of Professional
    Psychology, Alliant International
    University, San Francisco

Jeanne Howard, Ph.D.
Research and Policy Director
Evan B. Donaldson Adoption Institute

Katie Katuzny
Doctoral candidate
California School of Professional
    Psychology, Alliant International
    University, San Francisco

Hansung Kim, Ph.D.
Assistant Professor
College of Social Sciences,
    Hanyang University

Gerald P. Mallon, DSW
Professor and Executive Director
National Resource Center for
    Permanency and Family
    Connections, Hunter College
    School of Social Work

Charlotte J. Patterson, Ph.D.
Professor of Psychology
University of Virginia

Adam Pertman
Executive Director
Evan B. Donaldson Adoption Institute

Heidi Peyser, M.A.
U.S. National Longitudinal
    Lesbian Study

Cynthia Russett, Ph.D.
Larned Professor of History
Yale University

Scott Ryan, Ph.D.
Dean and Professor
University of Texas at Arlington
    School of Social Work and
Senior Research Fellow
Evan B. Donaldson Adoption Institute

Jennifer L. Wainright, Ph.D.
University of Virginia

Leslie H. Wind, Ph.D.
Clinical Associate Professor
    of Social Work
University of Southern California

Adoption by Lesbians and Gay Men

American Adoption

A Brief History

CYNTHIA RUSSETT ∎

The story of adoption is one without beginning and without end—without beginning because adoption has existed in some form throughout human history and without end because the story continues to unfold. What the story does have is a few fundamental fixed elements—parents and children and homes—but the meanings of these terms have been defined and redefined over time. Historically contingent, the institution of adoption has responded to changing conceptions of proper parenthood, the value of childhood, the needs of adults, the best interests of children, and the form of the ideal family. Today it encompasses a multiplicity of family forms, of which the most recent, at least in terms of public visibility, is the gay/lesbian family.

ADOPTION IN EARLY AMERICA

Children have lived with adults who were not their birthparents for many reasons. In America, during the colonial period and well into the nineteenth century, parents placed children in other homes in apprenticeships and indentures to learn a trade. Economic hardship was not always the reason, and historian Edmund Morgan has even speculated that colonial parents feared spoiling their children, and sent them out to another family that could train them in a useful skill while avoiding the dangers of coddling (Morgan, 1944). Destitute children could even be sold into apprenticeships. In these cases, they were not infants, but children of an age to work and learn, and the arrangement would last only for a specific number of years, not continuing into adulthood. Though bonds of affection might form between apprentices or indentured servants and the families into which they were placed, and indeed such children might be remembered in a householder's will, the emphasis in such situations was primarily economic: Children helped out with the work and, in turn, they learned the basics of a trade (Askeland, 2006).

Many children were, of course, in a very different situation: left homeless and dependent because of some kind of family breakdown—usually the illness, death, poverty, or desertion of one or both parents. They might be taken under the care of the state and placed in an almshouse until old enough (sometimes no more than 6 or 7 years) to be put out to indenture or apprenticeship. More fortunate children would be taken into the home of relatives or family friends in a kind of informal adoption, as had long been common in both Native American and African-American cultures. John Hancock, the signer of the Declaration of Independence, was raised by a childless uncle and aunt after his father died, and inherited their property (Berebitsky, 2000). This kind of informal adoption was not yet recognized in law, since colonial America had taken on the system of English common law, which did not recognize legal adoption because all inheritance had to follow bloodlines.

By the early nineteenth century, it became evident that better provision needed to be made for children who did not have a kinship network to take care of them. These children were becoming ever more numerous as America industrialized and urbanized, and immigration swelled the ranks of those without an extended family. The majority of dependent children lived in almshouses, or poorhouses, until after the Civil War; yet these were increasingly seen as undesirable institutions for the dependent young, since they also accommodated adults, who might be delinquent or insane, as well as children (Nelson, 2003). In her book *Minding the Children*, Geraldine Youcha cites an 1857 report of a New York State Senate committee lamenting the mixing of young and old in almshouses, "an association with their destitute parents, and their necessary poor house companions, [which] is not only a deprivation of the attention and comforts which they ought to enjoy during their tender years, but it is a fatal exposure to examples of most evil tendency. Their chance to become virtuous and exemplary citizens is the most desperate of all human chances" (Youcha, 1995). Orphanages, which had existed since before the Revolutionary War, offered an alternative. They remained the most important locus of temporary or permanent care of children without familial support until well into the twentieth century (Askeland, 2006).

THE RISE OF THE ORPHANAGE

Dolley Madison helped found one of the earliest orphanages, the Washington City Orphan Asylum (WCOA), in 1815. Designed to care for children orphaned by the British raid on Washington during the War of 1812, the WCOA was, like many such institutions, supported by local Protestant congregations. Catholics and Jews founded their own orphanages. In fact, the earliest orphanage in the United States seems to have been Catholic, established in 1729 by Ursuline nuns in Natchez, Mississippi, after an Indian massacre. Spurred in good part by fears that Protestant orphanages would proselytize Catholic children, Catholics founded 16 orphanages by 1840, largely staffed by orders of religious sisters. Urgent local conditions, notably epidemics such as cholera and yellow fever, sometimes motivated the creation of orphanages; one of the earliest Jewish orphanages, for instance, opened in New Orleans in 1856 in response to a yellow fever epidemic that had left women without husbands and orphaned many children. African-American children remained largely excluded from these institutions; New York's Colored Orphan Asylum, opened in 1836 by Quaker women, was one of the first to serve their needs. As the nineteenth century progressed, the number of children at risk increased with the carnage of the Civil War and the enormous post-war industrial expansion that opened the floodgates to immigration.

The term "orphanage" was actually a misnomer: Orphanages most frequently served children with at least one living parent who, for whatever reason, could not care for them. They were to be "second homes" until the children could be discharged, either to be reunited with their parents, placed in some form of indenture, or adopted into a new family. Though our image of nineteenth-century orphanages may picture them as residences until adulthood, this was infrequently the case.

Many people genuinely believed that institutionalization was the best solution to the problem of the growing numbers of dependent children. Orphanages gave children a reasonably safe place to live, adequate food to sustain life if not health (disease was a constant threat), discipline, and some basic schooling (Youcha, 1995). Still, in the mid-nineteenth century, these children overwhelmed the institutional resources of Eastern cities. And not everyone agreed that orphanages were the best answer to childhood dependency. Charles Loring Brace held that institutional care was detrimental to children, who would be much better off in families. As one of the founders and then secretary of the Children's Aid Society of New York, he created the most famous (or infamous) alternative to the orphanage: taking children from Eastern city streets and sending them to a more healthful rural environment. His "orphan trains" transported children to farm families, first in New York, New Jersey, and Connecticut and then to the Midwest. The majority of these trains ran from 1854 to 1904, though the practice continued sporadically until 1929, and in all carried perhaps 200,000 children to new homes. The *New York Sun* wrote favorably of this system of placing children into new families rather than into orphanages: "We mean no condemnation of the asylum system itself. As compared with the abandonment of children, it is an immense good. No one can deny it. But a new system, we claim, has been discovered, which is nearly as much in advance upon the asylum system as that is in advance of nothing at all" (Youcha, 1995, p. 208).

Though hailed at the time for its benevolence, the orphan train project has been reevaluated by historians, who find its record mixed at best. Some farmers looked upon the children simply as sources of labor. Some children were abused by the families who took them in and wound up as miserable as they had been in New York. In some cases, birthparents had not given consent for their children to be transported. Yet there are also stories with happy endings. Two orphan train riders became governors, one became a Supreme Court justice, and others grew up to be mayors and congressmen. Somewhat ironically, a great many of them returned from the salubrious countryside to the streets of New York and other major Eastern cities (Sokoloff, 1993; Youcha, 1995). Most of the orphan train riders were treated as foster children, but some were adopted, and perhaps the most lasting legacy of the orphan trains is their influence on the subsequent history of adoption. According to Stephen Presser (1972), "The origins of America's first adoption laws can be traced to the increase in the number of middle-class farmers desiring to legalize the addition of children to their families."

EMERGENCE OF THE ADOPTION AGENCY SYSTEM

Before the middle of the eighteenth century, some states recognized individual adoptions through the passage of private adoption acts in their legislatures. These acts were fairly frequent but obviously cumbersome and difficult to obtain without some degree of social influence on the part of the would-be adopters. State legislatures grew weary of providing these increasingly numerous individual remedies, and in addition felt a need to safeguard child welfare.

Legal adoption is usually dated from the year 1851, when Massachusetts passed the first general adoption law. It provided that either the parents, the surviving parent if one had died, the legal guardian, or the next of kin if both had died, or "some discreet and suitable person" appointed by the judge, had to give written consent to the adoption. A child of 14 years and older had to give his or her own consent. The judge would then determine that the individuals or couples hoping to adopt were "of sufficient ability to bring up the child, and furnish suitable nurture and education." The adopted child would then be deemed "the same to all intents and purposes as if such child had been born in lawful wedlock of such parents or parent by adoption" (Herman, 2007). This law is noteworthy for its requirement that a child 14 years or older had to consent to the adoption and that the adoptive parent or parents had to make adequate provision for the child's welfare. In the latter nineteenth century many states followed the lead of Massachusetts, enacting laws to codify the placement of children into new families and to give them the same inheritance rights as the family's biological children.

Claudia Nelson begins her study of the ways in which adoption and foster care have been portrayed in the literature with a clever comparison of "Little Orphan Annie," James Whitcomb Riley's 1855 bound-out girl, to the twentieth-century's Little Orphan Annie, adopted daughter of Daddy Warbucks. Riley's orphan washes the dishes, dusts the hearth, makes the fire, bakes the bread, and shoos the chickens. Daddy Warbucks' Annie lives to be cherished and protected (Nelson, 2003). The difference highlights the profound change in attitudes toward children that took place in the late nineteenth and early twentieth centuries. Children had been an economic asset, highly valued for their labor and often essential to family maintenance, since the colonial period. When children were placed in the homes of adults who were not their kin, they normally went to work. The benefits were multiple: to a family that gained another pair of hands, to a child who was given shelter and maintenance, and to a society that did not have to take on a public charge. As the economy moved away from agriculture and toward industrialization, however, children's labor, though still all too common, became less important as an economic factor. At the same time, the American conception of childhood was changing into one more nearly like that of today: Children were increasingly seen as vulnerable and in need of protection; they should be loved and nurtured. Their value no longer depended on their ability to work; it was emotional, and as such, priceless. One tangible result of this new attitude was a rise in the number of potential adoptive families who sought infants rather than children old enough to work. By the 1930s, a Minnesota study showed, most adoptive parents refused to take older children and, instead, favored babies because they perceived that those children would be entirely their own (Creagh, 2006).

Child welfare workers came to believe that the "best interests of the child" were served in families, rather than institutions, so their emphasis turned increasingly to making it possible for poor families to keep their children at home, and to finding permanent homes for children without parents. This view reached the highest levels in 1909 with the first White House Conference on the Care of Dependent Children, which concluded:

> Home life is the highest and finest product of civilization. It is the great molding force of mind and of character. Children should not be deprived of it except for urgent and compelling reasons. Children of parents of worthy character, suffering from temporary misfortune, and children of reasonably efficient and deserving mothers who are without the support of the normal breadwinner, should as a rule be kept with their parents, such aid being given as may be necessary to maintain suitable homes for the rearing of children... Except in unusual circumstances, the home should not be broken up for reasons of poverty, but only for considerations of inefficiency or immorality. (Hart, 1910, p. 386)

President Theodore Roosevelt gave his hearty approval to these sentiments.

Although the population of orphanages remained substantial well into the twentieth century, several factors led to their gradual decline—most notably, the emphasis on being in a family prompted greater and greater use of foster care and adoption instead of institutional settings. Progressive Era reforms such as mothers' pensions, and finally, under the New Deal, Aid to Dependent Children, were also designed to privilege families over institutions.

Interest in adoption on the part of childless couples grew markedly in the first half of the twentieth century. Some of its early manifestations—such as unregulated "baby brokers" and "black market adoptions"—were undesirable and prompted regulatory legislation in most states (Sokoloff, 1993). More legitimate institutions also responded to this awakened interest. In the years after 1910, philanthropic women founded the first specialized adoption agencies, such as the

Spence Alumni Society, the Alice Chapin Nursery, and the Cradle. These agencies took shape almost by chance. In New York, Alice Chapin began caring for the abandoned infants brought to her husband's hospital, and then placed them with couples who asked for them. She formalized her work in 1919 with the founding of the Alice Chapin Adoption Nursery. Similarly, in Chicago, Florence Walrath found a baby for her sister, whose infant had died, and was then approached by friends and acquaintances seeking babies of their own. She opened the Cradle in 1923, and it achieved national recognition when Hollywood stars sought out its services (Berebitsky, 2000).

The efforts of private agencies such as these were not always appreciated by social workers, who were still establishing themselves as legitimate professionals and were anxious to claim child welfare as their own field. Social workers disparaged the founders of private agencies as amateurs. Moreover, in their eagerness to place children, private agencies did not always investigate adopting parents with the scrutiny social workers felt was essential; in addition, in their commitment to adoption as the solution to illegitimacy, social workers felt private agencies were not sufficiently concerned about the possible consequences of "inferior" heredity, an issue of growing importance among social science scholars during this time period.

Fears that children from impoverished homes—or to their minds, worse, children born out of wedlock—were likely to turn out badly, received support from prevalent theories of eugenics. Two developments encouraged this concern: the rediscovery of Mendel's laws of heredity and the beginning of intelligence testing. At the time, inheritance was believed to follow simple Mendelian patterns, meaning that traits leading to success or failure in life were directly inheritable from one's parents. Moreover, such traits were believed to be fixed and immutable. Henry H. Goddard, perhaps the most influential eugenicist of this period, sounded the alarm at the possibility of "disease and mental deficiency and possibly crime" among the thousands of children being annually placed in homes, about whom almost nothing was known (Herman, 2007). Goddard used the Binet Scale, which he brought to the United States from France in 1908, to assess intelligence in children; his position as head of the Vineland School for Feeble-Minded Boys and Girls made him particularly sensitive to the problem of mental deficiency. In his mind, and in the mind of many eugenicists, feeble-mindedness was linked to illegitimacy, that is, feeble-minded unwed mothers gave birth to feeble-minded children.[1]

For Goddard, the remedy was obvious. He wrote,

> We must use every means to learn all the facts before we place these children in the care of other unsuspecting fathers or mothers… It means that the family history of every homeless and neglected child must be ascertained just as far as possible, and that no pains or expense be spared to get all the information that can possible be had… It is neither right nor wise for us to let our humanity, our pity and sympathy for the poor, homeless, and neglected child, drive us to do injustice to and commit a crime against those yet unborn. (Goddard, 1911)

Carrying out these recommendations meant establishing minimum standards in the adoption process, including certification of child-placers (eliminating amateurs and private agents), investigation of the fitness of both prospective adopting parents and the child to be adopted, and professional supervision of newly formed families. Almost all states had enacted minimum standards laws by mid-century, though the laws were totally unsuccessful in halting private adoption arrangements. One element of these standards was the search for the "normal" family. Social worker Dorothy Hutchinson, in her widely read text *In Quest of Foster Parents*, asserted that "selection of foster homes has at best been based on the assumption that although there is no such thing as a perfect home there is such thing as a normal family." What would "normal" mean? "Normality is something that is hard to define, yet easy to feel and see. In it is assumed a wider range of behavior and attitude, not a narrowly fixed concept" (quoted in Carp, 2002).

In fact, normality had a specific meaning: The normal family consisted of the traditional biological unit of mother, father, and child(ren). Adoption agencies worked diligently to replicate this traditional form. They could not, of course, make the adoptive family biological, but they could do the next best thing: create the appearance of biology. They did this by matching physical characteristics, including race, ethnicity, and body type, as well as eye, hair, and skin color. It was believed that matching physical traits would not only eliminate derogatory comments about adoption by others, especially biological children, but would also enhance family bonds—and this would also be true for intelligence and personality. Accordingly, agencies matched for temperament and intelligence as best they could on the basis of the temperament and intelligence of the biological parents. As one California adoption worker explained, "Natural parents derive a normal satisfaction from the similarity of their children to themselves. It is understandable that adopting parents experience this need as well, and the physical and mental traits of an adopted child which seem like those their own child might have shown are a tie which helps to bind them together more closely" (Berebitsky 2000, p. 138). Over time, however, adopters increasingly desired very young children, and, if possible, newborns. Since newborns could not be tested for intelligence, the concept of matching by intelligence had to be abandoned.[2]

Finally, but every bit as important and often more important, agencies matched for religion. As late as the 1950s, Melosh found that religious matching was a concern. The Delaware Children's Bureau that she studied followed the state mandate that "at least one of the prospective adopting parents shall be of the same religion as the natural mother" (Melosh, 2002). And even when a specific religion was not at issue, child placement workers looked for some kind of religious practice in adoptive homes. Religion in some form was considered one sign of parental fitness.[3]

If creating the ideal family meant finding the perfectly matched child, it also meant excluding the "defective" child, one with disabilities of body or mind. A hereditary history of psychosis, feeble-mindedness, epilepsy, addiction, criminality, or general emotional instability, even if the child showed no signs of any of these, signaled danger. For some child placement professionals, any defect consigned a child to ineligibility for adoption. Most troublesome of these was feeble-mindedness; agencies often had staff psychologists who could "ensure that feeble-minded children shall not be adopted." Such children belonged in institutions (Gill, 2002, pp. 162–168).

Prospective parents also came under growing scrutiny. The ideal family model not only excluded defective children as adoptees, it excluded single women as adopters. (At the time, men were not considered suitable adopters.) This attitude represented a change from the late nineteenth century, when single women had often been favorably viewed in light of the maternal instincts they shared with their married sisters. Before the 1920s, single women often raised their adopted children in a community of women or with a female partner. When two women lived together, the arrangement was often referred to as a Boston marriage and these were common and accepted. As the twentieth century moved away from the patriarchal family structure and toward a more companionate image of marriage, however, women were expected to focus on their roles as wives and romantic partners. New studies of sexuality brought homosexuality out into the open, and female partnerships, once completely respectable, came under hostile scrutiny.

Nor did single women escape: This new emphasis on romance and marriage by definition left them on the margins, branded as odd or deviant. Healthy adulthood required marriage: "Deprived of the outlets which a satisfactory marriage provides, the foster parent, whether bachelor or spinster, may unconsciously warp or thwart the child development by bestowing upon and accepting from him the full measure of affectional regard usually shared by the other parent" (Letter of U.S. Children's Bureau staffer Elsa Castendyck to Miss Charlotte Whitton, quoted in Berebitsky, 2000, p. 119). Increasingly, child placement professionals counseled against placing children with single women. Moreover, Freudian theory, growing increasingly important during this time period, lent weight to this negative view. Boys and girls, Freudians insisted, needed both a mother and a father to achieve "[n]ormal Oedipal development" (Berebitsky, 2000, p. 120). Helene Deutsch, a psychoanalyst and author of *The Psychology of Women*, described the phenomenon of single adoptive motherhood as pathological (Berebitsky, 2000). By the 1950s, guidelines for adoption unequivocally excluded single women. Adoption standards developed by the Child Welfare League of America in 1958 envisioned a single adoptive family model: one with both a mother and a father (Herman, 2007).

ADOPTION PRACTICE FOLLOWING WORLD WAR II

The landscape of American adoption changed profoundly in the years after World War II. Liberalized sexual mores reduced the stigma of unwed motherhood, leading many women to choose to parent their babies. Somewhat later, beginning in the 1960s and extending into the 1970s, the birth control pill and the legalization of abortion resulted in fewer unplanned pregnancies. As a result, the availability of white babies for adoption shrank significantly. Furthermore, as more and more children entered foster care, especially in the late 1970s and into the 1980s, the numbers of African-American children available for adoption grew. For white prospective adopters, two possible solutions to the reduced number of white babies existed: adoption of children transracially in this country or, somewhat later, intercountry adoption. Transracial adoption, primarily the adoption of black children by white families, raised a host of controversial issues, and was never a large-scale phenomenon. It reached its peak in 1971, when agencies reported 2574 placements of African-American children in white homes (Carp, 2002). With the enactment of the Multiethnic Placement Act (MEPA) and Interethnic Adoption Provisions Act (IEPA), as well as the Adoption and Safe Families Act (ASFA), during President Clinton's administration, the number of transracial placements, once again, had begun to rise (Smith, McRoy, & Kroll, 2008).

International adoption began as a direct outgrowth of World War II, which had left many foreign-born children orphaned or abandoned. A second war shortly thereafter, the Korean War, resulted in a much greater influx of Korean adoptees, profoundly changing the face of American adoption. Whereas the European children looked similar to their white American parents, the Korean children did not. Adoptions from Korea continued to be the most common kind of intercountry adoption until 1991. In the 1970s and 1980s, Latin America became a major source of children for adoption, and later still, Russia, Rumania, and China. In her article "Intercountry Adoption: A Frontier without Boundaries," Joan Heifetz Hollinger notes that in the last decades of the twentieth century and the first years of the twenty-first century, adoption of children from abroad more than tripled in number from the 1980s, although in recent years it has dropped off significantly (Hollinger, 2004).

Some opponents of international adoption argued that children are best cared for in their countries of origin, where they can grow up within their ethnic and cultural heritage. They also insisted that such adoptions constitute a vicious form of exploitation by rich countries of the dearest resources of poor countries. Advocates of international adoption, however, suggested a healthy empiricism. Elizabeth Bartholet summarizes their position as a call to realism: How can children of the streets and orphanages actually participate in their native culture? Although most people involved in intercountry adoption have avoided taking part in this controversy, the views of critics, and, more importantly, recent international baby-selling and kidnapping scandals, have had a major impact; countries have begun to institute restrictions on the numbers of children they will permit to be adopted, and international adoption has become a great deal more difficult (Bartholet, 2006), resulting in a dramatic drop-off in the total number of intercountry adoptions in the past few years.

The most controversial issue in the history of adoption after World War II was adult adoptees' access to their original birth certificates. Contrary to public perception, closure of these records for reasons of confidentiality was for the most part instituted quite late in the twentieth century, in the decades of the 1960s, 1970s, and 1980s. Those favoring closure gave several reasons, including the right of birth parents to privacy and the right of adoptive parents to raise their children without any interference from the birth family. At the same time, a movement was

gathering force on the part of adult adoptees to regain access to their birth certificates (which they had until the states began sealing them). This movement came
to public attention in 1973 with the popular film, "The Search for Anna Fisher,"
which told the story of activist Florence Fisher's successful discovery of her birthmother and their reunion.[4]

For a variety of reasons, including the reluctance of birthmothers to place
their babies if they had to lose all contact with them, open adoption has become
increasingly common. Those who favor an end to secrecy have worked to create
continuing contact between birth families and adoptive families. Such contact
would begin with an exchange of information at the time of adoption. Thereafter
contact might go no further than an occasional letter or photograph, or it might
be much more sustained, including regular visits between birth parents and
adopted child. Although there have been many skeptics, as well as outright opponents, of open adoption, nearly a quarter-century of research and social casework practice have found that this type of adoption arrangement has a positive
impact on most birthparents, adoptive parents, and, most importantly, adopted
individuals (Grotevant & McRoy, 1998; Grotevant, Perry, & McRoy, 2005; McRoy,
Grotevant, Ayers-Lopez, & Henney, 2007).

Adoptive families represent an important break with the concept that a "real"
or "normal" family is one with a mother and a father and their biological children.
As long as adoption agencies attempted physical matching, the illusion of that
concept could be maintained. But once children of different races and ethnicities
entered the homes of Americans, that "perfect" family model no longer accorded
with reality. The process of reinventing the family had begun (see Pertman &
Howard, this volume). It changed the profiles of both the adopted children and
the adoptive parents. Increasingly, children once thought to be unadoptable—
older children, those with mental or physical challenges, sibling groups, children
of color—came to be seen as deserving of homes. Meanwhile, the difficulty of
placing such children led to a relaxing of the strictures that had governed the
definition of suitable parents. In a society in which high rates of divorce left
women and some men to raise children alone, single applicants began to be considered, and in the 1970s a support group for single adoptive parents was formed.
Today, single women and, to a lesser extent, single men, although making up a
fairly small percentage of adoptions of domestically born infants, as well as adoptions of children from abroad, now represent a sizable percentage of those adults
adopting children from the foster care system. Over the past few decades, adoption agencies also began to accept as prospective adopters others previously considered ineligible to adopt, including foster parents, older adults, disabled adults,
racial minority adults, those in the working class, and those with low incomes.
Even more remarkably, gay and lesbian individuals and couples increasingly have
been viewed as resources in the fostering and adoption of children, especially
those youngsters with special needs (see Brodzinsky, this volume; Pertman &
Howard, this volume; Gates et al., 2007; Howard & Freundlich, 2008). In short, in
the past several decades the landscape of adoptive families has grown increasingly
diverse. Gay and lesbian adoption adds one more element to that diversity.

GAY AND LESBIAN ADOPTION: THE NEW FRONTIER

Daniel Luke Lippin-Hayes lives with his two dads, Thad Hayes and Adam Lippin, in Montclair, New Jersey. Like so many suburbanites, Daniel's parents moved out of the city because they thought suburban life was better for children. Montclair is a prosperous, liberal community, and the two dads say they have not experienced discrimination. When Daniel goes on play dates, his playmates' parents are sometimes straight and sometimes gay. Were it not for having two dads, Daniel's story would be entirely unremarkable, but his family, together with others like it, represents the new frontier of adoption (*New York Times*, 2007).

Same-sex couples are writing the latest chapter in the American adoption story (see Brodzinsky, this volume; Pertman, 2011; Pertman & Howard, this volume). Gay and lesbian people have always raised children, but until fairly recently they did so quietly, so it is impossible to know exactly how common this was in the past.

The implications of gay and lesbian adoption need to be understood in the broader context of the psychology of family formation, which examines desires, intentions, and actions taken to become parents. A stereotype held by many people is that sexual minority individuals do not wish to bear and/or raise children. Yet research suggests that this stereotype is wrong. For example, a sizable number of lesbians and gays have children from previous marriages (Martin, 1993; Patterson, 1994; Patterson & Friel, 2011). Based on Census 2000 data, Gates et al. (2007) report that one in three lesbian women and one in six gay men in the United States are raising children—either from previous marriages, surrogacy, or adoption. They also reported that 41 percent of childless lesbians and 52 percent of gay men expressed a desire to parent a child. In addition, a study by D'Augelli, Rendina, Grossman, and Sinclair (2006/2007) found strong expectations of future parenthood among a sample of urban lesbian and gay youth, with 86 percent of the young women and 91 percent of the young men reporting that they expected to rear children in the future. Furthermore, another recent study by Riskind and Patterson (2010) found that although lesbians and gays expressed less of a *desire* for parenting children than did heterosexual individuals, lesbians displayed the same strong *intention* as heterosexuals to become parents in the future; gay men expressed less future parenting intention than other participants in the study. Moreover, although showing less desire to parent children than heterosexuals, both lesbian women and gay men endorsed the *value of parenthood* just as much as heterosexual women and men. In short, contrary to stereotypes, sexual minority individuals are motivated to become parents and strongly value the role of parenthood. However, because they cannot directly procreate with their life partners, lesbians and gay men often seek alternative routes to parenthood, including adoption.

Over the past several decades more and more gay and lesbian individuals and couples living openly gay lives have sought adoption (see Brodzinsky, 2008; Brodzinsky, this volume; Gates et al., 2007). They have done so in the context of a society that has become a great deal more tolerant of homosexuality, although gay adoption remains a controversial subject (Rye & Meaney, 2010). We see those changes most easily in the laws governing same-sex adoption (see Appell, this volume). State-by-state, laws are being modified to permit gay and lesbian individuals, and in many cases same-sex couples, to petition to adopt. Florida, which for many years was the only state to explicitly forbid adoption by gays and lesbians, now allows such adoptions after the Third District Court of Appeal ruled that the law was unconstitutional (*Department of Children and Families v. In the Matter of the Adoption of X.X.G. and N.R.G.*, 2010). Mississippi bars "same-gender" couples from adopting; individual gays and lesbians, however, are eligible to adopt in Mississippi. In addition, in 2008 Arkansas voters approved a measure that banned . . . persons "co-habiting outside of a valid marriage" from adopting. Although this statute could also apply to heterosexual couples, it is widely perceived as intending to bar gay and lesbian couples from adopting;[1] Utah has a similar law. In both these states, an individual—gay or straight—would not be prohibited from adopting. Almost all the other states permit individual gays and lesbians to adopt; and in many states, same-sex couples also are allowed to adopt (Appell, this volume). By contrast, 11 states and the District of Columbia have policies that prohibit using sexual orientation as a basis for excluding gays and lesbians from adopting. In many other states, lower courts have concluded that gay and lesbian adoption is allowed (Howard, 2006).

In situations in which one of the same-sex partners is the biological parent of the couple's child, or has previously adopted a child, most jurisdictions allow the other partner to petition to adopt as a second parent (Appell, this volume). Both parents are then the legal guardians of the child. Gay and lesbian advocates have increasingly focused their attention on the importance of second-parent adoption to ensure that both partners have the full measure of legal parental rights over the child and to enhance the stability of the family.

The number of children being raised by gay and lesbian adoptive parents is large; it is probably larger than most people recognize. Gates et al. (2007), using the Census 2000 and the National Survey of Family Growth (NSFG) datasets, report that approximately 65,500 adopted children, or more that 4 percent of all adopted children in the United States, were being raised in lesbian and gay households. Many of these households were headed by a single parent, representing close to one in six of all single parents with adopted children. Same-sex couples, in contrast, were raising about 1 percent of all adopted children. It should be noted, however, that these figures could be an underestimation of the prevalence of gay and lesbian adoption, since some respondents undoubtedly were not fully "out," which could have resulted in a reluctance to acknowledge their sexual orientation in the surveys.

One interesting aspect of gay male adoption is that men may enter into the raising of children free from the cultural expectations that formerly defined women as mothers. Feminists had to fight the belief that a woman's place was in the home taking care of the children, and in so doing they sometimes devalued

---

1. See update on Arkansas law in footnote of Preface.

the role of a stay-at-home parent. Gay men may be more willing to take on that role. Mike Farina left his job as an engineer to take care of the twins he and his partner adopted. He explained, "I wanted the kids to bond with us. I didn't want any help. In those first few years, I didn't even get baby sitters. I thought, 'That's my job'" (*New York Times*, 2004).

Meanwhile lesbian women are shaping a new understanding of equity in relationships that cannot define roles by gender. Some scholars have theorized that lesbians, having experienced oppression in many aspects of their lives, are particularly sensitive to unfairness and inequality. In fact, research does indicate that lesbian couples do tend to share housework more equally, and in general to practice more equality in their relationships, than heterosexual couples (Chan, Brooks, Raboy, & Patterson, 1998; Goldberg, 2010; Patterson, Sutfin, & Fulcher, 2004).

Of course gay adoption remains controversial (Rye & Meaney, 2010). Not all communities are as accepting as Montclair, New Jersey. The arguments against gay adoption are familiar. Many stem from a religious conviction that homosexuality is wrong, and therefore gay partnerships are wrong, and so, obviously, are gay adoptions. Another argument stresses the value of the traditional family with one man and one woman and their children. Although this view may be biblically based (God created Adam and Eve, not Adam and Steve), it need not be religious in origin. Rather, it emphasizes the purported necessity of role models of both sexes in order for children to grow up comfortable with both and psychologically healthy. One moment in the cultural conflict over gay adoption came in 1989 with the publication of *Heather Has Two Mommies*, a children's book that portrayed Heather's family positively. One minister removed the book from the library; it subsequently became the eleventh most frequently banned book in the country.

A rather more amusing media episode occurred with the publication in 2005 of *And Tango Makes Three* by Justin Richardson and Peter Parnell. The book told the true story of two male penguins, Roy and Silo, in New York's Central Part Zoo who had bonded and formed a couple. They were given an egg to hatch and raise together. Zookeepers named the female chick that resulted Tango. If Heather had two mommies, Tango had two daddies.

In seeming to validate gay behavior and parenting in penguins, the book was immensely controversial; it became the most banned book in the country in 2009. Its impact was diminished subsequently, however, when Silo abandoned Roy in favor of a female penguin named Scrappy. Conservatives were pleased at this denouement, but the real message of the affair is probably that seeking to find lessons in sexuality in the animal kingdom is a misguided endeavor.

Adoption, whether by traditional or nontraditional parents, almost always takes place in the context of the best interests of the child, so there has been intense interest in the effects of gay and lesbian parenting on children. The landmark research review by Judith Stacey and Timothy Biblarz, "(How) Does the Sexual Orientation of Parents Matter?" is the most frequently cited work to address this question (Stacey & Biblarz, 2001). Social science research had almost unanimously found that there were no discernible differences between children raised in same-sex families and those raised in heterosexual families (see also Goldberg, 2010). Conservative critics of gay parenting argued, however, that the social science literature was biased in favor of gay rights and therefore was flawed and unreliable. Stacey and Biblarz did not fully agree with either side. They dismissed the conservative critique as distorted by heterosexual norms of healthy family life, which led—in the case of lesbian parents—to charges of a pathology of "fatherlessness." On the other hand, they could not agree with the literature that said children of gay parents showed no differences at all from those children raised by heterosexuals. They viewed this conclusion as a defensive one in the face of the heterosexual family norm, whose proponents understandably feared that "difference" would be interpreted as "deficient." In fact, Stacey and Biblarz found what they called "modest" but significant differences between the children of gay and straight parents. Not surprisingly, perhaps, both boys and girls raised by gay parents were less apt to fulfill the roles of stereotypical masculinity and femininity. Girls of lesbian parents, for example, "more frequently dress, play, and behave in ways that do not conform to sex-typed cultural norms" (Stacey & Biblarz, 2001, p. 169). They were also more interested in the traditionally male professions of medicine and law as well as engineering and space science. A very recent examination of the literature (Goldberg, 2010) has confirmed these findings, noting that children of lesbian and gay parents appear to be more flexible in their gendered role behavior.

Rather than interpreting these modest differences as deficits, Stacey and Biblarz suggested that the behavior of children from lesbian households was well within the normal range, and therefore of no great importance as a societal concern. Moreover, on the all-important issue of mental and emotional health, they noted that research has found no significant differences between children raised by gay and lesbian parents compared to those youngsters raised by heterosexual parents (see also Patterson & Wainright, this volume; Gartrell, Peyser, & Bos, this volume). These findings should reassure us that American children of gay and lesbian parents are not at risk for unhealthy development but are very much—if not entirely—the same as those of straight parents. And that is surely good news.

The adoption of children by gay and lesbian parents will continue to be controversial so long as homosexuality is not fully accepted into the social fabric of the country, but advocates have had considerable success. Five states have now legalized gay and lesbian marriage, which essentially opens a direct door to adoption. Many other states recognize civil unions, a somewhat shakier basis for adoption, since in most cases only one of the partners is recognized as the legal parent and the other partner must seek a second-parent adoption. It is very likely that more states will legalize gay marriage in the coming years. Meanwhile, acceptance of gay adoption, whether in marriage or in civil union, is substantial and growing, and is highlighted by the recent overturning of Florida's statute barring such adoptions (*Florida Department of Children and Families v. In the Matter of the Adoption of X.X.G. and N.R.G.*, 2010), as well as a similar ruling by the Arkansas supreme court in 2011.

CONCLUSIONS

American adoption is a story intimately linked to larger social changes over three centuries. Once thought of as little laborers, children increasingly became cherished for themselves. Once imagined as a single model, family structure bent and reshaped itself to the winds of change. We now have families with stepchildren, with half-brothers and half-sisters and blends of both, families with children and parents of different races and colors, families with two mothers, and families with two fathers. Adoption has always been a kind of front line of social change in reimagining the family, the place where change has been most evident, most scrutinized, and most controversial. Over time, it has helped to lead the way to acceptance of a diversity of family forms. Perhaps it can be the place where we learn to acknowledge that first and foremost, families are constructs of love, and love between parents and children should be honored wherever it is found.

Notes

1. For more information on intelligence testing of children and matching intellectual levels in adoption, see Berebitsky (2000).
2. Historian Barbara Melosh points out, however, that even today, childless couples remain concerned about intelligence as evidenced in the many ads for Ivy League egg donors (Melosh, 2002).
3. For a thorough discussion of matching, see Melosh (2002).
4. On the adoption rights movement and the search for the birthmother, see Melosh (2002).

References

Askeland, L. (2006). Informal adoption, apprentices, and indentured children in the colonial era and the new republic. In L. Askeland (Ed.), *Children and youth in adoption, orphanages, and foster care: A historical handbook and guide*. Westport, CT: Greenwood Press.

Bartholet, E. (2006). International adoption. In L. Askeland (Ed.), *Children and youth in adoption, orphanages, and foster care: A historical handbook and guide*. Westport, CT: Greenwood Press.

Berebitsky, J. (2000). *Like our very own: Adoption and the changing culture of motherhood, 1851–1950*. Lawrence: University Press of Kansas.

Carp, E. W. (2002). *Adoption in America: Historical perspectives*. Ann Arbor: University of Michigan Press.

Chan, R. W., Brooks, R. C., Raboy, B., & Patterson, C. J. (1998). Division of labor among lesbian and heterosexual parents: Associations with children's adjustment. *Journal of Family Psychology, 12*, 402–419.

Creagh, D. (2006). Science, social work, and bureaucracy: Cautious development in adoption and foster care, 1930–1969. In L. Askeland (Ed.)., *Children and youth in adoption, orphanages, and foster care: A historical handbook and guide.* Westport, CT: Greenwood Press.

D'Augelli, A. R., Rendina, H. J., Grossman, A. H., & Sinclair, K. O. (2006/2007). Lesbian and gay youths' aspirations for marriage and raising children. *Journal of LGBT Issues in Counseling, 1,* 77–98.

Florida Department of Children and Families v. In the Matter of Adoption of X.X.G and N.R.G., No. 3D08–3044, 2010 WL 3655782 (Fla. Dist. Ct. App., Sept 22, 2010).

Gates, G. J., et al. (2007). *Adoption and foster care by gay and lesbian parents in the United States.* Washington, D.C.: Urban Institute.

Gill, B. P. (2002). Adoption agencies and the search for the ideal family, 1918–1965. In E. W. Carp (Ed.), *Adoption in America: Historical perspectives.* Ann Arbor: University of Michigan Press.

Goddard, H. H. (1911). Wanted: A child to adopt. In E. Herman, Adoption history project. http://www.uoregon.edu/~adoption/archive/GoddardWCA.htm, not paginated

Goldberg, A. (2010). *Lesbian and gay parents and their children.* Washington, D.C.: American Psychological Association.

Grotevant, H. D., & McRoy, R. G. (1998). *Openness in adoption: Connecting families of birth and adoption.* Thousand Oaks, CA: Sage Publications.

Grotevant, H. D., Perry, Y. V., & McRoy, R. G. (2005). Openness in adoption: Outcomes for adolescents within their adoptive kinship networks. In D. Brodzinsky & J. Palacios (Eds.), *Psychological issues in adoption: Research and practice* (pp. 167–186). Westport, CT: Praeger.

Hart, H. H. (1910). *Preventive treatment of neglected children.* New York: Charities Publication Committee.

Herman, E. (2007). Adoption History Project. http://www.uoregon.edu/~adoption/ archive.htm, not paginated.

Hollinger, J. H. (2004). Intercountry adoption: A frontier without boundaries. In N. R. Cahn & J. H. Hollinger (Eds.), *Families by law: An adoption reader.* New York: New York University Press.

Howard, J. (2006). *Expanding resources for children: Is adoption by gays and lesbians part of the answer for boys and girls who need homes?* New York: Evan B. Donaldson Adoption Institute. Available online at www.adoptioninstitute.org

Howard, J., & Freundlich, M. (2008). *Expanding resources for waiting children II: Eliminating legal and practice barriers to gay and lesbian adoption from foster care.* New York: Evan B. Donaldson Adoption Institute. Available online at www.adoptioninstitute.org

Martin, A. (1993). *The lesbian and gay parenting handbook: Creating and raising our families.* New York: Harper Collins.

McRoy, R. G., Grotevant, H. D., Ayers-Lopez, S., & Henney, S. M. (2007). Open adoptions: Longitudinal outcomes for the adoption triad. In R. A. Javier, A. L. Baden, F. A. Biafora, & A. Camacho-Gingerich (Eds.), *Handbook of adoption: Implications for researchers, practitioners, and families* (pp. 175–189). Thousand Oaks, CA: Sage Publications.

Melosh, B. (2002). *Strangers and kin: The American way of adoption.* Cambridge, MA: Harvard University Press.

Morgan, E. (1944). *The Puritan family.* Boston: Trustees of the Public Library.

Nelson, C. (2003). *Little strangers: Portrayals of adoptions and foster care in America, 1850–1929*. Bloomington: Indiana University Press.

New York Times, January 12, 2004. Two fathers, with one happy to stay at home. Front page.

Patterson, C. J. (1994). Lesbian and gay couples considering parenthood. An agenda for research, service, and advocacy. *Journal of Lesbian and Gay Social Services, 1*, 33–55.

Patterson, C. J., & Friel, L. V. (2000). Sexual orientation and fertility. In G. Bently & N. Mascie-Taylor (Eds.), *Fertility in the modern world: Biosocial perspectives* (pp. 238–260). Cambridge: Cambridge University Press.

Patterson, C. J., Sutfin, E. L., & Fulcher, M. (2004). Division of labor among lesbian and heterosexual parenting couples: Correlates of specialized versus shared patterns. *Journal of Adult Development, 11*, 179–189.

Pertman, A. (2011). *Adoption nation: How the adoption revolution is transforming our families - and America*. Boston: Harvard Common Press.

Presser, S. B. (1972). The historical background of the American law of adoption. *Journal of Family Law, 11*, 442–516.

Riskind, R., & Patterson, C. J. (2010). Parenting intentions and desires among childless lesbian, gay, and heterosexual individuals. *Journal of Family Psychology, 24*, 78–81.

Rye, B. J., & Meaney, G. J. (2010). Self-defense, sexism, and etiological beliefs: Predictors of attitudes toward gay and lesbian adoption. *Journal of GLBT Family Studies, 6*, 1–24.

Sokoloff, B. Z. (1993). Antecedents of American adoption. *Future of Children, 3*, 19–22.

Smith, S., McRoy, R. G., & Kroll, J. (2008). *Finding families for African American children: The role of race and law in adoption from foster care*. New York: Evan B. Donaldson Adoption Institute. Available online at www.adoptioninstitute.org

Stacey, J., & Biblarz, T. (2001). How does the sexual orientation of parents matter? *American Sociological Review, 68*, 159–183.

Winerip, M. (2007). A reason to take the early bus home. *New York Times*, August 19, no page number.

Youcha, G. (1995). *Minding the children: Child care in America from colonial times to the present*. New York: Scribner's.

2

Emerging Diversity in Family Life

Adoption by Gay and Lesbian Parents

ADAM PERTMAN AND JEANNE HOWARD ■

Extraordinary changes have occurred in the American family over the past several decades—changes that have expanded both our understanding of what constitutes a family and our acceptance of a broad range of family forms. In a historic heartbeat, we have witnessed a radical reduction in the social stigmas against nontraditional families associated with divorce, single parenthood, interracial marriage, and nonbiological parent–child relationships. The result is a growth in the diversity of families—from ones in which children are raised by single parents, stepparents, grandparents, and parents of different races or ethnicities, to ones with parents who are lesbian or gay, or who are foster parents, adoptive parents, and even parents whose families have been created through artificial reproductive techniques such as egg and sperm donation, surrogacy, and, most recently, embryo transfers. These and other changes signal a fundamental, presumably permanent shift away from the "Leave it to Beaver" stereotype of a married mom, dad, and the children born to them, to recognition of an array of family forms within which children can thrive.

Many people view this transformation as personally and culturally beneficial. For example, greater acceptance of family diversity has provided more freedom for couples to end unhappy marriages and has reduced stigma for single parents and their children. These cultural shifts have also allowed more adults to experience the joys and vicissitudes of parenting and have advanced broader social equality. Others in our country, however, view these changes negatively, asserting that they are leading to a weakening of social responsibility and represent a threat to the very institution of family itself. For example, the Family Research Council, a conservative policy and lobbying group active in movements against both gay marriage and gay adoption, holds the view that being gay itself is dangerous and should never receive social approval. Its website states:

> *[The] Family Research Council [FRC] believes that homosexual conduct is harmful to the persons who engage in it and to society at large, and can never be affirmed. It is by definition unnatural, and as such is associated with negative physical and psychological health effects… We oppose the vigorous efforts of homosexual activists to demand that homosexuality be accepted as equivalent to heterosexuality in law, in the media, and in schools… Sympathy must be extended to those who struggle with unwanted homosexual attractions, and every effort should be made to assist such persons to overcome those attractions, as many already have.* (Family Research Council, 2009)

No matter how the changes in family composition in our country are perceived, however, this much appears to be true: These emerging family forms represent a new American (and Western) reality. Consequently, as a society, we must ensure—through our laws, policies, and practices—that all family types in which children are being raised are supported to enable children to be as strong and healthy as possible.

Adoption provides a useful prism through which to view the unprecedented, ongoing transformation in American family life. A short time ago, in historical terms, adoption was used as a remedy for children who had no living parents, whose parents could not care for them, or whose parents were deemed unfit by society. Poverty and pregnancy outside of marriage were the primary triggers for the placement of children for adoption. Growth in out-of-wedlock pregnancy after World War II, continuing social reproach for "illegitimacy," and shame associated with infertility led to a set of practices that moved adoption from privacy to secrecy (Carp, 1998; Esposito & Biafora, 2007; Russett, this volume). The matching of children with parents who they resembled physically and intellectually was seen as critical to adoption success, the better to make the process invisible. Stigma relating to illegitimacy (including very real limitations on the rights and opportunities of "bastards") reinforced practices whereby mothers-to-be hid their pregnancies, relinquished children—often without seeing them—to people they had never met, and were expected to return to their lives free of the ostensible burden of an unplanned child. In fact, during this period, for a single woman to parent her child was viewed as selfish and a violation of important social norms. As one adoption book put it:

> The laws and customs of our society have been set up to give children a sound and stable upbringing through marriage and the two-parent family. The family which consists of an unmarried mother and her child is disapproved of, and stands out as different from other families in the community. It is a constant reminder that this girl has failed to conform with the approved customs and values of society. (Rondell & Michaels, 1962, p. 55)

Not only was the identity of the mother kept secret from the adopting parents, but so were most aspects of the child's biological, medical, and social history. Although some information was provided to the new family, the idea that the parties should meet, or that a relationship might develop between the family of creation and the family of nurture, was nearly unheard of as part of the formal adoption practice until relatively recently.

If illegitimacy and single parenthood were the problems, adoption by childless, infertile, married, white couples was the solution. Although single-parent adoption did occur, it was a distant second choice to the supposed ideal. And not all potential parents were viewed as "acceptable"; for instance, even when growing numbers of children were entering foster care in the 1970s and were in need of permanent families, foster parents—whether married or single—were deemed unsuitable except as temporary caretakers. It was not until 1973 that the Child Welfare League of America, the primary standard-setting body in adoption, revised its Adoption Standards to state that adoption by foster parents was acceptable. Even so, as late as the mid-1970s, over two-thirds of the states either prohibited or discouraged adoption by foster parents (Meezan, 1983).

The landscape of adoption has changed remarkably. In contemporary America, the majority of mothers (and sometimes fathers) placing infants for adoption do so under arrangements in which they select their children's new families, and most have the opportunity for ongoing contact (Grotevant & McRoy, 1998; Pertman, 2011; Smith, 2006). Furthermore, single parents today adopt infants domestically, adopt children from other countries, and, in the highest numbers, adopt children from the foster care system. For example, in 2006, 29 percent of foster care adoptions were by single parents (26 percent by females and 3 percent by males); an additional 2 percent of such adoptions were by unmarried couples. And foster parents, once seen as poor candidates for providing permanency, are currently the primary source of adoptive mothers and fathers for children from foster care (U.S. Children's Bureau, 2008).

MARRIAGE, ADOPTION, AND THE "HOMOSEXUAL AGENDA"

Another historic change in American society, and in Western societies generally, has been the fast-growing recognition of gay and lesbian family relationships (Gates, Badgett, Macomber, & Chambers, 2007; Mallon, 2007a; Pertman, 2011; Russett, this volume). That recognition comes with cultural ambivalence, to be sure, with some states granting protection from discrimination based on sexual orientation, as well as legally recognizing same-sex couple relationships and extending protections to their families, and with others denying such recognitions and protections.

Marriage by same-sex couples and adoption by gays and lesbians are intertwined. Movements against both trends gained momentum after the landmark 2003 U.S. Supreme Court decision striking down laws that criminalized homosexual behavior. In Lawrence et al. v. Texas (539 U.S. 558, 2003), the court held that laws prohibiting gay and lesbian behavior violate the due process clause of the

14th Amendment. The majority found that "the liberty protected by the Constitution allows homosexual persons the right to choose to enter upon relationships in the confines of their homes and private lives and still retain their dignity as free persons… [T]his Court's obligation is to define the liberty of all, not to mandate its own moral code."

Although Lawrence ended the criminalization of homosexuality, the fight over same-sex marriage (and civil unions and other formal recognition of gay and lesbian relationships) continues. Even prior to Lawrence, Congress had passed the Defense of Marriage Act, which banned federal recognition of same-sex marriages and allowed states to refuse recognition of such unions. In the year following Lawrence, however, the Supreme Court of Massachusetts held that banning same-sex marriage was a violation of the state Constitution and, in 2004, Massachusetts became the first state to allow marriage by two people of the same gender. This landmark decision, as well as passage of statutes and court findings in several states allowing same-sex marriage, civil union, or domestic partnership,[1] fueled concerns among social conservatives. They rallied with a movement to fight what they called the "homosexual agenda." Use of the term, which was first used by the Family Research Council as early as 1992, grew as gay and lesbian Americans began to achieve legal victories. The "homosexual agenda" was represented as a campaign to gain legitimacy, to normalize immoral behavior, and to carve out "special rights" for gays and lesbians. This campaign for legitimacy, including adoption by gays and lesbians, was presented as a threat to the social order and a danger to children. According to James Dobson of "Focus on the Family," the goals of the "homosexual agenda" include:

> … *universal acceptance of the gay lifestyle, discrediting of scriptures that condemn homosexuality, muzzling of the clergy and Christian media, granting of special privileges and rights in the law, overturning laws prohibiting pedophilia, indoctrinating children and future generations through public education, and securing all the legal benefits of marriage for any two or more people who claim to have homosexual tendencies.* (Dobson, 2005, p. 19)

At present, 30 states have passed constitutional amendments prohibiting same-sex marriage, and 41 have enacted statutes expressly restricting marriage to one man and one woman (National Conference of State Legislatures, 2009).

The denial of the right to marry has implications for the many adopted children with same-sex parents. For example, when states prohibit adoption by cohabiting couples, full legal protections are denied to boys and girls whose parents are not allowed to marry because they are lesbian or gay. These protections include health insurance, inheritance, Social Security benefits, family leave, child support, or visitation should the couple separate, and, most important, the right of a surviving parent to have automatic guardianship in case of the death or disability of the other. All of these rights and protections are guaranteed to children born to married parents, born to one parent and adopted by a stepparent, or adopted by married couples.

Recognizing this legal vulnerability, some states permit unmarried, same-sex parents to adopt the children born to their partners through second-parent adoption (see Appell, this volume). Such adoption has long been a remedy for stepparents who wish to have legal standing with their spouses' children, and, in many states, it has become a method by which a same-sex partner can gain legal standing. For children being adopted by same-sex couples, some states also allow both partners to become legal parents simultaneously (joint adoption) or consecutively (through second-parent adoption) (see Appell, this volume). Fourteen states[2] and the District of Columbia provide such protection through appellate or state supreme court rulings.

For most same-sex partners who adopt, the picture is a confusing one. Parents in states that recognize marriage or civil union for gay and lesbian partners generally provide protections similar to those for heterosexual married partners who adopt. For the majority of Americans, however, the ability to jointly adopt or to have a second-parent adoption depends on where they happen to live. Illinois allows both processes. In Michigan, joint adoption by same-sex partners is prohibited, but there is no express prohibition against second-parent adoption, although at least one judge has moved to block it. In Colorado, legal statute permits second-parent adoption, but there is no case law on joint adoption. North Carolina's statute bars joint adoption to those who are unmarried, but has allowed second-parent adoption at the trial court level. In addition, Florida, Nebraska, Ohio, Utah, and Wisconsin have ruled that existing second-parent or "stepparent" adoption laws do not apply to same-sex couples (Human Rights Campaign, 2009a). In these states, as well as in Mississippi, Utah, and most recently Arkansas (where adoption by unmarried couples was barred, the ban was struck down and the State has appealed the case to the state supreme court), children are legally vulnerable; that is, although they may have two (unmarried) adults serving as parents, only one can provide them with legal rights and protections.

Although marriage has been the battleground for the culture wars on the rights of gays and lesbians, family formation—and, in particular, adoption by gays and lesbians—has been under attack as well. Several state legislatures have considered banning such adoptions, though from 2006 forward none has yet done so through statute. However, in November 2008, Arkansas voters passed a referendum that bars unmarried couples from adopting children or serving as foster parents. Although the ballot measure's language did not specify gays or lesbians, materials in support of it made it clear that they were the targets. In a flyer backing the proposal, Family Council Action Committee President Jerry Cox stated:

> This act is a response to a homosexual political agenda at work in other states. This agenda uses children to advance the goals of special interest groups… Activists [in other states] have successfully used adoptive or foster care children by homosexuals to advance their agenda. Arkansas has no law on the books to prevent this. The children of Arkansas should never be used to promote the social or political agenda of any special interest group. (Family Council Action Committee, 2008)

The ban was struck down in April 2010 by an Arkansas court. The State appealed the case to the Arkansas supreme court, as Cox and the Family Council Action Committee had promised.[1]

Paradoxically, despite the continuing controversy about whether gays and lesbians should be permitted to marry, as well as the public discussion about whether same-sex couples should be allowed to adopt, all the states allow lesbian and gay *individuals* to form families through adoption[3] (see Appell, this volume). As noted, just three states prohibit unmarried couples from adopting; by default, they exclude gay and lesbian couples because they cannot marry in those states. When state statutory or case law does not expressly permit or protect adoption by gays and lesbians, children remain vulnerable.

SUPPORT FOR ADOPTION BY GAYS AND LESBIANS

The arguments of opponents to adoption by gays and lesbians are not supported by the leading professional organizations in child welfare, medicine, psychology, sociology, law, and adoption—nearly all of which are on record in support of adoption by all qualified, nurturing individuals and couples, irrespective of their sexual orientation. These organizations include the American Bar Association, the American Medical Association, the American Psychological Association, the American Psychiatric Association, the Child Welfare League of America, the Evan B. Donaldson Adoption Institute, the National Association of Social Workers, and many others. For example, the North American Council on Adoptable Children, an organization of over 1000 parents, professionals, and groups representing the needs of children awaiting permanent families, states that children should not be denied homes due to the sexual orientation of prospective parents, recommends that all prospective parents be considered fairly and equally, and opposes rules that exclude prospective parents on the basis of sexual orientation (Howard & Freundlich, 2008).

The position of these organizations is based on a quarter-century of research showing that growing up in a gay- or lesbian-headed household does not undermine the psychological, social, or educational adjustment of children. Although research into lesbian and gay parenting has been confronted with many challenges, especially in terms of sample selection, more recent studies have overcome many of these earlier difficulties (Gartrell, Peyser, & Bos, this volume; Meezan & Rauch, 2005; Patterson & Wainright, this volume). The sum of social science research, to date, finds few substantive differences in adjustment between children raised in gay- or lesbian-headed families and those raised by heterosexual parents. Furthermore, no significant differences have been found between children of lesbian mothers and those of straight mothers on a range of measures of psychological and social adjustment such as self-esteem, anxiety and depression,

1. On April 7, 2011 the Arkansas supreme court rejected the appeal, declaring the law banning gay/lesbian adoption to be unconstitutional.

behavior problems, social relationships, and emotional problems. Children also fare similarly in cognitive ability and school performance (Anderssen, Amlie, & Ytteroy, 2002; Brewaeys, Ponjaert, Van Hall, & Golombok, 1997; Flaks, Ficher, Masterpasqua, & Joseph, 1995; Golombok, Perry, Burston, Murray, Mooney-Somers, Stevens, & Golding, 2003; Golombok, Spencer, & Rutter, 1983; Meezan & Rauch, 2005; Tasker& Golombok, 1995; Wainright, Russell, & Patterson, 2004). A few studies have found that children of lesbian and gay parents fare better than their peers on some measures, such as in school involvement (Wainwright et al., 2004) and comfort in discussing sexual development with parents (Tasker & Golombok, 1995). Other studies have found more equality in parenting and greater parental involvement by both parents in lesbian- or gay-headed families (Chan, Brooks, Raboy, & Patterson, 1998). Although the majority of studies, to date, have been conducted on lesbian-headed families, the limited findings on families headed by gay fathers also indicate positive adjustment for children and healthy family functioning (Anderssen, Amlie, & Ytteroy, 2002; Patterson, 2000). (For a more thorough discussion of existing research see Gartrell et al., this volume, and Patterson & Wainright, this volume.)

Parenting by lesbian and gay adults has always existed—typically within traditional marriages in which one partner was "in the closet." Meanwhile, adoptions by lesbians and gays have been steadily increasing for decades, primarily as the process has opened to Americans who are not married (Brodzinsky, Patterson, & Vaziri, 2002; Brodzinsky, 2003; Brodzinsky, this volume; Gates et al., 2007).

American public opinion on this issue has also shifted significantly during the past decade. As recently as 1999, the majority of Americans (57 percent) opposed adoption by gays and lesbians, with only 38 percent approving it. By 2006, the public was almost evenly divided, with 48 percent opposed and 46 percent in favor (Pew Research Center for People and the Press, 2006)—and the trend line appears to be continuing in that direction. Indeed, opinion has shifted positively in every age group, among both male and female respondents, in every region of the country, in both political parties, in many religions, and among secular Americans. Those under 30 years old were far more open to the idea of gay and lesbian adoption, by a margin of 58 percent in favor to 38 percent opposed, suggesting that the shift in sentiment will continue and probably accelerate (Pew Research Center for People and the Press, 2006). Even in Florida—which until recently explicitly prohibited adoption by both gay and lesbian individuals and couples[4]—responses by voters indicate attitudes that would favor allowing these individuals and couples to adopt (Ryan, Bedard, & Gertz, 2004).

As public opinion has shifted, so have the practices of adoption agencies. For example, research by Brodzinsky et al. (2002) found that 63 percent of the 214 adoption agencies surveyed accepted applications from gay or lesbian prospective parents, and 38 percent had made at least one adoptive placement with such parents in the 2-year study period. The researchers found that policies and practices of agencies, as well as attitudes about gays and lesbians as adoptive parents, varied by agency. Public agencies, whose focus was placing children with special needs, Jewish agencies, and traditional Protestant agencies were more likely to approve of and to have accepted applications from gays and lesbians, whereas Catholic and fundamentalist Christian agencies were much less likely to consider them. Female respondents were more open to gay and lesbian adoption than males. In addition, agencies primarily placing children who were older and/or had special needs were more open to working with sexual minority individuals and couples than were agencies primarily placing healthy infants (Brodzinsky et al., 2002; Brodzinsky, 2003; Brodzinsky, this volume).

The numbers of children who are fostered by gay and lesbian parents or have been adopted by them are difficult to determine, particularly because many placement agencies do not request information about parents' sexual orientation. A joint study by the Urban Institute and the Williams Institute, however, estimates that 14,000 children are currently being fostered by gay or lesbian parents and that over 65,000 have been adopted by sexual minority individuals and couples. The report also notes that lesbians actually show greater interest in adoption (46.2 percent) than heterosexual women (32.1 percent), and more often take concrete steps toward adopting a child (5.7 percent versus 3.3 percent, respectively). Moreover, in response to conservative calls to restrict fostering and adopting to heterosexual adults, the report goes on to estimate that the economic impact of doing so would add from $87 million to $130 million to state expenditures each year (Gates et al., 2007).

Most of what we know about children growing up with lesbian or gay parents comes from research into families in which one of the adults is the birth parent. Recent studies of adoptive families formed by gay or lesbian parents, however, have found similar results to those of studies of nonadoptive families: Adoption by gay or lesbian parents does not lead to negative outcomes for children's behavior, family functioning, or youth and parent attachment. For example, a comparison of three types of adoptive families—43 families with children with special needs (in which the sexual orientation of the parents was not determined but who were presumed to be straight), 32 non-special needs families headed by gays or lesbians, and 25 non-special needs families headed by heterosexual parents—found higher levels of family functioning for those with younger children, as well as those with children who experienced fewer placements and who were free of disabilities or histories of abuse. In contrast, parental sexual orientation was not associated with the quality of family functioning, with the exception of families with older children. In those cases, being parented by gay and lesbian individuals was associated with higher levels of family functioning (Leung, Erich, & Kanenberg, 2005). In addition, a more recent study by Erich, Kanenberg, Case, Allen, and Bogdanos (2009) of 154 adoptive families (27 headed by gay or lesbian parents and 127 headed by heterosexual parents) found no relationship between parent sexual orientation and level of parent–child attachment in adolescence. Other factors, however, were associated with attachment. Specifically, higher levels of attachment were linked to more positive levels of life satisfaction among youth, greater parental satisfaction in the relationships with their children, fewer placements prior to adoption, and younger age among youth. Although there is much more to learn about the adjustment

and well-being of adopted children generally, and specifically about those factors correlated with different levels of adjustment in children being parented by
gay and lesbian individuals and couples, investigations to date suggest that
children are not disadvantaged by being adopted by lesbian or gay parents rather
than heterosexual ones.

GROWING INTERNATIONAL ACCEPTANCE OF GAY
AND LESBIAN ADOPTION

The United States is not alone in allowing adoption by lesbians and gays. At present, nine European nations,[5] Canada (in some provinces), Australia (in some
areas), and South Africa permit such adoptions. Israel's Welfare Ministry has
moved to facilitate adoption for same-sex couples and granted lesbian couples
permission to adopt a child together or to adopt the children of their partners
(Regev, 2007). A recent decision by the European Court of Human Rights, striking down French denial of a lesbian's request to adopt, found that France had
engaged in a violation of the European Convention of Human Rights by failing to
assess the woman's adoption as it would one by a single heterosexual. Although
the finding did not guarantee that gay and lesbian adoption would be mandated
throughout the European Union, it set a precedent for the 27 member nations,
opening the way for suits by other gay and lesbian prospective adopters (Crumley,
2008). Thus, both internationally and domestically, the trend is toward greater
recognition of these adoptions.

LAW, POLICY, AND PRACTICE

This shift in public opinion—as well as in legal statute and practice—is playing out
in most of the United States. As previously stated, only three states tailor their
prohibitions—Mississippi by barring gay and lesbian partners from adopting, and
Utah and Arkansas[2] by restricting adoption only to married couples. So, in all 50
states and the District of Columbia, gay and lesbian *individuals* can and do adopt
children. The debate is far from settled, however, with most states expanding their
pools of potential parents by including gays and lesbians, with a few other states
appearing to be headed in the opposite direction.

More than 100,000 of the children in foster care are legally free to be adopted.
The major child welfare, legal, psychological, and medical associations recognize
that many gay and lesbian adults are willing and able to parent such children and
the law now permits such adoptions in all states.[6] How, then, can policy and practice best serve the children who need homes and support the families formed by
gay and lesbian parents?

---

2. See previous note on the recent ruling affecting adoption by gays and lesbians in Arkansas.

The Child Welfare League of America's Standards of Excellence for Adoption Services (2000) (CWLA) state, "All applicants should be assessed on the basis of their abilities to successfully parent a child needing family membership and not on their race, ethnicity or culture, income, age, marital status, religion, appearance, differing lifestyles, or **sexual orientation**" [emphasis added]. Furthermore, the CWLA suggests that applicants for adoption should be accepted "on the basis of an individual assessment of their capacity to understand and meet the needs of a particular available child at the point of adoption and in the future." Yet, far too often, this is not the case.

Children Needing Homes

Most adopted children in the United States (other than those adopted by stepparents) come either from foster care, from other nations, or from parents who placed them for adoption as infants. Although there is no national count of domestic infant adoptions, they clearly have declined steadily in number since the 1970s. Of the approximately 135,000 adoptions occurring annually in the United States today, after excluding those by stepparents, 15 percent are of infants domestically born in this country, 26 percent are of children from other nations, and 59 percent are from foster care (Smith, 2006).

Many more couples and individuals seek to adopt domestically born healthy infants than currently are available. Even as the number of these adoptions has decreased, the number of adoptions from foster care has grown substantially— supported by federal legislation and state efforts to find homes for these boys and girls. The Adoption Excellence 2000 initiatives of the Clinton Administration and the related Adoption and Safe Families Act of 1997 led to dramatic increases in adoptions from the child welfare system (Figure 2.1).

In 1995, fewer than 26,000 children were adopted from foster care annually. By 2004, that number doubled to 52,000. That means, today, that the significant

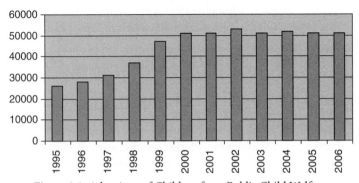

Figure 2.1 Adoptions of Children from Public Child Welfare.
SOURCE: Derived from U.S. Department of Health and Human Services, Administration for Children, Youth and Families, U.S. Children's Bureau. *Adoptions of Children with Public Child Welfare Agency Involvement by State FY 1995-FY 2006.*

majority of adoptions in the United States are not of newborns or of children from other countries, but of boys and girls who were removed from their homes of origin following maltreatment or risk of harm. Although there is an "oversupply" of parents interested in adopting infants domestically and children from abroad (particularly of young children), there is a significant "undersupply" of parents for children in foster care who need permanent families. In 2006, the most recent year for which data were available, 129,000 of the over half-million children in the public system were awaiting adoptive homes (U.S Children's Bureau, 2008).

Lesbian and gay adults in America have become parents by adopting infants, children from overseas,[7] children from foster care, and the biological children of their partners, and through artificial reproductive techniques and surrogacy arrangements. But they have fewer opportunities to adopt infants (anecdotally, we know that birthparents most often choose to place their children with married, heterosexual couples) or from abroad (because other countries also explicitly prefer or require married heterosexuals), so their greatest prospects of becoming adoptive parents are through the foster care system (Brodzinsky, this volume; Howard & Freundlich, 2008; Pertman, 2011). Although this reality clearly reflects an ongoing social bias, one of its consequences is that a significant and growing number of gays and lesbians look to the child welfare system to become parents.

There is clear consensus, based on solid research and extensive clinical and social casework experience, that children's prospects for growing up whole and normal are undermined by temporary or institutional care, that is, no matter how good they may be, these forms of care do not achieve results as positive as those for children raised in the emotionally and legally secure environment of a permanent family. Furthermore, the consequences of long-term foster care are stark. Recent studies on the outcomes of youths "aging out" of the child welfare system point to a host of risks: early parenthood, poverty, unemployment, homelessness, incarceration, and problems in mental and physical health (Courtney, Dworsky, Ruth, Keller, Havlicek, & Bost 2005). Adults are obviously the intended targets of states that exclude or discourage adoption by lesbians and gays, but these women and men can become parents though other means (or in other states); so the clearest harm done by shrinking the pool of qualified parental applicants is to children in need of permanent homes.

REDUCING BARRIERS

A combination of legal, policy, and organizational actions is needed to expand the pool of prospective parents to include qualified gays and lesbians. These are delineated in a recent report by the Evan B. Donaldson Adoption Institute (Howard & Freundlich, 2008). The report recommends—among many other actions—that child welfare advocates continue their work to revoke laws and policies that exclude qualified parents, and that they combat efforts to expand bans against lesbian and gay adoption. This work should also include advocacy for the right of same-sex couples to adopt children either simultaneously or in tandem, both as a matter of fairness and in order to afford their sons and daughters optimum legal and social protections.

One way in which progress could be made is simply to better inform the social workers and other professionals involved in adoptions—because the research shows that many of them misunderstand or do not know what is permissible, and therefore assume that gays and lesbians are not allowed to adopt in their states (Brodzinsky, this volume; Brodzinsky et al., 2002; Kenyon et al., 2003; Ryan, 2000). This education process is accelerating as organizations such as the Human Rights Campaign—with its *All Children–All Families* initiative (Human Rights Campaign, 2009b)—embark on initiatives to help agencies recruit more gay and lesbian adoptive parents, and as attitudes among adoption professionals and the general public change.

Knowledge of law and policy is a critical first step toward substantive change. To sensitively and openly incorporate sexual orientation into the preparation process, however, professionals who place children into new families must also be aware of their own stereotypes and biases (Mallon, 2007a; Mallon, this volume). Like racism, sexism, ageism, and other negative valuations, homophobia can influence beliefs and judgments (as well as actions) without being intentional or even conscious. Workers therefore may need education and training to assess their views and how they may disadvantage children waiting for permanent families.

Examining beliefs and stereotypes is critical, but professional competence is the key to successful adoption practice. To best serve children who need homes, as well as the families formed by gay and lesbian parents, workers and the agencies that employ them must be open to emerging knowledge and experience. Training specific to serving this population is therefore needed and, increasingly, is being desired and provided (see Brodzinsky, this volume). Similarly, a growing number of agencies are recruiting gay and lesbian employees, board directors, and members of advisory boards, understanding that they bring experience and expertise comparable to adding diversity in race, gender, and other areas. And, at the same time (albeit more slowly), professionals are connecting to organizations in gay and lesbian communities from which knowledge and resources can be obtained.

OPEN DISCUSSION—WITH SENSITIVITY

Child welfare authority Gary Mallon (2007a, 2007b, and this volume) asserts that prospective gay and lesbian adoptive parents are subject to both heightened scrutiny and oversensitivity. He argues that workers should be forthright, recognizing that not acknowledging gay and lesbian orientation can lead to the loss of important information about parental strengths as well as challenges, and can undermine the adoption preparation and support process. Furthermore, avoiding dialogue about sexual orientation prevents discussion of how parents can legally protect the children involved and can undercut their ability to get the assistance needed to plan for the discrimination that they and their children may face.

Most of the children who are awaiting adoption from foster care are older. Preparing them for placement with gay or lesbian parents must include helping them understand differences in sexual orientation, answering their questions openly and fully, and helping them learn to cope with the potential intolerance and prejudice of others.

Finally, because discrimination against gays and lesbians remains legal in most states, professionals working with these adoptive parents must be sensitive to the need for confidentiality. So adoption workers must be aware that some of their clients cannot safely be "out" and, therefore, in the home study process or other aspects of preadoption work, they must be careful not to inadvertently subject gay and lesbian prospective parents to the loss of employment or housing, or to necessarily view the decision to remain "closeted" in certain life contexts as reflecting adjustment difficulties (Mallon, this volume).

The primary role of those who help families grow through adoption is to find safe, loving, and permanent homes for children who need them. But doing so also has another consequence: demonstrating that gays and lesbians can and do form strong families, thereby presumably accelerating the movement of more children into families and simultaneously promoting positive social change.

CONCLUSIONS

Millions of children around the world, including over 100,000 in the United States, need families to raise them. The future for children who grow up without stable families is bleak for them and costly—and not only in terms of money—to society as a whole. To make genuine advances for these boys and girls, the social changes taking place in our country need to include the consideration of all qualified parents for them. The movement in that direction has been accelerating for decades—for single mothers and fathers, for cohabiting heterosexual couples, and, most recently, for gay and lesbian Americans. A transformation of the family, indeed of the very meaning of the word family, is taking place as a result. Whatever we may feel as individuals about this historic shift, both research and experience strongly indicate it is a positive one for children who need permanent homes. Primarily for their sake—but also in order to provide equal rights to all adults—- this social revolution warrants support. In the context of adoption, this means the removal of legal and policy barriers to adoption and foster parenting by gays and lesbians, enabling them to undergo the same scrutiny and consideration as other potential foster and adoptive parents; it means the expansion of joint and second-parent adoptions, so that children receive maximum protection and security; and, perhaps most critically, it means public education about the needs of waiting children and the ability of gay and lesbian adults (and many others) to meet their needs, so that—quite simply—more boys and girls can live fulfilling, happy lives.

Notes

1. Massachusetts, Connecticut, Iowa, Vermont, New Hampshire, and the District of Columbia allow or will soon allow the issuance of marriage licenses to two persons of the same gender. California (despite its recently passed ban on same-sex marriage), Oregon, New Jersey, and Washington offer most state level spousal rights, and Hawaii, and Wisconsin offer some protections (National Conference of State Legislatures, 2009). Maine's law allowing same-sex marriage, passed in May 2009, was repealed through voter referendum in November 2009.

2. Arkansas, California, Colorado, Connecticut, Florida, Illinois, Indiana, Maine, Massachusetts, New Jersey, New York, Oregon, Pennsylvania, and Vermont.

3. Florida's 1977 statutory ban on all adoptions by gays and lesbians was recently declared unconstitutional; the ruling was upheld by the Third District Court of Appeal (*Florida Department of Children and Families v. In the Matter of the Adoption of X.X.G. and N.R.G.*, 2010).

4. As previously noted, the Florida law was held to be unconstitutional by the Third District Court of Appeal in the October 2010 decision, *Florida Department of Children and Families v. In the Matter of the Adoption of X.X.G. and N.R.G.*

5. Belgium, Denmark, Germany, Iceland, The Netherlands, Norway, Spain, Sweden, and the United Kingdom.

6. The exceptions being for gay and lesbian *couples* in Mississippi and Utah.

7. International adoption has become more difficult for gay and lesbian adopters in recent years, with more countries such as China prohibiting adoption by single adults and others implementing specific bans against adoption by gay or lesbian adults, or at least by unmarried couples.

References

Anderssen, N., Amlie, C., & Ytteroy, E. A. (2002). Outcomes for children of lesbian and gay parents: A review of studies from 1978 to 2000. *Scandinavian Journal of Psychology, 43*, 335–351.

Brewaeys, A., Ponjaert, I., Van Hall, E. V., & Golombok, S. (1997). Donor insemination: Child development and family functioning in lesbian mother families. *Human Reproduction, 12*, 1349–1359.

Brodzinsky, D. (2003). *Adoption by gays and lesbians: A national survey of agency policies, practices and attitudes.* New York: Evan B. Donaldson Adoption Institute. Available at www.adoptioninstitute.org.

Brodzinsky, D. M., Patterson, C. J., & Vaziri, M. (2002). Adoption agency perspectives on lesbian and gay prospective parents: A national study. *Adoption Quarterly, 5*, 5–23.

Carp, E. W. (1998) *Family matters: Secrecy and disclosure in the history of adoption.* Cambridge, MA: Harvard University Press.

Chan, R. W., Brooks, R. C., Raboy, B., & Patterson, C. J. (1998). Division of labor among children conceived via donor insemination by lesbian and heterosexual mothers. *Child Development, 69*, 443–457.

Child Welfare League of America. (2000). *Standards for excellence in adoption.* Washington, D.C.: Child Welfare League of America.

Courtney, M. E., Dworsky, A., Ruth, G., Keller, T., Havlicek, J., & Bost, N. (2005). *Midwest evaluation of the adult functioning of former foster youth: Outcomes at age 19. Chapin Hall Working Paper.* Chicago, IL: Chapin Hall Center for Children.

Crumley, B. (2008). France overruled on gay adoption. *Time World,* January 23, 2008. Retrieved from http://time.com/time/world/article/0,8599,1706514,00.html June 15, 2008.

Dobson, J. (2005). *Marriage under fire: Why we must win this battle.* Carol Stream, IL: Tyndale House.

Erich, S., Leung, P., & Kindle, P. (2005). A comparative analysis of adoptive family functioning with gay/lesbian and heterosexual adoptive parents and their children. *Journal of GLBT Family Studies, 4,* 23–60.

Erich, S., Kanenberg, H., Case, K., Allen, T., & Bogdanos, T. (2009). An empirical analysis of factors affecting adolescent attachment in adoptive families with homosexual and straight parents. *Children and Youth Services Review, 31,* 398–404.

Esposito, D., & Biafora, F. A. (2007). Toward a sociology of adoption: Historical deconstruction. In R. Javier, A. Baden, F. Biafora, & A. Camacho-Gingerich (Eds.), *Handbook of adoption: Implications for researchers, practitioners, and families* (pp. 1–14). Thousand Oaks, CA: Sage Publications.

Family Council Action Committee. (2008). Jerry's Remarks. Retrieved from http://adoptionact.familycouncilactioncommittee.com/index.asp?PageID=14. June 30, 2009.

Family Research Council. (2009). *Human Sexuality (web publication).* Retrieved from http://www.frc.org/human-sexuality (accessed June 30, 2009).

Flaks, D. K., Ficher, I., Masterpasqua, F., & Joseph, G. (1995). Lesbians choosing motherhood. *Developmental Psychology, 31,* 105–114.

Gates, G., Badgett, L. M. V., Macomber, J. E., & Chambers, K. (2007). *Adoption and foster care by lesbian and gay parents in the United States.* Technical report issued jointly by the Williams Institute and the Urban Institute. Available at www.urban.org.

Golombok, S., Perry, B., Burston, A., Murray, C., Mooney-Somers, J., Stevens, M., & Golding, J. (2003). Children with lesbian parents: A community study. *Developmental Psychology, 39,* 20–33.

Golombok, S., Spencer A., & Rutter, M. (1983). Children in lesbian and single parent households: Psychosexual and psychiatric appraisal. *Journal of Child Psychology and Psychiatry, 24,* 551–572.

Grotevant, H. D. & McRoy, R. G. (1998). *Openness in adoption: Exploring family connections.* Thousand Oaks, CA: Sage Publications.

Howard, J., & Freundlich, M. (2008). *Expanding resources for waiting children II: Eliminating legal and practice barriers to gay and lesbian adoption from foster care.* New York: Evan B. Donaldson Adoption Institute. Available at www.adoptioninstitute.org.

Human Rights Campaign. (2009a). *Laws.* Retrieved from http://www.hrc.org/issues/parenting/adoptions/adoption_laws.asp, November 12, 2009.

Human Rights Campaign. (2009b). *Promising practices in adoption and foster care: A comprehensive guide to policies and practices that welcome, affirm, and support gay, lesbian, bisexual, and transgendered foster and adoptive parents.* Washington, D.C.: Human Rights Campaign.

Kenyon, G. L., Chong, K. E., Enkoff-Sage, M., Hill, C., Mays, C., & Rochelle, L. (2003). Public adoption by gay and lesbian parents in North Carolina: Policy and practice. *Families in Society, 84,* 571–575.

Leung, P., Erich, S., & Kanenberg, H. (2005). A comparison of family functioning in gay/ lesbian, heterosexual and special needs adoption. *Children and Youth Services Review, 27*, 1031–1044.

Mallon, G. (2007a). *Lesbian and gay foster and adoptive parents: Recruiting, assessing and supporting an untapped resource for children and youth.* Washington, D.C.: Child Welfare League of America.

Mallon, G. P. (2007b). Assessing lesbian and gay prospective foster and adoptive families: A focus on the home study process. *Child Welfare, 86*, 67–86.

Meezan, W. (1983). Toward an expanded role for adoption services. In. B. McGowan (Ed.), *Child welfare: Current dilemmas, future directions* (pp. 425–478). Itasca, IL: Peacock.

Meezan, W., & Rauch, J. (2005). Gay marriage, same-sex parenting and America's children. *Future of Children, 15*, 97–115.

National Conference of State Legislatures. (2009). *Same sex marriage, civil union and domestic partnerships.* Retrieved from http://www.ncsl.org/programs/cyf/samesex.htm, July 1, 2009.

Patterson, C. J. (2000). Family relationships of lesbians and gay men. *Journal of Marriage and the Family, 62*, 1052–1067.

Pertman, A. (2011). *Adoption nation. How the adoption revolution is transforming our families - and America.* Boston: Harvard Common Press.

Pew Research Center. (2006). *Less opposition to gay marriage, adoption and military service.* Retrieved from http://people-press.org/report/273/less-opposition-to-gay-marriage-adoption-and-military-service, December 1, 2008.

Regev, D. (2007). State to help same-sex couples adopt. *Israel News*, July 29, 2007. Retrieved from www.nhetnews.com/articles/07340,L-3430923,00.html, June 15, 2008.

Rondell, F., & Michaels, R. (1962). *The adopted family.* New York: Crown Publishers.

Ryan, S., Bedard, L., & Gertz, M. (2004). Florida's gay adoption ban; What do Floridians think? *University of Florida Journal of Law and Public Policy, 15*, 261–283.

Ryan, S. D. (2000). Examining social workers' placement recommendations of children with gay and lesbian parents. *Families in Society, 81*, 517–528.

Smith, S. (2006). *Safeguarding the rights and well-being of birth parents in the adoption process.* New York: Evan B. Donaldson Adoption Institute. Available at www.adoptioninstitute.org.

Tasker, F., & Golombok, S. (1995). Adults raised as children in lesbian families. *American Journal of Orthopsychiatry, 65*, 203–215.

U.S. Children's Bureau. (2008). *Trends in Foster care and Adoption FY 2002–FY 2006.* Retrieved from www.acf.hhs.gov/programs/cb/state_research/afcars/trends.html, June 1, 2008.

Wainright, J., Russell, S. T., & Patterson, C. J. (2004). Psychosocial adjustment, school outcomes, and romantic relationships of adolescents with same-sex parents. *Child Development, 75*, 1886–1898.

3

Legal Issues in Lesbian
and Gay Adoption

ANNETTE R. APPELL ■

Lesbians and gays adopt for any number of reasons, including the desire to parent, provide homes for children in need, protect nonlegally sanctioned parent–child relationships, adopt their partners' children, and formalize relationships to children created through reproductive technology. They adopt as singles, couples, or second parents. In fact, because lesbians and gays cannot marry or enter into other civil unions in most of the United States, couples choosing to have children together generally must adopt if they wish to establish legal ties between the partner who is the nonbiological or nonlegal parent and the child. Moreover, unlike adoption-seeking heterosexuals, lesbians and gays face additional legal burdens to establishing and protecting parent–child relationships. These obstacles include bans or limitations on lesbian and gay adoption and barriers to adopting as unmarried couples. In addition, although the ubiquitous best interests of the child standard most often affords a rationale for granting such adoptions, it also provides ammunition to challenge or more heavily scrutinize lesbian and gay adopters.

Despite these obstacles, adoption provides an important vehicle for lesbians and gays to create and formalize parent–child relationships in the United States. Courts and even legislatures have been knowingly permitting lesbian and gay individuals and couples to adopt children since at least the early 1990s (Appell, 2001a), well before the push for legal protection of adult same-sex relationships—rights that have developed more slowly and with greater controversy (Forman, 2004). Whereas same-sex couple adoption remains entangled with opposition to gay marriage, same-sex adult relationships are beginning to receive protections akin to, if not on par with, marriage. For those lesbian and gay life partners who can marry, or who are in states with civil union or enhanced domestic partnership laws, marital presumptions apply in adoptions. In those states, adoption may not be necessary because such statutory schemes provide that the parent–child relationship between the nonbiological parent and the child conceived in the relationship is automatic, just as the husband is presumed to be the legal father in heterosexual marital relationships (Appleton, 2006). In addition, the common law recognition of de facto parents also serves to create bundles of parental or quasiparental rights and obligations, such as ongoing visitation or even child support after the couple's relationship dissolves (Appell, 2001b). Nevertheless, adoption remains an important tool for lesbians and gays to create and protect their families.

This chapter provides an overview of adoption law and principles in the United States, situates lesbian and gay adoption within those norms, and illustrates how the courts and legislatures have responded to the increasing numbers of openly identified lesbians and gays who are seeking to adopt children as individuals and couples. It also addresses issues surrounding enforcement of adoption decrees and concludes with a consideration of practical implications of the variety and indeterminacy of legal rules regarding lesbian and gay adoption. The chapter does not address equitable and nonadoptive methods of creating quasi or actual parent–child relationships, such as de facto parenthood (Appell, 2001b) and parenthood created through the statutory parentage presumptions (Joslin, 2005).

OVERVIEW OF ADOPTION LAW AND PRINCIPLES

As a legal matter, parenthood includes a bundle of rights, obligations, and entitlements for both parent and child. Parents determine what is in the best interests of their children and the law presumes this determination is correct (Appell, 2001b; *Troxel v. Granville*, 2000). Thus, parents have the right to make decisions regarding child rearing, child custody, medical treatment, education, and religion, all within general parameters established by state and federal law regarding health, safety, and education. Children in turn have a liberty interest in the parent–child relationship and freedom from undue state intervention (*Santosky v. Kramer*, 1982). Benefits that flow from the parent–child relationship include the rights to inheritance, insurance coverage, survivor benefits, certain tort claims, parental obligations of care and support, and relationships with siblings and extended kin.

Adoption is by definition the legal transfer of parenthood from one to another parent or couple. This transfer normally operates to completely terminate parental rights and relations between the parent and child, including relations between the child and the terminated parent's kin, such as the child's siblings, grandparents, aunts, uncles, and cousins; in their stead, adoption creates a new set of family relationships through the adoptive parent or parents. In addition, because formal adoption was created before the rise of divorce, adoption statutes initially contemplated termination of the rights of any legal parent and complete transfer to an entirely new family.

Before the development of adoption law, parent–child relationships were primarily established through biological and marital relationships. Legal adoption, an extraordinary addition to the Anglo-American lexicon, was not part of the English law during the time the United States was inheriting its law from Britain (Carp, 2004). Adoption was, therefore, unknown in the common law of the United States. The common law is more organic and flexible than statutory law, and courts may interpret matters of common law more liberally, modifying it over time as the needs and mores of the people change. In contrast, statutory law, especially law that, like adoption, creates a new legal action, reflects the specific will of a democratically elected legislature and courts are constrained to strictly construe the law to reflect the legislature's intent.

It was not until 1851 that the first comprehensive general adoption statute was enacted in the United States, in Massachusetts; within decades, every state enacted a general adoption statute (Presser, 1971).[1] These laws, passed during a time of growing concern about the welfare of children whose parents could not care for them, regularized adoption procedures and codified two core principles of adoption: (1) the termination of one family and the creation of another when (2) such an action would serve the child's interests (Appell, 1998; Presser, 1971). Despite its progressive and salutary origins, adoption law is conservative and resolute, partially because it is statutory and less pervious to judicial modification and because adoption law is based on a heterosexual, nuclear family form that continues to be normative even though it is no longer, if it ever was, descriptively accurate (see Russett, this volume; Coontz, 2000; Stacey, 1996). Adoption absorbs and reflects tensions between deeply held traditional and postmodern values regarding nuclear families, biological connection, and marriage.

Slowly, these changing norms regarding children and families surfaced in domestic relations and adoption law. For example, as parental status received increasing constitutional recognition during the twentieth century, adoption laws added special protections against terminating parental rights and instituted limitations to the establishment of nonmarital fathers' rights (Appell & Boyer, 1995); the rise in divorce and remarriage rates pushed adoption law to add special stepparent adoption provisions (Carbone, 2006); changing notions of anonymity, identity, and exclusive parenting led to regulation of postadoption contact agreements (Appell, 2003); and most recently, increasing recognition and visibility of lesbian and gay families have pushed courts and legislatures to contemplate samesex couple adoption.

Despite such changes, state adoption laws still reflect remarkably similar norms regarding families and parenting. These norms consider exclusive parenting by no more than two legal parents and when there are two parents, they should be married. Adoption generally does not allow as parents two fathers, two mothers and a father, or a grandmother and her daughter; instead, most state adoption laws project single or married parents. Statutes generally provide for termination of both parents' rights before an adoption can occur, unless a stepparent is adopting a spouse's child. These special stepparent adoption provisions reflect a departure from adoption's complete substitution of one set of parents for another and instead permit one parent to retain parental rights while the other parent's rights are relinquished or otherwise terminated; this exception enables the stepparent to become the second parent to the child and the former spouse's parental status to be terminated. In addition, when a married person seeks to adopt, both spouses must join in the adoption petition because of the various legal presumptions related to marital status and the parent–child relationship.

Just as adoption navigates between conservative and progressive norms, adoption laws reflect two common, though often conflicting, principles of construction and interpretation. First, adoption law is a creature of statute and is subject to strict construction, so courts may be constrained to embellish or disregard the terms of the adoption act they are applying. Second, and sometimes in opposition to the strict construction rule, the best interest of the child generally is paramount in matters involving children, including adoption cases. This rule requires at a minimum a case-specific factual inquiry into the best interests of the prospective adoptee before the court can enter an adoption decree and, in some jurisdictions, the rule guides construction and interpretation of the adoption statute itself.

LESBIAN AND GAY ADOPTION

Adoption norms have been flexible enough to accommodate lesbian and gay adoption in many states; however, adoption law remains heavily based on marriage, so it does not always accommodate two-parent, nonmarital adoptions. The trend seems to be away from various barriers to and outright bans of lesbian and gay single or nonmarital, same-sex couple adoptions and toward statutory interpretation and legislative enactments that permit lesbian and gay adoption (see also Brodzinsky, this volume). Single lesbians and gay men are no longer categorically prohibited from adopting in any state, including Florida, where a state appellate court recently struck down as unconstitutional the state's statutory ban on lesbian and gay adoption (*Florida Department of Children and Families v. In the Matter of the Adoption of X.X.G. and N.R.G.*, 2010). Only Arkansas[1] (An Act Providing That an Individual Who Is Cohabiting Outside of a Valid Marriage May Not Adopt, 2008), Mississippi (Mississippi Code Ann., 2007), and Utah (Utah Code Ann., 2011) statutorily ban same-sex couple adoptions.[2] In other states, the best interests of the child mandate leaves courts with wide discretion to assess in individual cases whether a gay man or woman is fit to adopt; the breadth and indeterminacy of the best interests standard can work for or against lesbian and gay adoption, permitting decision-makers—judges, social workers, and guardians *ad litem*—to exercise their own positive, neutral, or negative views regarding lesbian and gay adoption petitioners.

It is difficult to assess conclusively how courts are responding to adoption petitions by single lesbians and gays, as well as same-sex couples, because adoption proceedings are closed, sealed, and rarely yield published decisions at the trial level. Moreover, because these proceedings are usually consensual and

---

1. Several times in this chapter, reference is made to Arkansas' ban on same-sex adoption. On April 7, 2011, the supreme court of Arkansas declared this law to be unconstitutional (Arkansas Department of Human Services v. Cole, 2011 Ark. 145).

uncontested, there is rarely an unsatisfied party to appeal a decision granting an adoption. As a result, few appellate decisions are available for those interested in following the development of adoption law and practice. However, national lesbian and gay human and legal rights organizations and their local or affinity groups monitor lesbian and gay adoptions in the states (Human Rights Campaign Foundation, 2008; Lambda Legal, 2009; National Lesbian & Gay Task Force, 2008). These organizations report that single lesbian and gay adoptions are permitted in nearly every state and the District of Columbia, including Utah and Mississippi, which have statutory bans applicable to same-sex couple adoption (Lambda Legal, 2009). It is not certain whether Arkansas, Nebraska, and North Dakota permit single lesbian and gay adoptions (Human Rights Campaign Foundation, 2008). Same-sex couple adoption appears to be widespread, but not as prevalent as single lesbian and gay adoption (Lambda Legal, 2009; National Lesbian and Gay Task Force, 2008).

The very fact that the adoption petitioners are lesbian, gay, or bisexual may trigger greater scrutiny than other adoptions when courts determine whether it is in the best interests of the child to be adopted (see also Brooks, Kim, & Wind, this volume; Mallon, this volume). For example, in Chicago, Illinois, where the adoption courts routinely permit lesbian and gay second-parent adoptions, the courts require home studies for those adoptions but do not require them for stepparent adoptions (In re C.M.A., 1999). This is true despite the fact that in both stepparent and second-parent adoptions, one of the parties petitioning for the adoption is already a legal parent and is presumptively better situated than a social services agency to assess whether it is in the child's interests to be adopted. The Tennessee Supreme Court found that a parent's "lifestyle" is a permissible factor to consider in the assessment of the child's best interests, but nevertheless approved the lesbian single-parent adoption of an infant against the challenge of the infant's grandparents (In re Adoption of M.J.S., 2000).

An Arizona adoption court utilized a heightened level of scrutiny regarding a bisexual petitioner while exercising its authority to assess the best interests of the child (In re Pima County Juvenile Action, 1986). In denying the adoption, the court disregarded the investigating social service agency's recommendation that the petitioner be permitted to adopt. Instead, the court found that the petitioner was not acceptable and appointed counsel to pursue further investigation of the petitioner. The court-appointed counsel recommended against adoption after finding that:

> Petitioner is a bisexual individual who has had, and may have in the future, sexual relationships with members of both sexes; he presently lives alone and is employed...; he has held at least eight different employment positions in eleven years; he has sought counseling for personal problems repeatedly in the last ten to eleven years; his family support system is limited at the present time. (In re Pima County Juvenile Action, 1986, p. 832)

The court denied the petition and the appellate court affirmed, holding, inter alias, that the petitioner's "ambivalence in his sexual preference was very appropriately a concern of the court. As we have stated previously, *the primary concern of the court, to the exclusion of all else, is the best interest and welfare of any child*" [In re *Pima County Juvenile Action*, 1986, p. 834 (emphasis supplied)].

In an unusual dispute, but one that exposes the open-endedness of the best interests determination, an Illinois adoption judge refused to grant adoption petitions in two separate lesbian coparent adoption cases, even though each couple received favorable home studies and the children's guardian *ad litem* concluded that the adoptions were in the best interests of the children (In re *C.M.A.*, 1999). In what should have been pro forma proceedings, the judge instead ordered hearings on the best interests of the children in each case. When the hearings revealed only positive evidence, the judge continued to refuse the request of the petitioners and guardian *ad litem* to grant the adoptions. The judge then appointed the Washington, D.C. based Family Research Council as a second guardian *ad litem* for the children because the Council opposes lesbian and gay adoptions. Ultimately, the judge was removed from the cases for cause and the adoption orders were entered.

Similar projection of value judgments about what is best for children prolonged the adoption of Charles B., a foster child with physical and mental disabilities whose parents had relinquished their parental rights years earlier (In re *Adoption of Charles B.*, 1990). The adoption petitioner, Mr. B., was employed as a psychological counselor and was in a committed relationship with another professional; in addition, Mr. B.'s extended family had embraced Charles as a member of the family. The adoption court granted the adoption over the objection of Charles' legal guardian with the right to consent to his adoption, the Licking County Department of Human Services. The guardian objected because Mr. B. did not meet the Department's "characteristic profile of preferred adoptive placement" (In re *Adoption of Charles B.*, 1990, p. 888). At the County's request, the intermediate appellate court reversed the adoption, but the Ohio Supreme Court ultimately upheld the adoption.

More often, however, the best interests standard militates toward permitting adoptions by lesbian and gay adopters, particularly if they appear to be ideal parents. For example, a Delaware court considering the second-parent adoption petition brought by the longtime partner of an adoptive parent of two foster children approved the adoption, despite the lack of clear statutory authority for nonmarital couple adoption (In re *Peter Hart*, 2001). The court granted the adoption because it was in the best interests of the children and to do "otherwise would be absurd, unreasonable, and unnecessary" (In re *Peter Hart*, 2001, p. 1182). The children in question were full brothers, each of whom was exposed to drugs in utero, was born prematurely, had experienced related physical problems arising therefrom, and had lived in multiple foster placements. The adoptive father and his partner were "life partners" who had been living together for 22 years at the time of the adoption, had merged their assets, and had each assumed a parental role with the brothers. The court concluded: "In fact and in law what does matter in the best interests of Peter and George is that they are thriving in the environment created by Gene Hart and Burke Shiri" (In re *Peter Hart*, 2001, p. 1191).

Statutory Bars or Impediments to Lesbian and Gay Adoption

As noted above, until recently, Florida was the only state to ban all adoptions by sexual minority individuals and couples as a matter of explicit public policy (i.e., by statute). Florida's ban, enacted in 1977, stated: "No person eligible to adopt under this statute may adopt if that person is a homosexual" (Fla. Stat. Ann., ch. 63.042(3)). This statute was overturned in the 2010 decision by the Florida Third District Court of Appeal that allowed Martin Gill, a gay man, to adopt the two brothers that he had been fostering for over 5 years with his partner.

A more recent approach to limiting adoption by unmarried couples, including lesbians and gays, is reflected in prohibitions of adoption in Utah and Arkansas by persons who are residing with a sexual partner in a relationship not sanctioned under that state's marriage laws (An Act Providing That an Individual Who Is Cohabiting Outside of a Valid Marriage May Not Adopt or Be a Foster Parent; 2008; Utah Code Ann., 2011). The adoption prohibition would, of course, also extend to heterosexuals in nonmarital sexual relationships, including those engaged in polygamous marriages. On their face, these adoption prohibitions do not extend to celibate same-sex couples or to sexually active lesbians and gays who are not residing with their sexual partners. The statutes appear then to promote single-parent adoption over two-parent adoptions for those persons who are not in a lawful marriage. The Mississippi adoption statute is more directly and exclusively applicable to lesbians and gay couples, but does not ban single gays and lesbians from adopting. Instead, it prohibits adoption "by couples of the same gender" (Miss. Code Ann., 2007) and, therefore, like Utah and Arkansas, privileges single-parent adoption. Otherwise, with certain exceptions discussed in the next section, state statutes are generally silent regarding lesbian and gay adoption.

Same-Sex Couple Adoption

Far more pervasive than outright bans on lesbian and gay adoption are indirect barriers to same-sex couple adoption because most adoption statutes do not address, and therefore may be interpreted to prohibit, adoption by unmarried heterosexual and same-sex couples. Instead, most adoption statutes appear to contemplate single-parent or marital adoptions, although there are a handful of statutes that explicitly permit same-sex or nonmarital two-parent adoption. Moreover, as discussed below, those domestic partnership and civil union schemes that treat registered relationships as akin to marriage permit same-sex nonmarital parents to adopt as if they were married.

Same-sex couple adoptions generally occur in two different situations: the would-be parents adopt an unrelated child at the same time, much as a single person or married couple would; or the partner of the birth or adoptive parent adopts the child, much like a stepparent would. The first same-sex couple adoption scenario, generally referred to as joint adoption, applies when a couple seeks together to adopt a child to whom neither is legally or biologically related (In re *Adoption of Carolyn B.*, 2004; In re *Infant Girl W.*, 2006). The second scenario, usually referred to as second-parent adoption, generally includes same-sex couples who formed a relationship after one or both of the partners already had a biological or adopted child.

Second-parent adoption is also utilized by same-sex couples who decide together to form a family usually through various technological forms of reproduction in which one of the partners is the birth mother or father; such arrangements might include artificial insemination, in vitro fertilization, or surrogacy (e.g., In re *Adoption of Two Children*, 1995; *Adoption of Tammy*, 1993). In this latter situation, although both members of the couple set out together to create a family and both assume parental roles for the child, only the biological parent has a legal relationship with the child unless the couple lives in a state that provides the equivalent of marital status to same-sex couples or otherwise interprets their parentage statutes to establish parenthood in these contexts.

In both the second-parent and joint-parent adoption scenarios, the purpose of coparent adoption is to establish legal recognition and protection of the nonlegal parents' prospective or de facto relationships to their children (*Adoption of Tammy*, 1993; In re *Jacob*, 1995). Although some courts interpret their state's statutory law to prohibit nonmarital couple adoption (e.g., In re *Adoption of T.K.J.*, 1996; In re *Angel Lace M.*, 1994), others courts conclude the opposite (e.g., *Adoption of Tammy*, 1993; In re *K.M.*, 1995; *Sharon S. v. Superior Court*, 2003). Twelve years after a Colorado appellate court construed the state's adoption statute to prohibit same-sex couple adoption (In re *Adoption of T.K.J.*, 1996), the Colorado legislature amended its adoption statute to explicitly permit second-parent adoption (Colo. Rev. Stats., 2008).

In addition, state attorneys general may be called upon to provide opinions about the legality of same-sex couple adoption under existing statutes. These opinions are not binding precedent, but are persuasive authority regarding state law. For example, Tennessee's attorney general issued an opinion on same-sex couple adoption at the request of a state judge and found that the Tennessee adoption statute permits same-sex couple adoptions (Tenn. Att'y Gen., 2007). Michigan's attorney general reached a different conclusion, determining that same-sex couples married in Massachusetts (at the time the first and only state to extend marriage rights to lesbians and gays) would not be permitted to adopt children as couples in Michigan because Michigan does not recognize such marriages and its case law does not permit two unmarried people to adopt a child (Mich. Att'y Gen., 2004).

SAME-SEX PARENT ADOPTION UNDER TRADITIONAL ADOPTION STATUTES: ADOPTION NORMS AND THE LAW

When state legislatures or attorneys general provide clear authority for or against coparent adoption, prospective adoptive parents, courts, government officials, and adoption professionals have some guidance as to whether state law permits same-sex couple adoption. When such explicit direction does not exist, as it does not in most states, courts utilize a variety of interpretive methods to determine whether such an adoption is permissible under statutes that are silent regarding same-sex couple adoption.

These statutes all reflect similar basic legal norms surrounding families and adoption: strict statutory construction, best interests of the child, exclusive parenting, and marriage-based, nuclear family structures. When the appellate courts first began to consider same-sex parent adoption, none of the adoption-seeking couples was married to each other and none was in a state that had special statutory provisions for nonmarital couple adoption. In these instances, there was not a clear answer regarding whether same-sex couple adoption was permitted. In reaching a decision on the adoptions in question, each court laboriously combed the statutory language and structure and employed norms regarding statutory construction, adoption, parents, and children to interpret those provisions. Courts that did not permit these adoptions tended to use formalistic interpretive methods whereas those courts that permitted same-sex couple adoptions utilized more functional approaches.

Formalistic Statutory Interpretation

Courts permitting and denying same-sex parent adoptions may rely on the strict construction rule, but this rule most strongly drove the courts that denied same-sex couple adoptions (In re *Adoption of T.K.J.*, 1996; In re *Adoption of Baby Z.*, 1999; In re *Angel Lace M.*, 1994; In re *Adoption of Jane Doe*, 1998). These courts took a formalistic approach and read the adoption statutes narrowly and literally to permit adoptions by single persons, married couples, or stepparents. Because those categories do not explicitly reference two adoptive parents who are not married, these courts found that the statute barred nonmarital couple joint adoption or, in the case of second-parent adoption, the existing parent must relinquish her parental rights for her partner to gain parental status. In the absence of explicit statutory language, the courts concluded that same-sex couple adoption was legally impossible.

Indeed, in each of these cases, the courts focused on the mechanics of adoption and heteronormative notions of marital and exclusive parenting and did not privilege other norms, including the profamily purposes of adoption or the best interests of the child. Even when these formalistic courts found that adoption by the second parent would serve the child's interests, they determined, nevertheless, that the child was not available for adoption unless the first parents' parental rights were terminated or relinquished (In re *Angel Lace M.*, 1994; In re *Adoption of Baby Z.*, 1999; In re *Adoption of Jane Doe*, 1998; In re *Adoption of T.K.J.*, 1996).

In a particularly formalistic interpretation of an adoption statute, the Connecticut Supreme Court construed the statute narrowly both because it was a statute in derogation of common law and because the adoption court has limited jurisdictional authority in Connecticut (In re *Adoption of Baby Z.*, 1999). The Supreme Court held that the child could be available for second-parent adoption without terminating the custodial parent's rights only if the couple were married, so there could be no action for adoption for an unmarried couple. The court concluded that "The members of our legislature, as elected representatives of the people have the power and responsibility to establish the requirements for adoption in this state. The Courts simply cannot play that role" (In re *Adoption of Baby Z.*, 1999, p. 1060). The Connecticut legislature responded to this prompt by enacting a nonmarital coparent adoption statute the following year (Conn. Gen. Stat. § 45a-727a, 2004).

The strict construction rule can also lead a court to permit same-sex couple adoption. A court reviewing two New York cases involving nonmarital heterosexual and homosexual second-parent adoptions recognized that the strict construction rule applied, but extended that strict construction to the "legislative purpose as well as legislative language" (In re *Jacob*, 1995, p. 399). That court ultimately decided that the purpose of the statute was to promote the child's interests and interpreted the language in a way that would advance that purpose. In this instance, it meant permitting nonmarital couples "who actually function as a child's parents to become the child's legal parents" (In re *Jacob*, 1995, p. 399).

It is worth noting that the strict construction of adoption statutes is important not just because such statutes derogate the common law, but also because adoption implicates fundamental rights—the rights of parents to raise their children. The U.S. Supreme Court has extended heightened protections to parental rights, particularly in the context of the termination of parental rights and adoption. Thus, there are heightened procedural and substantive protections for parents in the termination of parental rights cases, including a higher burden of proof of parental unfitness (*Santosky v. Kramer*, 1982), free trial transcripts for use in an appeal of a termination of parental rights decision (*M.L.B. v. S.L.J.*, 1996), and the right of nonmarital fathers to establish or preserve a relationship with their children (*Stanley v. Illinois*, 1972; *Caban v. Mohammed*, 1979; *Lehr v. Robertson*, 1983). Moreover, even when children have formed deep psychological attachments to parent-like figures, those attachments do not take precedence over the rights of biological or legal parents (*Smith v. Organization of Foster Families for Equality & Reform*, 1977). There are good reasons, therefore, for courts to be mindful, and even rigid, when determining which children are available for adoption and who has the standing to adopt.

It is not clear, however, that the narrow reading of the adoption statutes by the courts denying the second-parent adoptions protects these important constitutional interests because those second-parent adoption cases involved either fathers who consented to the adoption (e.g., In re *Adoption of Charles B.*, 1990; In re *Angel Lace M.*, 1994), parents whose parental rights previously had been lawfully terminated (e.g., In re *Adoption of Baby Z.*, 1999; In re *Peter Hart*, 2001), or fathers who were sperm donors without paternal rights (e.g., In re *Adoption of Luke*, 2002).

Ironically, those courts utilizing strict construction to prohibit the adoption presented a choice to the same-sex couples of terminating the biological, custodial mother's parental rights so that her partner could gain the legal privileges and burdens of parenthood. That choice also, arguably, inured to the detriment of the children's interests by constraining them to have only one parent or the other. Similarly, in the case of the joint nonmarital foster parent adoptions, narrow construction can result in dismissal of the adoption petition and deprive children of *any* legal parents.

Functional Statutory Interpretation

Courts permitting same-sex couple adoptions tended to apply more liberal and purposive interpretive devices to reach a result that would permit nonmarital couples to adopt in the absence of explicit statutory authority for such adoptions. These courts take a more functional approach, employing methods that promote the outcome of adoption. As discussed below, the best interests of the child mandate was perhaps the predominant leader in these decisions, but the courts also employed other statutory interpretation methods to support a construction of the statutes that would permit adoptions by lesbian and gay couples.

Some courts apply the common statutory interpretation rule that singular words include the plural, unless such an interpretation would be unreasonable (In re *Adoption of M.A.*, 2007; In re *Infant Girl W.*, 2006; In re *Jacob*, 1995; In re *M.M.D.*, 1995; *Adoption of Tammy*, 1993). Utilizing that rule, courts relied on the language in almost all adoption statutes that permits single persons to adopt children. For example, a Washington D.C. court read the language, "any person may petition the court for a decree of adoption" as "any persons may petition the court for a decree of adoption" (In re *M.M.D.*, 1995, pp. 846–7). This way, the courts effectively treat the second-parent adoption as a joint adoption petition by two people.

According to another principle of statutory construction, courts cannot assume that the omission of an issue means that the legislature considered and rejected that issue. This provision is the converse of the statutory construction principle *expressio unius exclusius*, which means that the statute's expression of an item or items (for example, in a list) dictates that other items not mentioned are excluded. Courts that chose the former interpretive device did not find a legislative policy or intention to preclude same-sex couple adoption just because the statutes said nothing about same-sex or nonmarital adoption. For example, the D.C. court reasoned that the D.C. adoption statute did not purport to "specify all eligible adopters, given its level of generality... and its use of 'ifs' when referring to married couples" (In re *M.M.D.*, 1995, p. 852). Therefore, the legislature's mention of married couples and failure to mention nonmarital couples did not present a situation of *expressio unius exclusius*; nor did the court find anything in the legislative history to suggest that Congress had ever considered the matter of unmarried couples adopting children and so could not have intended to exclude it (In re *M.M.D.*, 1995).

The Indiana Court of Appeals also relied on this type of reasoning when it permitted lesbian foster parents to adopt their foster child over the objection of the child welfare agency, stating "it does not follow" that requiring married persons to petition jointly meant that "the legislature was simultaneously denying an unmarried couple the right to petition jointly" (In re *Infant Girl W.*, 2006, p. 243). Similarly, the highest courts of Maine (In re *Adoption of M.A.*, 2007), Massachusetts (*Adoption of Tammy*, 1993), and Pennsylvania (In re *Adoption of R.B.F.*, 2002) found the absence of preclusive language supported the lesbian and gay coparent adoptions

under consideration, even while recognizing that the legislature may not have contemplated same-sex partner adoption (*Adoption of Tammy*, 1993, p. 319).

The courts granting coparent adoption relied most heavily on the best interest
of the child standard. These courts utilized this standard in a variety of ways to
support the granting of adoption decrees to reflect both parents. Some courts used
this best interest standard as an interpretive device to affect the purpose of the
statute (In re *Adoption of Carolyn B.*, 2004; In re *Adoption of Two Children*, 1995; In
re *Adoption of R.B.F.*, 2002; In re *Jacob*, 1995; In re *K.M.*, 1995; In re *M.M.D.*, 1995).
Courts in Illinois and New Jersey were aided by statutory language that mandated
a liberal construction of the statute to affect the child's best interests (N.J. Stat. Ann.
9:3–37, 2000; 750 Ill. Comp. Stat. 50/20 & 50/20a, 2007). In Indiana, the court
found that "the guiding principle of statutes governing the parent–child relationship is the best interests of the child" (In re *Adoption of K.S.P.*, 2004, p. 1257).

Nearly every court granting same-sex couple adoptions privileged the best
interests of the child standard and equated these interests with the psychological
parent principle associated with that standard (Appell & Boyer, 1995; Goldstein,
Freud, & Solnit, 1973; Spinak, 2007) along with recognition that it is often better
for a child to have two legal parents rather than one. Most of the cases involved
families that had been together for years during which time the second parents
participated in child rearing, childcare, and financial support of the child. These
courts then found ways to permissibly construe each statute in a manner that
would permit same-sex parent adoption without mandating the termination of
the legal parents' rights to preserve and protect the child's relationships with both
psychological parents (In re *Adoption of M.A.*, 2007; In re *Adoption of B.L.V.B.*,
1993; In re *Adoption of Two Children*, 1995; In re *Jacob*, 1995; In re *Adoption of
K.S.P.*, 2004; In re *M.M.D.*, 1995; In re *Adoption of R.B.F.*, 2002; *Adoption of
Tammy*, 1993).

In re *Jacob* (1995), for example, held that the adoption statute must "be applied
in harmony with the humanitarian principle that adoption is a means of securing
the best possible home for a child" and could do so "by allowing the two adults
who actually function as a child's parents to become the child's legal parents"
(p. 400). Another New York court would later rely on this same case and standard
to construe the adoption statute as permitting two lesbians in a long-term relationship to jointly adopt a child whom they had not yet parented; the court reasoned that requiring the women to file successive adoption petitions would
deprive the child "of two legal parents during the interval between finalization of
two separate adoptions" (In re *Adoption of Carolyn B.*, 2004, p. 230).[3]

Similarly, in *Adoption of Tammy* (1993), the Supreme Judicial Court of
Massachusetts seemed motivated to protect the child's relationship to both of her
parents, legal and de facto. Besides the ample testimony supporting the strengths
and integrity of the family, the court noted that the child had "strong emotional
and psychological bonds" to both the legal and de facto mothers along with the
benefits to the child of having the legal support of two parents, rather than of just
the one parent (*Adoption of Tammy*, 1993, p. 316). Courts in Indiana (In re
Adoption of K.S.P., 2004; In re *Infant Girl W.*, 2006) and Maine (In re *Adoption of*

M.A., 2007) also recognized the value of protecting these lived relationships and the rights and benefits that flow to the child through those relationships when they are legalized.

These various judicial responses to same-sex couple adoption cases suggest how malleable statutory interpretation principles can be. Indeed, they provide direction for either outcome. For example, Wisconsin's adoption statute explicitly exempts itself from strict construction (Wis. Stat. § 48.01(1)), but the Wisconsin Supreme Court strictly construed the statute to preclude second-parent adoption (In re *Angel Lace M.*, 1994). Massachusetts adoption law did not provide such an exemption, yet that court interpreted its adoption statute in a manner to promote the child's best interests (*Adoption of Tammy*, 1993). Neither state's statute explicitly permitted nonstepparent second-parent adoption.

It appears then that these interpretive principles, as malleable as family forms, provide both cover and support for judicial value determinations regarding which families are entitled to legal recognition and, in turn, which children will have the legal benefits of a second parent and the opportunity to have the person who is in fact a parent make the type of decisions reserved under the law to legal parents. An example of these obverse and perhaps thinly veiled judicial- and family-value determinations is evident in comparing the following judicial opinions in Ohio and Vermont, respectively:

> Until such time as the General Assembly of Ohio changes the law pertaining to same-sex marriages or rewrites the adoption statutes to specifically allow the requested legal relationship, I cannot interpret the existing adoption statute as contemplating a spousal relationship between two individuals of the same-sex such as to create a stepparent relationship in a legal context. (In re *Adoption of Jane Doe*, 1998, concurring opinion, p. 1072)

The Vermont Supreme Court came to an opposite, but equally valid (and prescient), view of the public policy of its state:

> We are not called upon to approve or disapprove the relationship between the two [co-parents]. Whether we do or not, the fact remains that Deborah has acted as a parent of B.L.V.B. and E.L.V.B from the moment they were born. To deny legal protection of their relationship, as a matter of law, is inconsistent with the children's best interests and therefore with the public policy of this state. ... (In re *Adoption of B.L.V.B.*, 1993, p. 1276)

Nonmarital Coparent Adoption Statutes

An increasing number of states make special provision for joint or second-parent adoptions in their adoption or civil union statutes. California [Cal. Fam. Code 9000(f), 2004], Colorado (Colo. Rev. Stat., 2008), Connecticut [Conn. Gen. Stat. § 45a-724(a) (3), 2004], and Vermont [Vt. Stat. Ann. Tit. 15A § 1–102(b), 2001] amended their adoption statutes to provide specifically for joint and second-parent adoptions for nonmarital couples. Connecticut's second-parent adoption statute includes legislative findings that reaffirmed state policy that marriage is heterosexual [§ 1 (4)], but also recognized the benefits to children of having persons "who manifest a deep concern for the child's growth and development" and that a child's best interests are

> promoted when a child has as many persons loving and caring for the child as possible… [and] when a child is part of a loving, supportive and stable family, whether that family is a nuclear, extended, split, blended, single parent, adoptive or foster family. [An Act Concerning the Best Interests of Children in Adoption Matters, § 1(2) & (3), 2000]

Subsequently, both Vermont (Vt. Stat. Ann. tit. 15, § 1204, 2001) and Connecticut (Conn. Gen. Stat. § 46b-38aa-38pp, 2006) enacted Civil Union statutes requiring that parties to civil unions receive the same benefits, protections, presumptions, and responsibilities as married people. California passed a robust domestic partnership law in 2003 that provided similar protections (California Domestic Partner Rights and Responsibilities Act of 2003). These statutes supplement the earlier second-parent adoption provisions. New Jersey (An Act concerning marriage and civil unions, establishing a commission and revising and supplementing various parts of the statutory law, 2006), New Hampshire (N.H. Rev. Stat. Ann. ch. 457-A, 2007), and Oregon (Oregon Family Fairness Act, 2007) have also passed civil union statutes. All of the civil union laws, as well as California's domestic partnership law, afford the rights and responsibilities of marriage to same-sex couples, including marital presumptions regarding parenthood. For example, if a child is born to a civil union, any parental presumptions normally afforded the person married to the mother would apply as well and civil partners could adopt as if they were stepparents (Anderson, 2006). Of course states that recognize lesbian and gay marriage would afford married same-sex partners the same rights as married heterosexuals enjoy. These rights include treating children born to the marriage as the lawful issue of both parents and permitting the couple to adopt jointly or under stepparent adoption provisions.

The question of what effect marital and quasimarital status laws would have on previously granted same-sex couple adoptions arose in California after it amended its stepparent adoption provisions in 2001 to include domestic partners [Cal. Fam. Code § 9000(f), 2004]. Until then, California courts had been granting second-parent adoptions with such regularity that the California Department of Social Services developed special second-parent adoption forms that permitted the legal parent to consent to the second parent's adoption without relinquishing parental rights (*Sharon S. v. Superior Court*, 2003). It was not clear what effect, if any, the 2001 law would have on same-sex couple adoption for couples not registered as domestic partners.

The California Supreme Court resolved that question in a closely watched case involving a lesbian couple who separated in the midst of their second second-parent adoption (*Sharon S. v. Superior Court*, 2003).[4] That case raised the questions of whether California's adoption law permits second-parent adoption for nonregistered domestic partners, whether second-parent adoption was lawful under the previous statute, and whether decades of second-parent adoptions could be invalidated.

The California Supreme Court held that second-parent adoptions have been and continue to be valid under California adoption law (*Sharon S. v. Superior Court*, 2003). In reaching this conclusion, the court engaged in a detailed analysis of the California adoption law and its history, ultimately holding that the law does not require termination of the custodial parents' parental rights for a second-parent adoption to occur. The court also relied on California administrative construction and practice regarding adoption and on the public policy in favor of second-parent adoption, including the benefits adoption affords children and the settled expectations of relinquishing parents and adoptive families (*Sharon S. v. Superior Court*, 2003).

Moreover, the California Supreme Court did not suggest that in the future second-parent adoptions would be permitted only under the new domestic partnership adoption provisions (available only to registered domestic partners). Instead the court held that nondomestic partners could adopt just as they had before the enactment of the domestic partnership adoption procedures. This holding is significant because the domestic partnership provisions are limited to persons who meet the domestic partnership criteria and exclude, for example, heterosexuals, relative care-givers, and persons no longer living together (*Sharon S. v. Superior Court*, 2003).

The Legal Effect of the Same-Sex Couple Adoption Decrees

Once same-sex couples receive an adoption decree, they are the legal parents of the child. The decree guarantees that the parents will be treated as parents for all legal purposes including custody, the authority to enroll the child in school, participate in health-care decision-making, travel with the child, and receive benefits for and through the child, and impart benefits to the child. As they would for any adoption decree, governmental agencies, courts, and other states ought to recognize these decrees as establishing for all legal purposes the parenthood of the adults named in the decree.

After the decree has been entered and the time for challenging it passed, the adoption cannot be challenged, ignored, or revoked. It is binding even against the parties to the adoption, even if the relationship between the adults ends. It is not surprising then that when a biological mother challenged the parental status of her partner who had adopted the child 3 years earlier in Texas, the Texas court held that the challenge came too late (*Hobbs v. Van Stavern*, 2006). In that case, the two women decided together to have a child through assisted reproduction and the nonbiological mother subsequently adopted the child in a second-parent adoption. After they separated, the biological mother claimed that the adoption was not valid. The court disagreed, holding that the birth mother could not challenge the adoption because the statutory time limit for such challenges expired 6 months after the adoption was entered (*Hobbs v. Van Stavern*, 2006, citing Texas

Family Code Ann. §162.012, 2002). Courts in other states have also refused to disregard or vacate second-parent adoptions in subsequent custody disputes between the same-sex coparents (*Giancaspro v. Congleton*, 2009; *S.J.L.S. v. T.L.S.*, 2008; *Schott v. Schott*, 2008).

Courts are also bound by adoption decrees entered in other states, even when the state being asked to enforce the decree does not itself permit same-sex couple adoption (*Embry v. Ryan*, 2009; *Giancaspro v. Congleton*, 2009; *Russell v. Bridgens*, 2002).[5] In *Russell v. Bridgens* (2002), Russell had adopted Bridgens' adopted daughter in Pennsylvania. When they separated 2 years later, Russell moved to Nebraska where she filed a petition for custody and support of the child. Bridgens filed a cross-petition for the same relief and moved to dismiss Russell's claims on the grounds that the adoption was not valid in Pennsylvania and therefore was not enforceable in Nebraska. The trial court granted the motion to dismiss, but the Nebraska Supreme Court reversed, applying the U.S. Constitution's Full Faith and Credit clause (U.S. Const. art. IV, § 1). That clause requires full faith and credit to "be given in each State to the public Acts, Records, and judicial Proceedings of every other State" (U.S. Const. art. IV, § 1). This clause, the Nebraska Supreme Court held, prohibits a state from "reviewing the merits of a judgment rendered in a sister state" (*Russell v. Bridgens*, 2002, p. 59). Therefore, the Nebraska Court assessed whether the Pennsylvania statutory requirements were met in the adoption, found they were, and did not look any further (*Russell v. Bridgens*, 2002).

Enforceability of adoption decrees also arises when adoptive parents seek amended birth certificates reflecting the adoption; they do so because birth certificates are a standard form of proof of parentage and the child's identity. After an adoption, the state or county office that issues birth certificates normally will seal the child's original birth certificate and issue a revised one reflecting the new legal truth established by the adoption decree (Samuels, 2001). When adoptive parents adopt a child in a state in which the child was not born, they may return to the state of the child's birth for an amended birth certificate that reflects the adoption. Just as courts are bound to enforce the adoption decree, public officials in the decree-granting state and in other states must honor the decree.

Most of the litigated contests regarding issuance of postadoptive birth certificates occur when parents seek new birth certificates in states other than the one that granted the adoption, particularly in those states that do not recognize same-sex parents. This was the scenario when three same-sex parent adoptive families, whose adopted children were born in Virginia but adopted in Washington, D.C., challenged the Virginia Registrar of Vital Records and Health Statistics' refusal to issue revised birth certificates reflecting the legal parentage of the children (*Davenport v. Little-Bowser*, 2005). The three couples filed suits seeking to compel the Registrar to issue the certificates, but the trial court held that as a matter of Virginia law, "birth certificates can only list the name of a mother and a father. Birth certificates cannot list the names of two mothers or the names of two fathers. It just cannot be done" (*Davenport v. Little-Bowser*, 2005, p. 369).

Although the adoptive parents raised federal constitutional grounds of equal protection (U.S. Const. amend. XIV, § 2) and full faith and credit (U.S. Const. art. IV, § 1) in support of their claim, the Virginia Supreme Court ruled on state statutory grounds that Virginia law clearly required the executive branch to issue new birth certificates for a person born in Virginia when presented with a certified copy of the decree of adoption and the information necessary to identify the original certificate of birth (*Davenport v. Little-Bowser*, 2005, referencing Virginia Code § 32.1–262, 2004).

A similar dispute arose in Oklahoma when government officials refused to issue birth certificates that reflected the adoptions for three same-sex parent adoptive families (*Finstuen v. Crutcher*, 2007). That case contained an additional wrinkle: Oklahoma had enacted a statute that prohibited the "state, any of its agencies, or any court of this state… [to] recognize an adoption by more than one individual of the same sex from any other state or foreign jurisdiction" [Okla. Stat. tit. 10, § 7502–1.4(A), 2006]. Although not as widespread as the defense of marriage laws that most states passed in response to increasing family rights of lesbians and gays, a number of states have considered enacting laws that would prohibit state actors from recognizing sister state same-sex couple coparent adoptions (Appell, 2001a; Caldwell, 2003; Stone, 2006). So far, only Oklahoma has enacted such a law.

Oklahoma enacted its ban in response to an opinion of the state's Attorney General requiring the Oklahoma State Department of Health to issue a revised birth certificate on behalf of two gay men from Washington who had entered into an open adoption of a child born in Oklahoma (*Finstuen v. Crutcher*, 2007).[6] Three same-sex adoptive couples, including the couple whose child's amended birth certificate instigated the Attorney General's opinion, challenged this new law. Although the couples claimed that the ban violated a number of constitutional rights, the federal trial court ruled on just one ground, holding "that final adoption orders by a state court of competent jurisdiction are judgments that must be given full faith and credit under the Constitution by every other state in the nation. Because the Oklahoma statute at issue categorically rejects a class of out-of-state adoption decrees, it violates the Full Faith and Credit Clause" (*Finstuen v. Crutcher*, 2007, 1141).

Similarly, in 2010, another federal appeals court held that Louisiana must comply with the Constitution's Full Faith and Credit Clause, requiring the state's Registrar and Director of the Office of Vital Records and Statistics to issue a new birth certificate for a Louisiana-born child adopted by two gay men in New York (*Adar v. Smith*, 2010). In refusing to issue the amended birth certificate, the Registrar had relied on Louisiana public policy and an opinion by the Attorney General of Louisiana, which concluded that the Full Faith and Credit Clause did not require Louisiana to issue new birth certificates to children adopted by same-sex couples (La. Att'y Gen., 2007).[7]

PRACTICAL IMPLICATIONS AND CONCLUSIONS

Lesbian and gay adoption pushes cultural buttons regarding intimate associations, including marriage and children, and raises fundamental questions about private and public values regarding the construction of families. It is not surprising that the law, which is by nature conservative, is struggling to balance policies promoting private values, communal life, personal responsibility, and the best interests of children. Despite meeting resistance and controversy along the way, the overall trajectory for lesbian and gay adoption has been toward acceptance and accommodation rather than exclusion.

In the decades since lesbians and gays openly sought and began to obtain adoptive parent status, they have confronted a series of barriers including increased scrutiny and being disadvantaged by norms that do not permit lesbian and gay couples to enter into legal marriages. These struggles appear to have more often resulted in the law positively recognizing lesbian and gay families as entitled to the same, or at least similar, privileges and obligations as heterosexual families. As the lesbian and gay civil rights movement gains traction, it achieves victories in courts and legislatures that guarantee increasing equality under the law to lesbian and gay families. These achievements include systemic legal reforms such as civil unions and even marriage, all of which make adoption more accessible and less necessary as other options become available for legalizing family relationships.

Still, this change is incremental and scattered. As the law struggles with whether and how to accommodate changing family forms, the legal landscape surrounding lesbian and gay adoption remains murky. This absence of clarity presents a number of practical implications. First, the absence of controlling legal authority in the form of statutes or appellate court rulings raises practical questions regarding access to justice and a lack of consistency and determinacy that in turn undermines the rule of law. Although over 20 percent of the states now have statutory or case law permitting same-sex couple adoption, at least 15 other states have permitted second-parent adoption without such higher authority and in 17 states it is unclear whether such adoptions are permitted (National Lesbian & Gay Task Force, 2009). Moreover, adoption practice is confidential and local, not only among the 50 states, territories, and districts of the United States, but also within the states, often varying by county and even within counties by judge. This absence of controlling, public authority regarding same-sex parent adoption in most states, particularly in combination with specific bans on or affecting lesbian and gay adoption in other states, obfuscates the legality of single and coupled lesbian and gay adoption in many states.

Because of these conditions, lesbian and gay families, their attorneys, and other adoption professionals may not know what the rules are or even which courts, attorneys, or agencies are open to same-sex parent adoption. In fact, Brodzinsky, Patterson, and Vaziri (2002) found that adoption agency directors in six states, none of which banned lesbian and gay adoption, believed that such adoption was illegal. Even more striking is that 29 other directors were unsure of the legality of lesbian and gay adoption in their own states (Brodzinsky, Patterson, & Vaziri, 2002). Similar findings are reported in a separate survey research study by Brodzinsky (this volume). The importance of adoption in the family and child welfare lexicons suggest that it is critical for policymakers and other leaders to provide information to child welfare professionals and for the professionals to educate themselves so they know when and where lesbians and gays can adopt children.

Second, in those jurisdictions without clear authority, all of the ancillary adoption issues, such as issuance of new birth certificates and rules regarding parental authority, remain unregulated, leaving families, courts, and adoption professionals without guidance or certainty. This lack of clarity may promote insecurity for parents and confusion for the public officials, teachers, and other professionals with whom the family interacts. This confusion is particularly problematic in the realm of parent–child relations, an area that calls for certainty and clarity. For example, in the *Finstuen v. Crutcher* (2007) litigation, the parents sought new birth certificates so that there would be no questions regarding whether the second parent could have access to the child and make decisions in educational and medical contexts. In *Adar v. Smith* (2010), the parents claimed that the unavailability of an amended birth certificate interfered with the child's medical insurance coverage. It is important for families and the professionals and public servants they encounter to know whom the family comprises and what rights and privileges belong to the adults and children.

A third set of practical challenges facing lesbian and gay adopters and their advocates arises out of the indeterminacy of the best interests of the child standard and the contentiousness that still surrounds lesbian and gay adoption. As shown above, courts and agencies have utilized the best interest of the child standard to more heavily scrutinize lesbian and gay adoptions and to hold homosexuality itself as relevant to the inquiry regarding the propriety of the adoption. Not only may the burden be placed on lesbians and gays to prove in individual cases that they will be good parents despite their nonheterosexual orientation, states may also ban lesbian and gay adoption until there is conclusive empirical or other proof that lesbian and gay adoption is categorically in the best interests of children (*Lofton v. Sec'y of Dep't of Children & Family Services*, 2004).

Moreover, although the best interests standard has served well those lesbian and gay families that reflect dominant norms, lesbians and gays who are not middle class or involved in stable, monogamous relationships may have a more difficult time establishing parent–child relationships (Shapiro, 1999) or even receiving children for adoption (Appell, 2008). These barriers may also disserve children by limiting their placement options. Moreover, no matter how normative the prospective adoptive parents may be, if courts and adoption professionals do not disaggregate opposition to same-sex marriage from their considerations of children's interests in having legal parents who love and care for them, adoption decision points will reflect adult interests, rather than the interests of the child (Table 3.1).

Table 3.1 REPORTED LAW REGARDING SAME-SEX COUPLE ADOPTION AS OF 2011

State	Permits Same-Sex couple Adoption by Statute	Permits Same-Sex Couple Adoption by Appellate Case Law	Same-Sex Couple Adoptions May Be Permitted	Prohibits Same-Sex Couple Adoption by Statute	Prohibits Same-Sex Couple Adoption by Case Law	Prohibits All Lesbian & Gay Adoptions
Alabama			▼			
Alaska			▼			
Arizona						
Arkansas		▼[1]				
California	▼[2]	▼				
Colorado	▼					
Connecticut	▼[2]					
Delaware		(Trial court decision)	▼			
D.C.	▼[2]	▼				
Florida		▼[3]				■##
Georgia			▼			
Hawaii			▼			
Idaho						
Illinois		▼				
Indiana		▼				
Iowa		▼[1]	▼[4]			
Kansas						
Kentucky			▼[4]			
Louisiana					(Attorney General Opinion)	
Maine		▼				
Maryland			▼			
Massachusetts		▼[2]				
Michigan			▼		(Attorney General Opinion)	

Table 3.1 (Continued)

State	Permits Same-Sex couple Adoption by Statute	Permits Same-Sex Couple Adoption by Appellate Case Law	Same-Sex Couple Adoptions May Be Permitted	Prohibits Same-Sex Couple Adoption by Statute	Prohibits Same-Sex Couple Adoption by Case Law	Prohibits All Lesbian & Gay Adoptions
Minnesota			▼			
Mississippi				■		
Missouri						
Montana						
Nebraska					■	
Nevada	▼²					
New Hampshire	▼²	▼				
New Jersey	▼²	▼				
New Mexico			▼			
New York	▼	▼				
North Carolina						
North Dakota						
Ohio					■	
Oklahoma						
Oregon	▼²					
Pennsylvania		▼				
Rhode Island			▼			
South Carolina						
South Dakota						
Tennessee		(Attorney General Opinion)				
Texas			▼³			
Utah				■		
Vermont	▼²	▼				

Table 3.1 (CONTINUED)

State	Permits Same-Sex couple Adoption by Statute	Permits Same-Sex Couple Adoption by Appellate Case Law	Same-Sex Couple Adoptions May Be Permitted	Prohibits Same-Sex Couple Adoption by Statute	Prohibits Same-Sex Couple Adoption by Case Law	Prohibits All Lesbian & Gay Adoptions
Virginia						
Washington			▼			
West Virginia						
Wisconsin					■	
Wyoming						

NOTES: [1]On April 7, 2011, the Arkansas supreme court ruled that the previous ban on adoption by lesbians and gay men was unconstitutional.

[2]Civil union, domestic partnership, or marriage laws that afford same-sex partners state rights equivalent to heterosexual married couples.

[3]On September 22, 2010, a Florida appellate court held that the state's statutory ban against gay adoptions was unconstitutional.

[4]Appellate courts have upheld this in collateral appeals of same-sex couple adoptions granted in that state.

Notes

1. Before then, adoption was informal or was effected through private legislative acts as a way to ensure that children could inherit from individuals who were not their birth parents (Presser, 1971).
2. New Hampshire revoked its ban in 1999 (Homosexual Person-Removing Ban, 1999); moreover, recently, a trial court in Arkansas struck down the Arkansas ban for violating individual liberty under the Arkansas constitution (*Cole v. Arkansas Dept. of Human Services*, Case No 60CV-08–14284; Order 4/16/10).
3. In 2010, New York amended its adoption laws to permit explicitly adoption by two unmarried adult intimate partners (N.Y. Domestic Relations Law § 110, as amended by An Act to amend domestic relations law in relation to authorizing two unmarried adult intimate partners to adopt a child, Session Law 1523-A, 2010).
4. Dozens of local and national groups appeared as friends of the court. These *amicus curiae* included the American Civil Liberties Union, the National Center for Youth Law, the Youth Law Center, Legal Services for Children, National Association of Children's Counsel, California Trial Lawyers, the National Center for Lesbian Rights, Lambda Legal Defense and Education Fund, a number of California bar associations, and representatives of state and local government (*Sharon S. v. Superior Court*, 2003).
5. In *Embry v. Ryan* (2009), a Florida appellate court upheld a Washington state same-sex adoption decree, even though Florida has a ban on lesbian and gay adoption.

In *Russell v. Bridgens* (2002), a Nebraska court upheld an out-of-state second-parent adoption decree even though Nebraska's Supreme Court had several months earlier interpreted its own adoption statute to not permit second-parent adoption (In re *Adoption of Luke*, 2002). In *Giancaspro v. Congleton* (2009), a Michigan appellate court enforced an Illinois second-parent adoption even though Michigan law arguably does not permit nonmarital (heterosexual) couple adoption (Giancaspro, 2009, p. 4).

6. The Oklahoma Attorney General's opinion found that the United States Constitution and Oklahoma law require Oklahoma agencies to "recognize adoption decrees issued to same-sex couples by other states." See Okla. Atty. Gen. Op. 04–8, PP 14, 16 (Mar. 19, 2004) (Specter, 2005, p. 467, n. 1).

7. The Louisiana's Attorney General Opinion also declared that same-sex couple adoption was not permitted under Louisiana state law (La. Atty. Gen. Op. 06–0325, 2007). The federal court decision did not reach that issue.

References

Adar v. Smith, 597 F.3d 697 (5th Cir. 2010).

Adoption of Tammy, 619 N.E.2d 315 (Mass. 1993).

An Act Concerning the Best Interests of Children in Adoption Matters, 2000 Conn. Pub. Acts 00–228 (2000).

An Act concerning marriage and civil unions, establishing a commission and revising and supplementing various parts of the statutory law, 2006 N.J. Laws ch. 103.

An Act Providing That an Individual Who Is Cohabiting Outside of a Valid Marriage May Not Adopt or Be a Foster Parent (2008).

Anderson, L. S. (2006). Protecting parent-child relationships: Determining parental rights of same-sex parents consistently despite varying recognition of their relationships. *Pierce Law Review, 5*, 1–30.

Appell, A. R. (1998). Increasing options to improve permanency: Considerations in drafting an adoption with contract statute. *Children's Legal Rights Journal, 18*(4), 24–51.

Appell, A. R. (2001a). Lesbian & gay adoption. *Adoption Quarterly, 4*(3), 75–86.

Appell, A. R. (2001b). Virtual mothers and the meaning of parenthood. *University of Michigan Journal of Law Reform, 34*(4), 683–790.

Appell, A. R. (2003). Survey of state utilization of adoption with contact. *Adoption Quarterly, 6*(4), 73–86.

Appell, A. R. (2008). Endurance of biological connection: heteronormativity, same-sex parenting and the lessons of adoption. *Brigham Young University Journal of Public Law, (22)* 289–325.

Appell, A. R., & Boyer, B. (1995). Parental rights vs. best interests of the child: A false dichotomy in the context of adoption. *Duke Journal of Gender Law & Policy, 2*, 63–83.

Appleton, S. F. (2006). Presuming women: revisiting the presumption of legitimacy in the same sex couples era. *Boston University Law Review, 86*, 227–294.

Brodzinsky, D. M., Patterson, C. J., & Vaziri, M. (2002). Adoption agency perspectives on lesbian and gay prospective parents: A national study. *Adoption Quarterly, 5*(3), 5–23.

Caldwell, J. (2003, June 10). Little victories for gay adoption: A Mississippi ruling in favor of two lesbian moms shows that states may be forced to allow gay parents even as they reject gay couples. The Advocate. Retrieved Dec. 31, 2007, from http://findarticles.com/p/articles/mi_m1589/is_2003_June_10/ai_105367670.

Caban v. Mohammed, 441 U.S. 380 (1979).

California Domestic Partner Rights and Responsibilities Act of 2003. 2003 Statutes 421.

Cal. Fam. Code § 297.5 (West 2005). (West 2004 & Supp. 2007)

Cal. Fam. Code § 9000(f). (West 2004 & Supp. 2007)

Carbone, J. (2006). The role of adoption in winning public recognition for adult partnerships. *Capital University Law Review, 35*, 341–398.

Carp, E. W. (2004). Introduction. In E. W. Carp (Ed.), *Adoption in America* (pp. 1–26). Ann Arbor: University of Michigan Press.

Cole v. Arkansas Dep't. of Human Services, Case No. 60CV-08–14284 (Order 4/16/10), available at www.scribd.com/doc/30313733/Cole-v-Arkansas-Dept-of-Human-Services-Et-Al-Slip-Op-No-60CV-08–14284-Ak-Pulaski-Circuit-Court-Apr-16–2010-PDF.

Colo. Rev. Stat. § 19–5–203(1), 19–5–208(5), 19–5–210(1.5), 19–5–211(1.5) (West Supp. 2008).

Conn. Gen. Stat. § 45a-724(a)(3) & 45a-727a (West 2004).

Conn. Gen. Stat. § 46b-38aa-38pp (West Supp. 2007).

Coontz, S. (2000). *The way we never were*. New York: Basic Books.

Davenport v. Little Bowser, 611 S.E.2d 366 (Va. 2005).

Embry v. Ryan, 11 So. 3d 408 (Fla. App. 2009).

Finstuen v. Crutcher, 496 F.3d 1139 (10th Cir. 2007).

Fla. Stat. Ann. § 63.042(3) (West 2005).

Florida Department of Children and Families v. Adoption of X.X.G. and N.R.G., 45 So.3d 79 (Fla. App. 2010).

Forman, D. (2004). Interstate recognition of same-sex parents in the wake of gay marriage, civil unions, and domestic partnerships. *Boston College Law Review, 46*, 1–81.

Giancaspro v. Congleton, 2009 WL 416301 (Mich. App. 2009) (unpublished decision)

Goldstein, J., Freud, A., & Solnit, A., (1973). *Beyond the best interests of the child*. New York: The Free Press.

Hobbs v. Van Stavern, 239 S.W.3d 1 (Tex. App. 2006).

Homosexual Person–Removing Ban, 1999 N.H. Laws C. 18 (amending N.H. Rev. Stat. Ann. § 161:2, 170-B:2, 170-B:4, 170-F:2 & 170-F:6 (Supp. 1999)).

Human Rights Campaign Foundation. (2008). Parenting Laws. Retrieved February 28, 2009 from http://www.hrc.org/documents/parenting_laws_maps.pdf.

Ill. Comp. Stat. 50/20 and 50/20a (2007).

In re *Adoption of Baby Z.*, 724 A.2d 1035 (Conn. 1999).

In re *Adoption of B.L.V.B.*, 628 A.2d 1271 (Vt. 1993).

In re *Adoption of Carolyn* B., 774 N.Y.S.2d 227 (N.Y. App. Div. 2004).

In re *Adoption of Charles* B., 552 N.E.2d 884 (Ohio 1990).

In re *Adoption of Jane Doe*, 719 N.E.2d 1071 (Oh. Ct. App. 1998), reconsideration denied, 711 N.E.2d 234 (Ohio 1999).

In re *Adoption of K.S.P.*, 804 N.E.2d 1253 (Ind. Ct. App. 2004).

In re *Adoption of Luke*, 640 N.W.2d 374 (Neb. 2002).

In re *Adoption of M.A.*, 930 A.2d 1088 (Maine 2007)

In re *Adoption of M.J.S.*, 44 S.W.3d (Tenn. Ct. App. 2000).

In re *Adoption of R.B.F.*, 803 A.2d 1195 (Pa. 2002).

In re *Adoption of T.K.J.*, 931 P.2d 488 (Colo. Ct. App. 1996).

In re *Adoption of Two Children*, 666 A.2d 535 (N.J. Super. Ct. App. Div. 1995).

In re *Angel Lace M.*, 516 N.W.2d 678 (Wisc. 1994).

In re *C.M.A.*, 715 N.E.2d 674 (Ill. App. Ct. 1999).

In re *Infant Girl W.*, 845 N.E.2d 229 (Ind. Ct. App. 2006).

In re *Jacob*, 660 N.E.2d 397 (N.Y. 1995).

In re *K.M.*, 653 N.E.2d 888 (Ill. App. Ct. 1995).

In re *M.M.D.*, 662 A.2d 837 (D.C. 1995).

In re *Peter Hart*, 806 A.2d 1179 (Del. Fam. Ct. 2001).

In re *Pima County Juvenile Action B-10489*, 727 P.2d 830 (Ariz. Ct. App. 1986).

Joslin, C. G. (2005). The legal parentage of children born to same-sex coupes couples: Developments in the law. *Family Law Quarterly, 39*(3), 683–705.

Lambda Legal. (2009). Overview of State Adoption Laws. Retrieved February 23, 2009, from http://www.lambdalegal.org/our-work/issues/marriage-relationships-family/ parenting/overview-of-state-adoption.html.

Lehr v. Robertson, 463 U.S. 248 (1983).

Lofton v. Sec'y of Dep't of Children & Family Services, 377 F.3d 1275 (11th Cir., 2004).

La. Att'y Gen. (April 18, 2007). Opinion 06–0325.

Mich. Att'y Gen. (September 14, 2004). Opinion No. 7160.

Miss. Code Ann. § 93–17–3(5) (West 2007).

M.L.B. v. S.L.J., 519 U.S. 102 (1996).

National Lesbian and Gay Task Force. (2008). *Second Parent Adoption in the U.S.* Retrieved February 23, 2009, from http://www.thetaskforce.org/reports_and_research/second_ parent_adoption_laws.

N.H. Rev. Stat. Ann. ch. 457-A (Supp. 2007) (effective January 1, 2008).

N.J. Stat. Ann. § 9:3–37 (West Supp. 2007).

N.Y. Domestic Relations Law § 110 (as amended by Session Law 1523-A, Sept. 17, 2010).

Okla. Stat. Ann. tit. 10, § 7502-1.4(A) (West 2007).

Oregon Family Fairness Act, Oregon Laws 2007, ch. 99, sec. 9.

Presser, S. B. (1971). The historical background of the American law of adoption. *Journal of Family Law, 11*, 443–516.

Russell v. Bridgens, 647 N.W.2d 56 (Neb. 2002).

Samuels, E. (2001). The idea of adoption: An inquiry into the history of adult adoptee access to birth records. *Rutgers Law Review, 53*, 367–436.

Santosky v. Kramer, 455 U.S. 745 (1982).

Schott v. Schott, 744 N.W.2d 85 (Iowa 2008).

Shapiro, J. (1999). A lesbian-centered critique of second parent adoption. *Berkeley Women's Law Journal, 14*(1), 17–39.

Sharon S. v. Superior Court, 73 P.3d 554 (Cal. 2003).

S.J.L.S. v. T.L.S., 265 S.W.3d 804 (Kent. App. Ct. 2008).

Smith v. Organization of Foster Families for Equality & Reform, 431 U.S. 816 (1977).

Specter, R. G. (2005). The unconstitutionality of Oklahoma's statute denying recognition to adoptions by same-sex couples from other states. *Tulsa Law Review, 40*, 467–477.

Spinak, J. (2007). When did lawyers for children stop reading Goldstein, Freud and Solnit? Lessons from the twentieth century on best interests and the role of the child advocate. *Family Law Quarterly, 41*, 393–411.

Stacey, J. (1996). *In the name of the family: Rethinking family values in the postmodern age*. Boston, MA: Beacon Press.

Stanley v. Illinois, 405 U.S. 645 (1972).

Stone, A. (Feb. 20, 2006). Drives to ban gay adoption heat up in 16 States. U.S.A. Today. Retrieved February 23, 2009, from http://www.usatoday.com/news/nation/2006–02–20-gay-adoption_x.htm.

Tenn. Att'y Gen. (October 10, 2007). Op. No. 07–140.

Texas Family Code Ann. § 162.012. (Vernon 2002).

Troxel v. Granville, 530 U.S. 57 (2000).

U.S. Const. art. IV, § 1.

U.S. Const. amend. XIV, § 2.

Utah Code Ann. § 78B-6-117(3) (2011).

Vt. Stat. Ann. tit. 15, § 1204 (2002).

Vt. Stat. Ann. tit. 15A, § 1–102(b) (2002).

Va. Code Ann. § 32.1–262 (2004).

4

Adoption by Lesbians and Gay Men

A National Survey of Adoption Agency Policies and Practices

DAVID M. BRODZINSKY ■

In the past few decades, considerable controversy has surrounded the issue of children growing up in lesbian- and gay-headed households. Cases such as the gay marriage trial in Hawaii (*Baehr v. Miike*), as well as child-custody cases around the county involving gay or lesbian parents, have focused the public's attention on societal beliefs and stereotypes regarding the parenting capacity and mental health of lesbians and gays, as well as the psychological outcomes for children raised by them. Other cases, such as the challenge to Florida's ban on adoption by gay men and women (*Lofton v. Kearney*) and the recent overturning of the Florida law (*FL. Department of Children and Families v. In the Matter of Adoption of X.X.G. and N.R.G.*, 2010), as well as the Arkansas referendum overturning the right of same-sex couples to adopt, have extended the nationwide debate about these issues to the practice of adoption (see Appell, this volume; Blanks, Dockwell, & Wallance, 2004).[1]

Although it is widely acknowledged by social casework professionals that lesbian and gay individuals have been adopting children for some time (Mallon, 2006; Sullivan, 1995), relatively little is known about adoption agency policies and practices in this area, or about the extent to which such placements are being made. The debate about adoption by lesbians, gays, and same-sex couples, as well as the development of best-practice standards in this area, requires sound empirical data and a thorough understanding of the parameters influencing such placements.

In an attempt to address these issues and to promote a more informed dialogue on this controversial topic, the Evan B. Donaldson Adoption Institute conducted

1. On April 7, 2001, after the book was in production, the supreme court of Arkansas declared the state law banning adoption by sexual minority adults to be unconstitutional.

a systematic, nationwide analysis of how agencies handle interest by lesbians and gay men in adopting children, the extent to which agencies are making such placements, and agency staff attitudes regarding adoption by this group of individuals. This chapter provides an overview of the results of this research and the implications of these results for adoption practice.[1]

BARRIERS TO ADOPTION BY LESBIANS, GAYS, AND SAME-SEX COUPLES

Although in the past there were many barriers preventing certain groups from adopting children—including single adults, low-income individuals, fertile couples, members of minority groups, older adults, disabled adults, foster parents, and lesbian and gay individuals—today those barriers have largely been eliminated (Brodzinsky & Pinderhughes, 2002; Brodzinsky, Smith, & Brodzinsky, 1998; Pertman & Howard, this volume). Only one group continues to be discouraged, and in some cases prevented from adopting: gay men and women, whether as individuals or as couples (Appell, this volume; Blanks, Dockwell, & Wallance, et al, 2004; Mallon, 2006).

Statutory barriers to same-sex adoption exist at present in two states[2]: Mississippi's law prohibits adoption by same-sex couples, whereas Utah's prohibition applies to all unmarried adults living with a sexual partner, regardless of their sexual orientation (Appell, 2001, and this volume; Blanks et al., 2004). Most states also impose statutory barriers to second-parent adoptions, prohibiting a lesbian or gay individual (or an unmarried heterosexual person) from adopting a partner's biological or adopted child (Appell, 2001, and this volume; Blanks et al., 2004). Furthermore, although most state adoption laws are silent on the issue or allow adoption by lesbians and gays, local judiciaries are often resistant to granting adoption petitions.

Several factors appear to underlie the resistance to adoption and parenting by lesbians and gays in the United States (Brooks, Kim, & Wind, this volume; Mallon, 2006, and this volume). In many cases, personal and religious beliefs, as well as homophobic attitudes within our culture, have led individuals to conclude that same-gender sexual attraction is deviant and sinful (Herek, 1995). These beliefs and attitudes, as well as the myths, stereotypes, and misconceptions that derive from social prejudice and institutionalized discrimination against lesbians and gays, often influence state legislators, the judiciary, social casework professionals, and others who are involved in the adoption process (Matthews & Cramer, 2006; Downs & James, 2006). Stereotypes affecting policy and practice related to gay and lesbian adoption also include the notion that only heterosexuals wish to bear or raise children. Yet a sizable number of lesbians and gay men have biological children from previous marriages or through artificial insemination and surrogacy (Agigian, 2004; Gates et al., 2007; Martin, 1993; Patterson, 1994, 1995, 2002; Patterson & Friel, 2000). In fact, approximately one-third of lesbian households and one-fifth of gay male households include children (Gates et al., 2007; U.S. Census Bureau, 2004). In addition, research on childless gay men and lesbians has found that many would like to become parents (Beers, 1996; Morris, Balsam, & Rothblum, 2000; Sbordone, 1993). Finally, barriers to same-sex adoption also reflect lingering cultural assumptions that gay and lesbian parents are more likely to be emotionally disturbed and pose a greater risk for abusing children than their heterosexual counterparts, and that their children are more likely to have psychological problems and to develop same-gender sexual attraction themselves compared to the children of heterosexual parents.[3] Yet social science research has not supported these assumptions (see Gartrell, Peyser, & Bos, this volume; Goldberg, 2010; Patterson, 2002; Patterson & Wainright, this volume; Stacey & Biblarz, 2001; and Tasker & Golombok, 1997 for reviews of this literature). Furthermore, what little is known about family relationships and child outcomes in same-sex adoptive households also fails to support the critics of this type of adoption practice (Bennett, 2003; Erich, Kanenberg, Case, Allen, & Bogdanos, 2009; Erich, Leung, & Kindle, 2005; Erich, Leung, Kindle, & Carter, 2005; Kindle & Erich, 2005; Farr, Forssell, & Patterson, 2010a, 2010b; Matthews & Cramer, 2006; Ryan & Brown, this volume).

CURRENT TRENDS IN ADOPTION BY LESBIANS AND GAY MEN

Data from the National Survey of Family Growth (NSFG) conducted by the National Center for Health Statistics in 2002 show that a significant percentage of lesbian and bisexual women are interested in adopting children (Gates et al., 2007). In fact, interest in adopting is greater for these women (46.2 percent) than for heterosexual women (32.1 percent).[4] Moreover, lesbian and bisexual women are also more likely to have ever taken concrete steps toward adopting a child (5.7 percent) compared to their heterosexual peers (3.3 percent). Gates et al. (2007) suggest that these figures translate into over a million lesbian and bisexual women being interested in adopting, with over 130,000 of these individuals actually having taken some steps toward achieving this goal. Although comparable data were not available for gay men, they suggest that there are probably another million gay or bisexual men who also are interested in adoption.

Based upon Census 2000 and NSFG data, Gates et al. (2007) report that of the nearly 3.1 million lesbian and gay households in the United States, approximately 1.6 percent (nearly 52,000) include an adopted child under the age of 18 years. In addition, they estimate that there are approximately 65,000 adopted children currently being raised by lesbian or gay parents, which accounts for over 4 percent of all adopted children in the United States. Lesbian and gay adoptive families are much more likely to live in New England, Mid-Atlantic, and West Coast states than in the Midwest or Southern states. Finally, Gates et al. (2007) reported that same-sex adoptive parents generally are older, better educated, and have higher incomes than heterosexual adoptive parents.

POLICIES AND PRACTICES RELATED TO LESBIAN
AND GAY ADOPTION

Almost all major professional organizations in the legal, child-welfare and health-care fields in the United States have issued statements supporting gay and lesbian parenting and adoption (Mallon, 2006). Moreover, the Child Welfare League of America, the preeminent professional organization in the United States setting best-practice standards for adoption and foster care, has recommended that sexual orientation should not be the sole criterion determining suitability of adoption applicants, and that lesbian and gay clients should be assessed the same way as any other prospective parents (see Mallon, this volume). Yet, despite these affirmative viewpoints, it remains unclear to what extent adoption agencies actually support and make placements with lesbians and gay men. A recent study by Brodzinsky, Patterson, and Vaziri (2002), however, sheds some light on these issues. Through a nationwide mailed survey, the investigators collected data from 214 adoption agencies with respect to their policies and practices regarding adoption by lesbians and gays during the 1995–1996 time period. Results indicated that 63 percent of agencies accepted adoption applications from these individuals, with 37 percent reporting that they had made at least one adoption placement with an individual and/or couple who self-identified as lesbian or gay. Only 16 percent of the agencies, however, reported reaching out to the lesbian and gay communities to recruit prospective adoptive parents. The research also identified two factors significantly influencing agency policies and practices in this area: the religious affiliation of the agency and the type of adoption program run by the agency. Public agencies and private, secular agencies, as well as Jewish-affiliated agencies, were more likely to accept adoption applications from lesbians and gays, and to make adoption placements with these individuals, than were agencies affiliated with the Catholic church or with fundamentalist Christian beliefs. In addition, agencies focusing on special needs adoptions were more likely to accept applications from, and make placements with, lesbians, gays, and same-sex couples than were agencies focusing on domestic infant adoptions. Agencies focusing on international adoption, and those with more varied adoption programs, fell between the other two groups with regard to their policies and practices.

Although the results reported by Brodzinsky et al. (2002) provided the first nationwide empirical data on adoption agency policies and practices related to same-sex adoption, a number of methodological issues potentially limited the study's conclusions. The return rate of the survey was only 26 percent and, because of limited resources, the researchers were unable to follow up with agencies that failed to respond to the initial mailed survey. Although the number of agencies in the sample was considerable, and varied widely in terms of their size, geographical location, religious affiliation, and program focus, the low response rate could have produced an unrepresentative pattern of findings. Furthermore, because the researchers had relatively little information about the nonresponders, it was impossible to determine if agencies that chose not to complete the survey were unsupportive of lesbian and gay adoption. If that were the case, the figures reported may have overestimated the percentage of agencies that accepted adoption applications or made placements with this group of individuals.

GOALS OF THE DONALDSON INSTITUTE STUDY

Because of the relative lack of information on lesbian and gay adoptions, and its relevance to the ongoing public debate about same-sex marriage and parenting, the Evan B. Donaldson Adoption Institute sought to expand on the research reported by Brodzinsky et al. (2002). Specifically, its goals were the following:

- Collect data from a larger number of agencies nationally;
- Improve the response rate for the agencies sampled;
- Collect more detailed information on nonresponding agencies;
- Gather more detailed information on agency policies regarding acceptance and processing of adoption applications by gays and lesbians;
- Collect more detailed information on agency outreach efforts to the lesbian and gay communities;
- Gather information on the training needs of agencies related to these adoptions;
- Develop a more detailed series of questions focusing on respondents' attitudes and beliefs regarding parenting and adoption by lesbians and gays.

METHODOLOGY

Survey Sample

Adoption agencies were identified from the National Adoption Information Clearinghouse 2001 database, which included 1692 agencies, 1641 private and 51 public (from all states and the District of Columbia). Surveys were mailed to adoption program directors from 820 private agencies (half of those listed, randomly chosen within each state), plus all 51 public agencies. After the returned surveys were examined, an additional 24 questionnaires were sent to private agencies randomly selected from those states that were underrepresented in the initially collected data. As a result, 895 agencies were targeted for inclusion in the study—51.4 percent of the private adoption agencies and 100 percent of the public ones in the database.

Three hundred and seven adoption agencies responded to the survey, 277 private and 30 public. An additional 106 questionnaires were undeliverable because the agency either had moved or no longer existed, and another 44 reported that they no longer made adoption placements. Excluding these agencies, the response rate for our study was 41.2 percent, a very acceptable rate for mailed survey research and an improvement over the study reported by Brodzinsky et al. (2002).

Public and private agencies in nearly all states, plus the District of Columbia, returned surveys; Mississippi and New Mexico were the only exceptions. On average, about 40 percent of the agencies sampled within in each state returned completed questionnaires.

Procedures and Survey Format

Questionnaires were sent to adoption program directors, asking them to respond anonymously and return the survey in a self-addressed, stamped envelope. Several months after the initial mailing, a follow-up letter was sent to those that had not responded. Included in the follow-up letter was a request for agencies that had decided not to participate in the research to provide information explaining the basis for their decision. The final stage of data collection involved telephoning agencies that had not responded to previous requests. About 50 percent of the nonresponding agencies were contacted directly by telephone; in other cases, messages were left but not returned. Two points need to be made regarding the telephone contact. First, a sizable minority of those agencies contacted reported they had never received a copy of the initial survey or the follow-up letter, strongly suggesting that a number of nonrespondents, with whom we had no contact, may also have failed to receive the survey. If so, the return rate may underestimate the extent of agency cooperation in the research, since those that were unaware of the existence of the study could not make an informed decision about whether to participate. Second, in 35 cases data were collected by telephone. Because this procedure offered the respondents no anonymity, they were not asked to respond to the last section of the survey focusing on personal attitudes regarding parenting and adoption by lesbian and gay individuals.

The questionnaire, which was a revision of the one used by Brodzinsky et al. (2002), was designed to identify adoption agency policies and practices regarding applications from and placements with lesbians and gays during the 2-year period covering 1999–2000, as well as to assess respondents' attitudes about parenting and adoption by sexual minority adults. The survey consisted of 18 questions addressing the following issues:

(1) agency type (public or private);
(2) agency religious affiliation, if any;
(3) total number of adoption placements completed in 1999 and 2000;
(4) percent of placements involving domestic infants and toddlers, children with special needs, and children from other countries;
(5) awareness of state law on adoption by lesbians and gays;
(6) awareness of state law regarding second-parent adoption;
(7) agency policy regarding gay and lesbian adoption;
(8) agency involvement in international adoption, and if it exists, the countries from which placements are made;
(9) willingness to accept adoption applications from openly, self-identified lesbian and gay individuals;

(10) estimated number of placements made with lesbians and gays;

(11) policies and practices regarding collecting information about an applicant's sexual orientation;

(12) what the agency would do if, during the course of the adoption application process, it became apparent that the applicant was lesbian or gay, although she or he had not acknowledged it previously;

(13) whether the agency had ever rejected an application from a gay or lesbian individual, and, if so, for what reasons;

(14) whether the agency recruits applicants from the gay and lesbian communities as parenting resources for "waiting" children, and if so, by what means;

(15) whether the agency was interested in receiving in-service training related to working with lesbians, gays, and same-sex couples as prospective adoptive parents, and, if so, in what areas the training would be most useful;

(16) whether the agency, as a matter of policy or routine practice, informs birth parents when the adoption plan involves placing their child with a gay or lesbian individual or couple;

(17) whether the agency has had instances in which birth parents have requested placement of their child with a gay or lesbian individual or couple, and, if so, how often this has occurred; and

(18) whether the agency has had instances in which birth parents specifically have requested that their child not be placed with such individuals, and, if so, how often this has occurred.

Finally, respondents also were asked to fill out an 18-item questionnaire, with each statement rated on a 5-point scale from strongly agree (5) to strongly disagree (1), focusing on their personal attitudes and beliefs related to lesbian and gay parenting and adoption. Data from the attitude questionnaire can be found in the technical report on the project and will not be reported in this chapter (Brodzinsky, 2003).

SURVEY FINDINGS

Agency Characteristics

As noted previously, of the agencies responding to the survey, 30 were public and 277 were private. The size of the adoption programs was highly variable across agencies. The average number of placements made by the public agencies across the 2-year period studied was 2050.3 (range from 60 to 13,556), while the average number of placements for private agencies was 116.9 (range from 0 to 902). The nature of the adoption programs run by the agencies also varied. Public agencies almost exclusively placed older children and those with special needs (94.9 percent), with only a small percentage of the placements involving domestically born infants

(5.1 percent). In contrast, 39.6 percent of the adoption placements made by private agencies involved domestically born infants and toddlers, 32.9 percent involved children with special needs, and 27.6 percent involved children from other countries. Agencies also varied in terms of their religious affiliation. Nearly one-half (48.7 percent) of the private agencies had no religious affiliation, 17 percent were affiliated with Catholicism, 6.1 percent with the Mormon church, 5.4 percent with Lutheranism, 5.4 percent with various Fundamentalist Christian denominations, 4.3 percent with Judaism, 3.6 percent with the Baptist church, 2.9 percent with the Methodist church, and 6.5 percent with other religious denominations.

Nonparticipant Characteristics

One of the study's goals was to collect information on nonparticipating agencies to enable more accurate interpretation of the findings. One hundred and twenty agencies, representing 25 percent of the nonparticipants, provided information through follow-up letters and telephone contacts. Over a third (34.1 percent) of the nonparticipating adoption directors indicated they did not respond because their agencies did not work with lesbian or gay clients. In the majority of these cases, this policy was connected to the agency's religious affiliation. In other cases, however, respondents indicated their agencies placed only children from other nations, and the countries they worked with prohibited placement of children with this group of individuals.

A slightly greater percentage (36.7 percent) of the nonparticipants decided not to fill out the questionnaire because their agencies were not directly involved in making adoption placements. In some cases, the agency's adoption program had closed; in others, the agency only did homestudies; in a few instances, the agency was an administrative office only and its adoptions were conducted through affiliated offices also included in the database. Another 13.3 percent of the nonparticipating adoption directors reported they were interested in the project but too busy to respond or their adoption programs were so large they had no way of knowing whether a prospective adoptive parent was lesbian or gay; state agencies accounted for many of the latter cases. In addition, 12.5 percent of the nonparticipating adoption directors stated they were not interested in filling out the survey, but gave no specific reason for their decision. Finally, included among the nonparticipants were four agencies (3.0 percent) that returned the survey with incomplete data.

As noted previously, in calculating our return rate, we eliminated those nonparticipating agencies that did not make adoption placements. For some of our key analyses, however, we were able to include information from those nonparticipating agencies reporting that they did not work with lesbian and gay clients. For example, when agencies declined to participate in the study for this reason, the following assumptions were made: (1) they were unwilling to accept adoption applications from these individuals; (2) they made no placements with self-identified lesbian and gay individuals; (3) they would reject any application submitted by self-identified lesbians or gays; (4) they did not recruit from this group for prospective adoptive parents; and (5) they were uninterested in staff training related to working with such clients. Based upon these assumptions, data from an additional 41 nonparticipating agencies were included in all data analyses for the areas of inquiry noted above, which increased our overall return rate to 46.7 percent for these critical analyses.

Awareness of Adoption Law

Adoption agency directors were asked to indicate their states' legal status regarding adoption by lesbians and gays. At the time the data were collected, only Florida, Mississippi, and Utah had statutory bans or prohibitive barriers to such adoptions. Nevertheless, 17 respondents (5.4 percent) from other states incorrectly reported that lesbians and gays were barred from adopting children in their states. Another 31 respondents (9.9 percent) were unsure of their states' laws on the subject.

Agency Policies Regarding Same-Sex Adoption

The survey asked whether agencies had any official policies regarding adoption by gays and lesbians, and, if so, their nature. Respondents were asked to select one or more policies listed in the survey that guided their agencies' decision-making process in this area. Nearly two-thirds (65 percent) of adoption directors reported that their agencies had specific, relevant policies. For those with formal policies, the following guidelines were acknowledged as factors in decision-making practices regarding adoption applications from this group of potential clients: 33.6 percent accepted such applications based upon a nondiscriminatory policy; 19.5 percent accepted such applications, but noted that adoption placements were guided by regulations set forth by the child's country of origin; 18.1 percent accepted such applications, but reported that the child's birth parents were allowed to make the final choice; 19.5 percent rejected such applications on religious or moral grounds; 8 percent rejected such applications because they placed children only with married couples; and 5.2 percent rejected such applications based on state law or country of origin prohibitions.

Acceptance of Adoption Applications from Lesbians and Gays

Respondents were asked whether their agencies accepted adoption applications from self-identified lesbian and gay individuals as well as same-sex couples. Sixty percent of adoption directors indicated their agencies accepted applications from single sexual minority women and men, with only a slightly smaller percentage reporting acceptance of applications from lesbian couples (59.2 percent) and gay couples (59.2 percent).[5] [These percentages, and others below, when appropriate, include data from those agencies declining to participate because they did not make adoption placements with this group. Furthermore, because all subsequent analyses of adoption agency policies and practices comparing single lesbians versus single gay men, and lesbian couples versus gay male couples, were not significant, only those for single lesbians will be presented. The reader should assume that the same pattern of findings applies for the other three groups. Finally, for ease of reading, all statistical data have been eliminated in the chapter, but can be found in the technical report on the Donaldson Adoption Institute website, www. adoptioninstitute.org (Brodzinsky, 2003).]

Acceptance of applications from lesbians and gays was associated with the type of adoption program run by the agency. An adoption program was defined in terms of the percentage of placements involving a particular type of child. For example, an agency was designated as focused on domestic infants and toddlers if more than 50 percent of its placements involved such children. Similarly, agencies were designated as focused on either special needs or internationally born children if more than 50 percent of the placements involved such youngsters, respectively. If no single category represented a majority of the agency's placements, it was designated as having a mixed adoption program. Overall, 33 percent of the agencies focused primarily on placing domestically born infants and toddlers, 35 percent predominately made placements of children with special needs, 21 percent were primarily involved in international placements, and 11 percent had mixed adoption programs. Statistical analysis indicated a significant difference in the acceptance of adoption applications from the different types of agencies: Special needs agencies were much more willing to accept applications from lesbians than agencies focusing on international placements, those with mixed adoption programs, and those focusing on domestically born infants and toddlers (Table 4.1).

Table 4.1 PERCENTAGE OF AGENCIES DISPLAYING VARIOUS TYPES OF INVOLVEMENT IN GAY AND LESBIAN ADOPTION AS A FUNCTION OF ADOPTION PROGRAM FOCUS

	Infant/ Toddler	Special Needs	International	Mixed
Willingness to accept adoption applications from lesbians and gays	48.0	85.3	68.2	65.7
Made at least one adoption placement with a lesbian or gay individual or couple	25.5	61.5	51.5	45.7
Made outreach recruiting efforts to lesbians and gays	14.7	32.1	19.7	11.4
Interested in training related to adoption by lesbians and gays	42.2	71.6	39.4	60.0

There was also a significant difference in the acceptance of adoption applications from lesbians as a function of the agencies' religious affiliations. In this study, Jewish-affiliated agencies were universally willing to work with lesbian clients, as were the majority of public and private secular agencies and the majority of Lutheran agencies. The rest were much less willing to accept applications from these individuals, although a sizable minority of Methodist and Catholic agencies did. No agencies affiliated with fundamentalist Christian beliefs or the Baptist church, and only one Mormon agency respondent, reported a willingness to accept applications from lesbians (Table 4.2).

Collection of Information on Sexual Orientation

When asked whether their agencies collected information on prospective adoptive parents' sexual orientation, 42.9 percent of adoption directors responded affirmatively. Nearly three-quarters (72.5 percent) of these agencies explored the issue of sexual orientation with all applicants as part of the homestudy; 12 percent indicated the information is included in the application process; 10.6 percent reported the information is sought only from individuals thought to be lesbian or

Table 4.2 PERCENTAGE OF AGENCIES DISPLAYING VARIOUS TYPES OF INVOLVEMENT IN GAY AND LESBIAN ADOPTION AS A FUNCTION OF RELIGIOUS AFFILIATION

	Pub	PrS	Jew	Lut	Bap	Cat	Mor	Met	ChF	Oth
Willingness to accept adoption applications from lesbians and gays	90.0	80.2	100.0	66.7	0.0	27.7	5.9	37.5	0.0	17.7
Made at least one adoption placement with a lesbian or gay individual or couple	83.3	55.9	72.7	53.3	0.0	2.0	0.0	0.0	0.0	11.8
Made outreach recruiting efforts to lesbians and gays	20.0	29.9	41.7	0.0	0.0	4.3	0.0	0.0	0.0	5.9
Interested in training related to adoption by lesbians and gays	66.6	64.4	83.3	53.3	10.0	23.4	0.0	25.0	0.0	11.8

NOTES: Pub, public agencies; PrS, private secular agencies; Jew, Jewish agencies; Lut, Lutheran agencies; Bap, Baptist agencies; Cat, Catholic agencies; Mor, Mormon agencies; Met, Methodist agencies; ChF, Christian fundamentalist agencies; Oth, other agencies.

gay; and 15.9 percent noted the information is collected by other means. (Because a respondent could indicate more than one means of collecting this information, the total percentage exceeds 100 percent.)

Respondents were asked what their agencies would do if, during the course of the application process or homestudy, it became apparent an applicant was lesbian or gay, although she or he had not acknowledged it previously. More than half (54.3 percent) reported they would include this information in the adoption preparation and education process; 29 percent stated they would reject the client's application; 9.5 percent indicated they would ignore the information and continue to process the application; 3.7 percent suggested they would refer the client for counseling as an adjunct to the homestudy process; and 8.9 percent reported they would choose other options, including referring the client to another agency that worked with lesbians and gays, or only allowing the applicant to adopt a child with special needs. (Once again, because a respondent could provide more than one answer to the question, the total percentage exceeds 100 percent.)

Agency Placement Practices in Relation to Lesbians and Gays

Over the 2-year period of 1999–2000, responding agencies reported making a total of 91,118 adoption placements, 1206 (1.3 percent) of which were with self-identified lesbians and gays. It should be noted, however, that this figure almost assuredly underestimates the true extent of such placements. For many agencies, especially private ones with large adoption programs, as well as for many state agencies, respondents noted that although their organization had made such placements, it was impossible to estimate the actual number. In such cases, for statistical purposes, only one adoption placement with a lesbian or gay client per year was counted. Because respondents often were unsure of the exact number of such adoption placements made by their agencies, we utilized the same strategy as Brodzinsky et al. (2002) and sought to determine the percentage of agencies that made at least one such placement during the study period. Our data indicate that 39 percent of all agencies made at least one such placement.

Adoption placements with lesbians and gays varied, however, as a function of the types of programs run by the specific agencies. Those focusing on special needs placements were significantly more likely to place a child with lesbian or gay clients than were agencies focusing on domestically born infants and toddlers; agencies with a strong international adoption focus or a mixed adoption program fell between the other two agency types (see Table 4.1).

Placement of children with lesbian and gay individuals or couples was also associated with the agency's religious affiliation. Jewish and Lutheran agencies, as well as public agencies, and private secular agencies were significantly more likely to make an adoption placement with a self-identified lesbian or gay client than were agencies affiliated with the Catholic, Mormon, Methodist, and fundamentalist Christian churches (see Table 4.2).

Respondents also were asked whether their agencies had ever rejected an application from a prospective lesbian or gay adoptive parent. Approximately 20 percent of all respondents reported their agencies, on at least one occasion, had rejected such an application. When asked their reasons, the following explanations were noted: applicant's unrealistic expectations regarding adoption (31.8 percent), psychological problems in the applicant (31.8 percent), questionable motives for adopting (24.6 percent), relationship problems for the applicant (24.6 percent), placement with lesbians and gays violates agency policy (23.2 percent), applicant's lifestyle was incompatible with adoption (20.3 percent), placement with lesbians and gays was prohibited by the child's country of origin (20.3 percent), the sexual orientation of the applicant was incompatible with adoption (14.5 percent), placement with lesbian and gay adults was prohibited by state law (13.1 percent), lack of adequate social support (11.6 percent), financial problems for the applicant (8.7 percent), same-sex placements violate community standards (4.3 percent), and medical problems of the applicant (2.9 percent). (Because the respondent could endorse more than one reason for the agency's decision to reject an application from a lesbian or gay client, the total percentage exceeds 100 percent.)

Almost half (47 percent) of the agencies that accepted applications from lesbians and gays indicated that as a matter of policy or routine practice, they informed birth parents when making an adoption placement with a lesbian or gay individual or same-sex couple. Furthermore, approximately 15 percent of these agencies indicated they have had birth parents request such placements or have chosen or agreed to such individuals as their child's adoptive parents. On the other hand, nearly 26 percent of respondents also noted their agencies have had birth parents object to the placement of their child with lesbian or gay individuals, or have specifically asked that their child not be placed with such individuals.

Recruitment of Lesbian and Gay Adoptive Parents

Approximately one-fifth (19 percent) of adoption directors reported their agencies made outreach efforts to recruit adoptive parent applicants from lesbian and gay communities. Among those agencies that did attempt to do so, a wide range of methods was employed. By far the most prevalent was word of mouth (86.6 percent), followed by efforts to work with lesbian and gay organizations (49.3 percent), adoption workshops targeting these individuals as prospective adoptive parents (38.8 percent), advertisements in targeted publications (23.8 percent), posting of information about same-sex adoption on the agency's website (19.4 percent), emailing or mailing adoption information to lesbian and gay groups (10.4 percent), and a variety of other recruitment efforts (7.5 percent). (Because respondents could indicate more than one type of recruitment effort, the total percentage exceeds 100 percent.)

Active recruitment of gay and lesbian prospective adoptive parents varied as a function of the focus of each agency's program. Agencies that predominately placed children with special needs were more likely to recruit gay men and women as parenting resources than were agencies focusing on international or domestic infant and toddler placements, as well as those with mixed adoption programs (see Table 4.1).

Recruitment of prospective adoptive parents from lesbian and gay communities, once again, was associated with the agency's religious affiliation. Jewish-affiliated agencies, as well as public agencies and private secular agencies, made some effort to reach out to lesbians and gays; Catholic-affiliated agencies displayed a minimal interest in recruiting such clients; the remainder of the agencies displayed no interest at all (see Table 4.2).

Training in Working with Lesbian and Gay Adoptive Parents

Respondents were asked whether their agencies would be interested in receiving in-service training geared toward working with prospective adoptive parents who are lesbian or gay, either in written form or through workshops. Nearly half (48 percent) indicated a desire for such training. Agencies focusing on the placement of children with special needs and those with mixed adoption programs expressed more interest in such training than did agencies focusing on domestic infant and toddler adoptions and international adoptions (see Table 4.1). In addition, interest in training also varied as a function of the agency's religious affiliation (see Table 4.2). Respondents from Jewish-affiliated agencies expressed the greatest interest in such training, followed by those from state agencies, private secular agencies, and Lutheran-affiliated agencies. A sizable minority of agencies affiliated with the Methodist and Catholic churches also displayed some interest in training. The remainder showed minimal (Baptist) or no interest at all (Mormon, Christian Fundamentalist). Furthermore, as would be expected, interest in training was greater among those agencies expressing a willingness to accept adoption applications from lesbian and gay individuals (74.4 percent) and those that had already made at least one adoption placement with this group (77.6 percent) compared to those that expressed no interest in working with such clients (8 percent) or that had not placed any children for such adoptions during the study period (27.9 percent).

Finally, adoption program directors were asked to indicate which training topics in relation to lesbian and gay adoption would be particularly useful for agency staff. The most frequently endorsed training areas were psychological issues in children raised by lesbian and gay parents (88.7 percent); social casework issues in working with such clients (88.1 percent); psychological issues in adoptive parenting by lesbians and gays (81.5 percent); attitudes, biases, and stereotypes about lesbian and gay individuals and couples (75 percent); and relevant legal issues (68.5 percent).

CONCLUSIONS AND IMPLICATIONS

The current study collected data on adoption by lesbians and gays from a large number of agencies across the United States—both public and private, and varying in size, program focus, and religious affiliation. Importantly, our return rate was slightly over 41 percent for most analyses, and nearly 47 percent for some of the more crucial analyses when data from nonparticipating agencies were included.

Our results confirm that adoptions of children by lesbians and gays are occurring regularly and in noteworthy numbers across the country, through both public and private agencies, a finding consistent with data reported by Gates et al. (2007). Slightly over 60 percent of respondents indicated that their agencies were willing to accept adoption applications from lesbian and gay individuals and same-sex couples, and 39 percent reported their agencies had made at least one placement with this group in 1999 and 2000. These figures are consistent with the ones reported by Brodzinsky et al (2002). Given our success in increasing the response rate from 26 percent to 47 percent (for these specific analyses), we are confident these data are reliable and valid indicators of the nationwide trend in adoption agency willingness to accept applications from, and place children with, lesbians and gays.

What our data cannot determine is the actual number of adoption placements being made with this group of individuals. Very few agencies reported that they keep such adoption statistics. In fact, only about 43 percent of respondents indicated their agencies collected information about an applicant's sexual orientation at all. Our study found 1.3 percent of all adoption placements were made with self-identified lesbians or gays compared to 1.6 percent reported by Brodzinsky et al. (2002). As noted previously, this figure probably underestimates the number of such placements, especially for public agencies and larger private ones.

Many respondents noted that although they were aware their agencies had made placements with lesbian or gay applicants during the target period, because of the size of their adoption program, or because they did not keep specific statistics on such placements, they could not provide an estimate of the number of children placed with gay individuals or couples. In such cases, for statistical purposes, we assumed only *one* adoption was made with a lesbian or gay individual or couple during the target period. For public and larger private agencies, this assumption is extremely conservative. Although it accurately represents the fact that the agency made adoption placements with lesbians and gays, it does not capture the actual extent of this practice over the 2-year period studied.

Furthermore, there are other reasons to believe that the 1.3 percent figure underestimates the prevalence of adoption by lesbians and gays in the United States (see also Gates et al., 2007). Because of homophobic and heterosexist attitudes, some lesbians and gays choose to withhold information regarding their sexual orientation when they submit applications to adoption agencies. With the growing acceptance of single adoptive parenthood, as well as the sensitivity among many social casework professionals regarding exploring issues of sexual orientation during the home study process (Brooks, Kim, & Wind, this volume; Mallon, 2006, and this volume), agency personnel often have no basis for knowing an unmarried applicant's sexual orientation. In addition, this study, like the one reported by Brodzinsky et al. (2002), focused only on adoptions facilitated by public and licensed private agencies. Yet many lesbians and gays choose to pursue adoption through private placement, by means of attorneys or other professionals, rather than through agencies of any type. The thousands of independent adoptions that occur each year are not represented in our data.

Although approximately 60 percent of public agencies responded to our survey, adoption directors from several states with very large adoption programs did not return questionnaires. Because the majority of public agency placements involve children with special needs, and the data suggest that agencies focusing on such children are the most likely to accept applications from and make placements with lesbians and gays, the percentage of adoptions by this group of individuals reported here is undoubtedly a significant underestimate.

Finally, it is important to note that the survey data reflect agency policies and practices from approximately 10 years ago. Given the growing acceptance for gay and lesbian parenthood and adoption in the general population (ABC News, 2002; Mallon, 2006; Miall & March, 2005; Schwartz, 2010), it is not unreasonable to expect that the figures reported here are lower than would be found for more current placement data.

The results also point to a clear disparity between the percentage of agencies indicating that they accept adoption applications from lesbians and gays (60 percent), the percentage that made at least one such placement during the target period (39 percent), and the percentage that actively recruited these individuals as prospective adoptive parents (19 percent). Several possible explanations account for this finding.

First, agency policies regarding same-sex adoption may not be well disseminated to the lesbian and gay communities. Only a small percentage of agencies reported that they actively target these women and men in their advertisements, training seminars, and websites. Many agencies willing to accept applications from these individuals may not openly advertise this fact because they do not want to create controversy and/or alienate possible funding sources. Such agencies are likely to have a passive approach to lesbian and gay adoption; in other words, they do not actively seek out gay individuals or couples. As a result, lesbians and gays who wish to adopt may assume their sexual orientation automatically eliminates them as applicants at most agencies. If so, they may be reluctant to apply, may choose not to reveal their sexual orientation, or may apply only to agencies that have developed a reputation, probably through word of mouth, as being gay friendly. [Projects such as the one initiated by the Human Rights Campaign recently have been developed to help agencies overcome barriers to working with sexual-minority individuals, as well as to reach out to this community as a viable option for children needing to be adopted (Human Right Campaign, 2009)].

Additionally, the disparity between the percentage of agencies willing to accept applications from lesbian and gay clients compared to the percentage that have made such placements could reflect a difference between formal policies and the attitudes, beliefs, and behavior of the casework personnel who process applications (Brooks, Kim, & Wind, this volume; Mallon, 2006, and this volume). Caseworkers who oppose such adoptions, for any reason, could ignore agency policies and obstruct placements with lesbian and gay clients.

Finally, the data on willingness to accept adoption applications could be somewhat inflated by a politically correct response bias. In other words, some respondents may have sought to portray their agencies as being antidiscriminatory and open to all potential applicants, even though, in practice, they do not support or allow adoption by lesbians and gays.

To reiterate, our results, like those of Brodzinsky et al. (2002), indicate that placements with lesbians and gays differ as a function of the agency's program focus and religious affiliation. Generally, agencies focusing on special needs adoptions are more willing to accept applications from lesbians and gays than all other types of agencies. These agencies also make more effort to recruit prospective parents from the lesbian and gay communities, and make more adoption placements with these individuals, than other agencies. Over the years, special needs agencies have been the most aggressive in breaking down the barriers to adoptive parenthood. With the significant number of children lingering in foster care, these agencies have increasingly become more inclusive in their policies, allowing certain groups to adopt (e.g., older adults, low-income families, foster parents, disabled individuals, single adults, minority individuals, lesbians and gays), who in the past were precluded from doing so (Brodzinsky & Pinderhughes, 2002; Brodzinsky et al., 1998; Cole & Donley, 1990; Howard, 2006; Howard & Freundlich, 2008).

In contrast, agencies focusing on the placement of domestic infants and toddlers were the least likely to have policies and practices supportive of same-sex adoption. Several factors may account for this finding. First, a growing number of biological parents today are choosing the families who adopt their children. As a result, although an agency may be willing to accept applications from lesbians or gays, birth parents' choices may well keep down the actual number of such placements. In fact, 26 percent of all agencies that accept applications from lesbians and gays reported that at one or more times, pregnant women (and their partners, when involved) have specifically requested that the agency not place their child with such individuals. (In contrast, 15 percent of these agencies indicated that at one or more times, expectant parents have actually requested, or approved of plans, to place their child with lesbians or gays.) Second, many infant-oriented agencies are also affiliated with religions that have very conservative beliefs about lesbians and gays. In the current study, these agencies reported little interest in working with lesbian and gay adults.

The situation for agencies focusing on international adoption is more complicated. To the best of our knowledge, no sending country has a policy specifically allowing the placement of children with lesbians and gays. In fact, some either specifically prohibit such placements or have regulations that indirectly impede them (e.g., requiring adoptive parents to be married). Yet more than two-thirds of the international agencies in our study reported that they were willing to accept applications from lesbian and gay clients, and half of these made at least one placement with such individuals. These results are very similar to those reported by Brodzinsky et al. (2002) and suggest that many international adoption agencies likely have a "don't ask, don't tell" policy regarding such placements. As Brodzinsky et al. (2002) noted, however, these agencies appear to face an ethical dilemma involving the choice between adhering to the cultural values, standards, and regulations of a child's birth country—which in many cases would preclude lesbian and gay adoption—and the desire to find a stable and nurturing home environment for a child in need, regardless of the adoptive parents' sexual orientation. To date, there has been relatively little discussion in the professional literature regarding this ethical issue, nor of possible ways for agencies to deal with this dilemma.

Our study also clearly links agency policies and practices regarding lesbians and gays to religious affiliation (or lack thereof). Consistent with the results reported by Brodzinsky et al. (2002), our data strongly suggest that public agencies and private secular agencies, as well as Jewish- and Lutheran-affiliated agencies, are much more willing to work with lesbian and gay clients than are most other religiously affiliated agencies, especially those associated with Catholic, Baptist, Mormon, and fundamentalist Christian churches.

Although many public and private agencies appear to support adoption by lesbians and gays, very few reported attempting to recruit prospective adoptive parents from these communities. The agencies that did report some type of recruiting effort indicated that word of mouth was by far the most common means of outreach. Efforts to work directly with lesbian and gay organizations and advocacy groups, as well as educational seminars targeting lesbian and gay individuals, also were relatively common strategies employed by agencies. It would appear, however, that this is an area in which agencies need much more education and training (Human Rights Campaign, 2009).

It is also clear that many agencies are interested in specific training to work with lesbian and gay clients. Specific areas of interest noted by the respondents were legal and social casework issues, myths and stereotypes associated with same-gender sexual attraction, and psychological issues related to same-sex parents and their children. In keeping with the pattern of findings previously reported, interest in such training was greater among agencies associated with special needs placements, as well as public agencies, private secular agencies, Jewish-affiliated agencies, and Lutheran-affiliated agencies. Despite this interest, until very recently, there had been no systematic effort made to develop and disseminate training materials on lesbian and gay adoption, with the exception of the work of the Human Rights Campaign (2009) and the Evan B. Donaldson Adoption Institute.[6]

Slightly more than 5 percent of adoption directors incorrectly reported that adoption by lesbians and gays was prohibited by their states' law, and another 10 percent were unsure of the legal standards in their states. These findings, which probably can be accounted for by the ambiguity, frequent challenges, and periodic amendments to state adoption laws, suggest the need for ongoing education of adoption agency personnel regarding the legal status of same-sex adoption (and second-parent adoption) in their states.

In evaluating the results of this study, several methodological issues need to be considered. The first is the sample representation. Although our return rate is reasonable for mailed survey research, it does leave open the possibility that the results are skewed by the nature of the participating versus nonparticipating agencies. We were able to gather information on the reasons for nonparticipation from 25 percent of these agencies. Approximately one-third of these respondents indicated they chose not to participate because their agencies did not work with lesbian or gay clients. It is possible that many of the other nonparticipating agencies that did not respond to our follow-up letter also had policies and practices that were unsupportive of placements with these individuals. An examination of the names of the nonparticipating agencies indicated that many (but still a minority) had Catholic, Baptist, Methodist, or Mormon affiliations. Our findings suggest that these types of agencies generally are unsupportive of same-sex adoption.

However, failure to participate in the study was related not only to the agency's lack of support for such adoptions. In fact, the most common reason for nonparticipation (39 percent) was that the agency's adoption program had closed or it conducted only homestudies. Furthermore, another 13 percent of respondents from nonparticipating agencies indicated they were interested in the study, but were simply too busy to fill out the questionnaire. In short, it is clear that there were many possible reasons for nonparticipation and that conservative attitudes and policies about lesbians and gays were not necessarily the dominant factor. Thus, given the random sampling of agencies within each state, coupled with the large number of agencies that responded to the survey, it is our belief that the results reflect a reliable and valid assessment of nationwide trends in adoption agency interest and willingness to work with prospective lesbian and gay adoptive parents.

A second limitation of the study is that it focused only on the policies and practices of licensed adoption agencies and excluded the many independent adoption placements made each year nationwide. As noted previously, many lesbians and gays choose independent adoption, typically with the help of an attorney. This study does not examine such placements.

Several implications can be drawn from our findings. On a broad sociological level, the clear picture is of a growing willingness by adoption agencies to place children with lesbians and gays, and of a desire by this group of individuals and couples to become adoptive parents (Gates et al., 2007; Mallon, 2006, and this volume). The consequences of this trend are beyond the scope of this study, but certainly warrant future research and analysis.

For those single gays and lesbians, as well as same-sex couples, who wish to become adoptive, the picture appears more encouraging than is often portrayed. Although homophobic and heterosexist attitudes undoubtedly influence the policies and practices of many agencies (Brooks, this volume; Mallon, this volume), the majority indicate they are willing to work with these individuals, even if their brochures, advertisements, and websites do not currently indicate that this is the case. This finding suggests that lesbians and gays should not only examine the written materials of an agency, but also talk with its personnel, as well as others who have worked with the agency, before making a determination about applying for adoption.

As noted previously, it is clear that many agencies need, and desire, better training in this area, including the best ways of reaching out to prospective sexual minority adoptive parents. The relatively passive approach utilized by the majority of agencies often reflects their lack of awareness of the interest in adoption among many lesbians and gays or the best ways of making contact with these individuals.

Finally, the passive approach to working with lesbian and gay clients, including agencies that employ a "don't ask, don't tell" policy, raises a number of problems in relation to both preplacement and postplacement services for these individuals. If agency personnel do not know that a client is lesbian or gay, or choose not to address this topic directly when they do know, then a variety of important issues may never be adequately addressed—even though they have a potentially significant impact on the children, parents, and families as a whole. For example, the following are just a few of the relevant questions to be raised with lesbian and gay clients: How do they expect their sexual orientation to affect their children over the course of their development? What plans do they have for discussing their sexual orientation with their children? How do they plan to help their children deal with homophobic attitudes and behaviors of others, including their extended families, teachers, neighbors, etc.? To what extent are the clients' extended families, friends, and co-workers aware of their sexual orientation, and what level of support have they received from these individuals? Just as caseworkers explore adoption-related expectations with, and provide support to, adoptive parents during the preplacement period, they need to explore the unique aspects of lesbian and gay adoptive family life with their clients (Goldberg & Gianino, this volume; Mallon, this volume). Unless adoption agency personnel are aware of their clients' sexual orientation and create an atmosphere of respect, understanding, and support, it is unlikely that these and related issues will be discussed in an open and forthright manner. In the long run, failure to address these issues may well increase the risk for adjustment problems for the children, parents, and families.

Acknowledgments

This research was supported by a grant from the Rainbow Foundation to the Evan B. Donaldson Adoption Institute. We wish to express our deep appreciation to the adoption directors who took part in the study.

Notes

1. For a more detailed analysis of the findings, see Brodzinsky (2003).
2. Until very recently, Florida banned adoption by sexual minority individuals and couples. However, in 2008, the ban was ruled unconstitutional and the ruling was

upheld by the Third District Court of Appeal in 2010 (*Florida Department of Children and Families v. In the Matter of Adoption of X.X.G. and N.R.G.*, No. 3D08–3044, 2010 WL 3655782 (Fla. Dist. Ct. App. Sept 22, 2010). It is possible, however, that opponents of this type of adoption could challenge the ruling in future cases in Florida.

3. In 1973, the American Psychiatric Association removed homosexuality from its list of mental disorders. The American Psychological Association, and all other health-care associations, supported this decision.

4. Data related to adoption among gay men were not included in this report because the survey did not ask straight or gay men adoption-related questions.

5. Accepting applications from gay and lesbian couples should not be taken to mean that agencies were facilitating joint legal adoptions by the partners. In fact, in many states this type of adoption was prohibited by law. For purposes of this study, applications by couples is simply an acknowledgment by the agency that they worked with partnered gays and lesbians as well as unpartnered ones.

6. For information on the work by the Human Rights Campaign (HRC), contact Ellen Kahn at HRC in Washington, D.C.; for information on the work being conducted by the Donaldson Adoption Institute contact Adam Pertman at the Evan B. Donaldson Adoption Institute in New York City.

References

ABC News (2002). *More Americans support gay adoption.* ABCNews.com telephone survey, March 27–31, 2002. Available from *www.abcnews.go.com/sections/us/dailynews/gayadopt_poll020402.html*.

Agigian, A. (2004). *Baby steps: How lesbian alternative insemination is changing the world.* Wesleyan, CT: Wesleyan University Press.

Appell, A. R. (2001). Lesbian and gay adoption. *Adoption Quarterly, 4*, 75–86.

Beers, J. R. (1996). The desire to parent in gay men. Unpublished doctoral dissertation, Columbia University, New York, NY.

Bennett, S. (2003). Is there a primary mom? Parental perceptions of attachment bond hierarchies within lesbian adoptive families. *Child and Adolescent Social Work Journal, 20*, 159–173.

Blanks, V., Dockwell, B., & Wallance, G. J. (2004). Adoption by gays and lesbians: A survey of the law in the 50 United States and the District of Columbia. Technical report available online at www.adoptionpolicy.org.

Brodzinsky, D. (2003). *Adoption by lesbians and gay men: A national survey of adoption agency policies, practices and attitudes.* Final report from the Evan B. Donaldson Adoption Institute. Available online at www.adoptioninstitute.org.

Brodzinsky, D., Patterson, C., & Vaziri, M. (2002). Adoption agency perspectives on lesbian and gay prospective parents: A national study. *Adoption Quarterly, 5*, 5–23.

Brodzinsky, D., & Pinderhughes, E. (2002). Parenting and child development in adoptive families. In M. Bornstein (Ed.), *Handbook of parenting. Vol 1: Children and parenting* (pp. 279–311), 2nd ed. Mahwah, NJ: Lawrence Erlbaum Associates.

Brodzinsky, D., Smith, D., & Brodzinsky, A. (1998). *Children's adjustment to adoption: Developmental and clinical issues.* Thousand Oaks, CA: Sage Publications.

Cole, E. S., & Donley, K. S. (1990). History, values, and placement policy issues in adoption. In D. Brodzinsky & M. Schechter (Eds.), *The psychology of adoption* (pp. 273–294). New York: Oxford University Press.

Downs, A. C., & James, S. E. (2006). Gay, lesbian, and bisexual foster parents: Strengths and challenges for the child welfare system. *Child Welfare, LXXXV*, 281–298.

Erich, S., Kanenberg, H., Case, K., Allen, T., & Bogdanes, T. (2009). An empirical analysis of factors affecting adolescent attachment in adoptive families with homosexual and straight parents. *Children and Youth Services Review, 31*, 398–404.

Erich, S., Leung, P., & Kindle, P. (2005). A comparative analysis of adoptive family functioning with gay, lesbian, and heterosexual parents and their children. *Journal of GLBT Family Studies, 1*, 43–60.

Erich, S., Leung, P., Kindle, P., & Carter, S. (2005). Gay and lesbian adoptive families: An exploratory study of family functioning, adoptive child's behavior, and familial support networks. *Journal of Family Social Work, 9*, 17–32.

Farr, R. H., Forssell, S. L., & Patterson, C. J. (2010a). Parenting and child development in adoptive families: Does parental sexual orientation matter? *Applied Developmental Science, 14*, 164–178.

Farr, R. H., Forssell, S. L., & Patterson, C. J. (2010b). Gay, lesbian and heterosexual adoptive parents: Couple and relationship issues. *Journal of GLBT Family Studies, 6*, 199–213.

Florida Department of Children and Families v. In the Matter of Adoption of X.X.G. and N.R.G., No. 3D08-3044, 2010 WL 3655782 (Fla. Dist. Ct. App., Sept 22, 2010).

Gates, G. J., Badgett, M. V., Macomber, J. E., & Chambers, K. (2007). Adoption and foster care by gay and lesbian parents in the United States. Technical report issued jointly by the Williams Institute (Los Angeles, CA) and the Urban Institute (Washington, D.C.).

Goldberg, A.E. (2010). *Lesbian and gay parents and their children: Research on the family life cycle.* Washington, D.C.: American Psychology Association.

Herek, G. (1995). Psychosocial heterosexism in the United States. In A. R. D'Augelli & C. J. Patterson (Eds.), *Lesbian, gay, and bisexual identities over the lifespan: Psychological perspectives* (pp. 321–346). New York: Oxford University Press.

Howard, J. (2006). *Expanding resources for children: Is adoption by gays and lesbians part of the answer for boys and girls who need homes?* Policy brief from the Evan B. Donaldson Adoption Institute. Available online at www.adoptioninstitute.org.

Howard, J., & Freundlich, M. (2008). *Expanding resources for waiting children II: Eliminating legal and practice barriers to gay and lesbian adoption from foster care.* Policy brief from the Evan B. Donaldson Institute. Available online at www.adoptioninstitute.org.

Human Rights Campaign. (2009). *Promising practices in adoption and foster care: A comprehensive guide to policies and practices that welcome, affirm, and support gay, lesbian, bisexual, and transgendered foster and adoptive parents.* Washington, D.C.: Human Rights Campaign.

Kindle, P., & Erich, S. (2005). Perceptions of social support among heterosexual and homosexual adopters. *Families in Society: The Journal of Contemporary Social Services, 86*, 541–546.

Mallon, G. P. (2006). *Lesbian and gay foster and adoptive parents: Recruiting, assessing, and supporting an untapped resource for children and youth.* Washington, D.C.: Child Welfare League of America.

Martin, A. (1993). *The lesbian and gay parenting handbook: Creating and raising our families*. New York: Harper Collins.

Matthews, J. D., & Cramer, E. P. (2006). Envisaging the adoption process to strengthen gay- and lesbian-headed families: Recommendations for adoption professionals. *Child Welfare*, LXXXV, 317–340.

Miall, C. E., & March, K. (2005). Social support for changes in adoption practice: Gay adoption, open adoption, birth reunions, and the release of confidential identifying information. *Families in Society: The Journal of Contemporary Social Services*, 86, 83–92.

Morris, J. F., Balsam, K., & Rothblum, E. D. (2000). Lesbian and bisexual mothers and non-mothers: Demographics and the coming-out process. *Journal of Family Psychology*, 16, 144–156.

Patterson, C. J. (1994). Lesbian and gay couples considering parenthood. An agenda for research, service, and advocacy. *Journal of Lesbian and Gay Social Services*, 1, 33–55.

Patterson, C. J. (1995). Adoption of minor children by lesbian and gay adults: A social science perspective. *Duke Journal of Gender Law and Policy*, 2, 191–205.

Patterson, C. J. (2002). Lesbian and gay parenthood. In M. Bornstein (Ed.), *Handbook of parenting. Vol 3: Being and becoming a parent* (pp. 317–338), 2nd ed. Mahwah, NJ: Lawrence Erlbaum Associates.

Patterson, C. J., & Friel, L. V. (2000). Sexual orientation and fertility. In G. Bently & N. Mascie-Taylor (Eds.), *Fertility in the modern world: Biosocial perspectives* (pp. 238–260). Cambridge: Cambridge University Press.

Sbordone, A. J. (1993). Gay men choosing fatherhood. Unpublished doctoral dissertation, City University of New York, New York.

Schwartz, J. (2010). Investigating differences in public support for gay rights issues. *Journal of Homosexuality*, 57, 748–759.

Stacey, J., & Biblarz, T. (2001). (How) does the sexual orientation of parents matter? *American Sociological Review*, 66, 159–183.

Sullivan, A. (Ed.). (1995). *Issues in gay and lesbian adoption: Proceedings of the fourth annual Peirce-Warwick Adoption Symposium*. Washington, D.C.: Child Welfare League of America.

Tasker, F. L., & Golombok, S. (1997). *Growing up in a lesbian family: Effects on child development*. New York: Guilford.

U.S. Census Bureau of Household and Family Statistics. (2004). *America's families and living arrangements: 2004*. Retrieved June 9, 2006. Available from http://www.census.gov/population/socdemo/hh-fam/cps2004.html.

5

Adolescents with Same-Sex Parents

Findings from the National Longitudinal Study of Adolescent Health

CHARLOTTE J. PATTERSON AND JENNIFER L. WAINRIGHT ■

Should the sexual orientation of prospective adoptive parents be considered as a factor when making placements of minor children into adoptive homes? This question is one of several legal and policy controversies surrounding lesbian and gay parents and their children (Patterson, 2007, 2009; Patterson, Fulcher, & Wainright, 2002). Like others, it is of special interest to many people, including social workers, attorneys, child advocates, prospective adoptive parents, and, most of all, children in need of permanent homes. Some have argued that there should be a presumption against placing children with adoptive parents who are not heterosexual (e.g., Wardle, 1997). Others have argued that sexual orientation should be considered irrelevant to such decisions (e.g., Mallon, 2004; Wald, 2006). The question of how children fare in adoptive homes provided by nonheterosexual parents is prominently featured in these debates.

There is considerable variation in laws and policies governing adoptions by lesbian and gay adults across the United States (Appell, this volume; Brodzinsky, this volume; Gates, Badgett, Macomber, & Chambers, 2007; Wald, 2006). At the time of this writing (i.e., October 2009), adoption of minor children by these adults is specifically barred by statute only in Florida; a challenge to this law is currently in the courts.[1] Adoption of minor children by same-gender couples is forbidden in Mississippi. In Utah, adoption by unmarried couples is forbidden; since same-sex couples do not have access to the legal institution of marriage in that state, this law effectively excludes same-sex couples. In other states, such as California, Maryland, Massachusetts, and New York, the law allows adoptions by

1. In 2008, the Florida supreme court declared the state's ban on gay/lesbian adoption to be unconstitutional.

openly lesbian and gay prospective adoptive parents. For instance, in a landmark New York adoption case, the court noted that "(t)he fact that the petitioners here maintain an open lesbian relationship is not a reason to deny adoption. ... A parent's sexual orientation or sexual practices are presumptively irrelevant..." (In re *Adoption of Evan*, 1992, pp. 1001–1002).

In many other jurisdictions, there is active debate of issues relevant to sexual orientation and adoption. Bills to bar lesbian or gay applicants from becoming adoptive or foster parents have been introduced in a number of states (e.g., Kentucky, Tennessee, and Virginia) in the past several years. To date, all of these efforts have been defeated, but observers expect more may emerge in the future.

In these debates, there is agreement among the parties that the interests of children should be considered ahead of other concerns. For this reason, discussions about sexual orientation and adoption often resolve to debates about how parental sexual orientation may affect children. Advocates of allowing adoptions by lesbian and gay adults argue that many children need homes, that sexual orientation is unrelated to parenting abilities, and that, therefore, lesbian and gay parents should be allowed to adopt children. Opponents of such adoptions suggest that lesbian and gay adults do not provide safe, supportive homes for children, and that any children adopted by them will suffer. In short, all agree that children's welfare should be paramount, but the two sides of the debate disagree about what policies best serve children's interests.

In this discussion, reliable information about the actual development and adjustment of children who are being reared by lesbian and gay parents can be useful. The most directly relevant research would assess the growth and development of children who have been adopted by lesbian or gay parents. Also relevant, however, are data about the development of children who have been born to lesbian or gay parents and who are being reared by them. In the next section, we consider the findings of such research.

RESEARCH ON OFFSPRING OF LESBIAN AND GAY PARENTS

At the time of this writing (i.e., October 2009), only two studies of children adopted by lesbian and gay parents have been published (Erich, Leung, & Kindle, 2005; Ryan, 2007). Working with a convenience sample of 68 families in which parents were lesbian or gay and 43 families in which parents were heterosexual, Erich and his colleagues studied family functioning and behavior problems of 6-year-old children. Their findings revealed that children and families were adapting well. They reported no significant differences in children's conduct or in family functioning associated with parental sexual orientation (Erich, Leung, & Kindle, 2005; for related information about this study, see also Erich, Leung, Kindle, & Carter, 2005; Kindle & Erich, 2005; Leung, Erich & Kanenberg, 2005).

Ryan (2007) studied 53 lesbian-parent and 41 gay-parent families with adoptive children. He found that not only did parents describe their parenting in positive terms, but they also described their children as having many strengths. Despite the fact that many children had histories of maltreatment, they were rated by their parents as being within the normal range of functioning, both at home and at school.

The studies by Erich and his colleagues (2005) and by Ryan (2007) are the only published research to date to compare the adjustment of adopted children in both types of families, but there is no reason to expect that children adopted by lesbians and gay men should fare any differently than children adopted by heterosexual individuals. Furthermore, the findings reported in this study are quite consistent with those of a substantial literature on the development and adjustment of children with lesbian and gay parents. Both in longitudinal and in cross-sectional studies, in the United States and abroad, children of lesbian and gay parents have been found to show good adjustment and to develop in ways that are very similar to other children (Gartrell, Peyser, & Bos, this volume; Gartrell, Deck, Rodas, Peyser, & Banks, 2005; Patterson, 2000, 2006, 2009; Perrin & Committee on Psychosocial Aspects of Child and Family Health, 2002). Many questions have been studied, including children's adjustment at home, at school, with peers, and in other domains of their lives. In all these domains, the strength of parent–child relationships has been an important predictor of child adjustment, but parental sexual orientation has been less important (Patterson, 2006, 2007). When small differences have been found in child outcome or parenting behavior as a function of parental sexual orientation, the data have indicated no risk of harm for children of lesbians and gays.

The strength of these findings has been reflected in statements by many mainstream professional organizations. For instance, after a careful review of the research findings, the American Psychological Association (2004) went on record opposing "any discrimination based on sexual orientation in matters of adoption, child custody and visitation, foster care and reproductive health services." After their review of the research in this area, the American Academy of Pediatrics (2002) similarly recognized "that a considerable body of professional literature provides evidence that children with parents who are homosexual can have the same advantages and the same expectations for health, adjustment and development as can children whose parents are heterosexual." These and other respected professional groups, including the American Bar Association, the Child Welfare League of America, the National Association of Social Workers, and the Evan B. Donaldson Adoption Institute have based their conclusions on findings from social science research suggesting that parental sexual orientation is not a good predictor of parenting ability or child adjustment.

Very little research, however, has been conducted on *adolescent* offspring of lesbian or gay parents, and it has been suggested that caution be used when generalizing the results of research conducted with young children to adolescents (e.g., Perrin & Committee on Psychosocial Aspects of Child and Family Health, 2002). Because adolescence is a time during which issues such as personal identity, peers, and dating become very important, and because of concerns about the possible effects of same-sex parenting during adolescence (e.g., Baumrind, 1995), it is an especially important period in which to examine the development of youth with nonheterosexual parents.

A small body of research exists that focuses on the development of adolescent offspring of families headed by lesbian couples. Huggins (1989) reported a study of 18 adolescents with divorced heterosexual and 18 with divorced lesbian mothers, in which she found no differences in adolescent self-esteem as a function of mothers' sexual orientation. O'Connor (1993) studied 11 young men and women who were the offspring of divorced or separated lesbian mothers. Her participants expressed strong loyalty and protectiveness toward their mothers, but also described worries about losing friends or being judged by others due to their mothers' sexual orientation. Gershon, Tschann, and Jemerin (1999) studied self-esteem, perception of stigma, and coping skills among 76 adolescent offspring of lesbian mothers, and reported that adolescents who perceived more stigma related to having a lesbian mother had lower self-esteem in five of seven areas, including social acceptance and self-worth.

A recent study of adolescents parented by same- and opposite-sex couples in the United Kingdom assessed victimization, social support, and psychosocial functioning (Rivers, Poteat, & Noret, 2008). Rivers and his colleagues reported that adolescents with same-sex parents did not differ from those with opposite-sex parents or from the general student population at their school on measures of peer victimization and bullying, psychological symptoms, or use of social support. They also did not differ in their reports of common adolescent concerns, such as school work, appearance, and relationships with teachers (Rivers et al., 2008).

A slightly older population was studied in Tasker and Golombok's (1997) longitudinal study of 23 young adult offspring of lesbian mothers and a matched group of 23 young adult offspring of heterosexual mothers. In this generally well-adjusted sample, young men and women who were reared by lesbian mothers were no more likely than those raised by heterosexual mothers to experience depression or anxiety, or to have sought professional help for psychiatric problems. They reported having close friendships during adolescence, and were no more likely to remember peer group hostility than were those from other families. Offspring of lesbian mothers were also no more likely to report same-sex sexual attraction or a gay/lesbian/bisexual identity than were those from heterosexual families. They were, however, more likely to have considered a gay or lesbian relationship as a possibility for themselves and to have been involved in a same-sex relationship, suggesting that although sexual attraction and identity may not be related to parental sexual identities, the likelihood of considering or entering a same-sex relationship may be associated with parents' sexual orientation.

In general, like the literature on younger children, the studies of adolescents have found few differences in adjustment as a function of parental sexual orientation. Research on younger children (e.g., Chan, Raboy, & Patterson, 1998) has found that variables representing families' organization of daily life, such as division of household labor and childcare, are more likely than parental sexual orientation to be associated with children's outcomes. The research on adolescent offspring of same-sex couples described above, however, did not address this issue.

A substantial body of research indicates that parenting style influences the effectiveness of parents' efforts to socialize their children (Steinberg & Silk, 2002). In particular, a warm and accepting style of parenting is related to optimal outcomes for adolescents (Rohner, 1999), especially if it is combined with appropriate limit setting and monitoring of adolescent behavior (Steinberg, Lamborn, Dornbusch, & Darling, 1992). The relationship between parental warmth and positive outcomes has been found for adolescents from a wide variety of ethnic, socioeconomic, and family structure backgrounds, and by researchers working with a variety of different methodological approaches (Khaleque & Rohner, 2002). That these linkages have been found among such a diverse group of adolescents suggests that they might also be expected among the offspring of gay and lesbian parents.

In summary, the research on adolescent and young adult offspring of lesbian mothers suggests that they are developing in positive ways. However, the research has been limited and most studies were based on small samples, the representativeness of which can be difficult to assess (Stacey & Biblarz, 2001). One recent study assessed adjustment of 7-year-old children with lesbian and heterosexual mothers, using data from a large geographic population study (Golombok et al., 2003), and another focused on a representative sample of adolescents drawn from schools in the United Kingdom (Rivers et al., 2008). To the best of our knowledge, however, the research described here is the first to assess adjustment of adolescents living with same-sex parents with data drawn from a large national sample. Our sample is drawn from the National Longitudinal Study of Adolescent Health (Add Health), which includes participants from many different backgrounds, from many parts of the United States (Bearman, Jones, & Udry, 1997; Resnick et al., 1997).

Examination of the existing research indicates that there is a need for analysis of a comprehensive set of outcomes for adolescents who live with same-sex parents. The Add Health study assessed adolescent adjustment in many different ways, including various aspects of psychosocial well-being, school functioning, romantic relationships and behaviors, risky behaviors such as substance use, and peer relations. This study also examined several family and relationship variables that have not been included in past research, such as adolescents' perceptions of parental warmth, care from adults and peers, integration into the neighborhood, and autonomy, as well as parental assessment of the quality of the parent–child relationship. The Add Health database thus afforded a broad overview of adolescent adjustment.

Our research assessed normative levels of adjustment among adolescent offspring of same-sex parents, and also explored factors that are associated with individual differences in adjustment and behavior within this group. We assessed structural variables such as family type (i.e., whether the parent has a same-sex or opposite-sex partner), as well as family and relationship variables such as adolescents' perceptions of parental warmth, care from adults and peers, autonomy, and integration into the neighborhood, as well as the parents' perceptions of the quality of their relationship with their child. Based on the previous findings with children (e.g., Chan et al., 1998; Flaks et al., 1995; Golombok et al., 2003), we expected to find few differences in adjustment between youth living with parents who had same-sex versus opposite-sex partners. Consistent with the literature on sources of individual differences among adolescents (e.g., Steinberg & Silk, 2002), however, we did expect to find associations between family and relationship variables and adolescent adjustment outcomes.

In summary, this chapter describes our research on adjustment and development among adolescents living with same-sex couples. Our data were drawn from the Add Health study, which provided a nearly representative sample of adolescents and their parents in the United States during the 1990s. By selecting those youngsters in Add Health who were living with same-sex parents, and comparing them both to a matched group of youngsters living with other-sex parents and to the overall sample, we aimed to address questions about adjustment among teens living with same-sex parents.

INTRODUCTION TO THE NATIONAL LONGITUDINAL STUDY OF ADOLESCENT HEALTH

For this research, participating families were drawn from a large national sample of adolescents in the United States collected by Quality Education Data for the National Longitudinal Study of Adolescent Health (Add Health; Bearman, Jones, & Udry, 1997). Add Health is a school-based study of the health-related behaviors of adolescents in grades 7–12. A sample of 80 eligible high schools was initially selected. Schools were stratified to ensure that this sample was representative of U.S. schools with respect to region of country, urbanicity, school type, ethnicity, and school size. More than 70 percent of the originally sampled high schools were recruited by Add Health. If a school refused to participate, a replacement within its stratum was selected. Participating schools provided rosters of their students and, in most cases, agreed to administer an In-School Questionnaire during one class period. They also assisted in identifying their feeder schools (i.e., those schools that include seventh grade and send their graduates to that high school). The final sample consisted of a pair of schools in each of 80 communities, with the exception of some high schools that spanned grades 7 to 12 and therefore functioned as their own feeder schools (Bearman et al., 1997).

All students who completed an In-School Questionnaire, plus those who did not complete a questionnaire but who were listed on a school roster, were eligible for selection into the core in-home sample. Students in each school were stratified by grade and gender, and approximately 17 were randomly chosen from each stratum, so a total of about 200 adolescents were selected from each of the 80 pairs of schools. A total core sample of 12,105 adolescents was interviewed.

Most interviews were conducted in 1995 in the participants' homes. All data were recorded on laptop computers. For less sensitive sections, the interviewer read the questions and entered the respondent's answers. For more sensitive sections, the respondent listened to prerecorded questions through earphones and entered the answers directly.

A parent, preferably the resident mother, was asked to complete a questionnaire covering topics including parents' marriages and marriage-like relationships; neighborhood characteristics; involvement in volunteer, civic, or school activities; education and employment; household income; and parent–adolescent relationships.

Data employed in the studies, described below, were collected through the in-home interviews and surveys, as well as in-school surveys of students (Wave I, collected in 1994–1995) and through the in-home questionnaires of parents.

IDENTIFICATION OF CURRENT SAMPLE AND OF COMPARISON GROUPS

Offspring of same-sex couples were identified using a two-step process. We first identified families in which parents reported being in a marriage or marriage-like relationship with a person of the same sex. Because no data had been collected on parents' sexual identities as such, families headed by gay, bisexual, or lesbian parents who did not report that they were in a marriage or marriage-like relationship at the time of data collection could not be identified.

In the second step, the consistency of parental reports about gender and family relationships was examined. To guard against the possibility that some families may have been misclassified due to coding errors, we retained only those cases in which parental reports of gender and family relationship were consistent (e.g., a parent reported being female and described her relationship to the adolescent as "mother"). This procedure was designed to ensure that insofar as possible, only adolescents whose parents reported being involved in a marriage or marriage-like relationship with a person of the same sex were selected for further study.

The number of families headed by *male* same-sex couples was very small ($n = 6$). Results of preliminary analyses that included these families were nearly identical to those including only families headed by female same-sex couples. Because of their small numbers, and to simplify interpretation of results, however, we excluded these six families from the final sample.

The focal group of families identified through this process included those of 44 adolescents, 23 girls and 21 boys. Approximately 68 percent of the adolescents identified themselves as European-American or white, and 32 percent identified themselves as nonwhite or as biracial. On average, the adolescents were 15 and their parents were 41½ years of age. Average household income for families in the focal group was approximately $45,500 per year, and 48 percent of the parents in this group had been college educated. Because only two adolescents in the focal group had been adopted, their data are not reported separately here.

The resources of the Add Health database allowed the construction of a well-matched comparison group of adolescents. Each of the offspring of same-sex parents was matched with an adolescent from the Add Health database who was reared by opposite-sex parents. This matching was accomplished by generating a list of adolescents from the Add Health database who matched each target adolescent on the following characteristics: sex, age, ethnic background, adoption status (identified via parent reports), learning disability status, family income, and parent's educational attainment. The first matching adolescent on each list was chosen as the comparison adolescent for that target adolescent. The final sample included

88 families, including 44 families headed by mothers with female partners and 44 comparison families headed by opposite-sex couples.

To assess the degree to which our focal group of 44 families with same-sex parents was representative of the overall population from which it was drawn, we compared the demographic characteristics of the focal group with those for the entire Add Health core sample (n = 12,105). Using one-sample t-tests and χ^2 tests, as appropriate, we compared adolescent age, parent age, household income, adolescent gender, racial identification, adoption status, and parental education in the two groups. None of these comparisons was statistically significant. We conclude that our focal group of 44 families was demographically similar to the population from which it was drawn.

PSYCHOSOCIAL ADJUSTMENT, FAMILY RELATIONSHIPS, AND SCHOOL OUTCOMES AMONG ADOLESCENTS LIVINGWITH SAME-SEX COUPLES

Our first set of questions concerned psychosocial adjustment and school outcomes among adolescents with same-sex parents. How strong was the adolescents' self-esteem? To what extent did these youth experience depressive symptoms, or anxiety? What were their grades at school? How much trouble had they encountered at school, and how connected did they feel to other people in their school environments? And how close were their relationships with parents? Information addressing these questions allowed us to obtain an overview of adolescent functioning in different domains of life.

Assessment of Psychosocial Adjustment, Family Relationships, and School Outcomes

We examined data from Add Health regarding different aspects of adolescent adjustment and relationships with parents. Composite variables were created from the Add Health Home Interviews and In-School Questionnaires for adolescents' self-reported levels of depressive symptoms, anxiety, self-esteem, school grades, trouble at school, and school connectedness. Composite variables were also formed for adolescents' reports of their perceptions of parental warmth, caring from adults and peers, their integration into their neighborhood, and their autonomy. Adolescents' romantic attractions, relationships, and behaviors were assessed with individual items. Unless otherwise specified, these are all self-report variables. Parent reports about their relationships with adolescent offspring were also included.

Psychosocial Adjustment
Adolescent depressive symptoms were assessed with a 19-question version of the CES-D (Radloff, 1977) scale from the In-Home Interview. This scale of depressive

symptoms included questions about the frequency of symptoms such as feeling lonely, depressed, or too tired to do things. Possible scores on this scale, based on the sum of the 19 items, ranged from 0 to 57, with higher scores indicating greater levels of depressive symptoms. Cronbach's alpha for this scale was 0.85 for this sample.

Adolescent anxiety was measured with a seven-item scale that included questions about the frequency of symptoms such as feeling moody or having trouble relaxing. Items were measured on a scale of 0 (never) to 4 (every day), with scores ranging from 0 to 28, and higher scores indicating higher levels of anxiety. Cronbach's alpha for this anxiety scale was 0.68 for this sample.

Self-esteem was assessed using a six-item scale that included items such as feeling socially accepted and feeling loved and wanted. Items were measured on a scale of 1 (strongly disagree) to 5 (strongly agree), with scores ranging from 6 to 30, and higher scores indicating higher self-esteem. Cronbach's alpha for this scale was 0.80 for this sample.

SCHOOL FUNCTIONING

School outcomes measured included grade point average (GPA), school connectedness, and trouble in school. GPA was measured on a four-point scale where 4 = A, 3 = B, 2 = C, and 1 = D or lower. It was assessed by taking the mean of grades received in four school subjects (English, Mathematics, History/Social Studies, and Science) in the current or most recent school year. Cronbach's alpha for GPA was 0.79 in this sample.

School connectedness was measured using a five-item scale that assessed respondents' feelings of integration into their school. Items, which were averaged to form the adolescent's score, included the degree to which they felt close to other students, felt like part of their school, and felt teachers treated students fairly. Possible scores ranged from 1 (strongly disagree) to 5 (strongly agree). Cronbach's alpha for the school connectedness scale in this sample was 0.82.

Trouble at school was assessed with a four-item scale that included items such as problems getting homework done and in getting along with classmates. Items were measured on a scale of 0 (never) to 4 (every day) and the mean of the four items was taken, with higher scores indicating more trouble in school. Cronbach's alpha for this scale was 0.71 for this sample.

ROMANTIC RELATIONSHIPS, ATTRACTIONS, AND BEHAVIORS

Adolescents' romantic attractions were assessed with two yes/no questions, "Have you ever been attracted to a female?" and "Have you ever been attracted to a male?" Females who answered yes to the first question and males who answered yes to the second question were classified as having had a same-sex attraction. To assess dating behavior, adolescents were asked three yes/no questions: whether they had a romantic relationship in the past 18 months, whether they had a same-sex romantic relationship in the past 18 months, and whether they had ever engaged in sexual intercourse.

FAMILY AND RELATIONSHIP VARIABLES

Parental warmth toward the adolescent was assessed using the mean of five items from adolescent reports. Self-report items included adolescents' perceptions of parents' warmth and caring toward them, perceived level of family's understanding and attention, and feelings of closeness to parents. For questions in which adolescents were asked about each parent, we used the response for the one described as more warm and loving. Scores ranged from 1 (not at all) to 5 (very much), with higher scores indicating greater warmth. Cronbach's alpha for the parental warmth scale was 0.70.

Adolescents' perceptions of their integration into their neighborhoods were measured using a scale of three yes/no (1 = yes, 0 = no) items. Items included whether they knew people in their neighborhood, talked with neighbors, or felt their neighbors look out for each other. The three items were summed, and possible scores ranged from 0 to 3, with higher scores indicating greater neighborhood integration. Cronbach's alpha for neighborhood integration was 0.54.

Adolescents' perceived autonomy was assessed with a scale of seven yes/no (1 = yes, 0 = no) items that addressed the extent to which they were allowed to make decisions about aspects of their lives such as food, bedtime, TV viewing, and friends. The seven items were summed, and possible scores ranged from 0 to 7, with higher scores indicating greater autonomy. Cronbach's alpha for autonomy was 0.60.

Adolescents' perceived care from adults and friends was measured with three items regarding how much they believed that adults, teachers, and friends cared about them. The mean of the three items was taken as the adolescent's score, and possible scores ranged from 1 (not at all) to 5 (very much), with higher scores indicating perceptions of more caring. Cronbach's alpha for this scale was 0.58 for this sample.

Parental perceptions of the quality of their relationship with their child were assessed with a scale of six items from the parent's in-home interview. Items included questions about the parent's assessment of trust, understanding, communication, and the general quality of their relationship with their child, and were measured on a scale of 1 to 5; scores ranged from 6 to 30, with higher scores indicating closer relationships. Cronbach's alpha was 0.70 for this scale.

Results for Psychosocial Adjustment, Family Relationships, and School Outcomes

We conducted analyses in two steps. The first set of analyses evaluated the degree to which adolescents living with same-sex couples differed in their adjustment from the comparison group. The second set of analyses explored associations of adolescent adjustment with assessments of family and relationship processes. We expected that the makeup of adolescents' households would be less important than the strength of family relationships in accounting for variation in adolescent adjustment.

Overall, adolescents reported positive psychosocial outcomes, with low levels of anxiety and depressive symptoms, and high levels of self-esteem. Similarly, adolescents reported positive school outcomes, with average GPAs of 2.8, high levels of school connectedness, and low levels of trouble in school.

As expected, we found no differences in adolescents' psychosocial adjustment—which included depressive symptoms, anxiety, and self-esteem—between offspring of same-sex couples and offspring of comparison families headed by opposite-sex couples. We found a significant multivariate effect for family type for the school outcomes, which was also significant in the univariate analyses for school connectedness. Unexpectedly, adolescents with same-sex parents reported feeling more connected at school than did those living with opposite-sex parents, but we found no differences as a function of gender for psychosocial adjustment or school functioning. As expected, there were no significant interactions between gender and family type for psychological adjustment or school outcomes. Demographic covariates (e.g., adolescent age, family income, and parent's education) were not associated with these outcomes.

Analyses of adolescents' reports of romantic attractions and behaviors revealed no differences between the groups in the percentage of adolescents who reported ever having engaged in sexual intercourse (34 percent of adolescents living with same-sex couples and 34 percent of those living with other-sex couples). There was also no significant difference between the groups in the percentage of adolescents who had had a romantic relationship in the past 18 months (68 percent of adolescents living with same-sex couples and 59 percent of those living with other-sex couples). Fewer than 10 adolescents reported same-sex attractions and same-sex romantic relationships in the previous 18 months, so under stipulations that permit use of these data, group comparisons are not presented. Reports of romantic relationships, attractions, and behaviors did not differ as a function of age or gender, except that older adolescents were more likely than younger ones to report having had a romantic relationship in the past 18 months. In summary, adolescent psychosocial, romantic attractions and behaviors, and school adjustment did not differ as a function of family type or adolescent gender.

Overall, adolescents reported positive family relationships. Adolescents' reports of parental warmth were high. Adolescents' perceptions of others' (teachers, adults, and friends) care for them were also high, as were their reports of autonomy. Their average assessment of their integration into their neighborhoods was just above the middle of the scale, with higher scores indicating greater integration. Parents' perceptions of the quality of the parent–child relationship were also high. In short, this was a well-adjusted sample.

Consistent with results for psychosocial and school outcomes, we found no differences in adolescent reports of family and relationship processes, including parental warmth, care from others, personal autonomy, or neighborhood integration, as a function of family type. We did, however, find a significant multivariate difference in family and relationship processes that was attributable to adolescent gender. Further analysis revealed, as expected from earlier research, that girls reported higher levels of care from adults and peers than did boys.

To what degree did outcomes for adolescents in our focal and comparison samples differ from those for the population from which the samples were drawn? To explore this question, we obtained mean scores (or percentages for categorical variables) for each of the dependent variables. Using one-sample t-tests and χ^2 tests, as appropriate, we compared means for our focal sample to those for the entire Add Health core sample. None of these comparisons was statistically significant. Thus, outcomes for adolescents with same-sex parents in our focal sample did not differ significantly from those for a representative group of adolescents.

Having found almost no associations between family type and adolescent adjustment, we wanted to examine possible associations between outcomes and processes in the adolescent's environment. In particular, we examined correlations among adolescents' perceptions of parental warmth, care from adults and peers, autonomy, and neighborhood integration; parents' perceptions of the quality of the parent–child relationship; and measures of adolescent adjustment. We also conducted simultaneous multiple regression analyses to determine whether these family and relationship variables were significant predictors of adolescent adjustment, while controlling for family type, adolescent gender, and socioeconomic status. Regression analyses were conducted separately for adolescents' depressive symptoms, anxiety, self esteem, GPA, school connectedness, and trouble in school. Family type, adolescent's gender, parental education, and family income were also included as predictors. We did not examine romantic attractions and behavior because of the small number of adolescents in either group reporting same-sex attractions or romantic relationships.

Our results showed that, as expected, quality of family relationships was significantly associated with many adolescent outcomes, including school connectedness, anxiety, and trouble in school. The association between adolescents' depressive symptoms and parental report of the quality of the parent–adolescent relationship was not statistically significant. There was, however, a nonsignificant trend in the expected direction, with more positive relationships associated with lower levels of depressive symptoms. Levels of self-esteem were significantly associated with the adolescents' reports of caring from adults and peers, with more care associated with higher self esteem. Adolescents' anxiety was associated with adolescent gender, with boys reporting lower levels of anxiety. Adolescents' reports of trouble in school were associated with the quality of the parent–child relationship and level of parental education; less trouble in school was associated with more positive relationships with parents and having parents with higher levels of education. School connectedness was associated with family type, the quality of the parent–child relationship, and care from adults and peers, with a significant interaction between family type and care from adults and peers. Greater school connectedness was associated with having same-sex parents, reporting higher levels of care from adults and peers, and having parents who reported a more positive parent–child relationship. Adolescents' perceived care from adults and peers had a stronger effect on school connectedness for adolescents living with same-sex parents than for those living with opposite-sex parents. Adolescents' GPAs were not associated with any family and relationship variable or socioeconomic status variable. In summary, adolescents' and parents' reports of family and relationship processes, such as quality of the parent–child relationship and care from adults and peers, were associated with several measures of adolescent functioning and were better predictors of adolescent adjustment than was family type or adolescent gender.

SUBSTANCE USE, DELINQUENCY, AND VICTIMIZATION AMONG ADOLESCENTS LIVING WITH SAME-SEX COUPLES

We also studied substance use, delinquency, and victimization among youngsters living with same-sex couples. To what extent did youth use alcohol, tobacco, or illegal drugs? To what extent did youth participate in delinquent activities? And to what extent were they victimized by others? Our methods and findings for these questions are described below.

Assessment of Substance Use, Delinquency, and Victimization

SUBSTANCE USE
All of the substance use assessments were based on adolescents' self-reports. Adolescents' use of tobacco was assessed with a composite self-report variable (Sieving et al., 2000) that uses four items to classify adolescents into one of seven levels of tobacco use (1 = "never smoked," 3 = "currently smoking 1–2 cigarettes/day," 5 = "currently smoking 6–10 cigarettes/day," 7 = "currently smoking >20 cigarettes/day"). Friends' use of tobacco was assessed by asking how many of their three best friends smoked at least one cigarette per day.

Use of alcohol was assessed with three variables. We used a composite variable (Sieving et al., 2000), which uses two items to create an eight-level variable about adolescents' use of alcohol in their lifetime and in the past 12 months (1 = "2–3 drinks in their lifetime," 3 = "drank alcohol on 1 or 2 days in the past 12 months," 5 = "drank 2–3 days a month in the past 12 months," 7 = "drank 3–5 days a week in the past 12 months," 8 = "drank every day or almost every day in the past 12 months"). Adolescents were instructed to exclude "a sip or taste of someone else's drink." Individual items measured how often in the past 12 months adolescents had binged on alcohol (5+ drinks in a row) and had gotten drunk. Scores for these items ranged from 1 (never) to 7 (every day or almost every day).

Lifetime and current marijuana use were assessed with a composite variable (Sieving et al., 2000), which uses two survey items to form a seven-level variable (1 = "never used marijuana," 3 = "more than three times in their lifetime, no use in the past 30 days," 5 = "two or three times in the past 30 days," 7 = "more than five times in the past 30 days).

Adolescents' risky use of alcohol and drugs was assessed with a scale of eight items (1 = yes, 0 = no; Cronbach's alpha = 0.78) that asked whether the respondent had driven a car, gone to school, gotten into a fight, or carried a weapon while consuming alcohol or drugs. The sum of the eight items was taken, with higher scores indicating more risky use.

Relationship and physical problems caused by adolescents' use of alcohol were assessed with a scale of nine items (Cronbach's alpha = 0.84), asking about the frequency of being hung over, sick, in a fight, in a situation that was later regretted, or in trouble with parents, school, or friends or dates because of alcohol use in the past 12 months. Items were measured on a scale of 0 (never) to 4 (five or more times) and the mean of the nine items was taken, with higher scores indicating more problems.

Joint occurrences of substance use and sexual activity were assessed using a scale of six items (1 = yes, 0 = no; Cronbach's alpha = 0.68) asking whether the adolescents had used drugs, alcohol, or been drunk the first time (three items) or most recent time (three items) they had sexual intercourse. The sum of the six items was taken, and higher scores indicated more joint occurrences.

DELINQUENT BEHAVIOR

Adolescent delinquent behavior was assessed with 10 items (Cronbach's alpha = 0.74) in which they listened to questions through headphones and recorded their answers on a laptop computer. These items ask about the occurrence of activities such as damaging others' property, shoplifting, or getting into fights in the past 12 months. Scores on this scale were the sum of the 10 items (1 = yes, 0 = no), with higher scores indicating more delinquent behaviors.

VICTIMIZATION

Adolescents' experiences as victims and witnesses of violence were assessed with five items (Cronbach's alpha = 0.97) asking how often they had been shot at, cut, or jumped, had a gun or knife pulled on them, or had seen someone shot or stabbed. Scores were the sum of five items (1 = yes, 0 = no). Higher scores indicated more victimization.

FAMILY AND RELATIONSHIP VARIABLES

Adolescents' perceived care from adults, teachers, and friends was measured with three items (described above) regarding how much they believed that others cared about them, with higher scores indicating perceptions of more caring. Parental perceptions of the quality of their relationships with their adolescents were assessed with a scale described above, on which higher scores indicated closer relationships.

Results for Substance Use, Delinquency, and Victimization

Twenty-five percent of the adolescents reported that they had ever smoked regularly and 44 percent reported that they had consumed alcohol when they were not in the company of their parents. Reports of adolescents' frequency of alcohol or tobacco use were low. Adolescents also reported low levels of alcohol abuse, including binge drinking and getting drunk. Their reports of physical and relationship problems because of alcohol use were also low, as were their reports of risky use of drugs or alcohol and their reports of joint occurrences of sexual activity and drug or alcohol use. They also reported low levels of delinquent behavior and victimization.

As expected, we did not find a statistically significant difference in adolescents' reports of their frequency of alcohol, tobacco, or marijuana use as a function of family type. In addition, our analyses revealed no significant difference in the number of three best friends who smoked or frequency of getting drunk or binge drinking. Consistent with results for the substance use, we found no significant difference in problems arising from alcohol or drug use (relationship and physical problems, risky use of alcohol and drugs, and sex while under the influence of alcohol or drugs) as a function of family type. Analyses also revealed no difference in adolescents' delinquent behavior between offspring of same-sex couples and offspring of comparison families headed by different-sex couples. Similarly, we found no difference in adolescents' experiences as victims or witnesses of violence as a function of family type.

Having found no associations between family type and adolescent risk behavior, we explored possible associations between processes in the adolescent's environment and adolescent outcomes. We conducted regression analyses separately for use of tobacco, alcohol, and marijuana, as well as victimization and delinquent behavior. Family type, gender, parental education, and family income were included as predictors. Variables and interactions that were not statistically significant predictors were removed from the models.

Results showed that, as expected, quality of family relationships was significantly associated with many adolescent outcomes. Adolescents' tobacco use was significantly associated with parental report of the quality of the parent–adolescent relationship and with adolescents' reports of caring from adults and peers. As expected, greater perceived care from others and more positive relationships were associated with lower levels of tobacco use. Adolescents' use of alcohol, use of marijuana, and delinquent behavior were significantly associated with parental report of the quality of parent–adolescent relationships. Closer parent–adolescent relationships were associated with less alcohol use, less marijuana use, and less delinquent behavior on the part of youth. Boys reported more victimization than did girls, but interactions between family type and predictor variables were not significant. In summary, adolescents' reports of family and relationship processes, such as quality of parent–child relationships and care from adults and peers, were associated with several measures of adolescent outcomes and were better predictors of adolescent risk behavior than was family type.

PEER RELATIONS AMONG ADOLESCENTS LIVING WITH SAME-SEX COUPLES

Another important dimension of adolescent adjustment is peer relations. To explore experiences with peers among the offspring of same-sex and other-sex couples, we studied not only the adolescents' self-reported friendships but also their popularity among their peers, as described by their peers. In this way, we sought a comprehensive view of peer relations among adolescents living with same-sex couples.

Assessment of Peer Relations

Adolescents' reports of the quality of their peer relationships were measured with a scale of nine items, including questions about how much the adolescent felt friends cared about him or her, felt close to people at school, and felt like a part of school, as well as frequency of trouble getting along with other students, feeling that people were unfriendly, getting into any physical fights or serious physical fights, and being jumped. Negative items were reverse coded. These items were standardized (M = 0, SD = 1) and the sum was taken, with higher scores indicating more positive relationships. Cronbach's alpha was 0.68 for this sample.

Perceived support from and amount of time spent with the adolescent's five best male friends and five best female friends were measured with 10 yes/no items (three items each about time with male friends and time with female friends; two items each about support from male friends and support from female friends). The support items asked whether the adolescent had talked to the friend about a problem or talked to the friend on the telephone during the past 7 days. The time items asked whether the adolescent had gone to the friend's house, hung out with the friend during the past 7 days, or spent time with the friend during the past weekend. The three support items were summed for all five friends of each gender, and possible scores ranged from 0 to 15. The two time items were summed for all five friends of each gender, and possible scores ranged from 0 to 10. Higher scores indicated more support from or time spent with friends. Cronbach's alpha was 0.88 for time with female friends, 0.83 for time with male friends, 0.82 for support from female friends, and 0.70 for support from male friends.

Adolescents' self-report data on their friendship networks were available for a subset (n = 56) of those in our sample. Analyses revealed that this subset of adolescents did not differ on family income or parental education from those for whom these data were not available. Our analyses of network variables are limited to this smaller sample.

The number of friends the adolescent reported having in school was measured as the number of friendship nominations (up to 10) the adolescent made for students in school. The presence of a best female friend was assessed with a yes/no item indicating whether the adolescent nominated a female in the school as a best friend. Similarly, the presence of a best male friend was assessed with a yes/no item that indicates whether the adolescent nominated a male in school as a best friend.

Peer-report network data were available to augment the information provided by adolescents regarding their friendship networks. As with the adolescent self-report network data, analyses of these data are limited to the subset of adolescents (n = 56) for whom network data were available. Variables constructed by Add Health staff (Carolina Population Center, 1997) from peer-report data include adolescent popularity, network centrality, network density, network heterogeneity, and several network traits.

Popularity was calculated as the number of times an adolescent was nominated as a friend by other students in school, with higher scores indicating greater popularity in the adolescent's several network traits. Adolescents' centrality within their friendship network (Bonacich, 1987; Carolina Population Center, 1997) assesses whether they are located in prominent positions within their friendship network and connected to many peers in their peer group. Higher numbers indicate greater centrality.

The density of adolescents' friendship networks, including students who were nominated by the adolescent as a friend and students who nominated the adolescent as a friend, assesses how many interconnections exist among students in the peer group, which is related to how likely adolescents are to know others in their school (Haynie, 2000). Higher numbers indicate greater network density.

To assess the degree of diversity in friendship networks, which included students who were nominated as friends by the adolescent and students who nominated the adolescent as a friend, we used heterogeneity measures of grade, age, and race computed by Add Health staff. Higher numbers indicate greater diversity in a trait. We assessed two characteristics of friendship networks, with the mean value on that characteristic or behavior for students in the adolescent's peer network. These characteristics included grades and number of extracurricular activities. Higher scores indicate higher grades or more activities (Carolina Population Center, 1997).

Adolescents' perceived care from adults and friends was measured with three items regarding how much they believed that adults, teachers, and friends cared about them. The mean of the three items was taken as the adolescent's score, and possible scores ranged from 1 to 5, with higher scores indicating perceptions of more caring. Cronbach's alpha for this scale was 0.58 for this sample.

Perceived parental warmth toward the adolescent was assessed using the mean of five items from adolescent reports. Self-report items included adolescents' perceptions of parents' warmth and caring toward them, perceived level of family's understanding and attention, and adolescents' feelings of closeness to parents. For questions in which adolescents were asked about each of their parents, the response for the parent who was described as more warm and loving was used. Scores ranged from 1 to 5, with higher scores indicating greater warmth. Cronbach's alpha for the parental warmth scale was 0.70 for this sample.

Adolescents answered eight yes/no items describing activities adolescents sometimes engage in with their mothers. Adolescents reported whether or not they had engaged in each of the activities with their resident mother in the previous 4 weeks. These items included going shopping, playing a sport, talking about someone the adolescent is dating, going to the movies, discussing a personal problem, talking about grades, talking about a school project, and talking about other things going on in school. The eight items were summed, with possible scores ranging from 0 to 8. Cronbach's alpha for this variable was 0.67 for this sample.

Results for Peer Relations

Analyses were conducted in two major steps. The first set of analyses evaluated the degree to which adolescents living with same-sex couples differed in their family relationships and peer relations from the comparison group, and they employed two-way (family type: same-sex versus opposite-sex parents × gender of adolescent) ANOVAs and MANOVAs. The second set of analyses explored associations of adolescent peer relations with assessments of family and relationship processes. Simultaneous multiple regression analyses were used to determine whether these processes were significant predictors of adolescent adjustment, while controlling for family type, adolescent gender, and socioeconomic status. We expected that family type would be less important than family relationships and processes in accounting for variation in the quality of adolescent peer relations, and that processes related to positive outcomes for adolescents would be similar, regardless of family type, and that no interactions between family type and relationship processes would emerge.

Overall, this sample reported positive peer relations, with adolescents reporting an average of about five friends in school. Adolescents also reported spending time with between one and two male friends and between one and two female friends, on average, in the past week, engaging in activities such as going to the friend's home, hanging out, and talking on the phone.

As expected, there were no differences in the number of friends that adolescents nominated in their schools, nor in the quality of their peer relations as a function of family type. Girls rated the quality of their peer relations slightly more positively than did boys, but this comparison did not reach statistical significance. There was no significant difference between groups in the percent of adolescents who reported having a best male friend; 64 percent of adolescents with same-sex parents and 68 percent of those with opposite-sex parents reported this. Adolescents who reported having a best female friend (68 percent of adolescents with same-sex parents and 40 percent of adolescents with opposite-sex parents, *ns*) were somewhat more likely to be living with same-sex couples, but this difference did not reach statistical significance. Analyses of adolescents' reports of time spent with and support received from male and female friends also revealed no significant differences as a function of family type. There was, however, a significant effect for gender; girls reported more support from female friends than did boys. All of the analyses were run again with family income and parent's education as covariates. As the results did not differ between the two analyses and as the influence of demographic characteristics was not a focus of our research, demographic results are not presented here. Overall, adolescent reports of peer relations did not differ as a function of family type.

With regard to peer reports of peer relations, adolescents in this sample were nominated as a friend by an average of almost five schoolmates. As expected, analyses of peer reports of the adolescent's peer relations, including popularity, network centrality, and network density, revealed no significant differences as a function of family type. There was, however, a significant effect for adolescent gender, with girls having higher popularity ratings than did boys.

We also used peer report data to calculate the heterogeneity of the adolescent's friendship network with respect to age, race, and school grades. On average, this sample of adolescents had networks that were moderately diverse, and there were no significant differences as a function of family type or adolescent gender. In summary, adolescents living with same-sex parents had friendship networks that were very similar in heterogeneity and member characteristics to those of adolescents living with opposite-sex parents.

In line with our expectations, there were no significant differences in adolescent reports of family and relationship processes, including parental warmth, activities with mother, or care from others as a function of family type. Girls did, however, report higher levels of care from adults and peers, and greater participation in activities with their mothers, than did boys. To assess the degree to which outcomes for adolescents in our focal and comparison samples differed from those for the population from which the samples were drawn, we obtained mean scores from the Add Health Core Sample for each of the dependent variables. Using one-sample t-tests and chi-squared tests, we compared means for our focal sample to those for the entire Add Health core sample. None of these comparisons was statistically significant. Thus, peer relations for adolescents with same-sex parents in our focal sample did not differ significantly from those of a nationally representative group of American adolescents.

We also explored possible associations between processes in the adolescent's environment and adolescent peer relations. Simultaneous multiple regression analyses were used to determine whether these family and relationship variables were significant predictors of adolescent peer relations, while controlling for family type, adolescent gender, and socioeconomic status. Regression analyses were conducted separately for adolescents' reports of the quality of their peer relations and the number of friends nominated by the adolescent as friends, as well as for peer reports of popularity, network centrality, and network density. Family type, adolescent's gender, parental education, and family income were also included as predictors, with family type and adolescent gender remaining in all models for comparison. Demographic variables and family and relationship variables that were not statistically significant predictors were removed from the models.

Results showed that, as expected, family and relationship variables were significantly associated with many measures of adolescent peer relations. Adolescents' reports of the quality of their peer relations were significantly associated with parents' reports of the quality of the parent–adolescent relationship and with the adolescents' reports of caring from adults and peers, with more positive parent–adolescent relationships and more perceived care from adults and peers associated with more positive peer relations. Similarly, the number of school friends reported by adolescents was associated with the quality of the parent–adolescent relationship and the number of activities done with mother, with more positive parent–adolescent relationships and more activities with mother associated with having more friends at school.

Peer reports of adolescent peer relations were also significantly associated with family and relationship variables. Peer reports of adolescents' popularity were significantly associated with the number of activities with mother, with more activities with mother associated with greater popularity. Adolescents' centrality in their peer networks was associated with the quality of the parent–adolescent relationship; more positive relationships were associated with greater network centrality. There was also a significant association between network centrality and parental education, with higher levels of parental education associated with greater network centrality. There were no significant associations among the density of adolescent's peer networks and family and relationship variables.

In summary, adolescent peer relations were associated in expected ways with several family and relationship variables. Adolescent reports of care from adults and peers and number of activities with mother, as well as parental reports of the quality of the parent–adolescent relationship, were significantly associated with numerous measures of adolescent peer relations. Also as predicted, family type was not significantly associated with any measure of adolescent peer relations, but several associations were found among these measures and adolescent gender. Overall, these results suggest that family and relationship process variables are more important predictors of adolescent peer relations than is family type.

DISCUSSION

The results of this research—which is the first to draw participants from a large, national sample to examine the adjustment, school outcomes, substance use, family, and peer relations of adolescents living with same-sex couples—have revealed few significant differences in adolescent functioning as a function of family type. Regardless of family type, however, family and relationship variables such as the quality of the parent–adolescent relationship were significantly associated with many aspects of adolescent functioning. These results, which are consistent with the findings of past research on children living with lesbian mothers, suggest that qualities of relationships within the family are more important in predicting adolescent psychosocial adjustment, substance use, school outcomes, family, and peer relations than is family type (Chan et al., 1998; Patterson, 2006).

Our research included assessments of multiple facets of adolescent adjustment, including psychosocial adjustment, school outcomes, substance use, and relationships with parents and peers. Indeed, assessments of each of these variables were themselves mutifaceted. For instance, our assessments of peer relations included adolescents' perceptions of the number of friends they have in school, the quality of their peer relations, and the amount of support they receive from both male and female friends. Our assessments of peer relations also included peer reports about adolescent popularity within the school, centrality within peer networks, network density, and network heterogeneity. The consistency of our results, which did not reveal significant differences among adolescents living with same-sex parents versus those living with opposite-sex parents in a geographically, racially, and economically diverse sample, leads to the conclusion that adolescents living with same-sex parents are developing well (e.g., Wainright & Patterson, 2006, 2008; Wainright, Russell, & Patterson, 2004).

We did not find significant associations between adolescents' functioning and family type, but we did uncover associations between several aspects of adolescent social and personal adjustment, on the one hand, and family and relationship variables, on the other. For instance, parents' reports of the quality of the parent–adolescent relationship were significantly associated with adolescents' self-reports of the quality of their peer relations, number of friends in school, and peer network centrality. Also supporting the view that adolescent peer relations are strongly associated with qualities of other relationships, results revealed that adolescents' reports of care from others were significantly associated with their reports of the quality of their peer relations. Similarly, adolescents who reported participating in many activities with their mothers were also likely to report having more friends in school. Peer reports of popularity showed the same associations; those who described more activities with their mothers were also described as more popular by peers. Overall then, these results support past findings that suggest that family processes are more important predictors of adolescent functioning than are structural variables such as family type (e.g., Allen, Moore, Kuperminc, & Bell, 1998).

Major theories of human development have often been interpreted as predicting that offspring of same-sex parents would encounter important difficulties in their adjustment, especially during adolescence (Baumrind, 1995). Results from this large sample of American adolescents have failed to confirm these predictions, suggesting that the theories may need reevaluation, especially in their application to outcomes for offspring of same-sex parents (Patterson, 2000, 2006). Results of numerous recent studies on children and adolescents who do not live with heterosexual parents (e.g., Gartrell, Peyser, & Bos, this volume; Patterson, 2000, 2006; Perrin & Committee on Psychosocial Aspects of Child and Family Health, 2002; Stevens, Golombok, Beveridge, & the ALSPAC Study Team, 2002), as well as those of the current research, suggest that theorists may need to reconsider the importance of being reared by opposite-sex parents for human personal and social development.

Our confidence in the present findings is bolstered by the strengths of the Add Health study (Bearman et al.,1997) from which the data have been drawn. The Add Health study was designed and conducted by experienced researchers who did not collect data for the purpose of studying adolescents living with same-sex parents. This fact addresses one of the concerns sometimes expressed about some earlier studies, namely that samples may have been biased toward lesbian mothers who have higher incomes and greater educational attainment, as well as toward those families whose children are developing well. Regardless of whether earlier samples were or were not biased in any way, the present sample cannot have been subject to any such limitations.

The use of the Add Health database has allowed us to identify an ethnically, economically, and geographically diverse sample of adolescents living with same-sex couples. This is one of the most heterogeneous samples employed in research with this population to date. The continuing but understandable reluctance of some same-sex parents to identify themselves as such, however, limits our ability to assess the exact degree to which the current sample is representative of all lesbian-headed families. In addition, the Add Health database does not make it possible to determine how long adolescents have lived in their current family situations, so we cannot reach any conclusions on that topic. Despite these limitations, the Add Health database was a useful resource for this research.

This research is the first to involve information collected from parents and peers, as well as from adolescent self-reports, in the study of adolescent peer relations among youth reared by same-sex couples. This feature of the study allowed us to evaluate the possibility that self-reports might provide overly optimistic estimates of adolescent development. To the contrary, we found that both adolescents themselves and their peers at school described the peer relations of youngsters reared by same-sex couples as satisfactory. Thus, our peer report data represent a major asset that is helpful in ruling out possible alternative interpretations of our findings.

Despite the issues in past research that were addressed by the design of our study, the current research has some limitations. Among these is the fact that parents were not asked directly about their sexual identities. As a result, we were forced to rely on indirect assessments of sexual identity such as parent-report items that asked parents whether they were in a "marriage or marriage-like relationship," together with information about the gender of that partner. The design of the Add Health study allowed identification and study of adolescents living with mothers who have female romantic partners, but not adolescents with lesbian mothers who lived in other types of households (e.g., single lesbian mothers or mothers who did not consider their relationship with a female romantic partner to be a marriage or marriage-like relationship). The current research would have been strengthened if parents had been asked to describe their sexual identities in terms of their sexual attractions, fantasies, behaviors, and identities. As in all studies with gay and lesbian populations, it is likely that some parents chose not to disclose their same-sex relationships and therefore could not be identified for study in this research. Despite limitations, the research makes a valuable contribution to knowledge about adolescent development in the context of diverse families.

ADOPTION LAW AND POLICY IN LIGHT OF RESEARCH FINDINGS

The current findings have implications for public policies that involve children of lesbian mothers (Patterson, 2007, 2009). Inasmuch as these findings suggest adolescents living with same-sex parents develop in much the same way as do those living with opposite-sex parents, they provide no justification for discrimination on the basis of sexual orientation in matters such as adoption, foster care, and/or child custody. Our results suggest that relationships and processes that occur within the family are more important in the adolescents' personal and social development.

Those who argue against allowing lesbian and gay adults to become adoptive parents (e.g., Wardle, 1997) suggest that placement in such homes would not be in the children's best interests. This argument would seem to rest on demonstrations of harm for the children of lesbian or gay parents. After more than 25 years of research, however, evidence of any such harm has yet to emerge. Meanwhile, in jurisdictions that do not permit adoptions by lesbian and gay adults, children are being denied homes and families. Minimizing children's chances of finding adoptive homes is not a credible way to pursue their best interests, and as the results of research on sexual orientation and parenting continue to accumulate, this position becomes increasingly difficult to defend.

Those who argue that sexual orientation should be seen as irrelevant to the qualifications of prospective adoptive parents (e.g., Wald, 2006), on the other hand, would appear to be responding to the actual needs of children. In the United States today, many thousands of children do not have homes. Prospective adoptive parents are in short supply. Children who grow up with lesbian and gay parents appear to develop well compared to others. In these circumstances, to deny adoptions to otherwise qualified prospective adoptive parents on the basis of sexual orientation alone is to deny loving homes to children who need them.

To suggest that the sexual orientation of prospective adoptive parents should be considered irrelevant is not to abandon careful evaluation of those adults who wish to adopt. Methods that have been found to be useful in screening other candidates should be applied in the screening of lesbian and gay prospective adoptive parents as well. It is important that such work be done carefully, so as to protect children's interests. What is not justified is any special scrutiny or added screening for lesbian or gay individuals.

In the United States today, lesbian and gay adults are less likely than others to have had children who are biologically related to them (Patterson, 2000). This greater frequency of childlessness may make lesbian and gay adults a relatively untapped resource for adoption professionals. Compared with heterosexual adults, lesbian and gay individuals and couples may be especially likely to have an interest in becoming parents through adoption. Recent research suggests that lesbians do indeed express greater interest in adopting children than do heterosexual women (Gates et al., 2007). In many parts of the country today, adoption agencies are open to this possibility, and children are being adopted into loving homes by lesbian and gay adults (Brodzinsky, Patterson, & Vaziri, 2002; Mallon, 2004). As the numbers of such families increase, and as knowledge about them grows, it is likely that sexual orientation and parenting will increasingly be seen as unrelated. Indeed, the sexual orientation of prospective parents is likely some day to be seen as irrelevant to the placement of minor children into adoptive homes.

As the numbers of placements of children into lesbian and gay parent homes continue to increase, new issues are beginning to emerge (Mallon, 2004). For instance, how can agencies assist lesbian and gay adoptive families in coping with the special challenges that they encounter? What postadoption services would best support lesbian and gay adoptive parents and their children, and how do these vary as a function of the legal and policy climates in which families live? Some individuals and groups are beginning to tackle such questions (e.g., Human Rights Campaign Fund, 2008). The results of such work should be valuable in supporting lesbian and gay adoptive parents and their children in the future.

CONCLUSIONS

The present study has assessed several aspects of overall functioning among adolescents living with same-sex versus opposite-sex couples. Although family type had few significant linkages with any aspect of adolescent social or personal development, the qualities of adolescents' relationships with parents were associated with many aspects of their personal adjustment, substance use, delinquent behavior, and relations with peers. Whether they lived with same-sex or opposite-sex couples, adolescents whose parents reported having close relationships with them were likely to report higher self-esteem, fewer depressive symptoms, less use of alcohol and tobacco, and less delinquent behavior. They were also likely to have more friends in school, to have more supportive friends, and to achieve greater centrality within their friendship networks than other adolescents. These results do not support the idea that adolescent outcomes are shaped by parental sexual orientation, but they are consistent with views that emphasize the importance of relationships with parents. Overall, the results suggest that important decisions about adolescents—such as placement into adoptive homes—should focus not on parental sexual orientation, but on the qualities of adolescents' relationships with parents.

References

Allen, J. P., Moore, C., Kuperminc, G., & Bell, K. (1998). Attachment and adolescent psychosocial functioning. *Child Development, 69,* 1406–1419.

Baumrind, D. (1995). Commentary on sexual orientation: Research and social policy implications. *Developmental Psychology, 31,* 130–136.

Bearman, P. S., Jones, J., & Udry, J. R. (1997). The National Longitudinal Study of Adolescent Health: Research Design. Available via the internet at http://www.cpc.unc.edu/addhealth.

Bonacich, P. (1987). Power and centrality: A family of measures. *American Journal of Sociology, 92,* 1170–1182.

Brodzinsky, D. M., Patterson, C. J., & Vaziri, M. (2002). Adoption agency perspectives on lesbian and gay prospective parents: A national study. *Adoption Quarterly, 5,* 5–23.

Carolina Population Center University of North Carolina at Chapel Hill (1997). National longitudinal study of adolescent health: Wave I network variables code book. Retrieved on March 23, 2004, from http://www.cpc.unc.edu/projects/addhealth/codebooks/wave1.

Chan, R. W., Raboy, B., & Patterson, C. J. (1998). Psychosocial adjustment among children conceived via donor insemination by lesbian and heterosexual mothers. *Child Development, 69*, 443–457.

Erich, S., Leung, P., & Kindle, P. (2005). A comparative analysis of adoptive family functioning with gay, lesbian, and heterosexual parents and their children. *Journal of GLBT Family Studies, 1*, 43–60.

Erich, S., Leung, P., Kindle, P., & Carter, S. (2005). gay and lesbian adoptive families: An exploratory study of adoptive family functioning, adoptive children's behavior, and familial support networks. *Journal of Family Social Work, 9*, 17–32.

Flaks, D. K., Ficher, I., Masterpasqua, F., & Joseph, G. (1995). Lesbians choosing motherhood: A comparative study of lesbian and heterosexual parents and their children. *Developmental Psychology, 31*, 105–114.

Gartrell, N., Deck, A., Rodas, C., Peyser, H., & Banks, A. (2005). The National Lesbian Family Study: 4. Interviews with the 10-year-old children. *American Journal of Orthopsychiatry, 75*, 518–524.

Gates, G. J., Badgett, M. V. L., Macomber, J. E., & Chambers, K. (2007). *Adoption and foster care by gay and lesbian parents in the United States*. Los Angeles, CA: The Williams Institute, UCLA Law School.

Gershon, T. D., Tschann, J. M., & Jemerin, J. M. (1999). Stigmatization, self-esteem, and coping among the adolescent children of lesbian mothers. *Journal of Adolescent Health, 24*, 437–445.

Golombok, S., Perry, B., Burston, A., Murray, C., Mooney-Somers, J., Stevens, M., & Golding, J. (2003). Children with lesbian parents: A community study. *Developmental Psychology, 39*, 20–33.

Haynie, D. L. (2000). The peer group revisited: A network approach for understanding adolescent delinquency. Unpublished doctoral dissertation, Pennsylvania State University, Hershey, PA.

Huggins, S. L. (1989). A comparative study of self-esteem of adolescent children of divorced lesbian mothers and divorced heterosexual mothers. In F. W. Bozett (Ed.), *Homosexuality and the family* (pp. 123–135). New York: Harrington Park Press.

Human Rights Campaign Fund. (2008). *Promising practices in adoption and foster care: A comprehensive guide to policies and practices that welcome, affirm, and support gay, lesbian, bisexual, and transgendered foster and adoptive parents*. Washington, D.C.: Human Rights Campaign.

In Re *Adoption of Evan*, 583 N.Y.S.2d 997 (Sur. 1992).

Khaleque, A., & Rohner, R. P. (2002). Perceived parental acceptance-rejection and psychological adjustment: A meta-analysis of cross-cultural and intracultural studies. *Journal of Marriage and Family, 64*, 54–64.

Kindle, P., & Erich, S. (2005). Perceptions of social support among heterosexual and homosexual adopters. *Families in Society, 86*, 541–546.

Leung, P., Erich, S., & Kanenberg, H. (2005). A comparison of family functioning in gay/lesbian, heterosexual and special needs adoptions. *Children and Youth Services, 27*, 1031–1044.

Mallon, G. P. (2004). *Gay men choosing parenthood*. New York: Columbia University Press.

O'Connor, A. (1993). Voices from the heart: The developmental impact of a mother's lesbianism on her adolescent children. *Smith College Studies in Social Work, 63*, 281–299.

Patterson, C. J. (2000). Sexual orientation and family life: A decade review. *Journal of Marriage and the Family, 62*, 1052–1069.

Patterson, C. J. (2006). Children of lesbian and gay parents. *Current Directions in Psychological Science, 15*, 241–244.

Patterson, C. J. (2007). Lesbian and gay family issues in the context of changing legal and social policy environments. In K. J. Bieschke, R. M. Perez, & K. A. DeBord (Eds.), *Handbook of counseling and psychotherapy with lesbian, gay, bisexual and transgender clients* (2nd ed., pp. 103–133). Washington, D.C.: American Psychological Association.

Patterson, C. J. (2009). Children of lesbian and gay parents: Psychology, law, and policy. *American Psychologist, 64*, 727–736.

Patterson, C. J., Fulcher, M., & Wainright, J. (2002). Children of lesbian and gay parents: Research, law, and policy. In B. L. Bottoms, M. B. Kovera, & B. D. McAuliff (Eds.), *Children, Social Science and the Law* (pp, 176–199). New York: Cambridge University Press.

Perrin, E. C., & Committee on Psychosocial Aspects of Child, Family Health (2002). Technical report: Coparent or second-parent adoption by same-sex partners. *Pediatrics, 109*, 341–344.

Radloff, L. S. (1977). The CES-D Scale: A self-report depression scale for research in the general population. *Applied Psychological Measurement, 1*, 385–401.

Resnick, M. D., Bearman, P., Blum, R. W., Bauman, K. E., Harris, K. M., Jones, J., et al. (1997). Protecting adolescent from harm: Findings from the National Longitudinal Study of Adolescent Health. *JAMA: Journal of the American Medical Association, 27* (10), 823–832.

Rivers, I., Poteat, V. P., & Noret, N. (2008). Victimization, social support, and psychosocial functioning among children of same-sex and opposite-sex couples in the United Kingdom. *Developmental Psychology, 44*, 127–134.

Rohner, R. P. (1999). Acceptance and rejection. In D. Livinson, J. Ponzetti, & Jorgenson (Eds.), Encyclopedia of human emotions (Volume 1, pp. 6–14). New York: Macmillan.

Ryan, S. (2007). Parent-child interaction styles between gay and lesbian parents and their adopted children. *Journal of GLBT Family Studies, 3*, 105–132.

Sieving, R. E., Beurhing, T., Resnick, M. D., Bearinger, L. H., Shew, M., Ireland, M., Blum, R. W. (2000). Development of adolescent self-report measures from the National Longitudinal Study of Adolescent Health. *Journal of Adolescent Health, 28*, 73–81.

Stacey, J., & Biblarz, T. J. (2001). (How) does the sexual orientation of parents matter? *American Sociological Review, 66*, 159–183.

Steinberg, L., Lamborn, S. D., Dornbusch, S. M., & Darling, N. (1992). Impact of parenting practices on adolescent achievement: Authoritative parenting, school involvement, and encouragement to succeed. *Child Development, 63*, 1266–1281.

Steinberg, L., & Silk, J. S. (2002). Parenting adolescents. In M. H. Bornstein (Ed.), *Handbook of parenting, Volume 1: Children and parenting* (2nd ed., pp. 359–397). Mahwah, NJ: Lawrence Erlbaum Associates.

Stevens, M., Golombok, S., Beveridge, M., and the ALSPAC Study Team (2002). Does father absence influence children's gender development? Findings from a general population study of preschool children. *Parenting: Science and Practice, 2,* 47–60.

Tasker, F. L., & Golombok, S. (1997). *Growing up in a lesbian family: Effects on child Development.* New York: The Guilford Press.

Wainright, J. L., & Patterson, C. J. (2006). Delinquency, victimization, and substance use among adolescents with female same-sex parents. *Journal of Family Psychology, 20,* 526–530.

Wainright, J. L., & Patterson, C. J. (2008). Peer relations among adolescents with female same-sex parents. *Developmental Psychology, 44,* 117–126.

Wainright, J. L., Russell, S. T., & Patterson, C. J. (2004). Psychosocial adjustment, school outcomes, and romantic relationships of adolescents with same-sex parents. *Child Development, 75,* 1886–1898.

Wald, M. S. (2006). Adults' sexual orientation and state determinations regarding placement of children. *Family Law Quarterly, 40,* 381–434.

Wardle, L. (1997). The potential impact of homosexual parenting on children. *University of Illinois Law Review, 833,* 335–340.

6

Planned Lesbian Families

A Review of the U.S. National Longitudinal Lesbian Family Study

NANETTE GARTRELL, HEIDI PEYSER, AND HENNY BOS ∎

In 2002, the American Psychiatric Association issued a position statement on adoption and co-parenting of children by same-sex couples. "Optimal develop-ment for children," it stated, "is based not on the sexual orientation of the parents, but on stable attachments to committed and nurturing adults" (American Psychiatric Association, 2002). The American Psychological Association, the American Academy of Child and Adolescent Psychiatry, and the American Academy of Pediatrics have implemented similar policies (American Psychological Association, 2004; American Academy of Child and Adolescent Psychiatry, 1999; Parke, 2004; Pawelski, Perrin, Foy, et al., 2007). These policies reflect a growing body of social science research demonstrating that being raised by same-sex par-ents is as advantageous to children as growing up in families with heterosexual parents (Wald, 2006).

Most of the early studies on lesbian families—in the 1970s and 1980s—focused on the psychological development of children who had been conceived in hetero-sexual relationships and raised in lesbian households after their mothers had come out as lesbians (Golombok, Spencer, & Rutter, 1983; Gottman, 1990; Green, 1978; Green, Mandel, Hotvedt, Gray, & Smith, 1986; Hoeffer, 1981; Huggins, 1989; Kirkpatrick, 1987; Kirkpatrick, Smith, & Roy, 1981; Rees, 1979). Beginning in the 1980s, assisted reproductive technologies made it possible for lesbians with eco-nomic access to sperm banks or adoption agencies, or personal arrangements with sperm donors, to choose motherhood unrestricted by the limitations and conventions of a traditional heterosexual framework. Since that time, planned lesbian families have become an integral part of the social structure of the United States (Parke, 2004). At the time of the 2000 U.S. Census, one-third of female-partnered households contained children (Simmons & O'Connell, 2003). This so-called "lesbian baby boom" is a phenomenon that, in turn, spawned a series of quantitative studies that compared children in planned lesbian families with children of heterosexual parents on various measures, including psychological development, social relations, gender identity, and academic performance (Bos, Van Balen, & Van den Boom, 2003, 2004a, 2007; Brewaeys, Ponjaert, Van Hall, & Golombok, 1997; Chan, Brooks, Raboy, & Patterson, 1998a; Chan, Raboy, & Patterson, 1998b; Golombok et al., 2003; Patterson, 1994, 2001; Patterson, Hurt, & Mason, 1998; Vanfraussen, Ponjaert-Kristoffersen, & Brewaeys, 2002, 2003a). Some of these quantitative studies focused on the differences among planned lesbian families (Vanfraussen, Ponjaert-Kristoffersen, & Brewaeys, 2001, 2003b) and the potential effects of such diversity on child rearing and children (Bos, van Balen, Van den Boom, & Sandfort, 2004b).

Qualitative, longitudinal research is considered one of the most effective methods of documenting the psychosocial evolution of contemporary families (Hicks, 2005; Lambert, 2005). In a world of fluctuating public opinion about the merits of same-sex parenting, long-term studies that follow individual families from conception or adoption until the child reaches maturity offer a three-dimensional perspective on the joys, difficulties, and everyday realities of growing up in lesbian and gay families. The U.S. National Longitudinal Lesbian Family Study (NLLFS) was initiated in 1986 to provide prospective, descriptive, longitudinal data on the first wave of planned lesbian families with children conceived through donor insemination (DI). It is the largest and longest-running study of its kind in the United States. The study was designed to follow a cohort of lesbian mothers with age-matched children from the conception of their child (hereafter designated the "index child") until that child reached adulthood. The aim of the NLLFS is to report on the growth, development, and mental health of the children; to describe the parenting experiences in lesbian-led families; to describe the lesbian mothers' lives, relationships, and careers; and to document the effects of homophobia on the mothers and the children (Gartrell & Bos, 2010; Gartrell et al., 1996, 1999, 2000; Gartrell, Deck, Rodas, Peyser, & Banks, 2005; Gartrell, Rodas, Deck, Peyser, & Banks, 2005). This chapter will present an overview of the data collected on the NLLFS families from conception of the index children until they reached the age of 17. The NLLFS is an ongoing study for which data continue to be collected and analyzed.

STUDY DESIGN AND DEMOGRAPHICS

In 1986, lesbians who were attempting to become pregnant or who were already pregnant, using a known or unknown donor, and any partners who planned to share parenting were eligible for participation. Recruitment was solicited via announcements at lesbian events, in women's bookstores, in lesbian newspapers, and at multicultural events. Prospective participants contacted the researchers by telephone, and the nature of the study, including the importance of planning for long-term participation, was discussed with each caller. Every caller who met the study criteria was invited to enroll in the study, which was closed to new families in 1992.

Eighty-four families with children conceived by DI began the study when the mothers were inseminating or pregnant, resulting in 85 index children (one set of twins). At the initial interview (T1) 70 households consisted of a prospective birthmother and a co-mother, and 14 were headed by a prospective single mother. Seventy-three families had both a birthmother and a co-mother at the time of the index child's birth. Subsequent interviews took place when the child was 2 years old (T2), 5 years old (T3), 10 years old (T4), and 17 years old (T5). By T5, 78 families (93% of the original families) were still participating in the study. The families will be interviewed again when the index offspring are 25 years old (T6).

The families originally resided in the metropolitan areas of Boston, Washington, D.C., and San Francisco, where the researchers also lived. Since the T1 and T2 interviews were conducted in person and, at that time, the U.S. government did not fund research projects on planned lesbian families, geographic proximity to the researchers was essential. By T3, 27 of the families had moved to other areas of the United States, resulting in the decision to conduct all subsequent interviews of the mothers by telephone. At T4 and T5, each mother completed a Child Behavior Checklist (CBCL) to assess the competencies and behavior/emotional problems of the index offspring so that their psychological development could be compared with national norms (Achenbach, 1991; Achenbach & Rescorla, 2001). As 10-year-olds, the NLLFS children were also interviewed by telephone. When they were 17 years old, they completed an in-depth online questionnaire that included standardized instruments.

The mothers are predominantly college-educated, middle- and upper-middle class, professionals and managers. At T1, the mothers were on average 34 years old. The mothers identified as primarily as white/Caucasian; their offspring are slightly more heterogeneous: 87.1 percent of the children are white/caucasian, 3.8 percent Latino, 2.6 percent African American, 2.6 percent Asian/Pacific Islander, 2.6 per cent Middle Eastern, and 1.3 percent Native American.

In 38 families, the index child had no siblings. Other family constellations included nine where the index child had a sibling born to the birthmother; six where the index child had a sibling born to the co-mother; three where the index child had an adopted sibling and a foster sibling; one where the index child had two siblings born to the birthmother; one where the index child had two siblings born to the birthmother and one born to the co-mother; one where the index child had four adopted siblings and one foster sibling; and one where the index child had an adopted sibling, a foster sibling, and a sibling born to the co-mother. Seven index children had stepmothers, two had stepfathers (one birthmother and one co-mother had repartnered with men), and two had stepsiblings at T4.

CREATING A HEALTHY HOME ENVIRONMENT

How Did the Prospective Mothers Prepare for the Birth of Their Children?

During pregnancy (T1), the participants eagerly awaited the birth of children for whom they had carefully planned for many years. The coupled participants had forged meaningful bonds with their partners, having been together a mean of 6.1 years. According to a study by van Balen (2005), older first-time parents tend to focus more on the personal development of their children than do younger first-time parents. The NLLFS participants chose to inseminate at a mean age of 34 years—almost 10 years older than the average age of first-time heterosexual mothers in the United States (Centers for Disease Control and Prevention, 2002a; U.S. Census Bureau, 2004). As a group, the participants were strongly lesbian-identified, valuing honesty rather than secrecy about their sexual orientation. They expected to be open with their children, in an age-appropriate manner, about the DI and their sexual orientation.

Nearly all prospective mothers had come out to their families of origin and most held jobs. Many already had flexible work schedules that could be adapted to their childcare needs. Friendships were important to the participants, who were also active in forming parenting groups for socializing, information sharing (regarding resources such as nonhomophobic health providers and childcare facilities), networking, and problem solving.

The prospective mothers were committed to being fully present for their children, as evidenced by their attention to their own physical and mental health. They were generally in good physical health, and they planned to rely on family and friends, as well as on religious and social communities, for emotional support. Substance abuse by the NLLFS mothers has been consistently lower than the national U.S. averages for heterosexual women and for other lesbians who are not parents (Centers for Disease Control and Prevention, 2001); for the most part, the NLLFS mothers drink moderately and eschew cigarettes and illegal drugs.

DONOR SELECTION AND MALE ROLE MODELS

What Factors Contributed to the Choice of a Known versus an Unknown Donor? How Did the Mothers Feel about Male Role Models for Their Children?

Although the prospective mothers (T1) were nearly equally divided in preferring known and unknown donors, 36 percent of the children were conceived through known donors, 40 percent through unknown donors, and 24 percent had the possibility of meeting their donor after the children reached the age of 18. Half of the mothers who chose a known donor anticipated that he would be involved in parenting. In discussing the pros and cons of using a known donor, the mothers' reasons for knowing the man's identity ranged from practical considerations—having information about his health and heritage—to emotional concerns regarding the child's needs—wanting the child to know the man who contributed to her or his conception. Those who chose an unknown donor either did not know a suitable donor, or they had concerns about losing custody if a heterosexual donor later attempted to terminate the mother's parental rights on the basis of her sexual orientation.

More than half of T1 mothers believed that their children needed good male role models, envisioned as men who demonstrate sensitivity, empathy, thoughtfulness, and morality—traits that are not gender specific. Those who considered male role modeling important had already begun networking at T1 among friends and relatives to identify men who might be suitable candidates for involvement in their extended families.

At the second interview, when the index children were 2 years old (T2), most of the known donors were either actively parenting or involved in the child's daily life. Many families had incorporated close friends as "aunts" and "uncles" in an extended family network. For the most part, the mothers planned to ensure that their children had contact with loving men who would be good role models.

When the children were 5 years old (T3), one-third of those with known donors saw them regularly, and the others saw their donor-dads occasionally. Yet only half the mothers felt they had successfully incorporated good, loving men into their children's lives. By T4, when the children were 10 years old, the mothers of those with known donors reported that the children benefited from having a father, from having information about his family, and from experiencing less stigmatization than their peers whose donors were unknown. The children who could eventually meet their donors were nearly evenly divided in regretting that they had to wait until they were 18 years old, and in not caring about the prospective meeting. Most children with unknown donors expressed no regrets about not having a father. Nearly all children had been informed about the DI, and most of them answered honestly when asked by their peers about their "fathers."

EXTENDED FAMILY AND SUPPORT NETWORK

How Did the Families of Origin Respond to Their Lesbian Daughters' Decisions to Have Children? Have the Index Children Been Welcomed by Members of the Extended Family?

At T1, most prospective mothers had regular contact with their own parents, and most expected at least some relatives to accept the child. Prospective birthmothers and co-mothers were equally likely to expect their own parents to acknowledge and act as grandparents toward the index child. One in four prospective mothers stated that her own parents were out as the parents of a lesbian, and would be similarly open about being grandparents of the index child.

Two-thirds of the mothers of two-year-old children reported that they had grown closer to their own parents since the birth of the children. Birthmothers rated their own parents as closer to the index children than co-mothers rated theirs. Most mothers participated in lesbian family support groups and social activities.

By T3, most of the children's grandparents were out about their grandchildren's lesbian families. Only a small minority of grandparents did not relate to the index child as a full-fledged grandchild. The lesbian mothers felt that their families had been accepted by their neighbors, and many of the mothers' close friends were parents themselves. Social outings often involved other lesbian or gay families. Three-quarters of the mothers were active participants in the lesbian community, which played an important role in their children's lives.

When the children were 10 years old (T4), even more of their grandparents had become public about having a lesbian daughter who was raising their grand-child, and nearly all treated the grandchild no differently from any other family member. Most mothers considered themselves participants in the lesbian com-munity. The mothers socialized with both lesbian/gay families and straight fami-lies, reflecting their children's choice of friends and playmates. Committed to creating a safe path for their children in schools, neighborhoods, and communi-ties, the mothers took an active role in educating others about diversity and discrimination.

MOTHER–CHILD BONDING

When There Are Two Mothers, Is the Child Equally Bonded to Both? How Do the Mothers Handle Work Responsibilities and Childcare?

The birthmothers and co-mothers shared the responsibilities of child rearing and considered themselves equal co-parents in three-quarters of the families at T2. When asked which factors most strongly affected mother–child bonding, in many families the mothers felt that time spent with the child was more influential than biological connections. Typically, the child called one mother "Mommy" and the other "Momma." Nearly half of the children carried both mothers' last names, and the rest carried only the birthmother's.

Coupled mothers at T2 cited many advantages of two-mother households, particularly the benefits of having two actively involved parents. Surprisingly, when conflict arose between the mothers, it often centered on competitiveness about whose turn it was to take care of the child, rather than criticism that one parent was not doing enough. Some co-mothers were sad that they missed out on the bonding experience of breastfeeding.

To spend more time with the child, more than half of the T2 mothers had reduced their work hours, even though they anticipated that the choice to leave the fast track might limit their career possibilities. Coupled mothers alternated their work schedules so that at least one mother could be at home with the child.

When a child was ill, couples typically determined on a day-by-day basis which parent would incur the least hardship by taking time off work to care for the child.

At T3, fewer couples were experiencing jealousy or competitiveness around bonding with the child than at T2. Most of the continuous couples reported that the child was equally bonded to both mothers, that the mothers continued to share family responsibilities, and that the mothers had similar child-rearing philosophies. Many of the co-mothers had officially adopted their children by T3, thereby enhancing the co-mothers' "official" parenting role.

The mothers of 10-year-old children (T4) juggled work and parenting. Although they successfully managed career and motherhood responsibilities, many felt that they never had enough time for either. Three-quarters of the mothers worked full-time, although in two-mother families, the birth mothers and co-mothers sometimes took turns working reduced hours to spend more time with the children. Among the couples who were still together at T4, most shared child rearing and felt that the child was equally bonded to both mothers. Nevertheless, the legacy of the co-mother's feeling jealous of the birthmother's bond with the child that began at T2 continued in some families. The single mothers typically felt happy with their decisions to parent alone—preferring autonomy in decision making and the special single mother–child bond—although some expressed disappointment that they had no co-parent with whom to share the joys and challenges of motherhood.

RELATIONSHIP STABILITY IN TWO-MOTHER FAMILIES

What Characteristics Contribute to Relationship Stability in Lesbian Mothers? What Are the Custody Arrangements When Couples Split Up? How Does Relationship Longevity in Lesbian Couples Who Are Mothers Compare with That of Their Own Heterosexual, Married Sisters Who Are Also Mothers?

Shared values and communication skills topped the list of relationship strengths reported by the prospective mothers who were coupled at T1. Nearly all couples were monogamous. Most coupled participants expressed concern about having less time and energy for the relationship after the child was born.

The early years of child rearing were stressful to the mothers' relationships. Many reported that they led child-focused lives. At T2, the couples had little time and energy to tend to the relationship, resulting in eight breakups. By T3, when the children were 5 years old, one-third of the original couples had separated. The separated couples had been together a significantly shorter time before the index child's birth than the continuous couples. Those couples who acknowledged competitiveness around bonding at T2 were no more likely to have divorced by T3 than were the other couples. By T4, when the children were 10 years old, nearly half of the original couples had separated. The separation was described as very stressful to the family in all cases. The separated mothers were equally divided in rating communication with their former partner as "excellent," and "mixed" or "poor." Most of the separated mothers said that having a child delayed the dissolution of their relationship. There was no significant difference in relationship duration when the NLLFS mothers' divorced heterosexual sisters who are also mothers were compared with the NLLFS mothers who had separated. At T5, 56% of the mothers who were co-parents when the index children were born had separated; in 71.4% of these separated-couple families, custody was shared. These findings on custody in separated-couple NLLFS families contrast to population reports on divorced heterosexual couples in the U.S. showing that 65% of mothers end up with sole physical and legal custody of their children (Emery, 2005; Kreider & Fields, 2001; Softas-Nall & Sukhodolsky, 2006).

Of the continuous couples, many mothers felt that having a child had strengthened their relationship, despite having limited time and energy for one another. These coupled mothers were enthusiastic about sharing the joys and responsibilities of child rearing.

CHILDREN'S GROWTH, DEVELOPMENT, AND HEALTH

Are the Children of Lesbian Mothers Physically and Emotionally Healthy? How Do the Children of Lesbian Mothers Compare with the Children of Heterosexuals?

Nearly all of the 2-year-old, 5-year-old, and 10-year-old index children achieved developmental milestones, related well to peers, and were physically healthy. At the age of 10, six children had asthma, although none of their mothers smoked. The percentage of smokers among NLLFS mothers is substantially lower than in women in the general U.S. population, and childhood asthma is correlated with growing up in households with smokers (California Environmental Protection Agency, 2005; Centers for Disease Control and Prevention, 2001). The prevalence of developmental disorders—including attention deficit disorders, disruptive behaviors, and tics as well as disorders of learning, motor skills, communication, eating, and elimination—in the index children was comparable to rates in U.S. children under the age of 18 (Centers for Disease Control and Prevention, 2002b).

By the age of 10, none of the index children had been physically abused. Also, none of the boys had been sexually abused, although two girls had been sexually abused by older, unrelated men outside the home (an unfortunate and unpreventable risk for all children). These rates of abuse are strikingly lower than U.S. national rates of child abuse. Higher rates of abuse are typically reported by children who grow up in homes with adult heterosexual males (Finkelhor, Turner, Omrod, Hamby, & Krack, 2009; Russell & Bolen, 2000).

The index offspring were assessed by the CBCL to compare their social competencies and behavioral/emotional problems with U.S. national norms (Achenbach, 1991; Achenbach & Rescorla, 2001). At 10, the NLLFS children demonstrated fewer problems than the norm in internalizing problem behavior (such as being depressed, anxious, or withdrawn), externalizing problem behavior (such as rule-breaking or aggression), and sexual problem behavior (such as inappropriate sexual activity in public).

Three-quarters of the 10-year-old children attended public schools. A majority were enrolled in schools that were multicultural, and in most cases, with children of other lesbian or gay parents also in attendance. Nearly half of the elementary schools had incorporated a lesbian/gay (LGBT) curriculum. Children who attended these schools had significantly fewer behavioral problems on the CBCL than their peers whose schools did not offer this type of educational program (Bos, Gartrell, Peyser, & van Balen, 2008a).

On the CBCLs completed at T5, the 17-year-old daughters and sons of lesbian mothers were rated significantly higher in social, school/academic, and total competence, and significantly lower in social problems, rule-breaking, aggressive, and externalizing problem behavior than their age-matched counterparts in Achenbach's normative sample of American youth. Also at T5, no psychological differences were found among adolescent offspring conceived by known, as-yet-unknown, and permanently unknown donors, nor between adolescents whose mothers were still together and offspring whose mothers had separated.

EXPERIENCES OF HOMOPHOBIA

How Do the Children Respond to Homophobia? How Do the Mothers Prepare Their Children for the Prospect of Discrimination?

At T4 and T5, nearly half of the index offspring had experienced homophobia in the form of other children saying mean things about their mothers. The NLLFS offspring felt angry, upset, or sad about the incidents. Experiencing homophobia was associated with higher CBCL problem scores at T4, even though the index children who reported these incidents had scores that fell within the normative range. Already by T4, the NLLFS children had been prepared by their mothers to expect such incidents; some mothers had taught their children constructive ways of responding to hostility from their peers. So when other children made homophobic comments about the NLLFS mothers, their own children defended them—calling the criticism "wrong," "not nice," or "stupid." For instance, one child recalled:

> "One kid said one time that he didn't like gays and lesbians and I said, 'You mean like my mom?' and he said, 'I didn't know your mom was.' So I told him that if he had a friend and he was black would he stop being his friend and he said, 'No.' I told him it was the same thing." (Gartrell et al., 2005)

At 10, the NLLFS children who experienced homophobia felt angry, sad, and upset after the incidents. Some said that children were chastised when they made homophobic comments only if the teacher overheard. Among children who had been targeted for homophobia, those whose mothers participated in the LGBT community had significantly fewer problems with rule-breaking and fewer somatic complaints than those whose mothers were uninvolved in LGBT activities (Bos et al., 2008a).

At T4, the NLLFS mothers continued to be open about their lesbianism, although many tried to accommodate their preadolescent children's concerns about fitting in by following their lead in disclosing information about the family to their peers. A majority of 10-year-old children were completely out with their peers about growing up in a lesbian household. Even among children who had not experienced homophobic bullying, those whose mothers participated in the LGBT community demonstrated fewer behavioral problems on the CBCL than those whose mothers did not (Bos et al., 2008a). Three-quarters of the children's grandparents were out about their daughter's lesbian family by the time the index children were 10 years old.

PREDICTIONS OF CHILD'S SEXUAL ORIENTATION

Are Children Raised by Lesbian Mothers More Likely to Be Gay or Lesbian as Adults?

The NLLFS mothers were asked at T3 and again at T4 if they felt they could predict their children's adult sexual orientations. More than half of the mothers said that they were not able to predict. Of those who chose to venture a guess at T4, 37 percent said they anticipated that their children might be heterosexual as adults, 6 percent thought they might turn out to be lesbian or gay, and 4 percent thought their children might be bisexual. Accompanying these responses were the mothers' assurances that they had no preferences concerning eventual sexual orientation.

COMPARABLE STUDIES

Brewaeys et al. (1997) examined the family relationships and the emotional and gender development of Belgian children conceived through DI and raised in lesbian families. The researchers compared 30 lesbian families with 4- to 8-year-old children, 38 heterosexual families with DI children, and 30 heterosexual families with naturally conceived children. The lesbian mothers had been inseminated at fertility clinics in Brussels between 1986 and 1991. No differences were found between the lesbian- and the heterosexually parented families in the quality of the couples' relationships or the mother–child interactions. The quality of the co-mothers' interactions with their children in the lesbian families was superior to the quality of the fathers' interactions with the children in the heterosexual families. The children raised by lesbian mothers were well adjusted; their gender role development did not differ from those raised by heterosexual parents.

In a follow-up study on 24 of the same lesbian families, Vanfraussen et al. (2001, 2003a, 2003b) compared the children's and their mothers' attitudes toward donor anonymity. At this interval, the participants included 41 children ranging in age from 7 to 17 years, and 45 mothers. Although fertility clinics in Belgium use only anonymous donors, when the mothers were asked whether they preferred anonymous or identified donors, most mothers preferred anonymity. The children were nearly equally divided between those who preferred donor anonymity and those who wanted to know more about the donor. There were more boys than girls in the latter group, and curiosity was the principal motive (Vanfraussen et al., 2003a). A majority of the children who preferred donor anonymity expressed loyalty toward their co-mothers (Vanfraussen et al., 2003b). The children's relationships with the birthmothers and the co-mothers were comparable. The researchers concluded that curiosity about the donors was not linked to the quality of the mother–child interaction.

Vanfraussen et al. (2002) compared the 24 lesbian families with 24 heterosexual families—matched as closely as possible with the highest educational level in the lesbian family, the age and gender of the child, and the family size—to assess harassment or teasing of the children and its effects on their psychological well-being. The researchers found that the children in lesbian families were out about their two-mother families and were more likely to experience homophobia. Their teachers described the children raised in lesbian families as having more attention problems than their peers who were growing up in heterosexual families.

In 1990, Patterson (1994, 2001; Patterson et al., 1998; see also Patterson & Wainright, this volume) initiated a study on the behavioral adjustment, self-concepts, and sex role behavior of 4- to 9-year-old children born to or adopted by a lesbian mother or mothers in the San Francisco Bay area. When compared on the CBCL with national norms, the children were rated as normal in social competence and behavior problems. The children's self-concepts were comparable to those of peers with heterosexual parents, except that the children with lesbian parents reported more negative reactions to stress and a more positive sense of themselves. The children were more likely to have regular contact with relatives of the birthmothers than the co-mothers. Children who communicated regularly with their grandparents were rated as having fewer behavioral problems on the CBCL than those who saw or talked with grandparents less frequently. The mothers fell within normal ranges in self-esteem and mental health. Consistent with the findings in heterosexual families, adjustment in the children was associated with maternal mental health.

In a related study, Chan et al. (1998a, 1998b; Fulcher, Sutfin, Chan, Scheib, & Patterson, 2006) examined the division of household labor in 30 lesbian and 16 heterosexual couples who were the parents of 5- to 11-year-old DI children. The researchers found that the lesbian couples shared domestic responsibilities more equally than did the heterosexual parents. Relationship satisfaction in the lesbian couples was correlated with the sharing of responsibilities. The children of those who shared household and childcare tasks also demonstrated fewer behavioral problems.

In 2003, Golombok et al. reported on the quality of parent–child relationships and the socioemotional and gender development in a community sample of 7-year-old children in lesbian families. Citing the limitations of research based on volunteer or convenience samples, this study recruited participants through a longitudinal population study of 14,000 mothers and their children in the United Kingdom that began in 1991. Among the 39 lesbian mother families who met the study criteria and agreed to participate, 28 had conceived their children in previous heterosexual relationships, and 11 had conceived their children through DI. The lesbian families were compared with 74 two-parent heterosexual families, and 60 families headed by single heterosexual mothers. The researchers found that lesbian co-mothers "smacked" their children less frequently than heterosexual fathers—noteworthy because hitting children increases their own aggressive behavior. No differences were found in the gender development and psychological adjustment of children raised by lesbians and heterosexuals. Golombok concluded that family structure (single-parent, two-parent, same-sex parent) is less important in children's development than the quality of parenting (Golombok, 2000).

The most recent report from Golombok's research team (Golombok & Badger, 2010) provided data from a comparative longitudinal study of children reared in fatherless and traditional families that began when the index offspring had a mean age of 6 years. At the third follow-up, the 18 young adults with lesbian mothers (mean age 19 years) and the 20 reared by single heterosexual mothers (mean age19.5 years) showed more positive family relationships and higher levels of self-esteem than the 32 reared in two-parent heterosexual households (mean age 18 years).

Bos et al. (2003, 2004a, 2004b, 2007) began a longitudinal study of planned lesbian families in the Netherlands in 2001. The researchers have been following 100 two-mother families with children conceived through DI and 100 heterosexual families with naturally conceived children. In the first phase of this study, when the children were between 4 and 8 years old, the researchers found that the lesbian mothers had spent more time considering their motivations for motherhood, had a stronger desire to parent, and placed a higher premium on happiness than did the heterosexual parents. The lesbian mothers were also less concerned about conformity as a child-rearing goal than were the heterosexual parents, although the lesbian co-mothers were more likely than the heterosexual fathers to justify the quality of their parenting.

Bos et al. (2007) also compared child adjustment and parenting in the two sets of families. The researchers found that the lesbian co-mothers were more satisfied with the co-parenting provided by the birthmothers than the heterosexual mothers were with the co-parenting provided by their spouses. The lesbian co-mothers had less need to assert power and expressed more parental concern than did the heterosexual fathers. Overall, the findings of Bos et al. indicate that child adjustment is more strongly associated with power assertion, parental concern, and satisfaction with the co-parent than with the sexual orientation of the parents.

Most of the lesbian mothers in the study by Bos et al. (2004b) demonstrated low levels of internalized homophobia; similarly, few felt stigmatized. The lesbian mothers who had experienced rejection or stigma, or who demonstrated internalized homophobia, were more likely to be defensive about their choice to parent. The lesbian mothers who had been rejected were also more likely to report parental stress and behavior problems in their children.

When the children were between 8 and 12 years old, Bos & Sandfort (2010) compared child adjustment and gender development in the lesbian and heterosexual samples. With respect to psychosocial adjustment, no significant differences were found between children in lesbian and heterosexual families. Compared with children in heterosexual families, children in planned lesbian families were less likely to consider their own gender as superior, and were less likely to identify as heterosexual (Bos & Sandfort, 2010).

In a comparison of the Dutch families in Bos' study with the American families in the NLLFS (Bos, Gartrell, van Balen, Peyser, & Sandfort, 2008b), the Dutch children were significantly more open about growing up in a lesbian family, scored significantly higher on measures of psychological adjustment, and experienced significantly less homophobia than the American children. Mirroring these findings, the World Value Survey (Sandfort, 2005) shows that among Western cultures, the Netherlands has the highest level of acceptance of homosexuality, whereas the United States has one of the lowest. Significantly more of the NLLFS couples had separated than Dutch couples of comparable-age children.

CONCLUSIONS

Overall, the studies of planned lesbian families find that the children are highly desired by mothers who thoughtfully arrange their own lives to be available and attentive parents. Typically, the mothers are lesbian identified, valuing honesty and openness about their sexual orientation. They are also health-conscious, loving parents who neither physically nor sexually abuse their children. Domestic child-rearing responsibilities are for the most part shared in two-mother households, the child is equally bonded to both mothers, and lesbian co-mothers provide higher quality parenting than heterosexual fathers. Although the co-mothers sometimes feel more peripheral during breast feeding, having the opportunity to adopt their children enhances the co-mothers' feelings of legitimacy as parents. Among families in which the mothers separate before the child reaches maturity, those with co-parent adoption agreements are more likely to share custody after the breakup. Having children brings lesbian mothers closer to their own parents, of whom increasing numbers have come out about their grandchildren's lesbian families.

There are no differences in the gender development or psychological adjustment of children raised by lesbians and those raised by heterosexuals. There are also no differences in the psychological well-being of children whose donors are known and those whose donors are unknown, nor in those whose mothers have separated and those whose mothers are still together. The latter finding may relate to the shared custody and continued involvement of both mothers in the child's life after the breakup.

Mental health in the children of lesbian mothers is enhanced by attending schools with lesbian/gay curricula, by having regular contact with grandparents, and—if they have two mothers—when the mothers share domestic responsibilities. Although the children who experienced homophobia demonstrated more behavioral problems, their psychological adjustment is still within the normal range. Among the children who are targeted for homophobic bullying, those whose mothers participate in the LGBT community demonstrate more resilience. Most mothers have no preferences or predictions about their children's eventual sexual orientation.

More lesbians than ever before would like to adopt a child (Gates, Badgett, Macomber, & Chambers, 2007; Matthews & Cramer, 2006), but they encounter numerous obstacles—chiefly related to homophobia—in their quest to become adoptive parents (Brooks & Goldberg, 2001). Yet the research indicates that American and European lesbian families are ideal for children in need of adoption. Study after study shows that children raised by lesbian mothers are thriving: They are psychologically well-adjusted, they demonstrate a sophisticated understanding of diversity, and they are resilient in the face of homophobic adversity. These children benefit from having mothers who are lesbian-identified participants in the LGBT community and who have taken an active role in educating others about discrimination and tolerance.

As the American, British, and Dutch longitudinal studies continue into the future, they will enhance our understanding of the critical ingredients that define successful parenting (Parke, 2004) and the unique contributions made by lesbian families to the changing sociopolitical landscape of our world.

References

Achenbach, T. M. (1991). *Manual for the child behavior checklist/4–18 and 1991 profile.* Burlington: University of Vermont, Department of Psychiatry.

Achenbach, T. M., & Rescorla, L. A. (2001). *Manual for the ASEBA school-age forms.* Burlington: University of Vermont, Department of Psychiatry.

American Academy of Child and Adolescent Psychiatry. (1999). Policy statement: Gay, lesbian, and bisexual parents, *available at* http://www.aacap.org/page.ww?=publications+store&name=Policy+Statements.

American Psychiatric Association. (2002). Position statement: Adoption and co-parenting of children by same sex couples, *available at* http://www.psych.org/edu/other_res/lib_archives/archives/200214.pdf.

American Psychological Association. (2004). Policy statement: Sexual orientation, parents, & children, *available at* http://www.apa.org/pi/lgbc/policy.parents.html.

Bos, H. M. W., Gartrell, N., Peyser, H., & van Balen, F. (2008a). The USA National Longitudinal Lesbian Family Study: Homophobia, psychological adjustment, and protective factors. *Journal of Lesbian Studies, 12,* 455–471.

Bos, H. M. W., Gartrell, K., van Balen, F., Peyser, H., & Sandfort, Th. G. M. (2008b). Children in planned lesbian families: A cross-cultural comparison between the USA and the Netherlands. *American Journal of Orthopsychiatry, 78*, 211–219.

Bos, H. M. W., & Sandfort, Th. (2010). Children's gender identity in lesbian and heterosexual two-parent families. *Sex Roles, 62*, 114–126.

Bos, H. M. W., van Balen, F., & van den Boom, D. C. (2003). Planned lesbian families: Their desire and motivation to have children. *Human Reproduction, 18*, 2216–2224.

Bos, H. M. W., van Balen, F., & van den Boom, D. C. (2004a). Experience of parenthood, couple relationship, social support, and child-rearing goals in planned lesbian mother families. *Journal of Child Psychology and Psychiatry, 45*, 755–764.

Bos, H. M. W., van Balen, F., van den Boom, D. C., & Sandfort, Th. G. M. (2004b). Minority stress, experience of parenthood and child adjustment in lesbian families. *Journal of Reproductive and Infant Psychology, 22*, 291–304.

Bos, H. M. W., van Balen, F., & van den Boom, D. C. (2007). Child adjustment and parenting in planned lesbian-parent families. *American Journal of Orthopsychiatry, 77*, 38–48.

Brewaeys, A., Ponjaert, I., Van Hall, E. V., & Golombok, S. (1997). Donor insemination: Child development and family functioning in lesbian mother families with 4 to 8 years old children. *Human Reproduction, 12*, 1349–1359.

Brooks, D., & Goldberg, S. (2001). Gay and lesbian adoptive and foster care placements: Can they meet the needs of waiting children? *Social Work, 46*, 147–157.

California Environmental Protection Agency. (2005). Respiratory Health Effect of Passive Smoking. Office of Environmental Health Hazard Assessment.

Centers for Disease Control and Prevention. (2001). Tobacco information and prevention source. Women and smoking: A report of the surgeon general. Retrieved May 23, 2003, from http://www.cdc.gov/tobacco/sgr_forwomen.htm.

Centers for Disease Control and Prevention. (2002a). American women waiting to begin families. Retrieved February 27, 2007, from http://www.cdc.gov/od/oc/media/pressrel/r021211.htm.

Centers for Disease Control and Prevention. (2002b). National Center on Birth Defects and Developmental Disabilities. Developmental disabilities. Retrieved May 17, 2003, from http://www.cdc.gov.ncbddd/dd/default/htm.

Chan, R. W., Brooks, R. C., Raboy, B., & Patterson, C. J. (1998a). Division of labor among lesbian and heterosexual parents: Associations with children's adjustment. *Journal of Family Psychology, 12*, 402–419.

Chan, R. W., Raboy, B., & Patterson, C. J. (1998b). Psychosocial adjustment among children conceived via donor insemination by lesbian and heterosexual mothers. *Child Development, 69*, 443–457.

Emery, R. E., Otto, R. K., & O'Donohue, W. T. (2005). A critical assessment of child custody evaluations: limited science and a flawed system. *Psychological Science in the Public Interest. 6*(1),1–29.

Finkelhor, D., Turner, H., Omrod, R. K., Hamby, S. L., & Krack, K. (2009, October). Children's exposure to violence: A comprehensive national survey. *Juvenile Justice Bullentin*, 1–11.

Fulcher, M., Sutfin, E. L., Chan, R. W., Scheib, J. E., & Patterson, C. J. (2006). Lesbian mothers and their children: Findings from the contemporary families study. In A. M. Omoto & H. S. Kurtzman (Eds.), *Sexual orientation and mental health* (pp. 281–299). Washington, D.C.: American Psychological Association.

Gartrell, N., Banks, A., Hamilton, J., Reed, N., Bishop, H., & Rodas, C. (1999). The national lesbian family study: 2. Interviews with mothers of toddlers. *American Journal of Orthopsychiatry, 69,* 362–369.

Gartrell, N., Banks, A., Reed, N., Hamilton, J., Rodas, C., & Deck, A. (2000). The national lesbian family study: 3. Interviews with mothers of five-year-olds. *American Journal of Orthopsychiatry, 70,* 542–548.

Gartrell, N., Deck, A., Rodas, C., Peyser, H., & Banks, A. (2005). The national lesbian family study: 4. Interviews with the 10-year-old children. *American Journal of Orthopsychiatry, 75,* 518–524.

Gartrell, N., Hamilton, J., Banks, A., Mosbacher, D., Reed, N., Sparks, C., & Bishop H. (1996). The national lesbian family study: 1. Interviews with prospective mothers. *American Journal of Orthopsychiatry, 66,* 272–281.

Gartrell, N., Hamilton, J., Banks, A., Mosbacher, D., Reed, N., Sparks, C., & Bishop H. (2006). The national lesbian family study: 5. Interviews with mothers of ten-year-olds. *Feminism & Psychology, 16,* 175–192.

Gates, G. J., Badgett, M. V., Macomber, J. E., & Chambers, K. (2007). Adoption and foster care by gay and lesbian parents in the United States. Technical report issued jointly by the Williams Institute (Los Angeles, CA) and the Urban Institute (Washington, D.C.).

Golombok, S. (2000). *Parenting: What really counts?* London: Routledge.

Golombok, S., Perry, B., Burston, A., Murray, C., Mooney-Somers, J., Stevens, M., & Golding, J. (2003). Children with lesbian parents: A community study. *Developmental Psychology, 39,* 20–33.

Golombok, S., Spencer, A., & Rutter, M. (1983). Children in lesbian and single parent households: Psychosexual and psychiatric appraisal. *Journal of Child Psychology and Psychiatry, 24,* 551–572.

Gottman, J. S. (1990). Children of gay and lesbian parents. In F. W. Bozett & M. B. Sussman (Eds.), *Homosexuality and family relations* (pp. 177–196). New York: Harrington Park Press.

Green, R. (1978). Sexual identity of 37 children raised by homosexual or transsexual parents. *American Journal of Psychiatry, 135,* 692–697.

Green, R., Mandel, J. B., Hotvedt, M. E., Gray, J., & Smith, L. (1986). Lesbian mothers and their children: A comparison with solo parent heterosexual mothers and their children. *Archives of Sexual Behavior, 15,* 167–184.

Hicks, S. (2005). Queer genealogies: Tales of conformity and rebellion amongst lesbian and gay foster carers and adopters. *Qualitative Social Work, 4,* 293–308.

Hoeffer, B. (1981). Children's acquisition of sex-role behavior in lesbian-mother families. *American Journal of Orthopsychiatry, 51,* 536–544.

Huggins, S. L. (1989). A comparative study of self-esteem of adolescent children of divorced lesbian mothers and divorced heterosexual mothers. In F. W. Bozett (Ed.), *Homosexuality and the family* (pp. 123–135). New York: Harrington Park Press.

Kirkpatrick, M. (1987). Clinical implications of lesbian mother studies. *Journal of Homosexuality, 13,* 201–211.

Kirkpatrick, M., Smith, C., & Roy, R. (1981). Lesbian mothers and their children: A comparative survey. *American Journal of Orthopsychiatry, 51,* 545–551.

Kreider, R. M., & Fields, J. M. (2001). *Number, timing, and duration of marriages and divorces: Fall 1996.* Washington, DC: Current Population Reports, US Census Bureau, 70–80.

Lambert, S. (2005). Gay and lesbian families: What we know and where to go from here. *Family Journal: Counseling and Therapy for Couples and Families, 13*, 43–51.

MacCallum, F., & Golombok, S. (2004). Children raised in fatherless families from infancy: A follow-up of children of lesbian and single heterosexual mothers at early adolescence. *Journal of Child Psychology and Psychiatry, 45*, 1407–1419.

Matthews, J. D., & Cramer, E. P. (2006). Envisaging the adoption process to strengthen gay- and lesbian-headed families: Recommendations for adoption professionals. *Child Welfare, 85*, 317–340.

Parke, R. D. (2004). Development in the family. *Annual Review of Psychology, 55*, 365–399.

Patterson, C. J. (1994). Children of the lesbian baby boom: Behavioral adjustment, self-concepts and sex role identity. In B. Greene & G. M. Herek (Eds.), *Psychological perspectives on lesbian and gay issues: Vol.1. Lesbian and gay psychology: Theory, research & clinical applications* (pp. 156–175). Thousand Oaks, CA: Sage.

Patterson, C. J. (2001). Families of the lesbian baby boom: Maternal mental health and child adjustment. *Journal of Gay and Lesbian Psychotherapy, 4*, 91–107.

Patterson, C. J., Hurt, S., & Mason, C. D. (1998). Families of the lesbian baby boom: Children's contact with grandparents and other adults. *American Journal of Orthopsychiatry, 68*, 390–399.

Pawelski, J. G., Perrin, E. C., Foy, J. M., Allen, C. E., Crawford, J. E., et al. (2007). The effects of marriage, civil union, and domestic partnership laws on the health and well-being of children. *Pediatrics, 118*, 349–364.

Rees, R. L. (1979). *A comparison of children of lesbian and single heterosexual mothers on three measures of socialization.* Unpublished doctoral dissertation. Berkeley, CA: California School of Professional Psychology.

Russell, D. H., & Bolen, R. M. (2000). *The epidemic of rape and child sexual abuse in the United States.* Thousand Oaks, CA: Sage.

Sandfort, Th. G. M. (2005). Homofobie: Welk probleem? Wiens probleem? *Tijdschrift voor Seksuologie [Journal of Sexuology], 29*, 11–18.

Simmons, T., & O'Connell, M. (2003). Married-couple and unmarried-partner households: 2000. Retrieved June 1, 2004, from the United States Census Bureau website at http://www.census.gov/prod/2003pubs/censr-5.pdf.

Softas-Nall, B., & Sukhodolsky, D. G. (2006). Family in the United States; social context, structure, and roles. In J. Georgas, J. W. Berry, F. J. R. Van de Vijver, C. Kagitcibasi, & Y. P. Poortinga (Eds.), *Families across cultures: A 30-nation psychological study* (pp. 483–490). Cambridge: Cambridge University Press.

van Balen, F. (2005). Late parenthood among subfertile and fertile couples: Motivations and educational goals. *Patient, Education, and Counseling, 59*, 276–282.

Vanfraussen, K., Ponjaert-Kristoffersen, I., & Brewaeys, A. (2001). An attempt to reconstruct children's donor concept: A comparison between children's and lesbian parents' attitudes towards donor anonymity. *Human Reproduction, 16*, 2019–2025.

Vanfraussen, K., Ponjaert-Kristoffersen, I., & Brewaeys, A. (2002). What does it mean for youngsters to grow up in a lesbian family created by means of donor insemination? *Journal of Reproductive and Infant Psychology, 20*, 237–252.

Vanfraussen, K., Ponjaert-Kristoffersen, I., & Brewaeys, A. (2003a). Why do children want to know more about the donor? The experiences of youngsters raised in lesbian families. *Journal of Psychosomatic Obstetrics and Gynecology, 24*, 31–38.

Vanfraussen, K., Ponjaert-Kristoffersen, I., & Brewaeys, A. (2003b). Family functioning in lesbian families created by donor insemination. *American Journal of Orthopsychiatry*, *73*, 78–90.

U.S. Census Bureau. (April 19, 2004). Retrieved March 16, 2007, from http://www.census.gov/Press-Release/www/releases/archives/facts_for_features_special_editions/001780.html.

Wald, M. S. (2006). Adults' sexual orientation and state determinations regarding placement of children. American Bar Association. *Family Law Quarterly*, *40*, 381–434.

7

Lesbian and Gay Prospective Foster and Adoptive Families

The Homestudy Assessment Process

GERALD P. MALLON ■

Despite widespread assumptions to the contrary, lesbians and gay men have been interested in and have been actively forming families for decades in a wide variety of ways—through kinship networks, domestic partnerships, foster parenting, adoption, surrogacy, co-parenting arrangements, and assisted reproductive technologies. Moreover, some have become parents through marriage prior to coming out as lesbian or gay.

The creation of lesbian- and gay-headed families has not been without historical controversy and, in some cases, legal and policy-driven barriers have been established to prevent nonheterosexuals from parenting and creating families. And yet, at the same time, in many regions of the United States and in many European countries, there has been a growing acceptance of gay and lesbian family life, as evidenced by the establishment of legal domestic partnerships, same-gender marriage, and an opening up of foster parenting and adoption to lesbians and gay men (Appell, this volume; Brodzinsky et al., 2002; Brodzinsky, 2003; Brodzinsky, this volume; Pertman & Howard, this volume; Russett, this volume).

An examination of how child welfare agencies manage applications from prospective families headed by lesbians and gay men, what unique issues are encountered in this process, and how gays and lesbians respond to the homestudy is important for better understanding and establishing best practice standards in this area. Consequently, these issues will be the focus of this chapter.

GAY AND LESBIAN FOSTERING AND ADOPTION

Lesbians and gay men in the United States have been creating families through adoption, foster care, and the establishment of kinship networks for decades

(Martin, 1993; Sullivan, 1995; Weston, 1991). In some cases, lesbians and gay men became parents without disclosure or discussion of their sexual orientation with adoption and foster care agencies. However, as many have become able to live their lives more openly, a growing number are considering parenthood in ways that are more transparent and honest than they might have thought possible in the past (Brooks & Goldberg, 2001).

For many lesbians and gay men, foster parenting or adopting is not a second choice, as it may be for heterosexual men and women who are infertile (Turner, 1999), but, rather, their preference from the start. Furthermore, there is a growing body of research showing that lesbians and gay men make good parents and raise children who show patterns of positive adjustment comparable to those of heterosexual parents (Erich, Kanenberg, Case, Allen, & Bogdanos, 2009; Erich, Leung, Kindle, & Carter, 2005; Farr, Forssell, & Patterson, 2010; Gartrell, Peyser, & Bos, this volume; Golombok, Perry, Burston, Murray, Mooney-Somers, & Stevens, 2003; Golombok & Tasker, 1996; Golombok, Tasker, & Murray, 1997; Leung, Erich, & Kanenberg, 2005; Patterson, 1992, 1994, 1995, 1996; Patterson & Wainright, this volume; Shuster, 2005; Stacey & Biblarz, 2001; Vanfraussen, Ponjaert-Kristofferson, & Brewaeys, 2002, 2003; Wainright & Patterson, 2006; Wainright, Russell, & Patterson, 2004). As a result, it is clear that lesbians and gay men represent an untapped resource of potential parents for some of the tens of thousands of children and youth who need permanent families. Although lesbians and gay men may have been historically discouraged from fostering or adopting, changes in legislation and policy over the past 10 years in some states reflect a more open attitude toward them as parents (Appell, this volume; Pace, 2006; Pertman & Howard, this volume; Ryan, Pearlmutter, & Groza, 2004).

ASSESSMENT OF LESBIAN AND GAY FOSTER AND ADOPTIVE FAMILIES

Deciding to adopt or become a foster parent for a child is a huge step. Potential parents are understandably apprehensive about what the process entails—and, given their history of discrimination, lesbians and gay men may have even greater cause for concern. Overall, far more lesbians and gay men have successfully fostered or adopted than is widely assumed, but there remains a widespread perception—an inaccurate one—that they are generally rejected as parental applicants (see Brodzinsky, this volume). One consequence of this assumption is that some lesbians and gay men who are interested in becoming parents do not pursue adoption or foster parenting.

Social workers in child welfare agencies play critical roles in deciding who will be licensed as a foster or adoptive parent and who will not. Social workers, like other professionals, display a range of attitudes, expectations, and beliefs, both positive and negative, about lesbian and gay people. These attitudes are critical in informing and influencing the assessment process. To help the profession create an atmosphere of respect and openness toward lesbians and gay men who are interested in becoming foster or adoptive parents, there is a clear need for appropriate training of social workers. Increasingly, adoption agencies are coming to recognize this reality (Brodzinsky, this volume). Before a sensitive and effective homestudy process for lesbian and gay individuals can be initiated, social workers need to be trained about the life realities of these prospective parents—as well as about their need to confront and deal with their own homophobia and heterocentrism.

The assessment processes for lesbians and gay men who are prospective foster or adoptive parents can become skewed if the assessing worker is either overfocusing on sexuality or totally ignoring it. Sexual orientation should not be ignored in the assessment process because the sexuality of individuals is an aspect of who they are as a total person and will have an impact on their life as a parent. What needs to be established early in the assessment is the applicants' ability to constructively manage the effects of homophobia or heterocentrism in their own lives.

As gay and lesbian parents have demonstrated their unique strengths as foster and adoptive parents (see Ryan & Brown, this volume), there has been less need among policymakers and child welfare professionals to argue that they "are just as good as straight parents," with the underlying presumption that the heterosexual model of family life is best. Rather, the child welfare field has witnessed a gradual shift toward a model of child care assessment that acknowledges the different experiences that being a gay or lesbian parent bring to fostering and adoption (Hill, 2009; Mallon, 2006). Incorporating an awareness and respect for these differences is now viewed as an increasingly accepted goal of the homestudy process.

States and child welfare agencies are required by law to carry out a full assessment of applicants before approving them as foster or adoptive parents. The information to be collected and required investigation are detailed in the relevant state regulations and standards. Although this process varies from state to state, prospective parents should be made aware of the flow of this process at the start of their initial engagement with the agency. The Texas Adoption Resource Exchange provides an excellent overview on its website about the steps to becoming a foster/adoptive parent (www.dfps.state.tx.us/adoption_and_foster_care, downloaded, June 28, 2005).

THE FIRST CONTACT

In initial interviews with the individual or couple, social workers must make clear in their language, affect, and tone that they are open and accepting of lesbians and gay men as parents. Social workers must also be aware that the applicant, at this initial interview, may not be "out." Many lesbian and gay applicants will be assessing both the social worker and the agency for "safety," trying to determine whether they will be supported or judged negatively. Although some lesbians and gay men come out directly at this first interview, others do so only as trust builds over time.

Pedro and his partner, Mark, who became foster parents in the late 1980s, made the following observations about approaching an agency and preparing for a first visit.

> We both wanted so much to become dads, but like most gay men we thought that we would never be able to do that. We loved our nieces and nephews, but being the greatest uncles in the world got old quickly and we wanted more—we wanted a family. We saw in the news that there were more and more children being born HIV positive and that their moms were either dying or unable to care for them or had already abandoned them in the hospital. AIDS was all around us, we had lost many friends or had others who were very ill, so AIDS and HIV, horrible as it was, was not foreign to us. We heard about this agency in New York called Leake and Watts that was among the first to license foster homes for HIV positive babies and we decided to contact them. We were cautious at first, but they sounded pretty open-minded, even to gay people becoming foster parents because they were really desperate to find families to love their children. So, we decided to pursue becoming foster parents, we didn't really even know the difference between foster care and adoption. We went to the orientation, we did the application, we got the references and the physicals, the financial statements, and we did the training and completed our homestudy in record time. In retrospect, we were as desperate to become dads as they were to get foster parents; it was a good match for all of us.

TRAINING GROUPS

Many lesbian and gay parents say they felt isolated and vulnerable in a MAPP (Model Approaches to Positive Parenting) or PRIDE (Parent Resource for Information, Development, Education) training group, and some parents who were interviewed for previous publications (Mallon, 2004, 2006; Mallon & Betts, 2005) noted that they were nervous about dealing with other group members' homophobia in the training setting. All the parents interviewed recalled that they had not been prepared by their assessing social worker for the group training, either in general or specifically in relation to their needs as lesbian or gay parents. Some parents observed that they felt the onus was on them to "come out" at the start of the group. Most of those interviewed commented that both social workers and other group facilitators "did not have a great understanding of what it meant to come out."

In truth, it is likely that there will be a range of reactions in such a group—from people who are shocked that lesbians and gay men would be allowed to adopt or foster to those who are comfortable and accepting of such parents. It is not the prospective parents' responsibility to either manage homophobia from group members or to educate the group; the onus for this rests with the facilitating social workers. In this respect, it is important that clear ground rules for the group should be set, and should make reference to accepting and valuing diversity while challenging discriminatory comments.

SHOULD THE HOMESTUDY BE DIFFERENT
FOR LESBIAN AND GAY PARENTS?

As lesbians and gay men seek to raise children in growing numbers, social workers increasingly have the opportunity to write homestudies for these families. Lesbian and gay adoption and foster parenting are changing quickly and dramatically across the United States (Brodzinsky, this volume; Gates, Badgett, Macomber, & Chambers, 2007). Because of the enormous variation in policies, expectations, practices, and cultures across the country, it may be impossible to agree on one best homestudy format. These vary from state to state, but recent changes in some state laws make the standardized development of these guidelines an important step in adoption practice. What is accepted practice in an urban area with large numbers of gay and lesbian prospective parents may be unheard of in a more suburban or rural area in which there is less experience with such applicants. Providing guidelines is useful because they (1) give social workers a sense of the formats other states and agencies are using to write homestudies for lesbian and gay clients and (2) provide general cultural competency information so that those who work with lesbians and gay men can do so in a sensitive, respectful manner.

A Continuum of Homestudy Formats

The sections below present several formats that are currently being used to write homestudies for prospective lesbian and gay adoptive and foster parents. As with heterosexual applicants, the issues can be quite different for single prospective parents than for couples. When single people adopt or foster, their sexual orientation is often not known, or it seems less important; the issues of adopting as a single person—rather than sexual orientation—often become primary (Marindin, 1997).

Single Lesbians and Gay People: Out or Not?

When a gay man or lesbian wishes to adopt as a single person, usually because he or she does not currently have a partner, the homestudy can be written as for any other single applicant. Applicants may voluntarily disclose information in the process of discussions about their sexuality, but if they do not openly discuss this topic, it is nevertheless an important area for social workers to explore.

If the worker does not know how the person identifies after the standard home visits, it is usually acceptable practice to write the homestudy without reference to the subject. It should not be assumed, however, that a single applicant is gay or lesbian. If the applicant is described as single, any major past relationships or marriages can be mentioned (sometimes applicants do not mention past partners' genders in their paperwork), and the homestudy can indicate the prospective parents' thoughts on relationships in the future.

If the applicant openly says that he or she is lesbian or gay, the worker may discuss with him or her how this information should be included in the home-study. It may be mentioned as descriptive (i.e., "Mary is a single lesbian woman living in a suburb of Hartford") or in more detail in the applicant's autobiography or description of past and anticipated future relationships. Some applicants feel more comfortable having this information included in the homestudy so that they do not have to worry about hiding information from social workers they may meet with in the future. This way, the applicants know that anyone who approaches them with a possible match is aware of their reality.

Other workers and applicants may feel that it is not necessary to share their sexual orientation, and that as a single person it has no relevance to the applicant's ability to parent a child. Some workers routinely advise single people who are gay or lesbian that they will not include this information in the homestudy because it is irrelevant. However, it is important to realize that failure to address the issue of sexual orientation could prevent the applicant from receiving important preparation and support related to how this issue could have an impact on future parenting. Moreover, should the individual be considering adopting an older child, failure to address sexual orientation in the homestudy also prevents appropriate preparation of the youngster about being raised by a gay or lesbian parent.

Same-Gender Couples

Two-Parent Family

Increasing numbers of social workers are writing the homestudies of gay and lesbian couples the same way they write the homestudies of heterosexual couples, with both people's names listed as the adoptive or foster parents. Some forms use the terms "parent one" and parent two," in a gender-neutral manner, with the intention that both parents receive an equal amount of attention within the homestudy.

The homestudy is written in the same format as if the couple were male–female, including information about the length of their relationship and its strengths and weaknesses. Because same-gender couples cannot marry in most states, information about marriage generally would not apply; however, in states in which the couple has been able to marry, this information should be noted.

Many social workers have said they prefer this type of straightforward home-study because it gives them a better understanding of the type of family that may be adopting or fostering a child or youth on their caseload, but some states' policies or laws may not allow homestudies to be written in this way. Importantly, by using this format, the homestudy makes it clear that the child will be placed with a gay or lesbian couple and paves the way for any relevant preparation and support of the clients and child that could be related to issues of sexual orientation.

This format is "groundbreaking" in some respects; it also is a very natural way to write this important document. But most lesbian and gay people are applying to adopt because they want to be parents, not because they want to be groundbreakers.

Single Parent with a Domestic Partner

A variation of the two-parent homestudy is one that examines a single parent with a "domestic partner." Some social workers choose this approach because of laws or policies that require one partner in a same-gender couple to adopt as a single person, or because their agency is more comfortable with this format. In this scenario, the homestudy is written primarily about one partner, focusing on that person's social history and interest in adoption, and listing his or her name alone as the adoptive or foster parent; the second partner is included in the homestudy process and is described as a domestic partner or friend. The length and quality of their relationship and cohabitation are described, and the homestudy explains that both partners will consider themselves parents of the child to be adopted.

This type of homestudy is clearly a hybrid: It is honest about the situation of the couple, but conforms to current policies about lesbian and gay adoption; and, like the previous format, it calls attention to any necessary preparation and support of clients and children related to sexual orientation. In agencies or states in which people are uncomfortable or unwilling to consider a homestudy with two same-gender parents, this approach may be a good fit. However, it can be confusing to see one person listed as the adoptive or foster parent when the reality is really a two-parent family. The format also may be misleading and suggest to those who read the document that this family consists of a "primary parent" and that parent's partner, instead of two adults who will share parenting responsibilities.

Single Person with a Roommate

Until recently, most homestudies of same-gender couples were written using this format. One partner is described as a single parent, and the entire homestudy focuses on this person alone. Because homestudies are required to list other individuals living in the home, the partner is listed as a roommate, and criminal clearances are obtained. Very little additional information about the relationship is mentioned, although a sentence is often included saying that this "roommate" is supportive of the applicant's plans to adopt.

This type of homestudy can be the safest in a state or agency that is extremely uncomfortable with gay and lesbian adoptions, or it may be mandated by policy or law. However, this format can be problematic if it is not clear to a person reading the homestudy what this family's structure really looks like. Some social workers reading the homestudy may take it at face value, assuming this is truly a single-parent family. Other social workers may read between the lines and wonder what the relationship is between the two "roommates." When a worker expresses interest in placing a child with the "single parent," he or she may be given more information about the situation verbally or in writing.

Although this approach to writing a gay or lesbian homestudy seemed the safest way to do so in the past, some families have found it can backfire today. For example, one worker thought a specific child on her caseload would do extremely well placed with a single man and selected a "single person" homestudy written in this way. After investing considerable time pursuing the match, she found out that it was actually a two-parent family, not the situation she believed could best meet this child's needs (although she had had positive experiences placing other children with gay and lesbian couples in the past). She also raised concerns that if the agency—not one with which she had worked previously—was willing to omit such major information about the family from the homestudy, she felt less willing to trust whether other important information had also been omitted. Social workers and agencies that choose to follow this format should do so with these concerns in mind, as well as the possibility that appropriate preparation and support of the family related to sexual orientation may not be offered to the client and child. Homestudies should always be written with the best interests of the child or youth, not of the potential parent, in mind. It is important to heed the words of adoption expert and therapist Joyce Maguire Pavao (2005), who reminds us that adoption is about finding families for children, not about finding children for families.

ISSUES TO ADDRESS IN A HOMESTUDY

Many issues are common to all homestudies, regardless of the sexual orientation of the prospective parents, but for lesbian and gay parents the following specific areas also should be addressed.

Comfort with Sexual Orientation and the Reaction of Others

Clearly, although most homestudies did not address sexual orientation in the past, it should now be an issue to be fully and openly discussed in the assessment process. Many lesbians and gay men who have been through this process have found that some social workers either excessively focused on their sexuality or, conversely, did not address the implications of sexuality at all. Most lesbian and gay applicants have spent a lot more time thinking about their sexuality than have most heterosexuals. Moreover, the reluctance to address this issue in the homestudy appears to lie more with the social worker than with most gay or lesbian applicants.

Many prospective applicants write their autobiographies as part of the assessment process, and they may choose to address issues relating to their sexual orientation as part of doing so. For many lesbians and gay men, realizing their sexual orientation and coming out to friends and family constitute a significant life event, as is meeting their partners. The autobiography should not focus exclusively on issues relating to sexual orientation, as this is only one part of a whole person's life experience. But neither should the applicants be encouraged to hide or downplay this aspect of their lives. Social workers should encourage prospective parents to be as honest as they can be, and to be as complete as they can be in writing their autobiographical statements.

It will be important to explore with potential parents their experience of coming out, and the impact this process has had on their significant relationships within their families and communities. The coming out process is so central in the identity development of lesbian and gay persons that social workers must have a strong understanding of the importance of this phenomenon (Cass, 1983/1984).

Assessing potential parents' level of "outness" and exploring with them at what point in their development they did actually come out are important elements of practice, as is understanding the need to conceal or selectively disclose one's orientation. Comfort level with one's "outness" is a key factor for prospective lesbian and gay adoptive and foster parents, as being uncomfortable about being out can complicate the parenting process. As one dad noted in Mallon's (2006) study, "if you are not out before you become a parent, you will be outed by your child, usually at an inopportune moment, like in school when they say things like 'I love to sleep on Saturdays in the big bed with my two daddies.'" Being comfortable with being out suggests that people have integrated their lesbian or gay sexual orientation into their lives, an essential aspect of identity and emotional adjustment that must be covered in a complete and accurate homestudy.

Some other questions social workers may wish to consider include the following:

- At what point did you consider coming out to others?
- Are you out in the community? At work? With your family? With friends?
- Are you out to your partner's parents and to extended family?
- What has been the attitude of your extended family to your partner? Have they been inclusive and welcoming, or not?
- Is your family supportive of you (and your partner) fostering or adopting a child?

Some lesbians and gay men, as well as their partners, are cut off from their extended families because of an inability or unwillingness to respect their identity. Of course, applicants should not be penalized because of their relatives' attitudes, but this information should be included so that a worker reading the assessment has a picture of the broader family system the child would join. In addition, a social worker should explore what support networks are available to the potential foster or adoptive parent.

Some additional questions social workers may wish to consider include the following:

- How have the effects of homophobia and heterocentrism affected your life? How have you dealt with these issues, both in the past and presently?
- How would you describe your current relationships—sexual, emotional, with family members, with the broader community? How do you negotiate homophobia within close relationships, for example, with your siblings, extended family members, friends, and neighbors?

- Have you thought about how you might relate to your child's birth parents, or to the parents of your child's friends—for example, at school or in a playgroup? How much research have you done in relation to attitudes of local institutions such as schools or healthcare systems? How would you help a child who experiences prejudice because of your sexual orientation?

Partnerships, Relationships, and Sexuality

There is some debate about whether social workers should ask applicants about their sexual relationships, and if they do, what should be done with this knowledge. There are distinctions between sexual orientation and sexual relationships, of course; the first has to do with one's attraction to a romantic and sexual partner, and the second has to do with one's behavioral expression of intimacy and sexuality. Many social workers may be reluctant to explore issues related to sexual orientation because they fear it will take them into areas having to do with discussions of sexual behavior. Questions about sexual relationships should be part of the assessment for *all* couples. Sexual expression is a form of communication and intimacy. How people feel about themselves, physically and sexually, is likely to have profound implications for the development of children in their care. How children feel about themselves, physically and sexually, will also have implications for how they relate to others and to society. This is all part of developing an acceptable sense of self, and helping with this development is a major task for any mother or father. Parents face challenges in dealing with their adolescents' sexuality, and they have a responsibility to provide information and help young people think about the nature of their sexuality and relationships. Thus, the ability to talk openly and honestly about relationship issues, including sexuality, in age-appropriate ways with their children, is an important aspect of parenting that needs to be considered in making placements with all families. This is especially true when the placements involve older children, who will soon be exploring these issues in their lives—or who already are.

The following questions need to be explored with *all* parental applicants who are in significant relationships:

- What qualities do you and your partner bring to the relationship?
- What makes the relationship positive for each of you? How do you support each other? How do you cope with stress and difficulties?
- How do each of you address issues of sexuality and intimacy in your relationship?
- How will a new child affect your relationship—for example, how will you cope with a child who becomes attached more readily to one of you than the other?
- Have you considered other options and explored other pathways to parenthood?
- How are decisions made in your relationship? Is there wider family involvement in the decision-making process?

- What are the strengths and vulnerabilities of your partnership? What areas of the relationship create the most conflict?
- Have there been previous significant relationships for either partner, and if so what has been learned from these? Do these previous relationships affect the present partnership? Are there children from any previous relationships, and if so, how will those children be affected by the decision to become parents?
- How comfortable are you and your partner likely to be in discussing issues related to intimacy and sexuality with your children, including same-gendered sexual attraction and behavior?
- When do you believe it is appropriate to begin discussing relationship issues and sexuality with children?

Other Adults in the Household or in the Applicant's Life

The reality of single, prospective parents' lives, including those who are lesbian and gay, includes significant adults who reside within the same household as well as those who do not but are nevertheless an important and regular part of the applicant's life; for example, a single applicant may not be in a current relationship, but may date occasionally or wish to date at some future time. Although no assessment can predict the future, social workers must be aware of the roles that other people in an applicant's life may play (including a person the applicant is dating or might one day date) and should consider the following questions:

- Although you are single now, how frequently do you date? Do your dates ever stay overnight? How would adopting a child have an impact on your dating plans?
- If you are dating someone in particular, is the relationship likely to become serious? If so, have you discussed with that person your intention to adopt a child? What was his or her reaction to your plan and how important is that attitude to you?
- How do you plan to discuss your romantic relationships with a child you are raising.

Motivation for Adoption

For most lesbian and gay families, parenting is a choice—but that is often not the case for heterosexuals, for whom the ability to become parents is perceived as a given. This may mean that lesbians or gay men who choose to create their families by fostering or adopting may be more motivated and deliberate as they embark on the decision-making process. For them, questions relating to motivation are very relevant for discussion since creating families by birth may not have been an option, and so fostering or adopting is often their first choice, as this case illustrates:

> *Charmaine and Anita, ages 32 and 36, respectively, are professional women living in a large southern city in the United States. Coupled for 10 years, both women thought about and discussed the possibility of parenting for the past three years. Neither woman was interested in creating a family via alternative insemination and once they made their decision to pursue parenting, they immediately started to learn about the foster care and adoption process. After completing the MAPP training for foster parents, Charmaine and Anita decided to foster/adopt a child through the public child welfare system. They were dually licensed as foster/adoptive parents with the hope that a child would be placed in their home. Within three months of completing the homestudy, a 6-month-old baby boy was placed in their home, first as a foster child and then, after parental rights were voluntarily surrendered, they moved toward adoption.*

Integrating the Child into the Family

For lesbian and gay prospective foster and adoptive families, an experienced and competent worker should inquire about the prospective parents' life, but should not overemphasize lesbian or gay issues. In reality, most such applicants have a gay or lesbian "life," not a gay or lesbian "lifestyle." Being lesbian or gay has become a part of who they are as people, but does not entirely define them. Some regularly attend venues and events such as lesbian and gay community centers or gay and lesbian pride parades—while some do not. The social worker may need to evaluate the ways in which individuals or couples spend their recreation and leisure time and how these will be impacted by raising a child and/or how the child will be impacted by these aspects of his or her parents' lives. However, it must be kept in mind that in most ways, integrating the newly placed child into their lives mirrors the same joys (e.g., feelings of nurturance and tenderness, positive attention from others) and stresses (e.g., increased fatigue, reduced intimacy in the couple relationship) as would be found for most straight parents.

Valuing Difference and Preparing Children for Prejudice

Although research and clinical experience suggest that growing up with gay and lesbian parents sometimes results in children being teased, this experience need not necessarily lead to adjustment difficulties. When parents are attuned to their children's experiences, and when they assertively prepare them for the possibility of homophobic comments from others, children typically develop appropriate coping strategies and learn to manage these difficult moments (see Gartrell et al., this volume). Because most lesbians and gay men have experienced prejudice themselves, they are likely to be particularly sensitive to the impact of discrimination on their children, and to their feelings of being different. In fact, gay and lesbian parents, like racial minority parents, may be in a unique position to foster positive attitudes about diversity issues and to support their children's ability to cope with prejudice. During the homestudy, social workers should help lesbian and gay prospective foster and adoptive parents explore their own experiences with discrimination to prepare them to help their children value diversity and cope with the prejudice and homophobic reactions of others.

Anticipating Concerns

Some social workers have success helping lesbian and gay families adopt by using a strategy in which they attempt to anticipate many of the concerns a child's placement social worker or even the child's birth parents might have. They first discuss these concerns openly with the prospective adoptive or foster parent(s), and then address each concern openly in the homestudy. This allows the family's worker to use the homestudy to educate the placement worker and/or the birth family. For example, in the homestudy, it might be noted that "Some workers worry that if they place a child with a gay or lesbian couple, he will grow up to be gay or lesbian. However, all the studies that have been done on this subject show that children raised by gay men and lesbians are no more likely to be homosexual than children raised by heterosexuals." Another example might be: "Bill and Sam realize that workers may fear that a child placed with them could be teased because s/he has 'two dads.' Here is how they plan to handle this issue if it arises." This approach also allows the family to address potential concerns before they become major barriers.

There are particular impediments to single men adopting because of unfounded stereotypes that they are less stable or want to adopt children to meet their sexual needs. A worker using the "anticipate everything" method may choose to emphasize in a single man's homestudy his healthy adult relationships, the stability of his life, and (if he agrees that it would be beneficial to the goal of adopting a child) how he is meeting his sexual needs. Obviously, any worker using this approach must explain the practical theory behind it and decide with the family whether it is a method they feel would be helpful.

Mistakes to Avoid

Keep in mind that sexual orientation and gender identity are only two aspects of who someone is; they should not be a major focus of a homestudy or of child placement decision (Nelson, 1997).

It is not appropriate to address who will parent the child if a same-gender couple splits up, unless this is a standard part of the agency's homestudy for a married male–female couple. If the professional assessment is that any couple's relationship—regardless of sexual orientation—is not strong enough to survive the challenges of parenting a child, it is questionable whether that couple should be approved to adopt. If, however, the worker's opinion is that the relationship is strong and stable, writing about a potential breakup inappropriately implies that a same-gender relationship cannot be as strong as a heterosexual marriage and that it cannot be expected to last.

It is not appropriate to address prospective parents' sex lives unless this is a standard part of the agency's homestudy for *all* applicants, whether single, married, cohabiting, straight, or lesbian or gay. At the same time, as noted above, questions about applicants' significant relationships, including their strengths and vulnerabilities, should always be included in the homestudy. At times, this may well include information about issues related to sexuality. The important point, however, is that caseworkers should not assume that an exploration of sexual issues is any more important or necessary among lesbian and gay clients than among heterosexual ones.

It is also appropriate to discuss the applicants' personal experiences with sexual abuse, how they have coped with any they have had, how well they are prepared to parent a child with a history of sexual abuse or sexual acting out behaviors, and how they expect to deal with issues of sexuality with their child. These discussions need not be different with lesbian and gay families than with those headed by heterosexuals.

It is also a mistake to assume that same-gender couples take on roles in their relationships wherein one plays the "man" and the other the "woman." Although this is a popular misconception, it is not the commonplace reality. However, it is appropriate with both straight and gay and lesbian couples to explore how they plan to distribute housework and parenting responsibilities. In fact, research suggests that there is greater sharing of everyday household and parenting responsibilities in lesbian and gay households than in straight households (Chan, Brooks, Raboy & Patterson, 1998; Patterson, Sutfin, & Fulcher, 2004).

Furthermore, it should not be assumed that children or adolescents whose words or behavior indicate they are questioning their sexual orientation or gender identity should be placed with families who can "cure" them and make them heterosexual. It might, however, be helpful for a youth who already has self-identified as lesbian or gay to be placed with lesbian or gay parents, as such a placement could provide an affirming environment of respect and support. But not all self-identified lesbian or gay youth in foster care need to be placed in lesbian- or gay-headed foster or adoptive homes. Such a decision should be made in response to the adolescent's needs, as well as preference, not as a result of the beliefs or stereotypes of the caseworker.

Final Decision Making

It is the responsibility of the social worker, his or her supervisor, and in some cases a treatment team to ensure that the assessor's recommendation is based on information that provides relevant and sufficient evidence of the applicant's ability to meet the requirements for being an adoptive or foster parent. The team must then decide whether to endorse the recommendation.

The values and attitudes of team members are often an issue in this process. Recurring themes from an untrained team with respect to lesbian and gay adopters or parents may include the following homophobic responses:

- "Where is the positive male or female role model?"
- "Who is the mother?"
- "How will you explain your relationship to children placed with you?"
- "Won't you make them gay?"

Arthur and Tom, who have had a baby girl placed with them, were asked by their social worker about role models; one of the issues that arose in connection with these questions was that they would not be able to teach a girl to put on make-up and do her hair. Both men laughed and said they were probably better able to teach these skills than many women that they knew given that both were hairstylists. Their social worker also observed that they had identified an "extensive list" of female role models in their support networks.

IMPLICATIONS FOR COMPETENT PRACTICE AND ASSESSMENT

The following are considerations for professionals developing policy around foster and adoptive parenting by gay men and lesbians; these are adapted from Sullivan's (1995, pp. 5–8) work:

1. The primary client is the child or youth in need of a family. All families are potential resources for the child or youth. The issue is not "Do gay men and lesbians have the right to adopt?" No family *ipso facto* has the *right* to adopt or to be a foster parent; rather, this is a *privilege* afforded to those families who meet set-out standards. The real issue is whether all individuals, including lesbians and gay men, will be given equal consideration to become foster or adoptive parents.
2. All placement considerations should focus on the best interests of the child or youth. Child welfare professionals should ask, "What is the best family resource for this young person at this time?"
3. No single factor, including sexual orientation, should be determinative in assessing the suitability for adoption or foster parenting (see Ryan, 2000).
4. The capacity to nurture a child or youth and a parent's sexual orientation are separate issues. These must not be confused in decision making.
5. Gay and lesbian applicants should be assessed using the same criteria as all other foster and adoptive parents. Although gay and lesbian applicants may present unique situations, they should not have to pass

extraordinary tests to prove their worthiness as parents. Those working
to certify gay and lesbian parents should ask themselves the following in
making such an assessment: What are the prospective parent's individual
strengths or weaknesses, and what is their capacity to nurture a child or
children who were not born to them?

6. Each placement decision should be based on the strengths and needs of
   the child or youth and the perceived ability of the prospective adoptive
   or foster family to meet those needs and develop those strengths.

There are unique considerations with respect to some aspects of foster parenting or adoption by gay or lesbian persons. Child welfare organizations should
evaluate the following issues:

1. In most states, only one same-gender partner can be legally recognized
   as a parent (Appell, this volume). Although this is changing in some
   states (e.g., New Jersey), child welfare professionals should be aware of
   the consequences of having a legal and nonlegal parent and must also
   assist potential adoptive parents in negotiating a careful discussion about
   this issue, including how to safeguard the child's relationship with the
   nonlegal parent in the event of potential future occurrences such as the
   couple's separation or the death or disability of the legal parent.

2. How willing are the parents to be open about their sexual orientation
   within their community? Having a child who attends school, makes use
   of healthcare services, and attends other child-oriented recreational
   events causes parents to make decisions about their own comfort level
   with being out in the community (see Mallon, 1999, 2000).

3. How willing are the parents to deal with and openly address the multiple
   levels of "differentness" that they and their child will experience? All
   foster and adopted children face issues related to their sense of
   differentness about being in foster care or being adopted. Some
   differences are easier to deal with than others. Being raised by lesbian
   and gay parents adds another layer of complexity and difference for the
   child, as does being placed with parents of a different race or ethnicity.

4. As in all placements, children should be involved in the decision-making
   process whenever possible. For example, in placing a 12-year-old child
   with a gay or lesbian couple, it would be important to determine what
   the child knows about gay and lesbian persons, and gauge his or her
   understanding of the benefits and challenges evident in placement with a
   specific family.

5. Although the differences between gay men and lesbians and straight
   persons as parents are frequently pointed out, it is also important to note
   that gay men and lesbians are resilient individuals and, as such, bring
   many strengths to a family. They know first hand, for example, how
   important it is to allow children to develop naturally without having
   preconceived notions about what they should be. Child welfare

professionals should be aware of the multiple strengths of a gay- or lesbian-headed family (see Ryan & Brown, this volume).

CONCLUSIONS

As is true for straight individuals, not all gay and lesbian people should be foster or adoptive parents. The question is not whether gay or lesbian applicants should be approved, but whether they will be offered the same fair process and open opportunity as nongay people who seek to adopt or foster. Sidestepping the issue of adoption and foster parenting by lesbians and gay men, or pretending that concern about the issue does not exist, does not protect children. It runs counter to the Adoption and Safe Families Act legislation and prevents some children and youth from becoming part of a loving and permanent family, which all children deserve (Howard, 2006; Howard & Freundlich, 2008). A publication by the Human Rights Campaign—*Promising Practices in Adoption and Foster Care* (Human Rights Campaign, 2009)—is a handbook that includes sample policies and tips from leaders of LGBT-welcoming child welfare agencies, researchers in the field, and LGBT adoptive and foster parents. In addition, the handbook offers an assessment tool and guidance to organizations seeking to enhance their organizational competence in working with lesbian and gay foster and adoption parents. A free copy of this important guide can be obtained at http://www.hrc.org/issues/parenting/7609.htm. *Promising Practices in Adoption and Foster Care* should be required reading for all child welfare administrators and professionals.

States and child welfare agencies are responsible for ensuring a timely and appropriate foster or adoptive family for every child who needs one. In meeting this responsibility, states and child welfare agencies must explore all potential resources for all children and youth awaiting placement in a family, including qualified lesbians and gay men who wish to parent and are eager to open their hearts and lives to children and youth in need.

References

Benkov, L. (1994). *Reinventing the family: The emerging story of lesbian and gay parents.* New York: Crown Publishers.

Brooks, D., & Goldberg, S. (2001). Gay and lesbian adoptive and foster care placements: Can they meet the needs of waiting children? *Families in Society, 46*(2), 147–157.

Brodzinsky, D. M., Patterson, C. J. & Vaziri, M. (2002). Adoption agency perspectives on lesbian and gay prospective parents: A national study. *Adoption Quarterly, 5*(3), 5–23.

Brodzinsky, D. M. (2003). Adoption by lesbians and gays: a national survey of adoption agency policies, practices, and attitudes. Evan B. Donaldson Adoption Institute. Retrieved October 6, 2006 (http://www.adoptioninstitute.org).

Cass, V. C. (1983/1984). Homosexual identity: A concept in need of definition. *Journal of Homosexuality, 9*, 105–126.

Chan, R. W., Brooks, R. C., Raboy, B., & Patterson, C. J. (1998). Division of labor among lesbian and heterosexual parents: Associations with children's adjustment. *Journal of Family Psychology, 12*, 402–419.

Erich, S., Kanenberg, H., Case, H., Allen, T., & Bogdanos, T. (2009). An empirical analysis of factors affecting adolescent attachment in adoptive families with homosexual and straight parents. *Children and Youth Services Review, 31*, 398–404.

Erich, S., Leung, P., Kindle, P., & Carter, S. (2005). Gay and lesbian adoptive families: An exploratory study of family functioning, adoptive child's behavior, and familial support networks. *Journal of Family Social Work, 9*, 17–32.

Farr, R. H., Forssell, S. L. & Patterson, C. J. (2010). Parenting and child development in adoptive families: Does parental sexual orientation matter? *Applied Developmental Science, 14*, 164–178.

Gates, G. J., Badgett, M. V. L., Macomber, J. E., & Chambers, K. (2007). *Adoption and foster care by gay and lesbian parents in the United States.* Technical report issued jointly by the Williams Institute (Los Angeles) and the Urban Institute (Washington, D.C.).

Golombok, S., Perry, B., Burston, A., Murray, C., Mooney-Somers, J., Stevens, M. & Golding, J. (2003). Children with lesbian parents: A community study. *Developmental Psychology, 29*(1), 20–33.

Golombok, S., Spencer, A., & Rutter, M. (1983). Children in lesbian and single-parent households: Psychosexual and psychiatric appraisal. *Journal of Child Psychology and Psychiatry, 24*(4), 551–572.

Golombok, S., & Tasker, F. (1996). Do parents influence the sexual orientation of their children? Findings from a longitudinal study of lesbian families. *Developmental Psychology, 32*(1), 3–11.

Golombok, S., Tasker, F., & Murray, C. (1997). Children raised in fatherless families from infancy: Family relationships and the socioemotional development of children of lesbian and single heterosexual mothers. *Journal of Child Psychology and Psychiatry, 38*, 783–791.

Hill, N. (2009). *The pink guide to adoption for lesbians and gay men.* London: British Association for Adoption and Fostering.

Howard, J. (2006). *Expanding resources for children: Is adoption by gays and lesbians part of the answer for boys and girls who need homes?* New York: Evan B. Donaldson Adoption Institute. Available at www.adoptioninstitute.org.

Howard, J., & Freundlich, M. (2008). *Expanding resources for waiting children II: Eliminating legal and practice barriers to gay and lesbian adoption from foster care.* New York: Evan B. Donaldson Adoption Institute. Available at www. adoptioninstitute.org.

Human Rights Campaign. (2009). *Promising practices in adoption and foster care: A comprehensive guide to policies and practices that welcome, affirm, and support gay, lesbian, bisexual, and transgender foster and adoptive parents.* HRC: Washington, D.C.

Leung, P., Erich, S., & Kanenberg, H. (2005). A comparison of family functioning in gay/lesbian heterosexual and special needs adoptions. *Children and Youth Services Review, 27*, 1031–1044.

Mallon, G. P. (1999). Lesbians and gay men as foster and adoptive parents. In *Let's get this straight: A gay and lesbian affirming approach to child welfare* (pp. 112–131). New York: Columbia University Press.

Mallon, G. P. (2000). Gay men and lesbians as adoptive parents. *Journal of Gay and Lesbian Social Services, 11*, 1–21.

Mallon, G. P. (2004). *Gay men choosing parenthood.* New York: Columbia University Press.

Mallon, G. P. (2006). *Lesbian and gay foster and adoptive parents: Recruiting, assessing, and supporting an untapped resource for children and youth.* Washington, D.C.: Child Welfare League of America.

Mallon, G., & Betts, B. (2005). *Recruiting, assessing and retaining lesbian and gay foster and adoptive families: A good practice guide for social workers.* London: British Association of Adoption and Foster Care.

Marindin, H. (1997). *The handbook for single adoptive parents.* Chevy Chase, MD: Committee for Single Parents.

Martin. A. (1993). *The lesbian and gay parenting handbook: Creating and raising our families.* New York: Harper Perennial.

Nelson, N. (1997). *When gay and lesbian people adopt.* Seattle, WA: Northwest Adoption Exchange.

Pace, P. R. (2006, February). Court upholds gay foster parents. *NASW News*, p. 5.

Patterson, C. J. (1992). Children of gay and lesbian parents. *Child Development, 63*, 1025–1042.

Patterson, C. J. (1994). Lesbian and gay couples considering parenthood: An agenda for research, service and advocacy. In L. A. Kurdek (Ed.), *Social services for gay and lesbian couples* (pp. 33–56). New York: Harrington Park Press.

Patterson, C. J. (1995). Lesbian mothers, gay fathers, and their children. In A. R. D'Augelli & C. J. Patterson, (Eds.), *Gay, lesbian, and bisexual identities over the lifespan* (pp. 262–292). Oxford: Oxford University Press.

Patterson, C. J. (1996). Lesbian mothers and their children: Findings from the Bay area families study. In J. Laird & R-J. Green (Eds.), *Lesbians and gays in couples and families: A handbook for therapists* (pp. 420–438). San Francisco: Jossey-Bass Publishers.

Patterson, C. J., Sutfin, E. L., & Fulcher, M. (2004). Division of labor among lesbian and heterosexual parenting couples: Correlates of specialized versus shared patterns. *Journal of Adult Development, 11*, 179–189.

Pavao, J. M. (2005). *The family of adoption.* Boston: Beacon Press.

Ryan, S. D. (2000). Examining social workers' placement recommendations of children with gay and lesbian adoptive parents. *Families in Society, 81*, 517–528.

Ryan, S. D., Pearlmutter, S., & Groza, V. (2004). Coming out of the closet: Opening agencies to gay and lesbian adoptive parents. *Social Work, 49*, 85–95.

Shuster, S. (2005). Can we speak freely? What research has told us about LGBT parenting. *In the Family, 10*, 14–17.

Stacey, J., & Biblarz, T. (2001). (How) Does the sexual orientation of parents matter? *American Sociological Review, 66*, 159–183.

Sullivan, A. (Ed.). (1995). *Issues in gay and lesbian adoption: Proceedings of the Fourth Annual Pierce-Warwick Adoption Symposium.* Washington, D.C.: Child Welfare League of America.

Turner, C. S. (1999). *Adoption journeys: Parents tell their stories*. Ithaca, NY: McBooks Press.

Vanfraussen, K., Ponjaert-Kristofferson, I., & Brewaeys, A. (2002). What does it mean for youngsters to grow up in a lesbian family created by means of donor insemination? *Journal of Reproductive and Infant Psychology, 20*, 237–252.

Vanfraussen, K., Ponjaert-Kristofferson, I., & Brewaeys, A. (2003). Family functioning in lesbian families created by donor insemination. *American Journal of Orthopsychiatry, 73*, 78–90.

Wainright, J. L., & Patterson, C. J. (2006). Delinquency, victimization, and substance use among adolescents with female same-sex parents. *Journal of Family Psychology, 20*, 526–530.

Wainright, J., Russell, S., & Patterson, C. (2004). Psychosocial adjustment, school outcomes, and romantic relationships of adolescents with same-sex parents. *Child Development, 75*, 1886–1898.

Weston, K. (1991). *Families we choose: Gay and lesbian kinship*. New York: Columbia University Press.

8

Supporting Gay and Lesbian Adoptive Families Before and After Adoption

DEVON BROOKS, HANSUNG KIM, AND LESLIE H. WIND ∎

For decades, adoption by gay men and lesbians has been controversial. For both the general public and adoption professionals, this controversy has stemmed sometimes from homophobia and at other times from arguably legitimate concerns about the impact of gay adoption on children (Brooks & Goldberg, 2001; Ryan, Pearlmutter, & Groza, 2004). Especially when it involves children in foster care, adoption practice is guided by the best interest standard of decision making (Ricketts, 1991; Ryan et al., 2004). This standard requires adoption professionals to base recommendations and placement decisions primarily on the best interests of an individual child rather than on the rights, needs, or wishes of adults. The standard, which serves as a professional (and moral) compass of sorts, has its roots in the *parens patriae* doctrine—the notion that the state is the supreme guardian of all children within its jurisdiction and therefore has the power to intervene in order to protect those children ("Parens Patriae," 2005).

Until recently, there was uncertainty about how gay and lesbian adoptive parents affect the adjustment and well-being of adopted children. A sizable body of research evidence, however, now shows that such parents—whether adoptive or biological—are as capable as straight parents of raising well-adjusted children, and that the sexual orientation of parents is not associated with children's outcomes (Gartrell, Peyser, & Bos, this volume; Goldberg, 2010; Ryan & Brown, this volume, Patterson & Wainright, this volume). If anything, studies suggest that gay men and lesbians may bring special strengths to the table as adoptive parents (Brooks & Goldberg, 2001; Brooks, Halloway, & Kim, in preparation; Matthews & Cramer, 2006; National Adoption Information Clearinghouse, 2000). Given the research-based evidence, along with changes in societal demographics and mores, it is not surprising that there has been dramatically growing acceptance of gay adoption in the United States and around the world (Brodzinsky, 2003; Brodzinsky, this volume; Brodzinsky, Patterson, & Vaziri, 2002; Mallon, this volume; Matthews & Cramer, 2006; Miall & March, 2005; Pertman & Howard, this volume).

Substantial research knowledge exists on adoption services and supports (Barth & Miller, 2000; Brooks, Allen, & Barth, 2002; Farber, Timberlake, Mudd, & Cullen, 2003; Kramer & Houston, 1998; Reilly & Platz, 2004; Wind, Brooks, & Barth, 2006), gay and lesbian parenting (Bigner & Bozett, 1990; Crawford, McLeod, Zamboni, & Jordan, 1999; Goldberg, 2010; Golombok & Tasker, 1996; Patterson, 1997), and gay and lesbian adoptive family functioning (Brooks & Goldberg, 2001; Brooks, Halloway, & Kim, in preparation; Erich, Leung, & Kindle, 2005; Farr, Forssell, & Patterson, 2010; Leung, Erich, & Kanenberg, 2005). There is even a small but growing knowledge base on informal social support for gay and lesbian adoptive and foster families (e.g., Kindle & Erich, 2005; Miall & March, 2005). Yet, to date, there has been no systematic investigation of the formal agency services that are needed and used by these families, the helpfulness of such services, or the relationship between services and various aspects of child and family functioning. As a result, adoption and child welfare professionals have little empirical knowledge to draw on when recruiting and preparing gay and lesbian parents for adoption, or when designing and providing supportive postadoption services.

This chapter offers a review of the social and political context of gay and lesbian adoption. It then describes common experiences that gay men and lesbians have as they journey toward and beyond adoptive parenthood. To address some of the gaps in empirical knowledge that are described above, the chapter also presents findings from a recently completed national study of adoptive families. The findings focus on the different service needs gay and lesbian families have before and after adoption, service use, and helpfulness of services used by families. Those involved in adoption practice with gay and lesbian families, as well as adoptive families themselves and the greater adoption community, should benefit from these findings.

THE SOCIAL AND POLITICAL CONTEXT OF GAY AND LESBIAN ADOPTION

Gay and lesbian adoption is not a new phenomenon (Mallon, 2000; Ryan, Pearlmutter, & Groza, 2004). Although there is no single, definitive source on the number of such adoptions, it is believed that about 65,500 children are currently being raised in the United States by their gay or lesbian adoptive parents. Accounting for more than 4 percent of all adoptions, this is almost certainly an underestimate of the actual number of gay adoptions (for reasons discussed below). It is estimated that an additional two million gay, lesbian, or bisexual people are interested in adopting (Gates, Badgett, Macomber, & Chambers, 2007). At the same time, almost 115,000 children across the country are waiting to be adopted (AFCARS, 2010).

Traditionally, adoption agencies (including adoption and permanency planning units of public child welfare agencies) have looked to heterosexual, two-parent or single-parent families as adoptive resources (Ryan et al., 2004). Over the past few decades, however, the types of individuals and relationships considered appropriate for potential adoptive parenthood have changed considerably; consequently, existing policies now reflect a more open attitude toward gay and lesbian adoptive parenting (Brodzinsky, this volume; Kenyon et al., 2003; Mallon, 2007, and this volume; Pertman & Howard, this volume). Federal law does not address whether gay and lesbian individuals or couples can adopt, nor are there uniform state standards. Instead, adoption practice is dictated by the statutes, agency regulations, and court opinions of each state (Appell, this volume; Howard & Freundlich, 2008; Kenyon et al., 2003; Pertman & Howard, this volume). Although all 50 states allow gay men and lesbians to adopt as single individuals,[1] only four states— California, Massachusetts, New Jersey, and Vermont—and the District of Columbia explicitly permit them to do so jointly. Eleven states and Washington, D.C., either implicitly or explicitly, state that sexual orientation cannot be used to prevent an adoption. Mississippi explicitly prohibits same-sex *couples* from adopting but leaves open the question of adoption by single lesbians and gays. Utah and Arkansas prohibit adoption by *couples who are not legally married*, effectively preventing gay and lesbian couples from adopting (although single gay men and lesbians can adopt as long as they are not cohabitating in nonmarital relationships) (Arkansas Code Annotated § 9-9-204; Utah Code Ann. § 78-30-1 et seq.).[1] All other states determine who can and cannot adopt on a case-by-case basis (Ryan et al., 2004). At present, legislators in several other states, including Alabama, Alaska, Michigan, Pennsylvania, Oregon, and Ohio, have introduced or are planning to introduce measures to end gay adoption (Ryan & Brown, this volume) within their borders.

ADOPTION RECRUITMENT, ASSESSMENT, AND SUPPORTT

Beyond legislative hurdles, prospective gay and lesbian adopters routinely experience service-related challenges. These challenges are related to recruitment and assessment of prospective gay and lesbian adoptive families, including being matched with a specific child or *type* of child. Most investigations of gay and lesbian adoption have revolved around its appropriateness as a placement option for children in need of permanent homes. Notwithstanding the lack of federal and empirical guidance, adoption and child welfare agencies are charged with identifying and providing safe and loving homes for available children, and findings from recent studies suggest that agencies generally are willing to place children with gay and lesbian adoptive families. Brodzinsky, Patterson, and Vaziri (2002) conducted the first nationwide survey of adoption agencies' policies and prac tices in relation to working with gay and lesbian prospective adoptive parents. Approximately 63 percent of respondents in their study indicated that their agencies accepted applications from gay and lesbian individuals and couples.

1. On April 7, 2011, the Arkansas supreme court declared the ban on gay/lesbian adoption to be unconstitutional.

Most agencies, however, do not appear to actively and aggressively recruit gay men and lesbians as adoptive parents. In some instances, they operate under a "don't ask, don't tell" policy. Only 16 percent of the agencies in the study by Brodzinsky and his colleagues (2002), for instance, reported reaching out to the lesbian and gay communities as a parenting resource for children needing adoptive homes. Similar findings are reported by Brodzinsky in this volume.

Despite reported openness at the agency level, available evidence suggests that gay men and lesbians interested in becoming adoptive parents continue to be overlooked, underappreciated, and discriminated against by the social workers, professionals, or judges they encounter as they attempt to adopt (Mallon, 2006, and this volume; Brooks & Goldberg, 2001). When conducting assessments and making decisions about the appropriateness of prospective adopters, all states allow the professionals involved in the placement of children to apply the "best interest of the child" standard. These professionals are responsible for assessing the strengths and needs of prospective adoptive families and the match between the short- and long-term needs of individual children awaiting adoptive placement.

As suggested by Ryan et al. (2004), the capacity of professionals to objectively and fully assess parenting ability among a range of family types may be limited. Rather than applying objective decision-making criteria, social workers' values, previous experience, and subjective judgment of particular families seem to drive approval and placement decisions. Furthermore, hidden or ambiguous policies provide no uniform guidance to staff, encourage individual interpretations of laws and regulations, and create misinformation among workers. Mallon (2000) points out that many adoption and child welfare professionals, ill-trained by schools of social work or the agencies in which they work, still hold firm to a belief system that is grounded in numerous negative myths and stereotypes about gay men and lesbians. These attitudes and beliefs are assumed to have a major effect on the professionals' work, including their assessment of nonheterosexuals as potential adoptive parents.

To assist adoption and child welfare professionals in their work with prospective gay and lesbian adopters, Mallon (2007) suggests that these applicants be assessed using the same criteria as for straight applicants (see also Mallon, this volume). Although they may present unique situations, Mallon further suggests that gay and lesbian applicants should not have to pass extraordinary tests to prove they are worthy and capable of adoptive parenting. Each placement decision should be based, instead, on the strengths and needs of the child and the perceived ability of the prospective adoptive family to meet those needs and to further develop the child's strengths. Such an approach is consistent with gay affirmative practice, a strengths-based, culturally sensitive approach to working with clients that recognizes lesbian and gay identity and behavior as healthy (Crisp, 2006).

Agencies and professionals engaging in culturally sensitive practices encourage prospective gay and lesbian adopters to be open and up-front about their sexual orientation. This enables the strengths and needs of the prospective adoptive families to be assessed early in the adoption process. Agencies known to reject applications by gay men and lesbians or that operate under an informal "don't ask, don't tell" policy obviously discourage openness in the process. Brooks and Goldberg (2001) warn that these kinds of policies have very real implications for practice and for children. Social workers who do not ask about sexual orientation and related issues may not invite gay and lesbian parents to acknowledge and address the unique challenges of raising children in their households. This effectively precludes adoption professionals from accurately assessing a prospective family's ability to raise a given child and the suitability of a particular placement.

Brooks and Goldberg (2001) go on to argue that if gay and lesbian prospective adoptive parents are expected to acknowledge and discuss their sexual orientation, it is imperative for the professionals they are working with to assure them that doing so will not jeopardize their chances of having a child placed with them or determine the type of child placed with them. Indeed, findings from Brooks and Goldberg's study and others (Kenyon et al., 2003; Matthews & Cramer, 2006) indicate that gay and lesbian prospective adopters are regularly discriminated against when being matched with specific children or types of children. In particular, these prospective parents reportedly tend to be matched more often with children who have disabilities or behavioral problems, are older, and/or are of nondominant cultural and ethnic backgrounds (regardless of the prospective parents' backgrounds). Kenyon et al. (2003) maintain that the informal practice of matching gay and lesbian parents with the most difficult, special needs, or "less preferred" children is indeed a form of discrimination as it denies choice on the part of the prospective adopters.

Other than these aspects of adoption practice, there has been very little attention in the professional literature to preadoption services and supports for gay and lesbian adoptive parents. There is also a dearth of information about the postadoption service needs of these families. Adopting a child can be stressful for any parent, as it involves changes in the financial, cultural and family system expectations. For gay and lesbian adopters, these stresses can be exacerbated by homophobic and heterosexist societal attitudes. Individuals facing taxing life situations fare much better if they have social support. More specifically, family social support has been identified as a key factor in adoptive family coping and functioning (Brodzinsky, 1990; Ji, Brooks, Barth, & Kim, 2010; Patterson, 2002; Pinderhughes, 1996). Higher levels of perceived social support have been associated with higher adopter satisfaction and improved parent–child interactions. In studies of the adoptions of children with special needs, in particular, higher levels of perceived social support seem to provide a protective buffer effect throughout the family life course (Elizur & Ziv, 2001).

Although most adoptions are successful, some can be quite challenging, especially when they involve children coming from foster care or from orphanages in other countries (Cadoret & Riggins-Caspers, 2000; Crea, Barth, Guo, & Brooks, 2008; Simmel, Barth, & Brooks, 2007; van der Vegt, van der Ende, Kirschbaum, Verhulst, & Tiemeier, 2009). The extent and nature of the need for postadoption services depend largely on whether the children have special needs and whether these needs can be met by existing approaches to service delivery. The dearth of information on postadoptive service needs of gay and lesbian families is particularly significant if, as has been suggested, the parents are often matched with children who have special needs. In light of the limited information in the social casework literature, we carried out a study in order to obtain a better understanding of the unique service needs of gay and lesbian adoptive families, both before and after adoption. Though not directly addressing the question of whether families experienced discrimination based on sexual orientation, our results will help us to better understand whether the biases of adoption professionals and agencies translate into unequal access to needed services and poorer quality of services for gay and lesbian adoptive parents, compared with their straight counterparts.

The study was guided by the following six questions: (1) What are the characteristics of gay and lesbian adoptive families? (2) How well are such families prepared for adoption? (3) What services are needed by and available to these families? (4) What unmet service needs exist for them? (5) What services do they use? (6) Which services do they find most helpful?

THE CURRENT STUDY

Recruitment of Respondents

Respondents in our research were adoptive parents who took part in a large, recently completed national study comparing transracial and within-racial adoptive families. The study was conducted under the auspices of a not-for profit adoption agency (hereafter referred to as "the Agency") located in Northern California. The Agency provides adoption-related services primarily to children of color, their adoptive parents, and their birth parents. Services include preadoption preparation, education, and counseling, postplacement supports, educational and informational services, referrals, and informal social supports.

Respondents were recruited by the Agency using various strategies, including recruitment from among its databases, posting of flyers, Internet and web-based notices, and advertisements in adoption-related publications and newsletters. The Agency also requested that adoption professionals, groups, organizations, and other agencies across the United States forward information about the study to their clients and members. Finally, families were solicited at local and national adoption conferences, and by encouraging adoptive families who expressed an interest or participated in the study to pass information about it to other adoptive families they thought might be willing to participate.

The Agency sent out over 22,000 notices about the study to adoption professionals, agencies, and organizations, adoption support groups, and adoptive families. Because it is not known how many of these individuals and groups actually received the notice and read it, it is impossible to accurately calculate a response rate. Given the nature of recruitment, particularly the snowballing approach that was used, it is also impossible to determine how representative respondents are of those targeted for participation. Approximately 38 percent of the recruitment sources were located in California; the remainder were from 30 different states.

Respondent Selection and Classification

Potential participants were asked to complete a demographic form and return it to the Agency. The information provided was then entered into a database and used to determine the eligibility of the family for participation and to identify a "target" adopted child who would be the focus of the study. Families and children were eligible for participation if each of the following parameters was met: The family had submitted a demographic form, the adoption was finalized, the child was currently over 2 years of age and under 20 years of age, the age at time of placement was under 5 years, the nature of the adoption was clearly identified as either within-racial or transracial, and at least one parent was the original adoptive parent of the child. Eligible families and target children within the families were then randomly selected based on sampling goals set by the agency. These goals were established to ensure a broad representation of families with respect to adoption type (i.e., transracial vs. within-racial), ethnicity of the child, age of the child, and gender of the child. Adoptive parents from families selected for participation were then mailed packets containing a cover letter, survey, and self-addressed, stamped envelope to be used to return the survey.

Among the questions included on the demographic form used to determine eligibility for participation was one asking respondents to describe their households. Response categories for this question included (1) heterosexual and (2) gay and lesbian. Of the 1196 families completing the survey, 1153 (96 percent) provided a response to this question. Of those, 82 (7.1 percent) were classified as gay and lesbian families and the remaining 1071 (92.8 percent) were classified as straight families. These comprised the comparison groups for the study.

Data Collection

Data were collected using the demographic form utilized to determine eligibility and an additional mailed survey. The demographic form contained questions pertaining to characteristics of respondents and their families, including information about their adopted children. The survey asked for additional information about the adopted children and the adoption experience, as well as information on family characteristics and well-being and adoption services and supports. The latter items addressed issues such as the need for particular services and supports, as well as their availability and helpfulness. Families were also asked how well prepared they felt for adopting their children and, separately, how well the professionals working with them prepared them for the adoption.

Analyses

Descriptive statistics are presented as frequencies, percentages, means, and standard deviations (SDs). Two sample Student's t tests were performed for between-group comparisons (i.e., gay and lesbian vs. straight) of continuous variables.

Pearson's χ^2 tests or Kolmogorov–Smirnov sample tests were performed for between-group comparisons of nominal and ordinal variables. For dichotomous data, binomial tests were used to determine if the proportion of gay and lesbian adoptive families falling in each category differed from observed probabilities of straight adoptive families falling into those categories. A p value less than 0.05 was used to indicate statistical significance.

RESULTS

Characteristics of Adoptive Families and Children

Tables 8.1 and 8.2 describe the characteristics of respondents, their families, and their adopted children. As noted previously, approximately 7 percent ($n = 82$) of the total sample of adoptive families in this study ($n = 1153$) was headed by gay men or lesbians. In many ways, the characteristics of gay and lesbian and heterosexual families were similar (see Tables 8.1 and 8.2), but there were differences as well. A greater percentage of mothers completed surveys in straight families than in gay and lesbian families. Compared with their straight counterparts, respondents from gay and lesbian families were more likely to have attained higher levels

Table 8.1 FAMILY CHARACTERISTICS

Characteristic	All Families (N = 1153)	Gay/Lesbian Families (N = 82)	Straight Families (N = 1071)	p
	%	%	%	
Respondent				
Mother	92.5	80.2	93.4	<0.05[a]
Father	7.5	19.8	6.6	
Respondent's current marital and relationship status				
Single	17.7	19.2	17.6	NS[a]
Living with partner or married	82.3	80.8	82.4	
Respondents' marital and relationship status at the time of adoption				
Single	16.7	18.2	16.6	NS[a]
Living with partner or married	83.3	81.8	83.4	
Current household characteristics among two-parent households				
Same race couple	87.9	86.2	88.0	NS[4]
Interracial couple	12.1	13.8	12.0	

Table 8.1 (Continued)

Characteristic	All Families (N = 1153)	Gay/Lesbian Families (N = 82)	Straight Families (N = 1071)	p
	%	%	%	
Respondent's mean age (years)	44.26 (SD = 6.95)	43.32 (SD = 6.38)	44.32 (SD = 7.00)	NS[b]
Respondent's partner and spouse's mean age (years)	44.76 (SD = 9.72)	43.36 (SD = 14.96)	44.86 (SD = 9.24)	NS[b]
Respondent's highest level of education				
Graduate school	50.1	71.3	48.5	
Four-year college	30.4	22.5	31.0	<0.05[a]
Junior and community college, AA, or	12.0	2.5	12.7	
vocational school	7.5	3.8	7.8	
Grade school and high school or GED				
Respondent's partner and spouse's highest level of education				
Graduate School	41.6	64.4	40.0	
Four-year college	31.9	22.0	32.6	<0.05[a]
Junior and community college, AA, or	13.8	10.2	14.1	
vocational school	12.7	3.4	13.4	
Grade school and high school or GED				
Respondent's race and ethnicity				
White or caucasian	74.5	81.7	73.9	
Black or African American	13.5	13.4	13.5	NS[a]
Asian or Pacific Islander	7.2	3.7	7.5	
Hispanic or Latino	3.9	1.2	4.1	
Other[c]	1.0	0.0	1.0	
Respondent's partner and spouse's race and ethnicity	74.8	78.8	74.4	
White or caucasian	13.1	12.2	13.2	NS[a]
Black or African-American	7.3	3.0	7.6	
Asian or Pacific Islander	3.9	4.5	3.9	
Hispanic or Latino	0.9	1.5	0.9	
Other[c]				
Household gross income				
Less than $39,999	9.9	8.8	10.0	
$40,000–$59,999	17.7	20.0	17.5	NS[a]
$60,000–$79,999	17.5	13.8	17.7	
$80,000–$99,999	18.9	20.0	18.8	
$100,000–$149,999	21.2	21.3	21.2	
$150,000 or more	14.8	16.3	14.7	

Table 8.1 (CONTINUED)

Characteristic	All Families (N = 1153)	Gay/Lesbian Families (N = 82)	Straight Families (N = 1071)	p
	%	%	%	
Community where family currently resides				
Urban (approximately 50,000 or more)	42.1	58.0	40.8	
Large town (approximately 10,000–50,000)	35.7	24.7	36.6	<0.05[a]
Small town (approximately 2,500–10,000)	15.8	7.4	16.4	
Rural or farm (approximately less than 2,500)	6.4	9.9	6.2	
Importance of role of religion or spirituality in family				
Very important	52.0	39.5	52.9	NS[a]
Somewhat important	38.5	54.3	37.3	
Not at all important	9.5	6.2	9.8	
Religion family practices				
Christian	73.5	39.4	76.1	
Jewish	8.4	22.5	7.3	<0.05[a]
Other[d]	18.1	38.0	16.6	
Mean number of children in family	2.62 (SD = 1.94)	1.94 (SD = 1.22)	2.67 (SD = 1.98)	<0.05[b]
Mean number of adopted children	2.45 (SD = 7.66)	1.67 (SD = 0.89)	2.51 (SD = 7.94)	NS[b]
Mean number of birth children	0.65 (SD = 1.14)	0.27 (SD = 0.80)	0.68 (SD = 1.16)	<0.05[b]

NOTES: [a]Chi-Square tests.
[b]Student's *t* test.
[c]Other includes Arab, Native American, or American Indian, and other racial groups.
[d]Other includes Buddhist, Hindu, Muslim, and other religious groups.

of formal education and to reside in urban areas. The percentage of families indicating that the role of religion or spirituality in their lives was "very important" was larger for straight families (53 percent) than for gay and lesbian families (40 percent). When asked what religion their family practices, respondents from straight families were nearly twice as likely as respondents from gay and lesbian families to indicate Christian (76 percent vs. 39 percent), whereas gay and lesbian respondents were more likely than straight respondents to indicate Judaism (23 percent vs. 7 percent) or some other religion (38 percent vs. 17 percent). For straight families, the total number of children (by adoption and birth) and the number of birth children was higher than for gay and lesbian families; the groups did not differ in the number of adopted children in the family.

Table 8.2 shows that adopted children were similar across the two groups in terms of their gender, ethnicity, type of adoption (i.e., within-racial vs. transracial), mean age at adoption, and how they were adopted (i.e., internationally, through a public or private agency, or independently). They differed in two

Table 8.2 CHILD CHARACTERISTICS

Characteristic	All Families (*N* = 1153)	Gay/Lesbian Families (*N* = 82)	Straight Families (*N* = 1071)	*p*
	%	%	%	
Child's gender				
Female	56.5	59.3	56.3	NS[a]
Male	43.5	40.7	43.7	
Child's race and ethnicity				
Black or African-American	40.4	53.7	39.4	NS[a]
Asian or Pacific Islander	32.4	25.6	32.9	
Hispanic or Latino	19.5	14.6	19.9	
White or Caucasian	6.1	3.7	6.0	
Other[c]	1.9	2.4	1.8	
Type of adoption				
Transracial	73.6	81.7	73.0	NS[a]
Interracial[d]	26.4	18.3	27.0	
Child's mean age at the time of adoption (years)	2.32 (SD = 2.15)	2.32 (SD = 2.24)	2.32 (SD = 2.14)	NS[b]
Child's mean age (years)	6.39 (SD = 4.07)	4.89 (SD = 3.00)	6.51 (SD = 4.12)	<0.05[b]
How adopted				
International	44.9	34.1	45.7	NS[a]
Public	21.8	29.3	21.2	
Private	26.0	28.0	25.8	
Independent	7.4	8.5	7.3	
Prior to adoption, child placed in out-of-home care				
Yes	80.2	69.5	81.0	<0.05[a]
No	19.8	30.5	19.0	

NOTES: [a]Chi-Square tests.
[b]Two-independent sample *t* test.
[c]Other includes Arab, Native American, or American Indian, and other racial groups.
[d]Either one or two parents have the same ethnic background as the adopted child.

respects, however. Contrary to findings in previous research, children in our study who were adopted by gay and lesbian families were significantly younger than those adopted by straight families ($x = 4.89$ years vs. 6.51 years), and less likely to have been placed in out-of-home care prior to adoption. Approximately 70 percent of children in gay and lesbian families had been in out-of-home care, compared to 81 percent of children in straight families.

Preparation for Adoption

The survey included two questions pertaining to respondents' preparation for adoption (see Table 8.3). The first one asked parents how prepared they felt to adopt their children, and the second asked how well the professionals working with their family prepared them for the adoption. Gay and lesbian families were similar to straight families in their responses to both questions. Approximately 95 percent of all respondents said they felt prepared to adopt, with 31 percent reporting they felt "very well prepared," 36 percent "well prepared," and 28 percent "somewhat well prepared." Fewer than 5 percent indicated they felt "not well prepared at all."

In terms of the preparation they received from the professionals working with them, the majority of all respondents (approximately 82 percent), regardless of

Table 8.3 PREPAREDNESS FOR ADOPTION

Characteristic	All Families (N = 1,153)	Gay/Lesbian Families (N = 82)	Straight Families (N = 1071)	p
	%	%	%	
How prepared did you feel to adopt this child?				
Very well prepared	31.4	27.0	31.7	NS[a]
Well prepared	36.0	37.0	36.0	
Somewhat well prepared	27.9	28.4	27.9	
Not well prepared at all	4.7	7.4	4.5	
How well did the professionals working with your family prepare you to adopt this child?				
Very well	25.0	25.1	22.5	NS[b]
Well	28.0	28.6	21.3	
Somewhat well	29.3	28.9	33.8	
Not well at all	17.7	17.4	22.5	

NOTES: [a]Kolmogorov–Smirnov $Z = 0.392$, $n = 1132$, $p > 0.05$.
[b]Kolmogorov–Smirnov $Z = 0.998$, $n = 1134$, $p > 0.05$.

sexual orientation, felt they had been well, somewhat well, or very well prepared to adopt, with the remaining 18 percent indicating that they felt "not well at all" prepared by such professionals.

Social Service Availability, Need, and Utilization

Next, we were interested in learning more about the needs and availability of different kinds of services and supports. Tables 8.4a (clinical services) and 8.4b (educational and information services) present respondents' reports of the services and supports they needed and the ones they believed were available to them. As can be seen in Table 8.4a, the clinical services most needed by adoptive families in our sample included opportunities for children to meet other children of the same racial and ethnic background (77 percent), support groups for preadoptive parents (66 percent), and support groups for parents adopting transracially. The groups differed in two ways: greater percentages of gay and lesbian families said they needed "marital" or individual counseling (43 percent vs. 27 percent) and respite care (35 percent vs. 20 percent). In terms of the availability of services, there were no differences between the groups.

As can be seen in Table 8.4b, substantial proportions of respondents expressed a need for educational and informational services, including reading material on adoption (91 percent), information on their children's medical or genetic history (85 percent), information on their children's social history or preadoption background (79 percent), lectures and seminars on adoption (77 percent), reading material on transracial adoption (75 percent), classes and workshops on understanding adopted children (71 percent), information about challenges associated with transracial adoption (70 percent), information about common experiences for transracial adoptive families (70 percent), information about their children's racial and ethnic groups (68 percent), Internet-based resources (64 percent), information about their children's racial and ethnic background (63 percent), lectures and seminars on transracial adoption (60 percent), classes on how to communicate with their children about adoption (55 percent), and legal advice (54 percent). Gay and lesbian families were more likely than straight ones to indicate that they needed the following services: information on their children's genetic history (93 percent vs. 84 percent), lectures and seminars on transracial adoption (73 percent vs. 59 percent), and information on how to search for their children's birth relatives (67 percent vs. 53 percent).

In terms of the reported availability of services, gay and lesbian families were more likely to report the availability of the following services: lectures and seminars on adoption (92 percent vs. 82 percent), classes and workshops on understanding adopted children (85 percent vs. 72 percent), lectures and seminars on transracial adoption (72 percent vs. 53 percent), and information about their children's racial and ethnic background (71 percent vs. 64 percent).

Table 8.4a Needs and Availability of Services: Clinical Services

Service	All Families (N = 1153)		Gay/Lesbian Families (N = 82)		Straight Families (N = 1071)	
	Needed %	*Available* %	*Needed* %	*Available* %	*Needed* %	*Available* %
Support group for preadoptive parents	65.7	71.1	57.3	69.5	66.4	71.2
Preadoptive support group for children being placed for adoption	23.2	21.1	26.8	14.6	23.0	21.6
Marital or individual counseling*	28.3	60.5	42.7	62.2	27.2	60.4
Child counseling	31.7	59.8	39.0	67.1	31.2	59.2
Family therapy	24.9	59.4	28.0	56.1	24.6	59.7
Intensive crisis counseling	13.3	44.5	14.6	41.5	13.2	44.7
Counseling group for preadoptive parents	33.8	41.5	28.0	39.0	34.3	41.6
Preadoptive counseling group for children being placed for adoption	15.4	18.0	11.0	15.9	15.7	18.2
Respite care*	20.6	23.3	35.4	29.3	19.5	22.9
Support group for parents adopting transracially	56.5	47.4	56.1	45.1	56.6	47.0
Support group for children being adopted transracially	40.0	26.5	35.4	20.7	40.3	27.0
Opportunities for children to meet other children of the same race and ethnic background	77.0	69.1	83.5	76.8	76.4	68.5

NOTES: *p < .05 (2-tailed). *Binomial tests were performed to test proportional difference between two groups in *services needed* (percentage of straight families were used as test statistic).

Table 8.4b NEEDS AND AVAILABILITY OF SERVICES: EDUCATIONAL
AND INFORMATIONAL SERVICES

Service	All Families (N = 1153)		Gay/Lesbian Families (N = 82)		Straight Families (N = 1071)	
	Needed %	Available %	Needed %	Available %	Needed %	Available %
Reading material on adoption	90.8	93.3	91.5	93.9	90.8	93.3
Lectures and seminars on adoption*	77.0	82.5	80.5	91.5	76.7	81.8
Classes and workshops on understanding adopted children*	70.6	72.9	76.8	85.4	70.1	71.9
Classes on how to communicate with your adopted child about adoption	54.9	55.9	51.2	59.8	55.2	55.6
Classes for extended family members on understanding adoption	31.3	15.4	29.3	13.4	31.5	15.6
Information on child's social history or preadoption background	78.9	56.7	84.1	63.4	78.5	56.2
Information on child's medical history or genetic history*	84.6	47.5	92.7	52.4	83.9	47.1
Legal advice†	53.7	64.4	67.1	69.5	52.7	64.0
Information on how to search for child's birth relatives	35.7	29.1	35.4	35.4	35.8	28.6
Information about child's racial and ethnic background	62.6	64.8	65.9	70.7	62.4	64.3
Reading material on transracial adoption*	75.2	76.4	84.1	86.6	74.5	75.6
Lectures and seminars on transracial adoption*,†	59.9	54.5	73.1	72.0	58.9	53.1

Table 8.4b (Continued)

Service	All Families (N = 1153)		Gay/Lesbian Families (N = 82)		Straight Families (N = 1071)	
	Needed %	Available %	Needed %	Available %	Needed %	Available %
Information about child's racial and ethnic group	68.4	65.9	74.4	75.6	68.0	65.2
Information about challenges associated with transracial adoption*	70.0	61.1	79.3	73.2	69.3	60.1
Information about common experiences for transracial adoptive families*	70.0	56.5	80.5	70.7	69.2	55.5
Web- or Internet-based resources	64.3	65.0	68.3	68.3	64.0	64.8

NOTES: *$p < 0.05$ (two-tailed). *Binomial tests were performed to test the proportional difference between two groups in *service availability* (percentage of straight families was used as the test statistic).

†$p < 0.05$ (two-tailed). †Binomial tests were performed to test the proportional difference between two groups in *services needed* (percentage of straight families was used as the test statistic).

   Information on and availability of needed services, as perceived by respondents, was used to calculate unmet clinical and educational and informational service needs variables. For all respondents, the greatest unmet clinical service needs (see Table 8.5a) were for preadoptive counseling groups for children being placed for adoption (75 percent), preadoptive support groups for children being placed for adoption (62 percent), respite care (59 percent), and support groups for children being adopted transracially (57 percent). Gay and lesbian respondents differed from their straight counterparts in only one instance: They were more likely to report an unmet need for preadoptive counseling groups for children being placed for adoption (100 percent vs. 73 percent).

   As can be seen in Table 8.5b, there is a particularly large unmet need for all respondents for classes for extended family members on understanding adoption (84 percent) and for information on how to search for their children's birth relatives (64 percent). Respondents differed in two respects: Straight families were more likely to have unmet educational and informational needs in terms of classes and workshops on understanding adopted children (16 percent vs. 5 percent), and classes on how to communicate with their children about adoption (25 percent vs. 8 percent).

Table 8.6 summarizes respondents' utilization of clinical and educational and informational services. Parents were asked to indicate the helpfulness of various services they had received (described later in Table 8.7). Responses indicating any level of helpfulness (i.e., "not helpful," "somewhat helpful," or "very helpful") were classified as having utilized the service. As can be seen in Table 8.6, our respondents seem to have utilized educational and informational services, overall, more than clinical services. Of the latter services, respondents were most likely to have utilized opportunities for children to meet other children of the same race and ethnic background (64 percent) and support groups for preadoptive parents (57 percent).

Table 8.5a UNMET NEEDS: CLINICAL SERVICES

Service	All Families		Gay/Lesbian Families		Straight Families	
	n	%	*n*	%	*n*	%
Support group for preadoptive parents	747	19.5	46	19.6	701	19.5
Preadoptive support group for children being placed for adoption	234	61.5	19	63.2	215	61.4
Marital or individual counseling	317	11.7	35	17.1	282	11.0
Child counseling	355	11.8	31	6.5	324	12.3
Family therapy	271	12.2	23	13.0	248	12.1
Intensive crisis counseling	144	31.9	9	33.3	135	31.9
Counseling group for preadoptive parents	370	38.1	19	31.6	351	38.5
Preadoptive counseling group for children being placed for adoption*	151	74.2	6	100.0	145	73.1
Respite care	226	58.8	28	60.7	198	58.6
Support group for parents adopting transracially	632	37.0	43	46.5	589	36.3
Support group for children being adopted transracially	435	56.8	24	66.7	411	56.2
Opportunities for children to meet other children of the same race and ethnic background	859	12.9	69	13.0	790	12.9

NOTES: *$p < 0.05$ (two-tailed). Binomial tests were performed to test the proportional difference between two groups in unmet need (percentage of straight families was used as the test statistic).

Table 8.5b UNMET NEEDS: EDUCATIONAL AND INFORMATIONAL SERVICES

Service	All Families		Gay/Lesbian Families		Straight Families	
	n	%	*n*	%	*n*	%
Reading material on adoption	1027	1.7	74	2.7	953	1.6
Lectures and seminars on adoption	872	7.8	66	3.0	806	8.2
Classes and workshops on understanding adopted children*	787	15.2	62	4.8	725	16.1
Classes on how to communicate with your adopted child about adoption*	607	23.9	38	7.9	569	25.0
Classes for extended family members on understanding adoption	344	84.3	22	81.8	322	84.5
Information on child's social history or preadoption background	886	32.3	69	29.0	817	32.6
Information on child's medical history or genetic history	939	45.5	74	44.6	865	45.5
Legal advice	598	12.4	52	11.5	546	12.5
Information on how to search for child's birth relatives	385	64.2	27	55.6	358	64.8
Information about child's racial and ethnic background	708	11.7	54	11.1	654	11.8
Reading material on transracial adoption	849	4.9	69	4.3	780	5.0
Lectures and seminars on transracial adoption	672	23.8	60	13.3	612	24.8
Information about child's racial and ethnic group	761	10.6	61	6.6	700	11.0
Information about challenges associated with transracial adoption	781	19.6	63	11.1	718	20.3
Information about common experiences for transracial adoptive families	784	25.9	66	16.7	718	26.7
Web- or Internet-based resources	702	15.2	55	14.5	647	15.3

NOTES: *$p < 0.05$ (two-tailed). Binomial tests were performed to test the proportional difference between two groups in unmet need (percentage of straight families was used as the test statistic).

Of the educational and information services, respondents were most likely to have utilized the following: reading material on adoption (89 percent), lectures and seminars on adoption (71 percent), reading material on transracial adoption (69 percent), classes and workshops on understanding adopted children (58 percent), information about their children's racial and ethnic groups (56 percent), information on their children's social history or preadoption background (54 percent), and information on their children's racial and ethnic background (51 percent). Gay and lesbian adopters differed from their straight counterparts in that greater proportions of the former group utilized respite care (16 percent vs. 8 percent), classes and workshops on understanding adopted children (71 percent vs. 57 percent), lectures and seminars on transracial adoption (61 percent vs. 44 percent), and information about common experiences for transracial adoptive

Table 8.6 SERVICES UTILIZED

Service	All Families (*N* = 1153)	Gay/Lesbian Families (*N* = 82)	Straight Families (*N* = 1071)
	%	%	%
CLINICAL			
Support group for preadoptive parents*	56.7	40.2	58.0
Preadoptive support group for children being placed for adoption	10.6	7.3	10.8
Marital or individual counseling	24.4	29.3	24.0
Child counseling	25.8	26.8	25.7
Family therapy	19.0	17.1	19.1
Intensive crisis counseling	9.3	6.1	9.5
Counseling group for preadoptive parents*	20.1	11.0	20.8
Preadoptive counseling group for children being placed for adoption	3.6	0.0	3.8
Respite care*	8.2	15.9	7.7
Support group for parents adopting transracially	34.4	24.4	35.2
Support group for children being adopted transracially*	15.4	4.9	16.2
Opportunities for children to meet other children of same race and ethnic background	64.4	73.2	63.8

Table 8.6 (CONTINUED)

Service	All Families (N = 1153)	Gay/Lesbian Families (N = 82)	Straight Families (N = 1071)
	%	%	%
EDUCATIONAL AND INFORMATIONAL			
Reading material on adoption	89.1	92.7	89.4
Lectures and seminars on adoption	71.1	84.1	70.8
Classes and workshops on understanding adopted children*	57.8	70.7	56.8
Classes on how to communicate with your adopted child about adoption	38.1	41.5	37.8
Classes for extended family members on understanding adoption	4.1	3.7	4.1
Information on child's social history or preadoption background	53.8	62.2	53.1
Information on child's medical history or genetic history	47.5	51.2	47.2
Legal advice	43.5	53.7	42.8
Information on how to search for child's birth relatives	10.6	11.0	10.6
Information about child's racial and ethnic background	50.8	53.7	50.6
Reading material on transracial adoption	69.0	78.0	68.3
Lectures and seminars on transracial adoption*	45.3	61.0	44.1
Information about child's racial and ethnic group	55.9	62.2	55.4
Information about challenges associated with transracial adoption	53.2	61.0	52.6
Information about common experiences for transracial adoptive families*	49.4	61.0	48.6
Web- or Internet-based resources	50.0	48.8	50.1

NOTES: *$p < 0.05$ (two-tailed). Binomial tests were performed to test the proportional difference between two groups in service utilization (percentage of straight families was used as the test statistic).

families (61 percent vs. 49 percent). Gay and lesbian adopters were *less* likely to
have utilized support groups for preadoptive parents (40 percent vs. 58 percent),
counseling groups for preadoptive parents (11 percent vs. 21 percent), and support groups for children being adopted transracially (5 percent vs. 16 percent).

Social Services and Support Helpfulness

Respondents were asked to indicate the level of helpfulness of the services they
had received using a three-point scale: 0 = not helpful, 1 = somewhat helpful, and
2 = very helpful. The mean values of helpfulness are reported in Table 8.7, with

Table 8.7 HELPFULNESS OF SERVICES RECEIVED[a]

Service	All Families (N = 1153)	Gay/Lesbian Families (N = 82)	Straight Families (N = 1,071)
	Mean (SD)	Mean (SD)	Mean (SD)
CLINICAL			
Support group for preadoptive parents	1.60 (0.57)	1.36 (0.74)	1.61 (0.55)
Preadoptive support group for children being placed for adoption	1.33 (0.79)	1.50 (0.84)	1.32 (0.79)
Marital or individual counseling	1.37 (0.68)	1.42 (0.78)	1.37 (0.67)
Child counseling*	1.38 (0.68)	1.64 (0.49)	1.36 (0.69)
Family therapy	1.39 (0.69)	1.57 (.65)	1.38 (.69)
Intensive crisis counseling	1.18 (0.77)	1.40 (0.89)	1.17 (0.77)
Counseling group for preadoptive parents	1.47 (0.65)	1.56 (0.73)	1.47 (0.65)
Preadoptive counseling group for children being placed for adoption	.98 (0.88)	n/a	.98 (0.88)
Respite care	1.48 (0.76)	1.62 (0.65)	1.46 (0.77)
Support group for parents adopting transracially	1.58 (0.56)	1.75 (0.55)	1.57 (0.56)
Support group for children being adopted transracially	1.42 (0.64)	1.75 (0.50)	1.41 (0.65)
Opportunities for children to meet other children of same race and ethnic background	1.68 (0.50)	1.73 (0.45)	1.68 (0.50)

Table 8.7 (CONTINUED)

Service	All Families (N = 1153)	Gay/Lesbian Families (N = 82)	Straight Families (N = 1,071)
	Mean (SD)	Mean (SD)	Mean (SD)
EDUCATIONAL AND INFORMATIONAL			
Reading material on adoption	1.70 (0.47)	1.62 (0.49)	1.71 (0.46)
Lectures and seminars on adoption	1.61 (0.53)	1.58 (0.60)	1.61 (0.52)
Classes and workshops on understanding adopted children	1.53 (0.55)	1.55 (0.73)	1.52 (0.55)
Classes on how to communicate with your adopted child about adoption*	1.52 (0.56)	1.71 (0.46)	1.51 (0.57)
Classes for extended family members on understanding adoption	.98 (0.79)	1.67 (0.58)	.93 (0.79)
Information on child's social history or preadoption background	1.49 (0.58)	1.45 (0.58)	1.49 (0.58)
Information on child's medical history or genetic history	1.43 (0.62)	1.36 (0.62)	1.43 (0.62)
Legal advice*	1.55 (0.58)	1.73 (0.50)	1.53 (0.59)
Information on how to search for child's birth relatives	1.31 (0.71)	1.44 (0.53)	1.30 (0.72)
Information about child's racial and ethnic background	1.53 (0.56)	1.64 (0.49)	1.52 (0.57)
Reading material on transracial adoption	1.61 (0.50)	1.58 (0.50)	1.61 (0.50)
Lectures and seminars on transracial adoption	1.56 (0.54)	1.58 (0.57)	1.56 (0.54)
Information about child's racial and ethnic group	1.54 (0.54)	1.61 (0.49)	1.53 (0.54)
Information about challenges associated with transracial adoption	1.50 (0.54)	1.56 (0.54)	1.50 (0.54)
Information about common experiences for transracial adoptive families	1.52 (.52)	1.56 (.54)	1.52 (.52)
Web- or Internet-based resources	1.50 (.58)	1.35 (.66)	1.51 (.57)

NOTES: [a]Helpfulness of service was measured with a three-point scale: 0 = not helpful, 1 = somewhat helpful, and 2 = very helpful. Higher values indicate greater levels of helpfulness.

*$p < 0.05$.

higher values indicating greater levels of helpfulness. The greatest levels of help-fulness of clinical services were for support groups for preadoptive parents, sup-port groups for parents adopting transracially, and opportunities for children to meet other children of their same racial and ethnic background. The greatest levels of helpfulness of educational and informational services were for reading material on adoption, lectures, and seminars on adoption, and reading material on transracial adoption. Worth noting is that the lowest levels of helpfulness for services were for preadoptive counseling for children being placed for adoption (a clinical service) and classes for extended family members on understanding adoption (an educational and information service).

The two groups of respondents differed in terms of their reported levels of helpfulness for child counseling (a clinical service), with gay and lesbian parents reporting a higher level of helpfulness than straight ones. The groups also differed in terms of the reported levels of helpfulness for two educational and information services; gay and lesbian respondents found classes on how to communicate with their children about adoption, as well as legal advice, more helpful than did straight respondents.

DISCUSSION

Findings from our research demonstrate both similarities and differences between gay and lesbian adoptive families and straight ones in relation to the characteris-tics of the two groups, their service needs before and after adoption, service use, and helpfulness of services that they utilized. We will briefly summarize these similarities and then highlight differences between these two adoptive family forms, before closing with implications for practice and future research.

What Are the Characteristics of Gay and Lesbian Adoptive Families?

To begin, findings show that approximately 7 percent of the respondents in the sample were gay and lesbian adoptive families. This is higher than previous estimates of the ratio of gay and lesbian families among the population of adop-tive families living in the United States. In their report on adoption and foster care by gay and lesbian parents, Gates et al. (2007) estimated that about 4 percent of adoptions are completed by gay men and lesbians. Brodzinsky et al. (2002) found in their study that 1.6 percent of all placements reported by the responding agencies involved placements with self-identified lesbian and gay individuals and couples. Some of the agencies in the study could not or would not attempt to estimate the actual number of placements they made with gay and lesbian clients. In these instances, the researchers coded the number of placements as "1." Furthermore, as Brodzinsky and his colleagues point out, families do not always self-disclose sexual orientation. Thus, the incidence of gay and lesbian placements in the study by Brodzinsky et al. likely underestimated the actual percentage of gay and lesbian adoptions. On the other hand, it is also quite possible that there was an overrepresentation of gay and lesbian adoptive parents in our latest study. This is a likely scenario given the large number of respondents from California and from urban areas in which larger numbers of gay men and lesbians reside. It is therefore reasonable to conclude that the true number of adoptive families currently in the United States lies somewhere between 2 percent and 7 percent of all adoptive families. Given demographic trends and increasing openness toward gays and lesbians, including their adoption of children, it is likely that the proportion of such adoptions will increase in the years to come.

Our findings are also important in that they offer empirical data about the types of children adopted by gay men and lesbians. There has been considerable speculation and some evidence (e.g., Brooks & Goldberg, 2001; Matthews & Cramer, 2006) that gay men and lesbian adopters are typically matched with children who have special needs—that is, children often considered hard to place. Yet our findings indicate that gay men and lesbians are adopting children similar to those placed with straight adopters. If anything, our data suggest that gay and lesbian families may be less likely to adopt special needs children, at least among those who adopt children under the age of 5 years. Only 70 percent of gay and lesbian respondents adopted children previously placed in out-of-home care, such as foster care, compared with 81 percent of straight adopters. Unfortunately, we did not ask respondents directly about the special needs characteristics of their children, so we are unable to say definitively whether the characteristics of the children in our study reflect those in the larger adopted child population.

Perception of Preparation for Adoption

Irrespective of the characteristics of the children who were adopted, respondents in our study were similar to one another in terms of the preparation they received prior to adoptive placement. Retrospectively, about two-thirds of all these adoptive parents reported feeling very well or well prepared to adopt overall. They were also similar in terms of their feelings about how well professionals working with their families prepared them for adoption, with over half indicating that they felt very well or well prepared by these professionals. Initially, these results are somewhat surprising given findings from past studies (Brooks & Goldberg, 2001; Mathews & Cramer, 2006) suggesting that gay men and lesbians regularly experience discrimination in the preadoption phase of their adoption process. However, numerous studies (Brooks & Goldberg, 2001; Downs & James, 2006; Brooks, Halloway, & Kim, in preparation) on gay and lesbian adoptive and foster parenting reveal that gay men and lesbians have special strengths and may be particularly resourceful. Studies also show that they are persistent. Gates et al. (2007) found that lesbians, on average, are more interested in adopting and more likely to take active steps toward doing so than are straight women. In their study of gay, lesbian, and bisexual foster parents, Downs and James (2006) found that 44 percent of the female and 56 percent of the male participants who had encountered legal challenges to becoming or remaining foster parents because of their sexual orientation were not initially approved, but challenged that denial and subsequently went on to become foster parents.

The available literature suggests it is quite likely that the gay and lesbian families in our study encountered discrimination in their adoption experiences. It is also likely that the kind of resourcefulness displayed by participants in the study by Downs and James (2006) allowed participants in our study to locate agencies and workers who were accepting and encouraging of them regardless of (or perhaps because of) their sexual orientation. Future studies should ask gay and lesbian adoptive parents about the specific experiences they have had with various agencies and workers at all stages of their adoption journey—not just the ones they were involved with when they eventually adopted—as well as specific questions regarding preparation for the unique challenges experienced by gay and lesbian adopters, such as coming out to the child, addressing discrimination in community settings, and more. Notwithstanding the possibility of a selection bias, our findings suggest that gay and lesbian adopters generally feel as well prepared as straight adopters and feel similarly well prepared by their adoption professionals.

Adoption Services Availability

With respect to the availability of services, our findings suggest that gay and lesbian and straight adoptive families are similar in most regards. When differences do exist, gay and lesbian adopters are more likely than their straight counterparts to report that a service *was available* to them. This is an important finding as it intimates that although gay men and lesbians may experience discrimination due to their sexual orientation (particularly during the preadoption phase), they are either not denied access to needed services or, consistent with their tenacity in engaging in the adoption process, they are more assertive in seeking them out. Our data do not, however, indicate whether gay men and lesbians must exert more energy to access services, or to the quality of service delivery. Future research examining the basis of perceived service availability could enhance actual access for all adoptive families.

Adoption Services Need, Use, and Helpfulness

SERVICE NEED
Overall, gay and lesbian adoptive families appear to be similar to straight adoptive families with respect to their needs for educational and informational services. There were some differences between the two groups, however. For instance, over two-thirds of gay and lesbian respondents reported needing legal advice, compared with just over half of straight families. This finding is almost certainly

related to the nature of gay and lesbian adoption as a family form (see Appell, this volume). In most states, gay and lesbian individuals cannot marry and therefore do not have the legal entitlements or protections afforded by marriage. As such, they are burdened with tasks that married couples are not. For example, the children with married parents are legally entitled to inheritance, Social Security, health insurance, parental care and support, and access to sibling and extended family relationships (Appell, this volume). A central issue, then, relates to the legal parental status in relation to the children.

Across the country, courts have struggled to address the legality of two-parent, nonmarital, same-sex adoption. Until recently, only one parent in lesbian and gay families has been recognized as the legal parent, either via biological means or formal adoption. In gay and lesbian adoptive families in which only one partner is considered the legal parent, the other partner has no legal standing. If the legal parent dies, the child becomes a legal orphan. If the couple separates, the nonlegal adult–child relationship is left unprotected, both in terms of visitation and the child's right to parental financial support (Adoption Education Center, 2007). Because in most states joint-parent adoption requires the partners to be married (Appell, this volume), the growing practice of second-parent adoption is the primary method for lesbian and gay couples to have both partners be considered legal parents of their child (Mallon, 2006), thereby providing equal legal protections for both adults and children. Considering the ramifications, it is no surprise that a greater proportion of gay and lesbian adopters in this study expressed a need for legal advice than did straight parents.

Gay and lesbian respondents were also more likely to express a need for lectures and seminars on transracial adoption, even though they were no more likely than straight respondents to adopt transracially. This finding may be related to their existing sensitivity regarding issues of family diversity. Studies have suggested that gay men and lesbians may be especially suited for adoptive parenting because of their experiences as members of a minority group, which contribute to an ability to accept differences and to better understand what it is like to be in a minority (Martin, 1993; Matthews & Cramer, 2006). In short, in preparing to adopt children of different racial and ethnic backgrounds, gay men and lesbians may be more attuned to issues of diversity and discrimination as a result of their own experiences, and therefore seek additional information and/or training related to the complexities associated with transracial adoption.

The finding that a greater percentage of gay and lesbian than straight respondents indicated a need for information about their children's medical or genetic history requires further examination. Children from both groups tended to be younger when adopted—just over 2 years of age. They were also similar in terms of how they were adopted. So it is not immediately clear why gay and lesbian respondents would be more interested in this information. Many adopted children, particularly those not adopted as infants, have experienced varying forms of adversity such as trauma, neglect, and disruption of prior placements. Children with these histories are likely to exhibit challenging behaviors at home and in the community (Mallon, 2006). Perhaps because of their personal experiences with adversity, gay and lesbian adoptive parents are less self-focused and are more likely to recognize that the child's development is influenced by a variety of factors prior to adoption; factors over which they had no control (e.g., medical and psychosocial history). Or, again, it may be that their attunement to family diversity issues, in general, sensitizes them to the complexity, variability, and spontaneity of contemporary adoptive family life.

Whereas gay and lesbian adoptive families appeared similar to their straight counterparts in terms of clinical needs, significant differences were found, with the former group reporting a greater need for couple or individual counseling and respite care. Although the reasons for this need are not readily obvious, previous studies may shed light on the dynamics contributing to this finding. Matthews and Cramer (2006) found that gay and lesbian adopters may be reluctant to utilize agency-based postadoption support groups due to a sense of exclusion and alienation; the poor fit with typical postadoption support groups may be related to the unique challenges faced by gays and lesbians. For example, James (2002) describes interconnected themes of identity and responsibility as lenses for organizing the experiences of lesbian and gay adoptive parents. He emphasizes the importance of understanding that issues common to adoptive families (e.g., loss, attachment, family reorganization) are experienced differently within the context of being a sexual minority in an often hostile society. In numerous settings, as gay and lesbian adoptive parents come out, they are then challenged to help their children address questions of individual and family identity and disclosure. In addition, for those with open adoptions, development of cooperative relationships with birth family members may present a significant challenge. Consequently, it seems likely that gay and lesbian parents would turn to their community for support.

Based on Belsky and Kelly's (1994) research that found involvement in the gay community changes once gay men and lesbians begin raising children, Matthews and Cramer (2006) propose that less-frequent participation may contribute to a sense of marginalization and stigmatization. Even though the community may offer support through parenting groups, gay and lesbian adoptive parents may feel excluded because the group composition is either one gender, couples (not singles), or parents with a biological child. Kindle and Erich (2005) also note the erosion of social support following the shift to parenthood. Gay and lesbian parents in their sample reported greater use of support from their partners and from day care centers. Stiglitz (1990) has also reported a strong reliance on partners in lesbian couples with children and has attributed couple dissolution to the advent of a child and related stressors. Consequently, poor fit with commonly offered postadoption support groups, a loss of previously felt support through the gay and lesbian community, and increased reliance on one's partner may all contribute to a greater need for couples or individual counseling and respite. In addition, the typical stressors associated with adoptive parenting may well be exacerbated by societal discrimination against them and their families due to their sexual orientation. Our finding may also reflect a greater sensitivity to problems—existing ones or those that may be emerging—by gay and lesbian adopters than straight ones Because nearly half of the gay men and lesbians in our study indicated a need for marital (couple) or individual counseling, further investigation of the nature of this unmet need is warranted.

SERVICES USE

Our findings also suggest that all the respondents tend to use similar types of services. In most instances, when differences existed between the two groups, the gay and lesbian families were more likely to utilize educational and informational services, whereas the straight families were more likely to utilize clinical services. Specifically, gay and lesbian adopters were less likely to utilize support or counseling groups for preadoptive parents. This may be due to differences in needs at this stage of the adoption process. For example, a common theme in preadoptive counseling and support groups is grief related to infertility. However, unlike most of their straight counterparts, many gay and lesbian adopters choose adoption as a first choice—so grief due to infertility is not a significant issue. In addition, gay and lesbian adopters may struggle with the decision to come out to fellow group members or to hide their sexual orientation and, thus, may not be able to utilize group processes as effectively (Mallon, this volume; Matthews & Cramer, 2006). Consequently, gay and lesbian parents may perceive education and information services as better fitting their needs than typically offered clinical services. If so, they likely would be well served by having adoption supports and services designed for and delivered specifically to gay and lesbian families, at least at this stage of the adoption process.

HELPFULNESS OF SERVICES

Next, we asked parents about the helpfulness of the services they received. As in our other analyses, we found that all the respondents were similar overall in terms of how they rated the helpfulness of services they received. However, gay and lesbian adoptive parents were more likely to find legal advice, child counselling, and classes on how to communicate with their children about adoption more helpful than did straight adoptive parents. In light of the unique challenges of gay and lesbian adoptive families related to identity and responsibility outlined by James (2002), adversities related to the U.S. legal system, and the cultural acceptance of psychotherapy within the gay and lesbian community (Balsam, Martell, & Safren, 2006), it is encouraging to know that respondents in our study not only pursued these types of supports, but also found them helpful. Further research is needed to delineate what aspects of these supports were particularly helpful and why. Such knowledge could contribute to the development of more effective services for gay and lesbian adoptive families.

UNMET NEEDS FOR ADOPTION SERVICES

Finally, we identified respondents' "unmet service needs," that is, the difference between needing a service and having it available. Again, all respondents in our study were very similar in all aspects, regardless of their sexual orientation. Although these are reassuring findings that demonstrate, by and large, that many needed services are available to gay and lesbian adoptive families, the areas of unmet need are also striking. There were two educational and informational needs that were found to be greater for straight adoptive respondents than for gay and lesbian ones: classes and workshops on understanding adopted children and on how to communicate with their children about adoption. We suspect that due to the unique needs of gay and lesbian adopters, the general preparation about these issues as presented in typical adoption trainings may be deemed insufficient.

With respect to clinical services, the only unmet need found to exist to a greater degree for gay and lesbian parents was for preadoptive counseling groups for children being placed for adoption. Mallon (2006) and Ryan (2000) stress the importance of preadoptive preparation of children placed in gay and lesbian families. As suggested by Ryan, gay affirmative practice requires workers to develop the capacity and willingness to openly and supportively explore and process fully children's related thoughts and concerns. Consistent with this perspective, Mallon highlights the importance of workers being prepared to confront heterocentric assumptions and comments from all participants throughout the process of adoption (e.g., from workers, supervisors, and birth family members).

Limitations of the Study

Although this is the first empirical study to systematically examine the service needs of gay and lesbian adoptive families compared with those of straight adoptive families, numerous limitations must be acknowledged (see Ryan & Brown, this volume). First, because it is not known exactly how many families were asked to participate in the survey, it is difficult to determine whether the adoptive parents who did participate were representative of the target population. It is likely that some sampling biases exist, given that most respondents submitted information through the Agency's website or had direct contact with the Agency prior to the study. This suggests that respondents may be more knowledgeable about and reliant on available services than the general population of adoptive families. It further suggests that respondents, the majority of whom were located in California and in urban areas, were unique in terms of their access to services and the openness of the agencies and workers with whom they worked. One other important limitation related to the characteristics of the sample has to do with the type of adoptions completed by the families. Nearly 75 percent of the adoptions were transracial. Though more common in recent years, transracial adoption historically has been less common and less encouraged than within-racial adoption (Brooks, Barth, Bussiere, & Patterson, 1999). It is likely that the agencies working with adoptive families in our sample were those that were more open to "alternative" adoption types, such as transracial adoption and gay and lesbian adoption. It is therefore possible that some of the similarities between groups that we observed were not a function of sexual orientation, but of adoption type and possibly geographic location. Although not significant, there was a slightly higher percentage of transracial adoption by gay men and lesbians than by straight parents, and respondents in the former group were significantly more likely than those in the latter to live in urban areas. These two factors could reflect the greater openness of adoption agencies and workers involved with gay and lesbian families than would otherwise be the case with within-racial gay and lesbian adoptive families, or gay and lesbian adoptive families not living in urban areas.

Another limitation of our study is related to the classification of respondents. We do not know whether parents in our sample self-identified as being gay or lesbian during the adoption process. Thus, it is possible that the journeys of gay and lesbian respondents toward adoption were not affected by their sexual orientation, if adoption workers assumed or were told that their clients were heterosexual. The majority (84 percent) of gay and lesbian respondents, however, reported living with their partners at the time of adoption. It is very likely, then, that their sexual orientation was known to the adoption agencies and workers working with them, particularly given the thoroughness of the adoption homestudy process.

Finally, the study is limited in that we did not include questions explicitly related to or addressing sexual orientation. For instance, we did not ask gay and lesbian respondents about their motivations for adopting, their support needs, or the unique preparation they received as a result of their sexual orientation. Nor did we ask them about the strategies they used on their way to adoption, particularly when they believed they encountered discrimination or other obstacles stemming from their sexual orientation.

CONCLUSIONS

Although findings from our study indicate that agency services are generally similar for all adoptive families, our research also identifies considerable differences that should be recognized in order to effectively prepare and support them for adoption. In nearly all aspects, gay and lesbian and straight adoptive family characteristics seem to be alike: They adopt similar kinds of children, receive similar kinds of support, and find the services they receive equally helpful. Overall, agency services that we asked respondents about seem to be equally needed, utilized, and helpful. Findings related to the helpfulness of the services identified in our study are especially encouraging, as they imply that despite reports of discrimination and homophobia in the adoption literature, many of the needs of gay and lesbian adoptive families are being adequately addressed and met. Yet significant differences also suggest the importance of some unique unmet needs of gay and lesbian adoptive parents. Given the increasing prevalence of this family form, it seems critical to use an affirmative practice approach that supports an open dialogue not only during recruitment and placement assessment processes, but also during adoption preparation of gay and lesbian adopters and adoptees and throughout the provision of postadoption services.

This systematic investigation makes a strong contribution to the literature on adoption services and support. However, research focusing specifically on gay and lesbian adoptive family issues is needed. As the number of such families grows, greater knowledge and skills supporting affirmative practice with this family form will be critical to effective adoption policies and procedures in general.

Acknowledgments

The authors wish to thank Karie Frasch, Beth Hall, and Gail Steinberg for their contributions to research described in this chapter. The research was supported by PACT: An Adoption Alliance.

Note

1. Florida's statute prohibiting all adoptions by lesbians and gays, dating back to 1977, was ruled unconstitutional in 2008. Recently, the Third District Court of Appeal upheld the lower court ruling (*FL. Department of Children and Families v. In the Matter of Adoption of X.X.G. and N.R.G.*, 2010).

References

Adoption and Foster Care Analysis and Reporting System (AFCARS). (2010). *The AFCARS report: Preliminary FY 2009 estimates as of July 2010 (17)*. Retrieved from http://www.acf.hhs.gov/programs/cb/stats_research/afcars/tar/report17.htm.

Adoption Education Center. (2007). Working with gay and lesbian adoptive parents. Retrieved December 9, 2007 at http://www.adoptiononline.com/aecgaylez.cfm. Arkansas Code Annotated § 9-9-204.

Balsam, K. F., Martell, C. R., & Safren, S. A. (2006). Affirmative cognitive-behavioral therapy with lesbian, gay, and bisexual people. In P. A. Hays & G. Y. Iwamasa (Eds.), *Culturally responsive cognitive-behavioral therapy: Assessment, practice, and supervision* (pp. 223–243). Washington, D.C.: American Psychological Association.

Barth, R. P., & Miller, J. M. (2000). Building effective post-adoption services: What is the empirical foundation? *Family Relations, 49*, 447–455.

Belsky, J., & Kelly, J. (1994). *The transition to parenthood: How a first child changes a marriage, why some couples grow closer and others apart*. New York: Dell Publishing.

Bigner, J. J., & Bozett, F. W. (1990). Parenting by gay fathers. In F. W. Bozett & M. B. Sussman (Eds.), *Homosexuality and family relations* (pp. 155–176). New York: Harrington Park.

Brodzinsky, D. M. (1990). A stress and coping model of adoption adjustment. In D. M. Brodzinsky & M. D. Schechter (Eds.), *The psychology of adoption* (pp. 3–24). New York: Oxford University Press.

Brodzinsky, D. M. (2003). *Adoption by lesbians and gays: A national survey of adoption agency policies, practices, and attitudes*. New York: Evan B. Donaldson Adoption Institute.

Brodzinsky, D. M., Patterson, C. J., & Vaziri, M. (2002). Adoption agency perspectives on lesbian and gay prospective parents: A national study. *Adoption Quarterly, 5*, 5–23.

Brooks, D., Allen, J., & Barth, R. P. (2002). Adoption services use, helpfulness, and need: A comparison of public and private agency and independent adoptive families. *Children and Youth Services Review, 24*, 213–238.

Brooks, D., Barth, R. P., Bussiere, A., & Patterson, G. (1999). Adoption and race: Implementing the Multiethnic Placement Act (MEPA) and the Interethnic Adoption Provisions. *Social Work, 44*, 167–178.

Brooks, D., & Goldberg, S. (2001). Gay and lesbian adoptive and foster care placements: Can they meet the needs of waiting children? *Social Work, 46*, 147–157.

Brooks, D., Halloway, I., & Kim, H. (in preparation). Family adjustment and well-being: A comparison of gay/lesbian and straight a adoptive families.

Cadoret, R. J., & Riggins-Caspers, K. (2000). Fetal alcohol exposure and adult psychopathology: Evidence from an adoptive study. In R. P. Barth, D., M. Freundlich, & D. M. Brodzinsky (Eds.), *Adoption of drug exposed children* (pp. 83–114). Washington, D.C.: Child Welfare League of America.

Crawford, I., McLeod, A., Zamboni, B. D., & Jordan, M. B. (1999). Psychologists' attitudes toward gay and lesbian parenting. Professional psychology: Research and Practice, 30, 394–401.

Crea, T. M., Barth, R. P., Guo, S., & Brooks, D. (2008). Behavioral outcomes for substance-exposed adopted children: Fourteen years postadoption. *American Journal of Orthopsychiatry, 78*, 11–19.

Crisp, C. (2006). The Gay Affirmative Practice Scale (GAP): A new measure for assessing cultural competence with gay and lesbian clients. *Social Work, 51*(2), 115–126.

Downs, A. C., & James, S. E. (2006). Gay, lesbian, and bisexual foster parents: Strengths and challenges for the child welfare system. *Child Welfare, 85*, 281–298.

Elizur, Y., & Ziv, M. (2001). Family support and acceptance, gay male identity, and psychological adjustment: A path model. *Family Processes, 40*, 125–144.

Erich, S., Leung, P., & Kindle, P. (2005). A comparative analysis of adoptive family functioning with gay, lesbian, and heterosexual parents and their children. *Journal of GLBT Family Studies, 1*, 43–60.

Farber, M., Timberlake, E., Mudd, H., & Cullen, L. (2003). Preparing parents for adoption: An agency experience. *Child and Adolescent Social Work Journal, 20*(3), 175–195.

Farr, R. H., Forssell, S. L., & Patterson, C. J. (2010). Parenting and child development in adoptive families: Does parental sexual orientation matter? *Applied Developmental Science, 14*, 164–178.

Florida Department of Children and Families v. *In the Matter of Adoption of X.X.G and N.R.G.*, No. 3D08–3044, 2010 WL 3655782 (Fla. Dist. Ct. App., Sept 22, 2010).

Gates, G. J., Badgett, M. V. L., Macomber, J. E., & Chambers, K. (2007). *Adoption and foster care by gay and lesbian parents in the United States.* Los Angeles, CA: Williams Institute.

Goldberg, A. E. (2010). *Lesbian and gay parents and their children.* Washington, D.C.: American Psychological Association.

Golombok, S., & Tasker, F. (1996). Do parents influence the sexual orientation of their children? Findings from a longitudinal study of lesbian families. *Developmental Psychology, 32*, 3–11.

Howard, J. & Freundlich, M. (2008). *Expanding resources for waiting children II: Eliminating legal & practice brriers to gay & lesbian adoption from foster care—policy and practice perspective.* New York NY: Evan B. Donaldson Adoption Institute.

James, S. E. (2002). Clinical themes in gay- and lesbian-parented adoptive families. *Clinical Child Psychology and Psychiatry, 7,* 475–486.

Ji, J., Brooks, D., Barth, R. P., & Kim, H. (2010). Beyond pre-adoptive risk: The impact of adoptive family environment on adopted youth's psychosocial adjustment. *American Journal of Orthopsychiatry, 80*(3), 432–442.

Kenyon, G. L., Chong, K., Enkoff-Sage, M., Hill, C., Mays, C., & Rochelle, L. (2003). Public adoption by gay and lesbian parents in North Carolina: Policy and practice. *Families in Society, 84,* 571–575.

Kindle, P. A., & Erich, S. (2005). Perceptions of social support among heterosexual and homosexual adopters. *Families in Society, 86,* 541–546.

Kramer, L., & Houston, D. (1998). Supporting families as they adopt children with special needs. *Family Relations, 47,* 423–432.

Leung, P., Erich, S., & Kanenberg, H. (2005). A comparison of family functioning in gay/lesbian, heterosexual and special needs adoptions. *Children and Youth Services Review, 27,* 1031–1044.

Mallon, G. P. (2000). Gay men and lesbians as adoptive parents. *Journal of Gay and Lesbian Social Services, 11,* 1–14.

Mallon, G. P. (2006). *Lesbian and gay foster and adoptive parents: Recruiting, assessing, and supporting an untapped resource for children and youth.* Washington, D.C.: Child Welfare League of America.

Mallon, G. P. (2007). Assessing lesbian and gay prospective foster and adoptive families: A focus on the home study process. *Child Welfare, 86,* 67–86.

Martin, A. (1993). *The gay and lesbian parenting handbook: Creating and raising our families.* New York: Harper Perennial.

Matthews, J. D., & Cramer, E. P. (2006). Envisaging the adoption process to strengthen gay- and lesbian-headed families: Recommendations for adoption professionals. *Child Welfare, 85,* 317–340.

Miall, C. E., & March, K. (2005). Social support for changes in adoption practice: Gay adoption, open adoption, birth reunions, and the release of confidential identifying information. *Families in Society, 86,* 83–92.

The National Adoption Information Clearinghouse. (2001). *Gay and lesbian adoptive parents: Resources for professionals and parents.* Washington, DC: The National Adoption Information Clearinghouse.

"Parens Patriae." (2005). In J. Lehman & S. Phelps (Eds.), *West's encyclopedia of American law,* 2nd ed. Farmington Hills, MI: Thomson Gale. eNotes.com. 2006. 1 July, 2007 http://law.enotes.com/wests-law-encyclopedia/parens-patriae.

Patterson, C. J. (1997). Children of lesbian and gay parents. In T. Ollendick & R. Prinz (Eds.), *Advances in Clinical Child Psychology,* Vol. 19 (pp. 235–282). New York: Plenum Press.

Patterson, J. M. (2002). Integrating family resilience and family stress theory. *Journal of Marriage and Family, 64,* 349–360.

Pinderhughes, E. E. (1996). Toward understanding family readjustment following older child adoption: The interplay between theory generation and empirical research. *Children and Youth Service Review, 18,* 115–138.

Reilly, T., & Platz, L. (2004). Post-adoption service needs of families with special needs children: Use, helpfulness, and unmet needs. *Journal of Social Service Review, 30*(4), 51–67.

Ricketts, W. (1991). *Lesbians and gay men as foster parents*. Portland: National Child Welfare Resource Center for Management and Administration, University of Southern Maine.

Ryan, S. D., Pearlmutter, S., & Groza, V. (2004). Coming out of the closet: Opening agencies to gay and lesbian adoptive parents. *Social Work*, *49*, 85–95.

Simmel, C., Barth, R. P., & Brooks, D. (2007). Adopted foster youths' psychosocial functioning: A longitudinal perspective. *Child & Family Social Work*, *12*, 336–348.

Stiglitz, E. (1990). Caught between two worlds: The impact of a child on a lesbian couple's relationship. *Women and Therapy*, *10*, 99–116.

Van der Vegt, E. J. M., van der Ende, J., Kirschbaum, C., Verhulst, F. C., & Tiemeier, H. (2009). Early neglect and abuse predict diurnal cortisol patterns in adults: A study of international adoptees. *Psychoneuroendocrinology*, *34*, 660–669.

Wind, L. H., Brooks, D., & Barth, R. P. (2006). Differences between adoptive families of children with and without special needs. *Adoption Quarterly*, *8*, 45–74.

9

Gay and Lesbian Adoptive Parents

Stressors and Strengths

SCOTT RYAN AND SUZANNE BROWN ■

Although no one knows exactly how many children are available for adoption internationally, estimates are in the millions. Just in the United States, about 115,000 children are legally available to be adopted from the child welfare system (Child Welfare League of America, 2008). To best meet the placement needs of these boys and girls, child welfare specialists must recruit and place children with all willing, qualified individuals and couples. Toward that end, adoption practice has moved from accepting only married, infertile, heterosexual couples, to placing children with myriad family forms—including those headed by gay and lesbian individuals and couples. In fact, every state (except Arkansas, Mississippi, and Utah) grants adoptions to gay and lesbian individuals and/or couples (Appell, this volume; Human Rights Campaign, 2009).[1]

Placement with these parents remains controversial in many segments of society, but the position among the primary child welfare, mental health, legal, and medical organizations is that gay men and lesbians can serve the needs of children and reduce the number of them in foster care (Ryan, 2008).

Contrary to the arguments of critics, no credible scientific evidence exists demonstrating that lesbian mothers or gay fathers organize their homes differently, are unfit parents, or have children who develop differently from those in homes headed by heterosexuals (Gartrell, Peyser, & Bos, this volume; Patterson & Wainright, this volume; Stacey & Biblarz, 2001). Research suggests that what matters most in the lives of children is not their parents' sexual orientation, but the love, caring, and maturity of these adults, along with their rearing of their children to become self-reliant and self-assured individuals.

Furthermore, success in adoption is not related to family form (i.e., single-parent, two-parent, transracial/cultural, or other structures), but depends on the balance of resources and stressors assisting and impacting the family (Groze, 1996). To optimize its prospects for success, any family adopting a child—especially one from the public system—needs community support; a well-developed network of social support; the ability to be flexible in its expectations and parenting; and accessible, affordable, and sensitive social services, including an array of therapies, respite care, and recreational activities.

More than is the case with most other groups of adults adopting children, there is much to be learned about how gay and lesbian individuals and couples respond to the stressors of being adoptive parents. In an effort to shed light on this issue, this chapter will outline the empirical and theoretical foundations of stressors and strengths in child development and family life, and subsequently apply these constructs to a large, national sample of gay and lesbian adoptive families. This information is intended to aid adoption professionals in identifying possible sources of strength and support in their work with gay and lesbian adoptive families, as well as to help these families plan for the common challenges they may face in raising their children.

LITERATURE REVIEW

Stress and Social Support

Some of the primary responsibilities of any family are the support, care, and nurture of its children. However, parents may encounter stressors that can undermine their care-giving efforts and, ultimately, their children's emotional well-being. These include stressors associated with "normative" child-related tasks (i.e., minor daily hassles), as well as those imposed by major life events such as illness, death, divorce, and loss of family income. Crnic and Greenberg (1990) posit that the frustration experienced by parents through daily hassles, although singularly having little significance, can cumulatively become a meaningful stressor without appropriate social support. Additionally, parent satisfaction with the parent–child relationship has an impact on child development (Groothues, Beckett, & O'Connor, 1998; Mahoney, Robinson, & Powell, 1992). These researchers suggest that many of the developmental problems manifested by children are related, at least partly, to difficulties in parent–child interactions. Their work supports the notion that social support and social interaction influence child development.

The mental health field has extensively explored the relationship between caregiver stress and social support. Indeed, in a seminal work in this area, Erickson (1968) used a stress-related concept to explain the impact of mental illness on family caregivers (i.e., parents). This development was significant, as it demonstrated that the problems caregivers develop are a direct result of stress caused by the impact of the care recipients' mental health problems. Although family members have been the first line of support for each other since antiquity, they were often thought of by professionals as part of the problem rather than as part of the solution. More recently, however, families have been seen as both helpful and supportive for individuals with myriad issues. For example, Solomon (1994) found that family members were sources of strength and support for individuals coping with mental illness, rather than casual factors in the development or exacerbation of the problem.

Social support, usually conceptualized as a positive factor, may intervene between a stressful event and the reaction to it by attenuating or preventing a stressful appraisal of the situation, thus increasing the person's ability to respond appropriately (Maguire, 1991; Monat & Lazarus, 1991); that is, the perception that others can provide necessary resources may redefine the potential for harm posed by a situation and/or bolster one's perceived ability to handle additional demands (Cohen & Wills, 1985). It can help prevent stress by making potentially harmful experiences seem less consequential or provide valuable resources for coping when stress does occur (Sarason, Sarason, & Pierce, 1990). Thus, socially supportive relationships may mitigate the effects of stress (House, 1981).

Within families, partner, friendship, and community supports may serve to alleviate the stress of daily hassles associated with parenting. Mitigating this stress may potentially improve parent–child relationship satisfaction, which, according to Mahoney, Robinson, and Powell (1992), will have a positive influence on child development. Colarossi and Eccles (2000) propose that the support parents provide could help their children cope with the stressors in their lives, leading to greater mental health and the ability to form better relationships with peers. Additionally, Van Ijzendoorn, Dikjstra, and Bus (1995) found that a strong parent–child relationship promotes healthier cognitive models of the world and self–other relationships—internal models that are embodied by feelings of safety, nurturance, predictability, and control. In short, this literature supports the idea that parenting stress, parent–child relationship satisfaction, and child development outcomes all have interactive effects on each other.

Stress and Social Support with Adoptions

According to Brodzinsky (1990), adoption can be a stressful experience for children and families, contrary to many prevailing beliefs and stereotypes. Leaving one's biological family for an adoptive home can constitute a major life stressor for a child; it also typically results in additional child-rearing challenges for parents (Kirk, 1964; Brodzinsky & Pinderhughes, 2002; Brodzinsky, Smith, & Brodzinsky, 1998). Adoption involves loss, which in turn can create stress for the child, thereby increasing vulnerability to emotional and behavioral problems (Brodzinsky, 1990).

Brodzinsky (1990) asserts that the most vital environmental factors affecting adopted children's adjustment are their experiences with biological and adoptive family members. Indeed, it is important to realize that adjustment for these children is influenced not only by the adoptive family environment, but—especially for those with histories of abuse and neglect—by the experiences they had with the biological family and previous foster families and/or institutional caregivers (Pinderhughes, 1998).

Berry (1990) also noted that adoptive families can have considerable stressors. For instance, many of the children have been removed from abusive environments, have been in foster care for extended periods, and often enter adoptive homes in which there are already other children (i.e., biological, adoptive, or foster). These prior experiences will affect the children's current appraisal of situations and coping processes. Berry (1990) also discussed the lack of social supports for older children with special needs adopted from the child welfare system. She noted their increased susceptibility to otherwise minor stressors of adoption and day-to-day coping, given that they have fewer resources and supports. These factors highlight the children's need for strong external support as they integrate with and attach to their new families.

Research suggests that higher levels of behavioral problems in adopted children are associated with lower levels of family functioning (Barth & Berry, 1988; Festinger, 1986; Leung & Erich, 2002; McDonald, Lieberman, Partridge, & Hornby, 1991; Rosenthal & Groze, 1992). It has also been found that greater rigidity in roles, rules, and interaction dynamics in adoptive families is related to increased risk for disruption (Kagan & Reid, 1986; Rosenthal, Schmidt, & Conner, 1988). Overall, these results suggest that the quality of family functioning is likely to be an important variable related to placement satisfaction.

Because highly challenging behavior is a significant risk factor for adoption disruptions, it is likely that adoptive parents' dissatisfaction with a placement may be connected to severe mental health problems (i.e., behavioral and/or emotional issues) on the part of their children. Parents who have ended or are contemplating ending an adoption are among those who view their adopted children as significantly more difficult to care for than others due to higher levels and severity of emotional, behavioral, physical, or other problems.

Despite the love and loyalty they invariably feel, the parents of adopted children with such intense issues experience many challenges, including the possibility of on-going therapeutic responsibilities and concerns about the future. To meet these challenges, parents need to marshal all the supports and resources available to them. This is true for all types of adoptive families, including those headed by lesbians and gays. However, given the majority of heteronormative models of family life in our society, and given the ongoing prejudice and homophobia experienced by nonheterosexuals who seek to adopt, there are questions about whether these individuals receive sufficient and effective supports for the challenges they face.

This chapter presents data on children adopted by gay and lesbian parents, and on the internal strengths of their families (parent–child relationships and family functioning) and external supports available to them. Specifically, the research seeks to answer the following questions: (1) What are the characteristics of the gay and lesbian adoptive parents and children within this sample? (2) What social supports are employed by these adoptive families, and how helpful did they find them to be? (3) What is the state of their parent–child relationships and overall family functioning? and (4) Are there significant differences in the adoptive parents' views of their children (i.e., whether they are harder to care for than other children) based on the number of mental health diagnoses, social support usage, parent–child relationship status, and level of family functioning?

Methodology

This study utilizes a cross-sectional survey design, which does not allow for comparisons over time. It does allow the study to present a multidimensional perspective on the adoptive parents' and children's demographics, however, as well as the adoptive parents' and children's relationship strength, the functioning level of the families, and the families' social support networks.

Analyses of these data will include univariate, bivariate, and multivariate statistical models to illustrate the adoptive families' overall level of functioning, the strength of the parent–child relationships, the mental health status of the children, and the social supports available to and employed by the families. These factors will be examined to determine how they predict the parents' views of their children, including the extent of child-rearing challenges they represent.

Research Participants

Research participants were recruited through a variety of media sources, including ads and/or announcements in several metropolitan gay and lesbian weekly newspapers, adoption magazines and gay parenting magazines, as well as on a designated website. Additionally, flyers were distributed to both gay/lesbian and adoption organizations, and through a gay and lesbian adoptive parent listserv.

A cover letter, consent form, and survey were sent to all individuals who were interested in participating in the research. Parents were encouraged to contact the researcher if they had any questions about the survey or the procedures. Two hundred and eighty-one surveys were sent to potential respondents. One hundred and eighty-three surveys were returned, for an overall response rate of 65.1 percent, which, according to Dillman (2000), constitutes an acceptable rate for mailed survey research.

Following inspection of data for errors in entry and initial frequency distributions, missing values were replaced using the expectation-maximization method of imputation (Hill, 1997). This technique was selected for its capacity to employ a broad range of variables (rather than, for instance, sample means for a single variable) in the replacement of missing values.

Measures

The survey consisted of 28 pages assessing a variety of domains, including (1) demographics of the parent(s), child(ren), target adopted child (i.e., the oldest adopted child in the home), and the family; (2) extent of involvement with the gay and lesbian community; (3) parental "out" status; (4) information on the adoption process and experiences, the adoption timeline, and adoption costs and subsidy; (5) the target adopted child's preadoption and postadoption experiences; (6) the overall adoption experience of the family; (7) parental satisfaction with adoption services; (8) family dynamics, social supports, and quality of the parent–child relationship; and (9) information on the target child's birth family. Included in the survey were several standardized psychometric instruments assessing different aspects of the domains noted above.

PARENT–CHILD RELATIONSHIP SATISFACTION

To gauge the overall level of parent–child relationship satisfaction, a previously developed scale based on concepts related to attachment theory was included (Groza & Ryan, 2002; Groza, Ryan, & Cash, 2003; Ryan & Groza, 2003). The scale focuses on interactive behaviors known to be related to attachment security versus insecurity—e.g., how well the parent and child get along, how much time they spend together, how well they communicate, how much trust and respect the parent has for the child, how close they are, and the nature of the impact of the parent–child relationship on the family. Responses to each question were based on a four-point Likert scale in which lower scores represent greater parent–child relationship satisfaction, as reported by the primary respondent. The responses were summed and divided by the number of questions (seven) to yield an average score. Reliability testing for the scale yielded a Chronbach's alpha $(\alpha) = 0.81$.

FAMILY FUNCTIONING

Family functioning was operationalized through the use of the Family Functioning Style Scale (FFSS), a 26-item instrument measuring five different family domains (Trivette, Dunst, Deal, Hamby, & Sexton, 1994); however, for purposes of this research, only the global scale, measuring overall family functioning, was used. The FFSS is based on the strengths perspective (Early & Glenmaye, 2000) and is intended to measure the extent to which family member(s) believe the family is represented by different strengths and capabilities. Family respondents were asked to rate items on a five-point Likert-type scale, with written anchor points ranging from "Not at all like my family" to "Sometimes like my family" to "Almost always like my family." Higher ratings are reflective of more positive family functioning. The coefficient alpha for the total scale is 0.92 (Trivette et al., 1990). Criterion-related validity, predictive validity, and construct validity have already been established for the measure (Trivette et al., 1990, 1994). The scale has also been validated on adoptive families (Nalavany, 2006), with a reported alpha coefficient for the global scale of 0.95. For this study, reliability testing for the scale yielded a Chronbach's alpha $(\alpha) = 0.91$, which is consistent with other adoptive and non-adoptive samples.

Results

ADOPTIVE PARENT AND FAMILY CHARACTERISTICS

The data in Table 9.1 provide basic information on the gay and lesbian adoptive parents who completed the survey. There were 182 adoptive families participating, of which 167 were headed by two parents. The sample had slightly more households led by lesbians than by gay men (54.9 percent vs. 45.1 percent);

furthermore, lesbian households were slightly more likely to have two parents than were gay-headed households (93.0 percent versus 90.2 percent). The sample was composed primarily of white individuals (90.1 percent for parent #1 and 87.4 percent for parent #2 in two-parent households). On average, adoptive parent respondents were in their early to mid-40s. The sample respondents also were quite well educated, with over 80 percent having a bachelor's degree or higher. About 70 percent were employed full-time outside of the home.

As noted in Table 9.1, almost 92 percent of respondents were partnered, for an average of 11.59 years (SD = 6.84 years). Only 57.1 percent of the respondent families contained two "legal" parents in which both partners adopted jointly or one formally adopted the biological child of the other. The remainder of the part- nered families were headed by a single legal parent and a parenting partner.

Table 9.1 ADOPTIVE PARENT AND FAMILY CHARACTERISTICS

Question	Distribution[1]	
	Parent #1 ($n = 182$)	Parent #2 ($n = 167$)
Gender (female)	54.9 percent	55.7 percent
Race/ethnicity (white)	90.1 percent	87.4 percent
Age	44.6 (6.45)	41.1 (6.30)
Education		
High school	19.8 percent	19.8 percent
Bachelor's degree	26.9 percent	29.3 percent
Master's degree	37.4 percent	34.1 percent
Doctoral degree	15.9 percent	16.8 percent
Employment (full-time)		
Relationship to child	69.8 percent	67.7 percent
Biological relative	—	6.1 percent
Adoptive parent	89.0 percent	68.3 percent
Would be if I could–adoptive parent	7.1 percent	17.7 percent
Other	3.8 percent	7.9 percent
Partnered (yes)	91.8 percent	
If partnered, for how long (in years)?	11.6 (6.84)	
Family income (in thousands)	$113,281 ($74,824)	
Community type		
Large urban	44.0 percent	
Small urban	15.4 percent	
Suburban	29.7 percent	
Rural	11.0 percent	

NOTES: [1]Mean (SD); percent = valid percent.

The majority of individuals in the latter category wanted to adopt their children but were prevented from doing so by state law. Most families in the sample earned a relatively high income, averaging $113,281 per year (SD = $74,824). The respondent families were dispersed across the United States, living in 32 states and the District of Columbia.

CHILD DEMOGRAPHICS, PLACEMENT, DEVELOPMENTAL, AND BEHAVIORAL INFORMATION

As shown in Table 9.2, the types of the children's adoptions were fairly evenly split among private and domestic (35.7 percent), public child welfare (34.6 percent), and international (29.7 percent) sources. Male adopted children made up over 60 percent of the sample. Children were, on average, 6.52 years old at the time of data collection (ranging from 0.42 to 17.75 years old). The distribution of race and ethnicity across the sample showed that the largest percentage of adopted children were identified as white (30.2 percent), followed by 22.0 percent Hispanic, 21 percent African American, 17 percent Asian, and almost 10 percent multiracial. This distribution, in light of the composition of the parent cohort, clearly demonstrates that a large number of these families were formed through transracial adoptive placements.

Table 9.2 ADOPTED CHILD'S DEMOGRAPHICS, PLACEMENT, DEVELOPMENTAL, AND BEHAVIORAL INFORMATION

Question	Distribution[1]
Child adopted	
Private/domestic	35.7 percent
International	29.7 percent
Public child welfare	34.6 percent
Child's gender (female)	38.5 percent
Test age (in years)	6.52 (4.52)
Race/ethnicity	
White	30.2 percent
Hispanic	22.0 percent
African American	20.9 percent
Asian	17.0 percent
Multiracial	9.9 percent
Special physical needs (n = 170)	
More serious than described	6.0 percent
About as described	65.9 percent
Less serious than described	28.0 percent

(*Continued*)

Table 9.2 (CONTINUED)

Question	Distribution[1]
Special behavioral needs (*n* = 180)	
More serious than described	10.4 percent
About as described	53.8 percent
Less serious than described	35.7 percent
Special emotional needs (*n* = 180)	
More serious than described	11.5 percent
About as described	52.7 percent
Less serious than described	35.7 percent
Mental health diagnosis (yes)	
Depressions	9.3 percent
Attention deficit hyperactivity disorder (ADHD)	15.4 percent
Oppositional defiant disorder (ODD)	7.7 percent
Anxiety	10.4 percent
Posttraumatic stress disorder (PTSD)	8.2 percent
Conduct disorder	4.4 percent
Reactive attachment disorder (RAD)	8.2 percent
Average number of mental health diagnoses	0.81 (1.62)
Taking medication for behavioral/emotional problems (yes)	11.5 percent
Harder to care for than most (yes)	36.8 percent

NOTES: [1]Mean (SD); percent = valid percent.

To assess whether reality differed from parental expectations, the survey asked adoptive parents about their children's physical, behavioral, and emotional needs, and whether any (or all) of these items were more serious, about as serious, or less serious than described by the agency at the time of placement. Only 6 percent of parents said that their children's special physical needs were more serious than expected, and slightly over 10 percent responded that the behavioral and emotional special needs were more serious than they were led to believe.

Of the 182 adopted children in the sample, almost 72 percent had no formal mental health diagnosis. Approximately 28 percent had at least one such diagnosis, and 12 percent had three or more diagnoses (of the seven diagnoses listed in Table 9.2). The most frequent diagnosis received by the adopted children was attention deficit hyperactivity disorder (ADHD) (15.4 percent), followed by anxiety disorder (10.4 percent). All others were reported in fewer than 10 percent of the children in the sample.

Although 28 percent of the children in the sample had some form of mental health diagnosis, only a relatively small portion (11.5 percent) were on any medication for emotional and behavioral problems. When asked if their children were harder to care for than most others, over 35 percent of parents replied affirmatively. As expected, those children identified as harder to care for had more diagnoses

(m = 2.00, SD = 2.15) than those identified as not hard to care for (m = 0.12, SD = 0.46), t = –7.05, df = 69.55, p < 0.001.

PARENT–CHILD RELATIONSHIP AND FAMILY FUNCTIONING STATUS

All individual items within the parent–child relationship scale suggested a strong positive bond between the adoptive parents and their children. Table 9.3 shows that substantially more than 50 percent of all respondents scored each item as "1," which reflected the strongest perceived parent–child relationship (m = 1.22, SD = 0.33). Additionally, the family functioning scale also indicated a high level of family strengths and resources (m = 4.14, SD = 0.44). As expected, parent–child relationship status (t = –7.53, df = 78.02; p < 0.001) as well as level of family functioning (t = 2.44, df = 180, p < 0.016) were worse when children were viewed as especially difficult to care for by their gay or lesbian parents.

Table 9.3 PARENT–CHILD RELATIONSHIP AND FAMILY FUNCTIONING STATUS

Question	Distribution[1]
Get along	
1—very well	85.2 percent
2—fairly well	13.7 percent
3—not so well	1.1 percent
4—very poorly	—
Spend time together	
1—about every day	98.4 percent
2—2 to 3 times per week	1.6 percent
3—once per week	—
4—once per month or less/not at all	—
Communication	
1—excellent	70.9 percent
2—good	26.4 percent
3—fair	2.7 percent
4—poor	—
Trust	
1—yes, very much so	73.1 percent
2—yes, for the most part	23.1 percent
3—not sure	1.1 percent
4—no	2.7 percent
Respect	
1—yes, very much so	64.8 percent
2—yes, for the most part	33.0 percent
3—not sure	1.1 percent
4—no	1.1 percent

(*continued*)

Table 9.3 (CONTINUED)

Question	Distribution[1]
Close	
1—yes, very much so	87.9 percent
2—yes, for the most part	11.5 percent
3—not sure	0.5 percent
4—no	—
Impact on family	
1—very positive	83.0 percent
2—mostly positive	12.1 percent
3—mixed	4.4 percent
4—mostly negative/very negative	0.5 percent
Parent–Child Relationship Scale[2] (α = 0.81)	1.22 (0.33)
Family Functioning Style Scale[3] (α = 0.91)	4.14 (0.44)

NOTES: [1]Mean (SD); percent = valid percent.
[2]Lower score is better.
[3]Higher score is better.

SOCIAL SUPPORT

Adoptive parents were asked to identify, from a list of 50 possible sources of social support, those available in their communities and, of those available and used, how helpful they had been. Due to space considerations, only those identified as available by 75 percent or more of the respondents are included here.

As shown in Table 9.4, the most helpful sources of support noted by the respondents, as identified by 50 percent or more indicating it as very helpful, included legal advice (58.3 percent); informal contacts with other adoptive families (67.5 percent), rated as the most helpful of all sources; contacts with the adopted child's family of origin (50.0 percent); the child's daycare/school (55.0 percent); lesbian, gay, bisexual, and transgender (LGBT) friends (50.6 percent); and non-LGBT friends (57.3 percent). Although all sources were, in general, identified as somewhat or very helpful, the category that ranked the lowest among the "very helpful" was the LGBT community (29.9 percent).

Eight sources were identified by 10 percent or more of adoptive parent respondents as "not helpful," including support groups for adoptive parents (12.4 percent), information on the child's racial and ethnic background (13.5 percent), adoption websites (13.3 percent), adoptive child's family of origin (13.9 percent), extended family (17.1 percent), co-workers (12.5 percent), neighbors (14.0 percent), and the LGBT community (17.4 percent, with which there was the highest level of dissatisfaction). Ultimately, even for the category scoring highest within the "not helpful" grouping, the majority of adoptive parents (82.6 percent) found these sources as somewhat or very helpful.

Several of the social support sources were found to be less helpful when the gay or lesbian parents experienced their children as more difficult to care for than

Table 9.4 SOCIAL SUPPORT

Question	Available[1] (yes)	Not Helpful[1] (−1)	Somewhat Helpful[1] (0)	Very Helpful[1] (1)
Support group for adoptive parents	84.1 percent	12.4 percent	45.1 percent	42.5 percent
Read books/articles on adoption	96.2 percent	2.9 percent	58.3 percent	38.9 percent
Attended lectures on adoption	79.1 percent	7.6 percent	57.6 percent	34.7 percent
Legal advice	79.1 percent	7.6 percent	34.0 percent	58.3 percent
Information on child's racial/ ethnic background	81.3 percent	13.5 percent	52.0 percent	34.5 percent
Adoption websites	86.8 percent	13.3 percent	51.9 percent	34.8 percent
Other websites/listservs	75.3 percent	7.3 percent	45.3 percent	47.4 percent
Informal contacts with adoptive families	92.9 percent	2.4 percent	30.2 percent	67.5 percent
Family of origin	91.2 percent	13.9 percent	36.1 percent	50.0 percent
Extended family	80.2 percent	17.1 percent	47.3 percent	35.6 percent
Co-workers	87.9 percent	12.5 percent	49.4 percent	38.1 percent
Neighbors	82.4 percent	14.0 percent	42.0 percent	44.0 percent
Daycare/school	81.9 percent	4.7 percent	40.3 percent	55.0 percent
Medical/health services	78.6 percent	5.6 percent	46.9 percent	47.6 percent
LGBT friends	94.5 percent	8.1 percent	41.3 percent	50.6 percent
Non-LGBT friends	97.8 percent	3.4 percent	39.3 percent	57.3 percent
LGBT community	79.1 percent	17.4 percent	52.8 percent	29.9 percent

NOTES: [1]Percent = valid percent.

most other children. These included adoption websites ($t = 1.95$, df $= 156$, $p < 0.053$), other websites ($t = 3.58$, df $= 135$, $p < 0.001$), non-LGBT friends ($t = 2.98$, df $= 176$, $p < 0.003$), neighbors ($t = 2.58$, df $= 148$, $p < 0.011$), daycare and school ($t = 3.30$, df $= 147$, $p < 0.001$), and medical and health services ($t = 3.17$, df $= 141$, $p < 0.002$).

PREDICTORS OF PARENT'S PERCEPTION OF CHILD
Based on the theoretical and empirical findings presented previously, three binary logistical regression models were run and are described in this section. The first one examines how the stressor (i.e., number of mental health diagnoses) increases

the chance of the adoptive parents viewing their children as harder to care for than most other children. The second builds upon the first by adding the internal resources available to the families (i.e., parent–child relationship status and family functioning) to offset this stressor. The final model examines how the addition of external social supports further influences the parents' perceptions of how hard their children are to care for compared to most others.

As shown in Table 9.5, the first model yielded a significant Chi-square, accounting for 21 percent of the variance in the level to which adoptive parents see their children as harder to care for than most others. The odds ratio for this model suggests that for *each additional diagnosis,* the likelihood doubles that the parent will see the child as harder to care for.

Table 9.5 BINARY LOGISTIC REGRESSION MODEL: IS THIS CHILD HARDER TO CARE FOR THAN MOST? (0 = NO/1 = YES)

$N = 182$; model Chi-square = 31.007 (df = 1, $p < 0.001$); Hosmer and Lemeshow Chi-square = 50.760 (df = 2, $p < 0.001$); Nagelkerke $R^2 = 0.21$

INDEPENDENT VARIABLES	COEFFICIENT β (SE)	ODDS RATIO
Total number of mental health diagnoses	0.72 (0.19)*	2.06

$N = 182$; model Chi-square = 101.16 (df = 3, $p < 0.001$); Hosmer and Lemeshow Chi-square = 5.11 (df = 8, $p < 0.75$); Nagelkerke $R^2 = 0.57$

INDEPENDENT VARIABLES	COEFFICIENT β (SE)	ODDS RATIO
Total number of mental health diagnoses	1.24 (0.29)*	3.46
Family Functioning Style Scale[1]	−1.15 (0.23)*	0.32
Parent–Child Relationship Scale[2]	2.96 (0.78)*	19.20

$N = 93$; model Chi-square = 77.64 (df = 9, $p < 0.001$); Hosmer and Lemeshow Chi-square = 51.29 (df = 8, $p < 0.74$); Nagelkerke $R^2 = 0.76$

INDEPENDENT VARIABLES	COEFFICIENT β (SE)	ODDS RATIO
Total number of mental health diagnoses	2.68 (0.73)*	14.56
Family Functioning Style Scale[1]	−1.54 (0.51)*	0.21
Parent–Child Relationship Scale[2]	3.70 (1.40)*	40.38
Adoption websites	0.36 (0.70)	1.43
Other websites/listservs	0.60 (0.81)	1.82
Neighbors	0.31 (0.77)	1.36
Daycare/school	−0.57 (0.54)	0.56
Medical/health services	−0.77 (0.64)	0.46
Non-LGBT Friends	−0.41 (0.70)	0.67

NOTES: *$p < 0.05$.
[1]Higher score is better.
[2]Lower score is better.

A second binary logistic regression model, utilizing the variables reflecting internal family resources, family functioning, and the parent–child relationship, as well as the number of mental health diagnoses, explained 57 percent of the variance in the dependent variable (i.e., perception of children's difficulty). A significant relationship was found among all three of the explanatory variables in this model. This enhanced model suggests that for *each additional diagnosis* found, the likelihood that the parents' view of their children as hard to care for will more than triple; for *each point reduction* in the level of family functioning (where lower is worse), the likelihood that the parents will see their children as harder to care for than most other children increases by over half; and for *each full additional point* increase in the parent–child relationship scale score (where higher is worse), the likelihood that the children will be viewed as harder to care for will increase more than 18-fold.

Finally, a third binary logistic regression model was run, adding external social support resources to the other predictor variables noted above. Only those social support variables previously found to be significant in their level of helpfulness were included in the analysis. The Chi-square for this model was significant, and explained 76 percent of the variance in the dependent variable. However, although significant relationships were found with all three of the previous explanatory variables, none of the individual social support variables predicted parents' perception of the child-rearing challenge represented by their children. In the current model, for *each additional diagnosis* found, the likelihood that the parents' views of their children as hard to care for increased over 13 times; for *each point reduction* in the family's level of functioning (where lower is worse), the likelihood that the parents saw their children as harder to care for than most other children increased by 75 percent; and, finally, for *each full additional point* increase in the parent–child relationship scale score (where higher is worse), the likelihood that the children were viewed as harder to care for increased 40-fold. In short, it is clear that these three variables—mental health diagnoses, level of family functioning, and quality of parent–child relationship—are strong indicators of gay and lesbian adoptive parents' perceptions of the child-rearing challenge represented by their children.

DISCUSSION

The current findings point to some of the stressors and strengths that are likely to be relevant for all adoptive families, gay or straight. First, adopted children with more mental health issues clearly are more challenging to care for. Of course, this finding is of no surprise, is supported by considerable research, and applies to nonadoptive families as well. Second, the impact of these challenges, although still significant, is alleviated by high levels of family functioning and strong parent–child relationships. Indeed, the study discussed here found a generally high level of family functioning and parenting skills in this moderately large sample of gay and lesbian adoptive parents, a result that is consistent with previous research on gay and lesbian parenting (Gartrell, Peyser, & Bos, this volume; Goldberg, 2010; Patterson & Wainright, this volume; Stacey & Biblarz, 2001).

The findings of this study clearly illustrate the strengths of gay and lesbian adoptive parents in this sample, and their strong relationship with their adopted children. The positively skewed scores reported by these respondents, indicating the families' positive level of functioning, mirror those found in studies of strengths of other adoptive families (Groza & Ryan, 2002; Groza, Ryan, & Cash, 2003; Groze & Rosenthal, 1993; Ryan & Groza, 2003, Hinterlong & Ryan, 2007; Nalavany, 2006). Gay and lesbian adoptive parents also reported numerous social supports that they found useful in coping with child-rearing stress; however, none of these sources independently predicted their perception of the child-rearing challenge represented by their children over and above the other variables studied. Still, taken as a whole, the availability and utilization of social supports did significantly increase the predictability of their perception of the child-rearing challenge of their children.

Practitioners working with adoptive families should be aware that family interventions specifically targeted to improve family-system coping may be the most likely to yield effective results. Using items from the Family Functioning Style Scale (Trivette, Dunst, Deal, Hamby, & Sexton, 1994) as a guide, some examples of areas of focus may include "making personal sacrifices for the family," "taking pride in small accomplishments," "trying to look at the bright side of things no matter what happens," and "a commitment to sticking together no matter how difficult things get." In addition, practitioners' efforts to strengthen parent–child relationships by building trust, having them spend time together doing favorite activities, and working on issues of communication will aid parents in building healthy connections with their adopted children (Brodzinsky, 2006). Intervening in these areas may not change the children's behavior or reduce the number of mental health diagnoses per se but, as shown by these data, it may help parents to better deal with these challenging behaviors and develop more realistic (and perhaps more hopeful) expectations about their children. This may, in turn, produce greater family commitment to the adoption and decrease the possibility of disruption.

Mallon (2006) identifies specific interventions that agencies and practitioners should implement in supporting gay and lesbian adoptive parents. These include helping parents understand the effects of trauma, abuse, separation, and loss on children's behavior and on the parent–child relationship; of course, such understanding clearly would be helpful for all adoptive families. Adoption practitioners should also be knowledgeable about issues specific to gay and lesbian parenting (such as stigma and secrecy), and provide information and appropriate referrals to peer support groups and resources specifically for gay and lesbian adoptive parents (see Brooks & Kim, this volume; Goldberg & Gianino, this volume). These resources can provide additional support to gay and lesbian parents by helping them navigate potential stigma and discriminative experiences in their larger social interactions as a gay and lesbian-headed family. Ryan (2000) also has argued that practitioners in adoption and child welfare should receive training regarding gay and lesbian issues, especially related to parenting, to improve supportive practices to gay and lesbian adoptive parents. These specific interventions can only enhance the responsiveness of gay and lesbian parents to their children's needs, further strengthen the parent–child relationship, and decrease the likelihood of placement disruptions.

The findings of this study provide additional support for those who assert that children growing up in gay and lesbian households are doing well, and should inform policymakers as they consider whether to support legislation allowing such family forms. It is clear that the children in this sample are growing up in healthy families with generally strong, capable parents. Although the findings are limited to this sample, this information may assist policymakers (and practitioners) in recognizing that gay and lesbian parents are capable of creating environments that support the development of emotionally healthy children. Still, some state adoption policies create hurdles for these families and others are unclear, with many departments of social services remaining silent on whether sexual orientation can be taken into account in making child placement decisions (Brooks & Goldberg, 2001).

Proposals for improving policy and practice to decrease barriers to adoption by gays and lesbians are few (see Mallon, this volume). The Child Welfare League of America suggests that adoption policy address the capacity of potential parents to nurture a child, rather than the potential parents' sexual orientation (Child Welfare League of America, 2000). Furthermore, agencies should create clear policy statements regarding assessments of and potential placements with adoptive parents who are gay or lesbian. Clear policies, along with the training of adoption workers regarding gay and lesbian parents, will reduce the likelihood that workers will make assessments based solely on personal beliefs—and increase the likelihood that evaluations will be based on applicants' parenting capacities rather than their sexual orientations (Mathews and Cramer, 2006; Mallon, this volume). Although the political debate may continue regarding who should be allowed to adopt, the data presented herein demonstrate that gays and lesbians should not be excluded from consideration as a group based solely on their sexual orientation. Instead, like any adoptive applicant, they should be assessed individually on what potential strengths they may (or may not) bring to the adoption process, and, most important, to a child in need of a family.

As noted, the study utilized valid, reliable, and widely used instruments, with both parents and children scoring at or above levels reported in other research. Nevertheless, as with all studies, this one contained limitations. Of primary concern is that the convenience sample may introduce selection bias, i.e., it is possible that the participants were limited to those who had positive experiences and believed they had strengths to discuss, thus not reflecting families who may have had negative adoption experiences. In addition, all of the results are based on parental self-reporting, so some or many of the respondents may have wanted to portray their experiences in the most positive light. In addition, there was no control or comparison group. Thus, one can talk about the experiences of these gay and lesbian adoptive parents, but generalizing beyond this sample to other gay or lesbian adoptive parents or to heterosexual adoptive parents is problematic.

Lastly, these data were collected cross-sectionally, so they do not permit us to understand the on-going, long-term dynamics of life in these and other adoptive families. It would be necessary to recruit families as they begin the adoption process and follow them over the child-rearing years to gain a more complete understanding of how factors such as parenting styles and child strengths interplay as children and adults come together as an adoptive family over time. However, it should be noted that the limitations above are not unique to research on gay- or lesbian-headed adoptive families, and similar longitudinal and developmental research is needed on all adoptive family forms [see, for example, Johnson (2006) and Nalavany (2006) for critical reviews of the literature on adopted adolescents and sexually abused adopted children, respectively].

While there is a growing body of literature describing gay and lesbian adoptive experiences, it is also clear that much more empirical work is needed to gain a complete understanding of adoptions in general, as well as of adoptive gay and lesbian parents and their children in particular. Future research should address some of the current gaps by obtaining a large representative sample, incorporating a comparison group of non-gay and lesbian adoptive parents, and, independent of parental reporting, collecting data from adopted children and others on how they grow and develop within such families. There is no evidence that such adoptions are harmful in any way, and there is growing evidence that such placements are as loving and supportive as adoptive families in general; nevertheless, more rigorous research will enable practitioners and policymakers to be more responsive to and supportive of the needs of these families—and, most pointedly, to the needs of children who do not yet have families.

Note

1. The Third District Court of Appeal recently upheld a lower court ruling that declared Florida's statutory ban on all adoptions by sexual minority individuals to be unconstitutional, thereby allowing adoption by lesbians and gays for the first time since 1977 (*FL. Department of Children and Families v. In the Matter of Adoption by X.X.G. and N.R.G.*, 2010).

References

Barth, R. P., & Berry, M. (1988). *Adoption and disruption: Rates, risks and responses.* New York: A. de Gruyter Publishers.

Berry, R. P. (1990). A study of disruptive adoptive placements of adolescents. *Child Welfare, 69,* 209–225.

Brodzinsky, D. M. (1990). A stress and coping model of adoption adjustment. In D. M. Brodzinsky & M. Schechter (Eds.), *The psychology of adoption.* (pp. 3–14). New York: Oxford University Press.

Brodzinsky, D. M. (2006). Family structural openness and communication openness as predictors in the adjustment of adopted children. *Adoption Quarterly, 9,* 1–18.

Brodzinsky, D. M., & Pinderhughes, E. (2002). Parenting and child development in adoptive families. In M. Bornstein (Ed.), *Handbook of parenting. Vol. 1: Children and parenting.* (pp. 279–311). Mahwah, New Jersey: Erlbaum & Associates.

Brodzinsky, D. M., Smith, D. W., & Brodzinsky, A. B.(1998). *Children's adjustment to adoption: Developmental and clinical issues.* New York: Sage.

Brooks, D., & Goldberg, S. (2001). Gay and lesbian adoptive and foster care placements: Can they meet the needs of waiting children? *Social Work, 46,* 147–157.

Child Welfare League of America. (2000). *Standards of excellence for adoption services.* Washington, D.C.

Child Welfare League of America. (2008). *Standards of excellence for adoption services.* Washington, D.C.

Cohen, S., & Wills, T. A. (1985). Stress, social support, and the buffering hypothesis. *Psychological Bulletin, 98,* 310–357.

Colarossi, L. G., & Eccles, J. S. (2000). A prospective study of adolescents' peer support: Gender differences and the influence of parental relationships. *Journal of Youth and Adolescence, 29,* 661–678.

Crnic, K. A., & Greenberg, M. T. (1990). Minor parenting stresses with young children. *Child Development, 61,* 1628–1637.

Dillman, D. A. (2000). *Mail and internet surveys: The tailored design method.* New York: Wiley & Sons Inc.

Early, T., & Glenmaye, L. (2000). Valuing families: Social work practice with families from a strengths perspective. *Social Work, 45,* 118–130.

Erickson, E. H. (1968). *Identity: Youth and crisis.* New York: W.W. Norton and Company.

Festinger, T. (1986). *Necessary risk: A study of adoptions and disrupted adoptive placements.* Washington, D.C.: Child Welfare League of America.

Florida Department of Children and Families v. In the Matter of Adoption of X.X.G and N.R.G., No. 3D08–3044, 2010 WL 3655782 (Fla. Dist. Ct. App., Sept 22, 2010).

Goldberg, A. E. (2010). *Lesbian and gay parents and their children.* Washington, D.C.: American Psychological Association.

Groothues, C., Beckett, C., & O'Connor, T. G. (1998). The outcome of adoptions from Romania: Predictors of parental satisfaction. *Adoption and Fostering, 22,* 30–40.

Groza, V., & Ryan, S. D. (2002). Pre-adoption stress and its association with child behavior in domestic special needs and international adoptions. *Psychoneuroendocrinology, 27,* 181–192.

Groza, V., Ryan, S. D., & Cash, S. J. (2003). Institutionalization, behavior, and international adoption: Predictors of behavior problems. *Journal of Immigrant and Minority Health, 5,* 5–17.

Groze, V. (1996). A 1 and 2 year follow-up study of adoptive families and special needs children. *Children and Youth Services Review, 18,* 57–82.

Groze, V., & Rosenthal, J. A. (1993). Attachment theory and the adoption of children with special needs. *Social Work Research and Abstracts, 29,* 5–13.

Hill, M. (1997). *SPSS missing values analysis 7.5.* Chicago, IL: SPSS Inc.

Hinterlong, J., & Ryan, S. (2007). Creating grander families: Older adults adopting younger kin and non-kin. *The Gerontologist, 48,* 527–537.

House, J. S. (1981). *Work stress and social support*. Reading, MA: Addison Wesley Publishing Company.

Human Rights Campaign. (2009). *Promising practices in adoption and foster care: A comprehensive guide to policies and practices that welcome, affirm, and support gay, lesbian, bisexual, and transgendered foster and adoptive parents*. Washington, D.C.: Human Rights Campaign.

Johnson, L. (2006). Adopted adolescents: Do social supports act as a buffer between stressors and adoptive parent-child relationships? Doctoral dissertation, Florida State University, 2006. *Dissertation Abstracts International*, AAT 3232393.

Kagan, R. M., & Reid, W. J. (1986). Critical factors in the adoption of emotionally disturbed youth. *Child Welfare*, 65, 63–73.

Kirk, S. A. (1964). Research in education. In H. Stevens & R. Heber (Eds.), *Mental retardation: A review of research*. Chicago: University of Chicago Press.

Leung, P., & Erich, S. (2002). Family functioning of adoptive children with special needs: Implications of familial supports and children characteristics. *Children and Youth Services Review*, 24, 799–816.

Maguire, L. (1991). *Social support systems in practice*. Silver Spring, MD: National Association of Social Workers Press.

Mahoney, G., Robinson, C., & Powell, A. (1992). Focusing on parent-child interaction: The bridge to developmentally appropriate practices. *Topics for Early Childhood Special Education*, 12, 105–120.

Mallon, G. P. (2006). *Lesbian and gay foster and adoptive parents: Recruiting, assessing, and supporting an untapped resource for children and youth*. Washington, D.C.: Child Welfare League of America.

Mallon, G. P. (2007). Assessing lesbian and gay prospective foster and adoptive families: A focus on the home study process. *Child Welfare*, 86, 67–86.

Mathews, J. D., & Cramer, E. P. (2006). Envisaging the adoption process to strengthen gay- and lesbian-headed families: Recommendations for adoption professionals. *Child Welfare*, 85, 317–340.

McDonald, T. P., Lieberman, A. A., Partridge, S., & Hornby, H. (1991). Assessing the role of agency services in reducing adoption disruptions. *Children and Youth Services Review*, 13, 425–438.

Monat, A., & Lazarus, R. S. (1991). *Stress and coping: An anthology*. New York: Columbia University Press.

Nalavany, B. A. (2006). The impact of pre-adoptive childhood sexual abuse on adopted boys. Doctoral dissertation, Florida State University, 2006. *Dissertation Abstracts International*, AAT 3216522.

Pinderhughes, E. (1998). Short term placement outcomes for children adopted after age five. *Children and Youth Services*, 20, 223–249.

Rosenthal, J. A., & Groze, V. K. (1992). *Special needs adoption: A study of intact families*. New York: Praeger.

Rosenthal, J. A., Schmidt, D., & Conner, J. (1988). Predictors of special needs adoption disruption: An exploratory study. *Children and Youth Services Review*, 10, 101–117.

Ryan, S. D. (2000). Examining social workers' placement recommendations of children with gay and lesbian adoptive parents. *Families in Society: The Journal of Contemporary Human Services*, 81, 517–528.

Ryan, S. D. (2008). Adoption, gay and lesbian. In V. Parrillo (Ed.), *Encyclopedia of social problems* (Vol. I, pp. 25–26). Thousand Oaks, CA: Sage Publications.

Ryan, S. D., & Groza, V. (2003). Romanian adoptions: A cross national comparison. *International Social Work, 47,* 53–79.

Sarason, B. R., Sarason, I. G., & Pierce, G. R. (1990). *Social support: An interactional view.* New York: John Wiley & Sons.

Solomon, P. (1994). Families views of service delivery: An empirical assessment. In H. P. Lefley & M. Wasow (Eds.), *Helping families cope with mental illness.* New York: Taylor & Francis.

Stacey, J., & Biblarz, T. J. (2001). (How) does the sexual orientation of parents matter? *American Sociological Review, 66,* 159–183.

Trivette, C. M., Dunst, C. J., Deal, A. G., Harer, A. W., & Propst, S. (1990). Assessing family strengths and family functioning style. *Topics in Early Childhood and Special Education, 10,* 16–35.

Trivette, C. M., Dunst, C. J., Deal, A. G., Hamby, D., & Sexton, D. (1994). Assessing family strengths and capabilities. In C. J. Dunst, C. M. Trivette, & A. G. Deal (Eds.), *Supporting and strengthening families.* Silver Spring, MD: NASW Press.

Van Ijzendoorn, M. H., Dikjstra, J., & Bus, A. G. (1995). Attachment, intelligence and language: A meta-analysis. *Social Development, 4,* 115–128.

10

Lesbian and Gay Adoptive Parent Families

Assessment, Clinical Issues, and Intervention

ABBIE E. GOLDBERG AND MARK GIANINO ■

Despite the substantial literature on adoptive families (Brodzinsky, 2006; Brodzinsky & Palacios, 2005; Brodzinsky & Pinderhughes, 2002; Palacios & Brodzinsky, 2010; van Korff, Grotevant, & McRoy, 2006) and the growing literature on lesbian and gay parent-headed families (Goldberg, 2010; Goldberg, Downing, & Sauck, 2008; Patterson, 2000), there remains limited research on lesbian and gay adoptive parent families (Gianino, 2008; Leung, Erich, & Kanenberg, 2005; Farr, Forssell, & Patterson, 2010). Much of the research on lesbian and gay parents focuses on couples and individuals who have had their children via alternative insemination (Gartrell, Banks, Reed, Hamilton, Rodas, & Deck, 2000; Gartrell, Peyser, & Bos, this volume) or who have had their children in a heterosexual relationship and later come out as lesbian and gay (Tasker & Golombok, 1997). Thus, this chapter will draw from multiple sources, including the literature on clinical work with lesbian and gay parent families and the literature on clinical work with adoptive families, as well as the general adoption literature and the lesbian and gay parent family literature.

The purpose of this chapter is to provide an overview of assessment and intervention issues in clinical practice with lesbian and gay adoptive parent families. It will begin by describing the context of lesbian and gay adoption and then will address the various phases of lesbian and gay adoptive parent family formation (from assessment to postplacement)—with an emphasis on the contexts influencing family development at these stages—as well as relevant assessment and intervention issues. Recommendations for adoption workers and therapists who work with lesbian and gay adoptive families at these phases will be made throughout. Case examples will also be provided to illustrate key issues and conflicts faced by these families, as well as opportunities and challenges for therapists.

THE CONTEXT OF LESBIAN AND GAY ADOPTION

Data from the U.S. Census suggest that the number of lesbian and gay adoptive parent households is increasing, and that these parents represent a sizable minority of adoptive mothers and fathers in the country. An estimated one in 20 male same-sex couples and one in five female same-sex couples were raising children in 1990; those figures rose to one in five for male couples and one in three for female couples by 2000 (Gates & Ost, 2004). Furthermore, of the 1.6 million adopted children under age 18 years, at least 65,000 live with lesbian or gay parents (Gates, Badgett, Macomber, & Chambers, 2007). This is likely a conservative estimate (in that some lesbian and gay individuals likely choose not to disclose their sexual orientation on the Census), and it does not include foster children.

Despite these growing numbers, as well as robust research findings demonstrating that children who are raised by sexual minorities are not disadvantaged with regard to emotional, social, and developmental outcomes (Goldberg, 2010; Patterson, 2000; Stacey & Biblarz, 2001), negative stereotypes of and misconceptions about lesbians and gays persist (Crawford, McLeod, Zamboni, & Jordan, 1999). As a result, they become parents in a societal context that alternately ignores and stigmatizes them. Such experiences of marginalization and stigmatization can have powerful implications for these parents' development and adjustment at various phases of the adoption process and the family life cycle. Consequently, therapists and evaluators who work with lesbian and gay adoptive families must be (1) cognizant of the ways in which, as a group, lesbians and gay men have been rejected and pathologized, (2) sensitive to the many ways in which heterosexism serves to directly and indirectly shape family members' experiences, (3) sensitive to the impact of racism on family members' experiences, among those lesbian and gay persons who adopt transracially, (4) familiar with the ways in which lesbian and gay adoptive families' experiences may be different from and similar to those of heterosexual adoptive families, and (5) active in identifying and building on family members' strengths and resources.

ASSESSMENT AND INTERVENTION ISSUES IN THE PREADOPTIVE PHASE (CONTEMPLATION)

Internalized Homophobia

In considering whether they wish to become parents, lesbians and gay men may confront internalized homophobia. Growing up in a heterosexist society, some sexual minorities have internalized the notion that (1) homosexuality is wrong, (2) they are less "fit" to parent than are heterosexuals, and (3) growing up with them is harmful to children's identity formation and psychosocial development. Thus, many lesbians and gay men may question whether they have a right to raise children, or they may worry that the barriers to becoming a gay parent are insurmountable (Gianino, 2008).

Therapists who work with lesbian and gay couples who are contemplating parenthood in general, and adoption specifically, may wish to probe these concerns and beliefs. For example, one or both partners may be holding back from fully committing to parenthood out of concern that they are being "selfish" in their desire to parent, and/or that they are being "unfair" to future children by knowingly subjecting them to potential stigma and heterosexism. Therapists can assist their clients in exploring the origins of these beliefs and worries (e.g., they may reflect the sentiments of family members, or they may stem from beliefs perpetuated by the broader society).

Professionals can also play an important role in countering some of the myths and false beliefs that sexual minorities have internalized, providing them with factual information and education about the research findings on the children of lesbian and gay parents. For example, they can help their clients understand that children's psychosocial development appears to be influenced more by the nature of familial relationships and interactions than by family structure per se (Stacey & Biblarz, 2001). At the same time, therapists may wish to explore their clients' feelings about and preparedness for the possibility that their children may be stigmatized based on their family form (Ray & Gregory, 2001). Always, however, therapists should seek to enable parents to locate the "problem" in society—that is, in the form of prejudice and discrimination—and not in their individual selves and sexual orientation (Martin, 1998).

Motivations for Parenthood and Adoption

Another area that therapists and evaluators may wish to address with lesbian and gay couples who are considering adoption is their individual motivation for parenthood. For some couples, the path to parenthood is initiated by one partner; that is, one partner broaches the topic, which initiates a process of discussion and negotiation that may ultimately result in the less-motivated partner developing a greater interest in the prospect of parenthood (Herrmann-Green & Gehring, 2007). Some partners, on the other hand, may fall short of this commitment: They may agree to *support* their partners in their quest to parent, and perhaps to "help out," but may be hesitant to embrace the notion of parenthood as a joint endeavor (Pies, 1990). Therapists can be instrumental in helping couples clarify and communicate their individual and collective motivations for parenthood, and guiding them to consider the potential implications of their similar or differing levels of investment. Exploration of the reasons for wanting to parent may also be useful, i.e., partners may have differing reasons for wanting to parent, and a discussion of such differences may be crucial to avoiding unexpected conflicts later on. Such issues are not unique to same-sex couples: Research suggests that men and women in heterosexual couples may also have differing motivations for parenthood (Mackey, White, & Day, 1992; van Balen, 2005).

Discussion of partners' motivations for adoption, specifically, is also warranted. Like heterosexual couples, some lesbians experience fertility problems, which ultimately lead them toward adoption (Goldberg & Smith, 2008; Goldberg, Downing, & Richardson, 2009; Shelley-Sireci & Ciano-Boyce, 2002). In turn, one or both partners may have unresolved feelings about infertility, which are important to address as couples actively move toward adoption. For example, the partner who tried to conceive may continue to experience feelings of anger and loss surrounding her inability to carry and bear a child. This can place a strain on the relationship, creating feelings of alienation and tension that may carry over into the adoption process if they are not directly addressed (Goldberg et al., 2009), and may have an impact on the capacity of the parents to effectively cope with specific adoption-related tasks (Brodzinsky, 1997). The need to address grief associated with infertility before fully committing to adoption is not specific to lesbian and gay individuals; this is also a salient issue among heterosexual couples (Brodzinsky, 1997).

Some lesbians and gay men choose to adopt because they do not feel strongly about having a biogenetically related child (Gagnon, Riley, Toole, & Goldberg, 2007; Gianino, 2008) or, in the case of lesbians, about experiencing pregnancy and childbirth (Goldberg et al., 2009). Furthermore, couples may opt for adoption over alternative insemination or surrogacy because they want each parent to have an equal connection to the child and, in the case of lesbians, may wish to avoid the potential inequities associated with one partner carrying the child (Goldberg et al., 2009). Also, similar to heterosexual couples (e.g., Brooks & James, 2003), altruistic motivations may underlie some lesbians' and gay men's desire to adopt; rather than bringing another child into the world, some wish to provide a permanent home to a child who needs one (Gagnon et al., 2007). Elaboration of motivations can be important in identifying potentially problematic or unrealistic beliefs and expectations or, alternatively, in revealing key strengths in couples' approach to or framing of adoption.

Although the existing literature on lesbian and gay adoption has tended to privilege couples as parents and omit consistent mention of single-parent families (J. Raible, personal communication, May 16, 2008), there is evidence that single sexual minorities are increasingly choosing to adopt (Matthews, 2004) for reasons that are similar to those of their coupled counterparts and of heterosexuals (e.g., a wish to fulfill a lifelong desire to parent; the altruistic desire to provide a child with a loving and stable home). However, single prospective parents, whether gay or not, face unique challenges.

For instance, they may question whether they possess the emotional and financial resources to care for a child on their own, particularly if their family and friendship networks are unsupportive or ambivalent about their parenting aspirations. They also might wonder how to balance the needs of a child and the demands of work. Finally, they may consider whether the decision to parent might curtail their options for future relationships or professional advancement. Therapists should support single lesbian and gay prospective adopters by helping them to engage in both emotional and practical preparation for the challenges that lie ahead. Furthermore, therapists and adoption professionals can provide practical assistance to their clients by helping them to locate gay-friendly resources for single adoptive and foster parents, whether in their own communities or in the form of "virtual," Internet-based communities.

CASE EXAMPLE: A LESBIAN COUPLE CONSIDERING PARENTHOOD

Maura and Louanne are a white lesbian couple who were together for 7 years before pursuing parenthood. Both women had strong desires to parent; in fact, their shared goal of parenthood was one of the factors that initially drew them to each other. The couple decided to pursue alternative insemination because of their initial perception of it as "easier" and "more straightforward" than adoption. Maura had a strong desire to carry and bear a child, and was also 5 years younger than Louanne; so, the couple mutually agreed that she was the obvious choice to carry the child. After a year of unsuccessful inseminations with an unidentified (anonymous) donor, the couple met with a fertility specialist. After a series of tests, Maura was advised to go on Clomid, a medication designed to stimulate ovulation. After 8 months of "pure and total hell"—Clomid often causes mood swings and other psychological and physical symptoms (Robinson & Stewart, 1996)—Maura decided to discontinue the medication, a decision Louanne fully supported. At this point, Maura broached the possibility of Louanne trying to conceive. Louanne was resistant, noting that she "never had a desire to carry a child."

Maura and Louanne presented for couples therapy, stating that they were "at a crossroads in terms of what to do next." Maura wanted Louanne to try to conceive because it seemed "easier" than pursuing adoption, but Louanne did not have a desire to do so. However, she said that this was not her biggest concern; rather, her greatest worry was that if she were to carry the child, Maura might find herself jealous or resentful, which might in turn cause conflict and tension in their relationship. The therapist encouraged both partners to consider the implications of such a decision. How would Louanne feel, committing to a course of action that she felt unprepared for and at least somewhat uncomfortable with? How would Maura feel, watching Louanne carry and give birth to a child when she herself still grieved her own inability to conceive?

Louanne acknowledged being a bit resentful of Maura's pressuring her, when she had been clear about her lack of desire to carry a child "from the moment we met." Maura acknowledged that this was true, but felt "so out of control and helpless" that she had wanted Louanne to change her mind. Maura also admitted that seeing Louanne pregnant might be difficult; how-ever, she felt that by being highly involved in the pregnancy and delivery, she could avoid feelings of loss and jealousy. The therapist validated Maura's desire to quickly "move on" from the painful process of infertility, while also suggesting that they explore more fully their feelings of loss and the per-ceived advantages or disadvantages of various routes to parenthood.

For the next several months, Maura and Louanne discussed their mutual sadness about Maura's inability to conceive, as well as their individual and collective fears and concerns about having Louanne try to conceive. Maura expressed the feeling that she "couldn't take another disappointment," causing Louanne to feel, as she humorously called it, "womb pressure." Thus, candid expression of their fears led both partners to feel more connected to and empathic toward each other. In this way, with the therapist's support, they were able to revisit their initial goal of becoming parents. The therapist encouraged them to discuss their concerns about adoption, and provided them with education about the various types of adoptions, as well as information about the unique barriers and challenges that they might experience because of their sexual orientation. Eventually, Maura and Louanne reached a mutual decision to pursue private domestic open adoption, which they both felt excited about and committed to pursuing.

This vignette illustrates the ways in which the "transitional period" between trying to conceive and moving to adoption may be stressful, particularly for lesbian couples who have differing sentiments toward becoming pregnant and giving birth (Goldberg et al., 2009). It also illustrates the potential usefulness of couples therapy during this transitional phase, especially with a therapist who is knowledgeable about gay adoption and is comfortable maintaining an affirming stance with respect to same-sex couples.

Decision Making about Adoption

Prospective lesbian and gay adoptive parents must make numerous decisions relating to which route to take (i.e., international, domestic infant, or foster care adoption). Professionals who assist lesbians and gay men in their decision making—such as adoption consultants, lawyers, and therapists—should encourage their clients to consider factors such as finances, feelings about the importance of being "out" during the adoption process, and preferences regarding child age, race, ethnicity, and level and type of special needs. For example, lesbians and gay men with limited finances may find that their best option is public domestic adoption—i.e., adoption through the child welfare (foster care) system. At the same time, they need to consider the possibility that the children available are most often older and may have histories of abuse or neglect (Brodzinsky & Pinderhughes, 2002).

Lesbians and gay men who place a strong emphasis on being open and honest about their relationship throughout the adoption process may be particularly ill-suited for international adoption, which requires that the couple "closet" their relationship and select one partner to adopt as a single parent (Gianino, 2008; Goldberg, Downing, & Sauck, 2007; Mallon, 2007). Indeed, couples should be cautioned about the potential stress and tension that may arise as a function of having only one partner recognized as the prospective parent (Goldberg et al., 2007). Furthermore, even if couples who pursue international adoption live in states that permit second-parent adoptions by lesbians and gay men,[1] they should be warned that such proceedings may take months to finalize, leaving a period of time during which the child has only one legal parent.

Lesbians and gay men who are uncomfortable with the secrecy inherent in "closed" adoptions may be particularly drawn toward open adoption, in which a pregnant woman (and the male partner, when he is involved) generally choose the adoptive parent(s), and which may involve ongoing contact with the birth parent(s) following adoption placement (Goldberg et al., 2007). Clients should be encouraged to think carefully about the level of openness they desire; clients with clear, shared expectations and goals will be in a better position to evaluate the potential "fit" of various potential matches. Finally, prospective parents who strongly desire a baby may wish to pursue domestic infant adoption, since children adopted internationally are often somewhat older (e.g., between 6 and 24 months) and there are few infants available from foster care.

Lesbian and gay prospective adoptive parents must also decide what child characteristics are important and/or too challenging for them. For example, they must assess their personal and social resources to determine whether they are willing and able to parent a child with special needs, and if so, what level or type of special needs they are open to. The term "special needs" refers to certain characteristics associated with increased challenges such as being older at the time of placement, having physical and/or cognitive disabilities, being a member of a sibling group, having diagnosed medical, emotional, and/or behavioral disorders, and having suffered drug or alcohol exposure in utero (Brooks & Goldberg, 2001; Ryan, Pearlmutter, & Groza, 2004).

Adoption professionals can help prospective parents to assess realistically their willingness and capacity to take on a child with such needs by emphasizing the need to be honest and forthright with themselves and their partners, even if it means appearing selfish or rigid. The would-be parents should be cautioned that a failure to be honest at the initial stages of decision making may result in unwanted or unfavorable circumstances later on. Specifically, they should consider their psychological and emotional preparedness for raising a child with emotional, physical, or medical issues. Do they feel capable of raising a child who might need a great deal of attention or specialized services? Do they feel prepared to care for a child who might never be independent or may have great difficulty in forming an emotional attachment to them? In addition to assessing their psychological resources, prospective parents should consider their financial, physical, and social resources. Are they prepared to make the financial commitment that may be necessary to provide for their child? Is their house equipped for a child with specific physical needs (e.g., is it wheelchair accessible, or could it be)? Would their parents and friends support their decision to adopt a child with special needs? What neighborhood and community resources in their geographic area are available for such a child?

In addition to considering the type of adoption they wish to pursue, prospective adoptive parents must also make important decisions about the race and ethnicity of the child they want to adopt. In doing so, they should be encouraged to consider their consciousness of and attitudes about race, their personal experiences as someone of a dominant or minority race, and their willingness and commitment to foster a strong racial and cultural identity in their child. They will need to consider the extent to which they feel prepared for and committed to becoming a multiracial family (if they are not already), as well as their level of preparedness for the visibility they will face as a multiracial lesbian and gay household—as such families are necessarily vulnerable to the stresses associated with both heterosexism and racism (Romney, 1995). Finally, prospective adoptive parents must also consider the extent to which their extended family members, friends, and neighbors are likely to be accepting of a transracial placement. Racism and resistance from social network members represent a major challenge faced by multiracial heterosexual (de Haymes & Simon, 2003) and lesbian (Bennett, 2003a) adoptive families, and this lack of support can contribute to familial tensions and stress (Deacon, 1997).

Interestingly, there is some evidence that white same-sex couples are more likely to be open to, and to adopt, transracially,[2] compared to white heterosexual couples (Farr & Patterson, 2009; Gates et al., 2007; Goldberg, 2009; Goldberg & Smith, 2009; Shelley-Sireci & Ciano-Boyce, 2002). This is important, given that transracial adoption, especially of African-American children by white couples, has been an area of considerable research interest over the past several decades and to this day remains the subject of considerable controversy (Carter-Black, 2002; de Haymes & Simon, 2003; Simon & Alstein, 2000; Smith, McRoy, Freundlich, & Kroll, 2008). One of the most prevalent arguments against transracial adoption is that no matter how well-meaning, white families cannot teach African-American children, in particular, how to cope in a society in which they are almost certain to encounter racism (Simon & Alstein, 2000). Thus, lesbian and gay parents who adopt transracially may be vulnerable to stigma related to their status as gay parents, as well as criticism related to their choice to adopt transracially.

A significant body of research suggests that although transracial adoption in and of itself does not create psychological and social problems in children (Smith et al., 2008), at the same time, transracially adopted children and their families do face numerous challenges, and the manner in which the parents cope with these challenges therefore is critical. Ideally, individuals and couples who choose to adopt transracially should be aware of their responsibility to create a new multiracial and multicultural identity as a family and to learn about their children's racial and ethnic heritage in order to foster a healthy self-image in them (Park & Green, 2000). Indeed, parents' level of competence in these regards has a significant impact on their children's racial and ethnic identity, self-image, and overall well-being (Baden & Steward, 2000; Massatti, Vonk, & Gregoire, 2004; Simon & Alstein, 2000; Vonk, 2001). And yet, although there is ample documentation of the *need* for specialized training for parents to help their children develop positive racial identities, there is little in the literature that documents *how* practitioners meet that need, especially for lesbian and gay adoptive parents. Given the conflicting narratives within the professional literature as well as in the mass media regarding the appropriateness of transracial adoption (Park & Green, 2000), it is no wonder that prospective adoptive parents are confused about whether they can meet the needs of children of racial and cultural backgrounds that are different from their own. The following illustration demonstrates the complexities of therapy with a white gay male couple considering transracial adoption, as well as the challenges and dilemmas that face the clinician.

Case Example: A Gay Couple Contemplating Transracial Adoption

Jonathan (34) and Rob (38) are a white gay male couple who had been together for 11 years when they began their pursuit of parenthood. They reported that each of them had always wanted to parent, which was one of the factors that drew them together. They began their parenting journey by attending a local parenting course for lesbians and gay men that was led by a lesbian social worker. The course assisted participants in clarifying their reasons for parenting, exploring obstacles to parenthood, identifying methods of family formation, and locating psychosocial resources that were needed to help them to fulfill their parenting quest. Early in the group, Jonathan and Rob cemented their desire to adopt rather than pursue other means of achieving parenthood, such as surrogacy. At this time, they also began to consider myriad questions regarding the type of adoption to pursue (domestic or international, open or not, transracial or interracial). Each option seemed to have its own costs and benefits. For example, they were attracted to the possibility of doing an open adoption as an openly gay couple; at the same time, however, they did not want to rule out international adoption, in which being open in their homestudy would inevitably lead to rejection since other countries typically allow adoption only by heterosexuals.

Over a period of several months after the class, Jonathan and Rob began to feel "stuck." They were unable to come to a decision about which direction to pursue and they began to feel overwhelmed by the process and the many decisions that needed to be made. In addition, they were inundated with conflicting "advice" from well-intentioned friends and family members. Disillusioned and uncertain about whether to proceed with adoption at all, they sought couples therapy to help sort out the best course of action: to move forward, or deal with the grief that would arise from a decision to foreclose their parenting aspirations. A transformative moment occurred in the first session when their therapist asked the following question: "When you close your eyes and picture your family, what do you see?" Rob quickly and instinctively responded that "having a child who could 'pass' as biologically ours is not important to either one of us."

What followed in subsequent sessions was an exploration of the partners' honest feelings and beliefs regarding transracial adoption. Initially, they were reluctant to share their feelings regarding adopting a child of another race, fearing that they would be judged by the therapist, who reassured them that such explorations were important for their best interests and a child's best interests. Jonathan offered that they had begun to consider adopting an African-American child but were uncertain how, as a white gay couple, they could socialize a child to prepare for and cope with societal racism. As the couple further explored the issue, they became increasingly unsure. Rob said: "I started reading stuff about interracial parenting and how dangerous that is, and then we did a lot of thinking. We made a conscious choice that we weren't sure if we were capable of handling an African-American boy because of the sort of racial stuff that goes with black men. I don't know if both of us were sure that we were capable of handling that as they got older. The only thing we knew is that neither one of us felt equipped to explain the racial history of this country to an African-American male child."

After further probing, Rob disclosed that his greatest fear was of rejection of their family by African-American parents (e.g., he worried that as gay white men, they would be judged by African-American parents as unfit to raise a black child). At this stage, it was important for the therapist to (1) assume a nonjudgmental stance in order to encourage the couple to honestly explore their own racial attitudes, (2) help clarify racial and ethnic stereotypes that might arise for the couple as part of their parenting journey, and (3) ascertain the couple's readiness to assume the opportunities and challenges inherent in transracial adoption.

Shortly thereafter, Rob reported that they became acquainted with another gay couple who had successfully adopted from Latin America. In turn, he was suddenly hit with the realization that "there's something that we really like about the thought of adopting internationally," so they began to research adopting from Latin America. The therapist was surprised to learn of their decision and wondered if Rob and Jonathan had considered that such an adoption would very likely be transracial as well as transcultural. In an effort to be respectful of the couple's need to make the choice that felt best for them, the therapist nonetheless felt compelled to ask them what experiences in their lives had better prepared them to deal with a Latin American child as compared to one who was African American. Jonathan said that as a teacher in an urban school setting and a fluent Spanish speaker, it suddenly made sense to him that their family would have more inroads into Latino communities and that the process of socialization would be a more comfortable fit for them and their child. The couple subsequently concluded therapy and began their pursuit of an international adoption from Latin America.

This vignette illustrates the challenges for any clinician working with a couple such as Rob and Jonathan in addressing the complexities of race and heterosexism. In facilitating adoptions for lesbian and gay clients, practitioners must be careful not to underplay the complexities of the transracial aspect of the adoption. Therefore, to achieve a measure of cultural competency in mental health service delivery to adoptees and their families, clinicians must examine their own attitudes and assumptions on the subject (Lee, 2003; Vonk, 2001).

Social Support

Research consistently indicates that lesbian and gay couples often perceive lower levels of support than their heterosexual counterparts (Kurdek, 2001); furthermore, a recent study of lesbian and heterosexual preadoptive couples found that low levels of perceived family support were related to higher levels of depression

(Goldberg & Smith, 2008). Additionally, a key predictor of adoption disruption is low levels of support from relatives or friends (Rosenthal, 1993). These data suggest that an important role for adoption professionals lies in the assessment and identification of clients' social resources and deficiencies. Specifically, professionals should seek to identify and address lesbian and gay prospective adopters' perceptions of familial resources and support, as well as their perceptions of other sources of potential support or nonsupport (e.g., friends, workplace, neighborhood, and community). By exploring these various sources of strength and/or stress, both clients and professionals can develop a more holistic picture of clients' overall network of resources, and may identify potential "gaps" that they wish to fill. For example, a couple might realize that their network of friends consists of very few parents; in turn, they may be motivated and encouraged to seek out other sources of support (e.g., joining a local parents' group, or, if this is not feasible in their community, joining an online/virtual parents' group). Adoption professionals can also directly support the development of healthy social networks. For example, adoption preparation classes can educate applicants about the importance of building and maintaining kin support; these classes may also function as important forums for connection and community building.

ASSESSMENT AND INTERVENTION ISSUES DURING THE ADOPTION PROCESS

Finding an Agency

Once lesbians and gay men have settled upon an adoption path, therapists, educators, and adoption professionals face new challenges in terms of assessing and supporting them in their quest to become parents. These prospective parents face challenges in locating agencies and lawyers that are willing to work with them (Brodzinsky, 2003, this volume; Goldberg et al., 2007); they may be turned away and/or told that the agency's "gay quota" has been filled, which can cause feelings of disempowerment and frustration (McPheeters, Carmi, & Goldberg, 2008), and/or they may experience insensitivity from individual caseworkers even in adoption agencies that do agree to work with them (Brooks, Kim, & Wind, this volume; Mallon, this volume). For example, some agencies communicate conflicting messages about whether lesbian and gay clients should disclose their sexual orientation during the adoption process, which is experienced as frustrating and misleading by clients (Mallon, 2004; Mallon, this volume; Matthews & Cramer, 2006). Additionally, practitioners may be uneducated about the legal issues inherent to lesbian and gay adoption—being unsure, for instance, of what to do if a lesbian or gay couple in California (a state that does permit same-sex couples to jointly adopt) is chosen as the adoptive parents by a birthmother living in Missouri (a state that does not permit co-parent adoption by same-sex couples). Furthermore, they may not be attuned to the unique context of lesbian and gay parenthood. For example, they may fail to consider the possibility that gay couples (and many lesbian couples) do not necessarily arrive at adoption after years of unsuccessful attempts to conceive (Goldberg et al., 2007; Matthews & Cramer, 2006). In turn, same-sex couples sometimes find themselves participating in trainings and support groups that focus heavily on infertility, which may be irrelevant to their experiences.

Professionals who work with lesbian and gay prospective adopters can support them in a variety of ways. Validating and normalizing perceptions of discrimination and feelings of frustration can help to strengthen clients' sense of empowerment, as well as the professional–client alliance. Additionally, professionals can actively support lesbians and gay men in their quest to identify sensitive and gay-friendly agencies. Lesbians and gay men might be encouraged to consider some of the following factors: Do the agency's materials (website, offices, printed brochures) contain images of same-sex couples? Does the agency explicitly state its openness to working with sexual minorities (in materials, website, mission statement)? Are staff members respectful and kind during initial in-person and telephone interactions? Does the agency have specialized support groups or services for lesbian and gay adoptive and prospective parents? Does the agency actively engage with and recruit from the gay community (Goldberg et al., 2007; Human Rights Campaign, 2009)?[3] By keeping a "scorecard" of their experiences with various agencies, lesbians and gay men may feel less vulnerable and more empowered in the adoption process.

The Waiting Stage

The waiting stage is an inherently stressful aspect of the adoption process. That is, once a couple has completed their homestudy (Mallon, this volume), they often wait an indeterminate period of time for a referral or child placement. Lesbian and gay couples may experience additional stress during this period. For example, research suggests that they often experience concerns that no pregnant woman will ever select a same-sex couple to adopt her child, and they therefore will be waiting "forever" (Goldberg et al., 2007). These concerns are not groundless: Some prospective birth mothers do express an unwillingness to place a child with lesbian and gay adoptive parents; and yet others willingly do so (Brodzinsky, 2003). Adoption professionals and clinicians can support lesbian and gay prospective parents as they cope with general feelings of impatience, lack of control, hopelessness, and fear (e.g., "Will it ever happen?"), as well as gay-specific fears (e.g., "Will a pregnant woman ever select a same-sex couple to adopt her child?") In particular, lesbian and gay prospective parents may find it helpful to be connected (e.g., by their adoption agencies or attorneys) to other waiting lesbian and gay clients, as well as ones who have successfully adopted. In this way, they are provided with supportive outlets for sharing their fears and anxieties, as well as models of successful placements that may instill hope. Of course, lesbian and gay prospective parents who have been waiting a particularly long time and/or who are feeling particularly hopeless may warrant special intervention; indeed, a recent study found that greater length of waiting time among both lesbian and heterosexual preadoptive couples was associated with increased symptoms of anxiety (Goldberg & Smith, 2008). Monthly check-in meetings with an adoption counselor and/or individual or couples therapy may be helpful for those who are having a particularly difficult time with the wait.

Legal Issues

Legal barriers pose another potential challenge for lesbian and gay couples as they prepare to adopt. Some live in states that do not permit same-sex couples to co-adopt their children (i.e., to perform joint adoptions). In this scenario, the couple must choose one partner to adopt the child as a single parent. Then, if the couple lives in a state that permits second-parent adoption by lesbian and gay partners, the nonlegal parent can subsequently adopt his or her partner's child, thereby ensuring two legal parents. Of course, for couples living in states that do not permit such second-parent adoptions, children have only one legal parent (Pawelski et al., 2006). Similarly, couples in which one partner adopts internationally as a single parent may also find themselves in this predicament if their home state does not permit second-parent adoption, either by sexual minorities or at all.

Adoption professionals and therapists should seek to educate their clients about the laws and policies surrounding adoption in their state. Additionally, clients who live in states that do not permit co-parent adoption should be encouraged to discuss who will be the "official" adoptive parent and how each of them feels about this decision. Many couples choose the partner with the higher income and/or higher job status, as this individual will be evaluated in part on the basis of her or his ability to provide for the child (presumably as a single parent). Although this decision may be straightforward for some couples, others may struggle with it (e.g., if they have comparable incomes, jobs, and health insurance). Of course, there is also an emotional component to this decision because neither partner may want to be the one formally "left out" as the legal parent. Furthermore, one partner may feel that he "wants it more" and is thus entitled to be the legal adoptive parent. Alternatively, one partner may feel that she should be the adoptive parent if her partner's family members are particularly hostile, i.e., she may worry that if her partner is the legal parent and if something happens to her, the partner's family members will sue for custody (Goldberg et al., 2009). Adoption professionals and therapists should support clients in exploring their fears and concerns related to legal and power inequity within the couple (Colberg, 1997). In turn, once couples have decided who will be the legal adopter, they should discuss and explore related feelings of worry, anxiety, and jealousy as they arise. As Colberg (1997) notes, lesbians and gay men "are already made to feel powerless in society. The safe haven of their relationship may be disrupted by their inability to equally share in the legal relationship to this child. The clinician should address this issue and help the clients to process their feelings" (p. 121). Finally, in particular, those living in states that do not permit second-parent adoptions should be encouraged to seek other legal safeguards for the nonlegal partner, such as wills and powers of attorney, which may help the nonlegal parent feel more secure. As Martin (1998) notes, parents who take on the emotional and physical responsibilities of raising a child—without any legal rights to parenthood—are exposing themselves and their children to significant risk.

Because of the potential for relatives and friends to view the legal parent as more "real," couples should be cautioned that they do not necessarily have to share the legal details of their adoption. Rather, this information can be treated by the couple as "privileged," at least in the initial stages of parenthood, when partners are establishing their parental roles in relation to the outside world.

CASE EXAMPLE: A LESBIAN COUPLE'S LEGAL DECISION MAKING

Carol (38) and Darlene (40) were in their relationship for 5 years at the time that they decided to pursue domestic, private adoption. As a couple living in rural Georgia, a state that does not permit same-sex couples to jointly adopt, they had to choose one partner to adopt as a single parent. Their hope, initially, was that after the first adoption went through, the other partner could pursue a second-parent adoption (they had several friends who lived in Georgia who had successfully pursued this path). The couple chose Carol to be the "official," legal adoptive parent because she had better health insurance (to which she could add a dependent child) and she made more money—and presumably would be perceived by the agency, as well as potential birth mothers, as a more "attractive" single parent than Darlene. Also, Carol's family was relatively unsupportive of their union and Carol feared that her family would reject an adopted child that was not even legally related to her. Darlene initially expressed concerns about her status as the "invisible parent" (i.e., in the context of the homestudy and adoption process), but was reassured by friends' success in obtaining second-parent adoptions and agreed that Carol should be the official legal adoptive parent as this seemed to be "the best way to ensure that we will get a child."

After 6 months of waiting, however, Carol and Darlene learned from a lawyer that no second-parent adoptions had been granted to lesbians or gay men in the county in which they resided; all of their friends who had successfully gone through that procedure lived in what Carol called "the hip suburbs." Devastated by this news, the couple sought counseling to determine the best course of action, and to discuss Darlene's increasing feelings of vulnerability and exclusion in the adoption process.

The therapist encouraged both partners to discuss their feelings of frustration about the likely impossibility of obtaining a second-parent adoption for Darlene. Both women were angry with their adoption agency and homestudy social worker for "not correcting our assumption that we would eventually both be legal parents of our child." The therapist empathized with their feeling that, as Darlene put it, "they don't know sh-t about gay adoption" but at the same time encouraged them to assertively address what they could do now to ensure that Darlene was not left legally vulnerable. The therapist facilitated a consultation with a local lawyer who was knowledgeable about gay adoption issues, and, in turn, he met with the couple and discussed the possibility of drawing up powers of attorney, wills, and other legal documents that would help to assert and hopefully protect Darlene's relationship with her partner and child. In addition, the therapist supported the couple in discussing the possibility of moving to a different county where second-parent adoption rulings were more favorable. Carol was initially resistant to this possibility, noting that it would extend her work commute from a half an hour to at least an hour. Her resistance, in turn, elicited a strong reaction from Darlene, who expressed feelings of frustration and hurt related to what she perceived as Carol's unwillingness to "make any sort of compromise so that I can share the same rights that she'll have."

The therapist sought to support the couple in regaining their strong alliance and reinstating their shared commitment to securing legal rights for Darlene. Specifically, she encouraged them to share their feelings of fear, frustration, and worry with one another. Darlene, of course, was concerned that she would not have legal rights to her child. Carol was somewhat hurt that Darlene was worried about her rights in the first place: "I would never take our child away from you, would never question your equal rights to them!" Darlene emphasized that she was confident that Carol would never purposefully try to interfere with her parental rights, but nevertheless "would really like to have them, for my own sense of security." Carol acknowledged that this was important and reiterated her own commitment to ensuring that Darlene was able to achieve this sense of security. At the close of therapy, Carol and Darlene had updated their legal documents, with the intention of more seriously considering moving once they had adopted.

This vignette illustrates the potential strain and stress that legal inequities can create in the couple relationship. It also highlights the importance of therapist knowledge about the state laws and community resources related to gay adoption.

POSTPLACEMENT ASSESSMENT AND INTERVENTION ISSUES

Experiences with Visibility and Stigma

Upon having a child, lesbians and gay men confront issues that are common to all adoptive parents, as well as some issues that are unique to their family structure. They may experience heightened visibility in society, due to the nature of their parental relationship (Gianino, 2008). Additionally, same-sex couples who adopt transracially are particularly visible, in that their children are immediately recognizable as having been adopted, are of a different race than their parents, and have lesbian or gay parents. These realities often invite unwanted questions and stares that may be challenging for couples and families who prefer to be left alone. Therapists and adoption professionals should support lesbian and gay parents in determining a course of action for responding to such queries. Do parents wish to function as educators—that is, do they wish to respond by educating strangers, acquaintances, friends, and relatives about their families (Chabot & Ames, 2004)? Or do they wish to ignore and/or avoid answering such questions in an attempt to maintain their privacy? Couples may need to consider the age of their children in deciding what approach is best for them. Indeed, parents of older children should be aware that in choosing to ignore an inquiry, they may be sending the message that their family is something to be ashamed of (Chabot & Ames, 2004). Thus, a challenging task for parents is to help their children learn about the difference between privacy and secrecy as they themselves begin to confront and respond to questions and comments from outsiders (Colberg, 1997). How parents choose to respond to inquiries regarding their sexual orientation and/or family structure may have implications for their children's sense of pride in their family structure, and provides a model for how their children may choose to handle such encounters themselves (Chabot & Ames, 2004; Gartrell et al., 2000).[4]

Socialization Challenges: Talking and Teaching about Race, Adoption, and Family

Sexual minorities are often described as having broad definitions of family. That is, they are often described as prioritizing the relational and affective components of relationships as opposed to the biolegal aspects of kinship (Weston, 1991). In support of this notion, there is evidence that lesbians and gay men may be more likely to seek out adoption as a means of becoming a parent compared to heterosexual couples (Gates et al., 2007; Goldberg & Smith, 2008; Tyebjee, 2003), as well as more open to adopting a child of a different race (Farr & Patterson, 2009; Gates et al., 2007; Goldberg, 2009; Goldberg & Smith, 2009).

This greater openness is not necessarily accompanied by greater preparedness, however, to cope with the challenges of living as an adoptive and, oftentimes, as a multiracial family. Lesbian and gay parents may find themselves wondering about how much attention and emphasis to place on their child's adoptive status and/or racial and cultural background. For example, they may feel conflicted about the number of "differences" that their child must hold in their identity, and may wonder whether it is beneficial or detrimental to prioritize their child's racial and cultural background as the focus of socialization. Alternatively, they may recognize that it is important to foster their child's racial and cultural identity, but lack sufficient personal or social resources to do so. For example, they may be unsure about how to go about facilitating a strong racial identity, especially if they live in a racially nondiverse area and/or have few family members or friends who share the same race as their child.

Therapists who work with lesbian and gay adoptive parents should educate their clients about the need to develop skills in openly and comfortably discussing with their child the facts of their adoption in a way that is developmentally appropriate, sensitive, and compassionate. Indeed, greater adoption-related communication and openness within adoptive families have been linked to positive adjustment outcomes in children (Brodzinsky, 2006). Additionally, adoptive families should be sensitized to the importance of developing an identity of themselves *as* adoptive families (as opposed to focusing solely and exclusively on their *child's* adoptive status as a factor that is relevant to their child's identity only).

Therapists who work with multiracial adoptive families should seek to educate the parents about the need to create a new multiracial, multicultural family identity and to learn about their child's racial and ethnic heritage so that they can help to foster a healthy self-image in their child (Park & Green, 2000). According to some scholars, transracial adoptive parents should ideally possess three areas of competence: *racial awareness*, or awareness of racism and the roles that race, ethnicity, and culture play in people's lives; *multicultural planning*, or facilitation of opportunities for their child to be exposed to and participate in his or her birth culture; and *survival skills*, or preparing their child with skills to externalize as opposed to internalize discrimination (Vonk, 2001). To promote these areas of competence, therapists should encourage parents to acknowledge and explore their own awareness of the role that race has played in their lives, and to consider how their experience of race may be different from or similar to that of their children. Parents should also be encouraged to recognize their responsibility to identify contexts and people that will enable their children to learn about their race and/or culture. Additionally, parents should seek to prepare their children for bias and discrimination; they should also equip them with the tools to cope with such experiences, while simultaneously working to instill in their children a sense of pride in their race and culture.

As transracially adopted children develop, they may experience feelings of alienation from and anger with their parents (Romney, 1995). That is, they may feel anger at their parents' apparent inability to truly understand the experiences of racism and discrimination that they face and/or may resent their parents for failing to provide them with a family and community in which they blend in more readily. In such cases, parents can be encouraged to engage in open dialogue with their children, and also to explore (by themselves, and/or alone with a therapist) their own feelings, attitudes, and beliefs about race. Additionally, parents should seek to establish a sense of themselves as a multiracial and/or multicultural family (e.g., by becoming active with their children in multiracial and/or multicultural events and groups) in order to (re)establish a sense of family cohesion (Romney, 1995).

In addition to cultivating an awareness of the role of racial—and possibly cultural—socialization in their children's upbringing, lesbian and gay adoptive parents also face the task of helping their children to develop a sense of pride in their family structure, as well as socializing them to anticipate and deal with heterosexism and homophobia. Clinical anecdotal evidence suggests that children may need help and supportive advice in dealing with the antigay sentiments of their peers (Martin, 1998). The limited research in this area suggests that lesbian and gay parents are often unsure of how to handle antigay teasing directed toward their children (Litovich & Langhout, 2004). Parents often worry that their children will be exposed to heterosexism and stigma, but they may be confused as to how to respond when such incidents occur.

Therapists should assist lesbian and gay clients in their efforts to counterbalance the heterosexist messages that their children receive from society. Specifically, parents should be encouraged to engage in open and developmentally appropriate discourse about sexualities and family diversity with their children. For younger children, it is often enough to explain that there is a diverse spectrum of relationships and family structures, emphasizing that some women love women and some men love men, and there are "all types of families." Parents of older children may find it useful to teach their children about the meaning of various words and to introduce appropriate terminology for describing sexuality and relationships in an effort to educate their children about the acceptability of a range of sexual expressions (Litovich & Langhout, 2004). Parents who adopt their children when they are older (e.g., school-aged and beyond) may encounter particular challenges in this area; that is, older children often have already formed ideas about homosexuality (e.g., as evil, immoral, or equivalent to pedophilia) that lesbian and gay parents may need to counter and address via education (Alexander, 2001). Adoption professionals should strive to prepare clients for the possibility that older children may experience initial or ongoing anxieties regarding placement in a lesbian and gay parent household, and should assess prospective adopters' comfort with and skills in addressing such anxieties. Likewise, child welfare professionals who work with children and adolescents should strive to assess for and correct any stereotypes or misconceptions about homosexuality, while remaining sensitive to the possibility that some youth—particularly those who exhibit strong negative feelings about homosexuality—should probably not be placed with lesbian and gay parents.

Adolescents (whether adopted early or at a later age) may struggle with acceptance and understanding of their parents' sexual orientation. Indeed, as they develop, youth increasingly understand the nature of same-sex sexuality, often at the same time that they begin to explore and deal with issues relating to their own sexuality. Additionally, adolescents often struggle with concerns about peer acceptance and conformity, which may heighten their concerns about their parents' sexuality and the possibility that they will be ostracized if "word get out" (Martin, 1998). As Martin points out, the therapist can serve an important role during adolescence, sensitizing parents to the particular concerns that their sexual orientation might raise for their child, and helping parents to establish the circumstances and language of disclosure. For example, parents who are extremely "out" and who are active participants in their local gay communities may need guidance regarding how open to be about their sexuality around their children's peers, thereby balancing their need for visibility with their children's desire for privacy (James, 2002; Martin, 1998). Such negotiations are likely to be particularly salient during adolescence, when youth typically experience a heightened need for privacy and independence from their parents. Alternatively, parents who are not open about their sexual orientation in all areas of their lives (e.g., at work) may be tempted to ask their children to maintain their secret in certain circumstances. Therapists can help parents to understand the potential negative impact of such requests (e.g., they communicate to children that their families are something to be kept hidden). Parents will also need to address issues related to their child's adoptive status, as there comes a time when children themselves become the decision makers as to whom and under what circumstances they will discuss their adoptions (James, 2002). Disclosure practices can become more complicated when the child is adopted transracially, as seen in the following vignette.

CASE EXAMPLE: THE "DO-RAG" AS A SYMBOL OF CULTURE AND PRIDE

Jake is an affable 15-year-old boy who identified his racial and ethnic background to the therapist as follows: "I'm sort of everything. I'm African American, Chinese, Spanish, and French." An energetic ninth-grader, Jake lives with his two mothers, Emma (42) and Paula (46), who have been together for 23 years and are both white. The family resides in a racially diverse, small Northeastern city where they are in contact with several other adoptive and lesbian and gay parent families. Jake was adopted at 2 weeks of age, is an only child, and his mothers say they all have always enjoyed a very close relationship. During the months preceding their initial contact with a therapist, Emma and Paula had become increasingly concerned about Jake's growing "secretiveness" with regard to his choice of clothes, who he was spending time with, and so on; they were also concerned by his general reluctance to spend time with the family. Although they recognized that much of his behavior was typical of adolescent development, they felt it could be beneficial for Jake to talk to someone about increasing tensions at home, and thus made contact with a therapist. In stating their concerns, they explained that Jake had always been "comfortable with and proud of our family but now he seems to want little to do with us. It is like we're going back in the closet again. The other day he pleaded with us not to come to his game. We feel like he's ashamed of us, and we don't want to make him feel guilty, but he gets irritated when we try to talk with him about it."

After an initial meeting with all three family members, it was determined that it would be most productive to meet with Jake individually. In session, Jake spoke of a recent change in schools as presenting new challenges regarding the visibility of his family as both lesbian parent-headed and transracial: "A lot of people ask you questions. Sometimes you just don't want to answer them. It sort of gets annoying. It depends on who I'm talking to 'cause the other people will be like, 'That's your mom?! She's white! Look at your skin, she ain't your mom!'" It became clear to the clinician that for Jake, the visibility of his family as transracial was as salient to him as was their status as a family with lesbian parents. Regarding his attitude toward his parents' sexual orientation, Jake was sanguine: "It was *never* really an issue. I was asked why don't I have a dad, or something like that, but I was never uncomfortable that I had two moms."

Jake volunteered that his parents did indeed try to foster pride in his cultural and ethnic identity; they had been actively involved in an adoptive family group in their community when he was younger, and he was still in contact with some of the children from that group. He expressed that lately, however, he had grown dissatisfied with conversations with his mothers around race, and was also tired of his peers judging his multicultural status: "Yeah, it's hard talking about racial issues to my parents because sometimes they just don't get it. Sometimes it's hard talking about issues like that, or trying to talk to kids when they're like, `Oh, why are you trying to do that. You're not ghetto' or like, 'You're not black.' And you're just like, you don't have to be ghetto or black to do that. Not all people are ghetto and black. Black people are upper-class too."

Efforts to claim his racial and ethnic identity were met with resistance from Jake's mothers, who worried about the increased level of risk he might be subjected to in the community. The specific symbol of this struggle was exemplified in his decision to wear a do-rag. Said Jake, in an early session: "My moms try to curb me, take me away from the way I dress. I like to wear baggy clothes, fitted hats, do-rags. But they won't let me wear do-rags because they're afraid I'm going to get hurt by a gang. But there's always that chance if you're *not* wearing a do-rag you're going to get it. If you're wearing the wrong color you can get it. I mean, I used to go to football games and there were loads of people wearing different color do-rags."

When asked how he and his parents resolved this issue, he reported that they simply would not let him wear the do-rag. But, having the last word, Jake added, "I usually take the do-rags outside the house and put them on, and then take them off when I see my moms again!"

Perhaps owing to their own marginalized status as a lesbian couple, Emma and Paula were fearful of the possible heightened risk to Jake due to his multiple statuses as a male child of color, as well as an adopted child with lesbian mothers. With encouragement from his therapist, Jake was able to open up to his mothers about his need to express his cultural identity in his own way, and his preference that, for now, they keep a low profile at his school. Emma and Paula agreed to try to respect his choices as long as they knew who his friends were and his whereabouts. It was also helpful for them to recall that in his middle school years, Jake was resistant to his parents coming to school as a two-mom family, and to understand that now, as his racial identity came into sharper focus for both himself and his peers, this may represent another stage of "coming out." It was also recommended that the family locate a mentor—perhaps a Big Brother in their community—in order to facilitate racial and ethnic identification with an adult male of color. Finally, the couple was encouraged to maintain connections with other lesbian and gay transracial families to address concerns related to heterosexism and racism that their child will continue to encounter.

This vignette illustrates how normative struggles of adolescence might manifest themselves within a multicultural context. It is critical that the therapist explore the quality and depth of the connections that each parent has within the various racial and cultural communities to which their child belongs. If these connections to racially and culturally different communities do not currently exist, it is important to support parents in considering how they envision themselves becoming more connected and credible. Finally, to help the parents create a multicultural identity for their family, it may be helpful to explore their fears about how they might be perceived as lesbian and gay by the various racial and cultural communities with which they may come in contact, and to help them overcome such apprehensions.

Attachment Issues

Adoptive parents often worry about attachment issues in their children. These fears are not groundless: Children who are adopted, particularly when they are older, may experience such challenges (Roberson, 2006). Indeed, adopted children have often experienced multiple separations (e.g., from birth parents, caregivers, foster parents, and so on), and thus may be vulnerable to feelings of loss and anxiety (Roberson, 2006). Additionally, children's preadoption history may include medical and/or nutritional deprivation, physical and/or sexual abuse, ineffective caregiving, and lengthy stays in orphanages, all of which tend to complicate the formation of attachment relationships (Shapiro, Shapiro, & Paret, 2001). Adoptive parents may be unprepared for the developmental problems and/or attachment difficulties that their children pose, and/or they may have unrealistic expectations about their children's readiness to bond, i.e., the parents are often eager to claim their children, whereas their children initially may not match their level of readiness (Shapiro et al., 2001). Therapists should validate their clients' feelings of frustration but also encourage them to acknowledge their children's losses and to maintain an appropriately empathic stance. Furthermore, clients should be encouraged to utilize adaptive and flexible caregiving strategies that facilitate their children's adjustment to their new home and family. These strategies will ideally contribute to a secure parent–child relationship that will help children develop confidence that their parents can be counted on to provide consistent protection and caregiving. In contrast, inflexible parenting and unrealistic expectations about children's progress and outcomes may contribute to low attachment security (Roberson, 2006).

Sometimes, children attach more quickly and/or easily to one parent (as can be the case in heterosexual families as well). Such dynamics can cause confusion and frustration on the part of the adults, particularly the "less desired" parent. In one study of 15 lesbian couples who adopted their children internationally, 12 reported that their children had primary bonds to one mother, despite the fact that all couples claimed to share parenting and childcare chores relatively equally (Bennett, 2003b). This preference for one mother sometimes caused feelings of competition and jealousy that were difficult to navigate during the early months and years of parenting. Therapists can support lesbian and gay couples in navigating such unequal attachments by (1) normalizing initial unequal attachments (e.g., similar patterns are often observed in nonadoptive heterosexual and lesbian parent families: e.g., Goldberg et al., 2008); (2) encouraging couples to recognize that a child's preference for one parent over the other may reflect nothing about each partner's "innate" caregiving capacity but, rather, may be a reflection of many factors including the child's personality, how much time each parent spends with the child, or the temperamental predisposition of the parent (e.g., a parent may respond confidently to a young child but may be more cautious with a preteen); and (3) encouraging couples to work *together* to address feelings of jealousy (and to promote more equal attachments) as opposed to allowing the child's parental preference to come between them.

Children are not the only ones who may struggle with attachment; adoptive parents—whether gay and lesbian or heterosexual—may also face this challenge. Some may feel that they should instantly bond with their child and are therefore disappointed and worried when they do not. Sometimes, one parent experiences a greater attachment to the child than the other, which may cause tension and conflict. For example, in interracial couples who adopt, the parent who is of the same race as the adopted child may feel more immediately attached (and/or may be the preferred attachment figure by the child), which may cause jealousy and strain—or the opposite may occur (i.e., it is possible that attachment may traverse racial boundaries, such that some parents may bond more readily with a child of a different race). Finally, some couples and individuals may find it challenging to maintain a continuous attachment when their child presents with complex emotional and behavioral challenges, which can create continuous stress and tension in the family system.

CASE EXAMPLE: A CRISIS IN ATTACHMENT

Luis is an outgoing, energetic, and engaging 13-year-old Latino boy who resides with his single gay adoptive father, Aaron (38). Luis was 8 when he was adopted by Aaron, prior to which he had resided in seven foster homes after being removed at the age of 4 from his abusive, drug-addicted, and developmentally disabled mother. Luis presented many challenges in the initial months, owing to so many years of disrupted attachments, trauma, and significant behavioral and learning difficulties. Over the years following the adoptive placement, social workers marveled at the progress Luis made in Aaron's home: temper tantrums decreased, he was excelling academically at school, and he made vast behavioral and cognitive improvements following Aaron's decision to have Luis removed from numerous medications that left him lethargic and confused. Further, Aaron made a regular effort to ensure that Luis had regular contact with his brothers and sisters, who were placed in various foster homes throughout the state, thus minimizing his separation and loss from key family members.

Luis and Aaron were referred to a therapist who worked with lesbian, gay, bisexual, and transgender (LGBT) clients and families. The referral arose from a crisis at home necessitating the involvement of Child Protective Services (CPS), when Aaron called the emergency hotline to report that he was absolutely overwhelmed with Luis' care and didn't know if he had the capacity to continue to parent him anymore. The catalyst for this crisis was

Aaron's discovery that his recent cable bill contained several hundred dollars' worth of charges that he did not make. Upon confronting him with this news, Luis adamantly and repeatedly denied that he had run up the charges. At that point, Aaron reports, "I was totally afraid I was going to lose it, so all I could think of doing was to call the CPS hotline. I felt really horrible about wishing I had never adopted Luis. Even thinking this made me feel, really, really badly." Indeed, for years Aaron had been struggling with managing Luis' behaviors with only sporadic assistance from state social workers.

Compounding his worries that he had insufficiently bonded with Luis, Aaron felt overwhelmed at the prospect of Luis' burgeoning adolescence. Recently, Luis had been inappropriately touching girls at school and had been asking his father about the meaning of terms like "hooking up" and "HIV." In a somewhat abstract way, Luis also expressed interest in Latino gangs. As a white man who was originally from Norway (he had moved to the United States 10 years earlier), Aaron sometimes felt his upbringing and background had inadequately prepared him for matters such as his son's sexuality and emerging ethnic and cultural interests. Furthermore, Aaron was quite isolated and had little social support: His large circle of friends had dwindled considerably over the years due to Luis' behaviors.

At the time that the referral was made to CPS, Aaron had been considering the possibility that Luis might be better off at a military boarding school—a plan that left Luis feeling scared and confused in that it may very well have replicated yet another abandonment in his young life. Indeed, Aaron was leery of mental health service providers after a recent visit with an outpatient therapist who suggested that she could help find a more "appropriate" adoptive family for Luis. Interpreting this remark as a disparagement of his parenting abilities based on his sexual orientation, Aaron was horrified that someone might actually suggest that the adoption should be "undone." It was at that moment that he realized that he needed to mobilize to locate professional mental health supports for himself and his son. He worked with CPS to locate a therapist for his son (an African-American practitioner), a family counselor for himself and Luis, and finally an individual therapist for himself. In therapy, Aaron was able to learn to better cope with stress. He also realized the importance of social support and began to rebuild informal networks of friends and community resources.

It was important for the therapist to empathize with Aaron's concerns about his attachment struggles with Luis, while at the same time inquiring about times past when he felt a deep emotional connection to his son—and there were many of them. It was crucial that Aaron felt supported by the therapist so that he did not feel left out or blamed for Luis' problems, most of which began prior to his adoptive placement. As stressors were addressed, Aaron felt greater efficacy as a parent and, in turn, much closer to Luis. He decided to forego boarding school for the time being, and father and son were ultimately able to derive greater enjoyment and satisfaction from their time together.

Finding Support and Resources

Lesbian and gay adoptive parents may encounter unique challenges in obtaining the support and resources they need during the postplacement parenting phase. For example, they may seek support and companionship from other adoptive parents (e.g., via attending adoption events and adoptive parent support groups) but encounter resistance or lack of understanding within traditional adoption circles based upon their sexual orientation. Additionally, they may seek support from their lesbian and gay friends and/or other lesbian and gay (nonadoptive) parents, but find themselves faced with racism and/or adoptism within these networks. Such encounters may lead lesbian and gay adoptive parents to feel frustrated, alienated, and alone. Therapists and adoption educators are in a position to provide support and guidance to families as they navigate these varied and complex forms of stigma. Practitioners are advised to regularly assess their clients' perceptions of and satisfaction with available support networks, and actively assist clients in identifying and obtaining desired supports and services. Toward this end, practitioners are also encouraged to maintain up-to-date knowledge of their community's resources related to gay adoptive families (e.g., knowledge of gay-friendly lawyers, parenting groups, and mental health professionals).

COMPETENCY ISSUES: TRAINING THERAPISTS AND ADOPTION PROFESSIONALS

Lesbian and gay adoptive parents are vulnerable to insensitive, inappropriate, and/or unhelpful treatment and interventions throughout the adoption process. That is, they may confront practitioners and adoption professionals who are insensitive to the unique issues facing sexual minorities and/or may blatantly stigmatize them (Goldberg et al., 2007). Such experiences may cause sexual minorities to avoid seeking support or therapy when they need it.

Training is needed for professionals and therapists who work with lesbian- and gay-parent families. Specifically, professionals in training should be encouraged to develop an awareness of their own comfort levels, biases, and prejudices about sex, gender, sexual orientation, and adoption, and how these might affect their interactions with clients. Additionally, professionals should be encouraged to develop a sophisticated understanding of how societal ideologies and practices affect LGBT persons (Godfrey, Haddock, Fisher, & Lund, 2006) and should recognize that sexual minority clients' problems may arise from or be exacerbated by societal heterosexism (Pachankis & Goldfried, 2004). Professionals should also be provided with education and reflection opportunities to help foster an awareness of lesbian and gay issues in general—for instance, coming out, discrimination, legal issues, etc. (Burckell & Goldfried, 2006).

Furthermore, practitioners who work with lesbian and gay *adoptive* parents and families need specialized training in the adoptive family life cycle and common challenges related to adoptive and foster parenting (Brodzinsky, 2008).

For example, practitioners must understand that the process by which individuals become parents via adoption is unique (Derdeyn & Graves, 1998) and, in turn, the experiences of adoptive parents during the contemplation, placement, and postplacement phases of adoption do not necessarily mirror the pregnancy, transition to parenthood, and parenthood experiences of biological parents. Clinicians and practitioners also need to understand how adoption-related challenges and life cycle issues may be different for lesbian and gay parent families. For example, in the preadoptive stage, lesbian and gay couples may experience heterosexism in their negotiations with adoption agencies and adoption professionals. In the postplacement stage, lesbian and gay adoptive families encounter heterosexism *and* adoptism in their interactions with society, which may create additional stress. And yet, at the same time that practitioners need to be sensitive to the additional challenges that these families face, they are encouraged to recognize and build upon the unique strengths of lesbian and gay adoptive families. For example, unlike their heterosexual peers, lesbian and gay parents may be more attuned to their children's experiences of feeling "different," based upon their own experiences of marginalization and difference. Simultaneously, however, professionals are encouraged to recognize the many commonalities in experience between lesbian and gay adoptive parents and heterosexual adoptive parents: e.g., both groups may have similar motivations for and concerns about adoptive parenthood, both groups may experience similar challenges during the postplacement adjustment phase, and both groups ultimately share in the joys of becoming a family.

In conclusion, therapists working with LGBT adoptive parents and their children can serve as allies and advocates for their clients by (1) being willing to educate themselves about the ways in which diversity can be both an asset and a challenge for these families, (2) recognizing the ways in which these families' experiences are not only different from but also similar to those of heterosexual adoptive families, (3) demonstrating empathic cross-cultural fluency, (4) maintaining an affirming and inquisitive stance in relation to their clients' struggles and triumphs, and (5) recognizing their role not only as providers of professional guidance and support, but also as catalysts for social justice.

Notes

1. Second-parent adoptions allow the nonlegal partner to adopt their partner's child(ren).
2. The term transracial adoption generally refers to an adoption in which a child's race or ethnicity is different from both parents when it is a couple that adopts, or one parent's if it is a single parent adoption (Smith, McRoy, Freundlich, & Kroll, 2008).
3. Of note is that the Human Rights Campaign, in conjunction with the All Children-All Families initiative, has published a "promising practices" guide, which is "the first comprehensive, practical tool aimed to help agency leaders actively improve policies and practices that affect their work with GLBT prospective adoptive parents." A copy of this guide can be requested from http://www.hrc.org/issues/parenting/adoptions/8941. htm. Also of note is that the Evan B. Donaldson Institute (http://www.adoptioninstitute.

org/index.php) has recently embarked on a project to enable practitioners to better recruit and train lesbian and gay adoptive parents.

4. Of note is that the W.I.S.E. Up Powerbook (Schoettle, 2000) is an excellent resource that therapists and adoption educators can use to help adopted children and their families learn useful coping strategies for managing the questions and curiosity of the nonadopted world.

References

Alexander, C. J. (2001). Developmental attachment and gay and lesbian adoptions. *Journal of Gay and Lesbian Social Services, 13,* 93–97.

Baden, A. L., & Steward, R. J. (2000). A framework for use with racially and culturally integrated families: The Cultural-Racial Identity Model as applied to transracial adoptees. *Journal of Social Distress and the Homeless, 9,* 309–337.

Bennett, S. (2003a). International adoptive lesbian families: Parental perceptions of the influence of diversity on family relationships in early childhood. *Smith College Studies in Social Work, 74,* 73–91.

Bennett, S. (2003b). Is there a primary mom? Parental perceptions of attachment bond hierarchies within lesbian adoptive families. *Child and Adolescent Social Work Journal, 20,* 159–173.

Brodzinsky, D. M. (1997). Infertility and adoption adjustment: Considerations and clinical issues. In S. R. Lieblum (Ed.), *Infertility: Psychological issues and counseling strategies* (pp. 246–262). New York: Wiley.

Brodzinsky, D. M. (2003). *Adoption by lesbians and gay men: A national survey of adoption agency policies, practices and attitudes.* Retrieved on May 1, 2008 from http://www.adoptioninstitute.org/whowe/Gay%20and%20Lesbian%20Adoption1.html.

Brodzinsky, D. (2006). Family structural openness and communication openness as predictors in the adjustment of adopted children. *Adoption Quarterly, 9,* 1–18.

Brodzinsky, D. (2008). *Adoptive Parent Preparation Project: Phase 1: Meeting the mental health and developmental needs of adopted children. Final policy and practice report.* Available at www.adoptioninstitute.org.

Brodzinsky, D. M., & Palacios, J. (Eds.). (2005). *Psychological issues in adoption: Research and practice.* Westport, CT: Praeger.

Brodzinsky, D. M., & Pinderhughes, E. (2002). Parenting and child development in adoptive families. In M. Bornstein (Ed.), *Handbook of parenting* (pp. 279–311). Mahwah, NJ: Erlbaum.

Brooks, D., & Goldberg, S. (2001). Gay and lesbian adoptive and foster care placements: Can they meet the needs of waiting children? *Social Work, 46,* 147–158.

Brooks, D., & James, S. (2003). Willingness to adopt Black foster children: Implications for child welfare policy and recruitment of adoptive families. *Children and Youth Services Review, 25,* 463–489.

Burckell, L. A., & Goldfried, M. R. (2006). Therapist qualities preferred by sexual minority individuals. *Psychotherapy: Theory, Research, Practice, Training, 43,* 32–49.

Carter-Black, J. (2002). Transracial adoption and foster care placement: Worker perception and attitude. *Child Welfare, 81,* 337–370.

Chabot, J. M., & Ames, B. D. (2004). "It wasn't 'let's get pregnant and go do it'": Decision-making in lesbian couples planning motherhood via donor insemination. *Family Relations, 53,* 348–356.

Colberg, M. (1997). Clinical issues with gay and lesbian adoptive parenting. In S. K. Roszia, A. Baran, & L. Coleman (Eds.), *Creating kinship* (pp. 115–123). Portland, OR: The Dougy Center.

Crawford, I., McLeod, A., Zamboni, B., & Jordan, M. (1999). Psychologists' attitudes towards gay and lesbian parenting. *Professional Psychology: Research and Practice, 30,* 394–401.

Deacon, S. A. (1997). Intercountry adoption and the family life cycle. *The American Journal of Family Therapy, 25,* 245–260.

de Haymes, M. V., & Simon, S. (2003). Transracial adoption: Families identify issues and needed support services. *Child Welfare, 82,* 1–23.

Derdeyn, A. P., & Graves, C. L. (1998). Clinical vicissitudes of adoption. *Child and Adolescent Psychiatric Clinics of North America, 7,* 373–388.

Farr, R. H., Forssell, S. L., & Patterson, C. J. (2010). Parenting and child development in adoptive families: Does parental sexual orientation matter? *Applied Developmental Science, 14,* 164–178.

Farr, R. H., & Patterson, C. J. (2009). Transracial adoption by lesbian, gay, and heterosexual couples: Who completes transracial adoptions and with what results? *Adoption Quarterly, 12,* 187–204.

Gagnon, A. C., Riley, A., Toole, M., & Goldberg, A. E. (2007). Motivations to parent in lesbian adoptive couples. Poster presented at the American Psychological Association annual conference, San Francisco, CA, August 2007.

Gartrell, N., Banks, A., Reed, N., Hamilton, J., Rodas, C., & Deck, A. (2000). The National Lesbian Family Study: 3. Interviews with mothers of five-year-olds. *American Journal of Orthopsychiatry, 70,* 542–548.

Gates, G., Badgett, M. V. L., Macomber, J. E., & Chambers, K. (2007). *Adoption and foster care by gay and lesbian parents in the United States.* Washington, D.C.: The Urban Institute.

Gates, G., & Ost, J. (2004). *The gay and lesbian atlas.* Washington, D.C.: The Urban Institute.

Gianino, M. (2008). Adaptation and transformation: The transition to adoptive parenthood for gay male couples. *Journal of GLBT Family Studies, 4,* 205–243.

Godfrey, K., Haddock, S. A., Fisher, A., & Lund, L. (2006). Essential components of curricula for preparing therapists to work effectively with lesbian, gay, and bisexual clients: A Delphi study. *Journal of Marital and Family Therapy, 32,* 491–504.

Goldberg, A. E. (2009). Lesbian and heterosexual preadoptive couples' openness to transracial adoption. *American Journal of Orthopsychiatry, 79,* 103–117.

Goldberg, A. E. (2010). *Lesbian and gay parents and their children.* Washington, D.C.: American Psychological Association.

Goldberg, A. E., Downing, J. B., & Richardson, H. (2009). From infertility to adoption: Perceptions of lesbian and heterosexual preadoptive couples. *Journal of Social and Personal Relationships, 26,* 938–963.

Goldberg, A. E., Downing, J. B., & Sauck, C. C. (2007). Choices, challenges, and tensions: Perspectives of lesbian prospective adoptive parents. *Adoption Quarterly, 10,* 33–64.

Goldberg, A. E., Downing, J. B., & Sauck, C. C. (2008). Perceptions of children's parental preferences in lesbian two-mother households. *Journal of Marriage and Family, 70,* 419–434.

Goldberg, A. E., & Smith, J. Z. (2008). Social support and well-being in lesbian and heterosexual preadoptive parents. *Family Relations, 57,* 281–294.

Goldberg, A. E., & Smith, J. Z. (2009). Predicting non-African American lesbian and heterosexual preadoptive couples' openness to adopting an African American child. *Family Relations, 58,* 346–360.

Herrmann-Green, L. K., & Gehring, T. M. (2007). The German lesbian family study: Planning for parenthood via donor insemination. *Journal of GLBT Family Studies, 3,* 351–395.

Human Rights Campaign. (2009). *Promising practices in adoption and foster care: A comprehensive guide to policies and practices that welcome, affirm, and support gay, lesbian, bisexual, and transgender foster and adoptive parents.* Washington, D.C.: HRC.

James, S. E. (2002). Clinical themes in gay- and lesbian-parented adoptive families. *Clinical Child Psychology and Psychiatry, 7,* 475–486

Kurdek, L. (2001). Differences between heterosexual-nonparent couples and gay, lesbian, and heterosexual-parent couples. *Journal of Family Issues, 22,* 727–754.

Lee, R. (2003). The transracial adoption paradox: History, research, and counseling implications of cultural socialization. *Counseling Psychologist, 31,* 711–744.

Leung, P., Erich, S., & Kanenberg, H. (2005). A comparison of family functioning in gay/lesbian, heterosexual and special needs adoptions. *Children & Youth Services Review, 27,* 1031–1044.

Litovich, M. L., & Langhout, R. D. (2004). Framing heterosexism in lesbian families: A preliminary examination of resilient coping. *Journal of Community and Applied Social Psychology, 14,* 411–435.

Mackey, W. C., White, U., & Day, R. D. (1992). Reasons American men become fathers: Men's divulgences, women's perspectives. *Journal of Genetic Psychology, 153,* 435–445.

Mallon, G. P. (2004). *Gay men choosing parenthood.* New York: Columbia University Press.

Mallon, G. P. (2007). Assessing lesbian and gay prospective foster and adoptive families: A focus on the home study process. *Child Welfare, 86,* 67–86.

Martin, A. (1998). Clinical issues in psychotherapy with lesbian-, gay-, and bisexual-parented families. In C. J. Patterson & A. R. D'Augelli (Eds.), *Lesbian, gay, and bisexual identities in families: Psychological perspectives* (pp. 270–291). New York: Oxford University Press.

Massatti, R. R., Vonk, M. E., & Gregoire, T. K. (2004). Reliability and validity of the Transracial Adoption Parenting Scale. *Research on Social Work Practice, 14,* 43–50.

Matthews, J. (2004). *A qualitative study of the lived experience of single gay adoptive fathers.* Retrieved June 26, 2006 from http://etd.vcu.edu/theses.

Matthews, J. D., & Cramer, E. P. (2006). Envisaging the adoption process to strengthen gay and lesbian-headed families: Recommendations for adoption professionals. *Child Welfare, 85,* 317–340.

McPheeters, A., Carmi, M., & Goldberg, A. E. (2008). *Gay men's experiences of sexism and heterosexism in the adoption process.* Poster presented at the American Psychological Association annual conference, Boston MA, August 2008.

Pachankis, J. E., & Goldfried, M. V. (2004). Clinical issues in working with lesbian, gay, and bisexual clients. *Psychotherapy: Theory, Research, & Practice, 41,* 227–246.

Palacios, J., & Brodzinsky, D. M. (2010). Adoption research: Trends, topics and outcomes. *International Journal of Behavioral Development, 34,* 270–284.

Park, S. M., & Green, C. E. (2000). Is transracial adoption in the best interests of ethnic minority children?: Questions concerning legal and scientific interpretations of a child's best interests. *Adoption Quarterly, 3,* 5–34.

Patterson, C. J. (2000). Family relationships of lesbians and gay men. *Journal of Marriage and Family, 62*, 1052–1069.

Pawelski, J. G., et al. (2006). The effects of marriage, civil union, and. domestic partnership laws on the health and well-being of children. *Pediatrics, 118*, 349–364.

Pies, C. (1990). Lesbians and the choice to parent. *Marriage and Family Review, 14*, 137–154.

Ray, V., & Gregory, R. (2001). School experiences of the children of lesbian and gay parents. *Family Matters, 59*, 28–34.

Roberson, K. (2006). Attachment and caregiving behavioral systems in intercountry adoption: A literature review. *Children and Youth Services Review, 28*, 727–740.

Robinson, G. E., & Stewart, D. E. (1996). The psychological impact of infertility and new reproductive technologies. *Harvard Review of Psychiatry, 4*, 168–172.

Romney, P. (1995). Reflecting on race and family identity: Therapy with a multiracial adoptive family. *In Session: Psychotherapy in Practice, 1*, 87–99.

Rosenthal, J. A. (1993). Outcomes of adoption of children with special needs. *The Future of Children, 3*, 77–88.

Ryan, S., Pearlmutter, S., & Groza, V. (2004). Coming out of the closet: Opening agencies to gay men and lesbian adoptive parents. *Social Work, 49*, 85–96.

Schoettle, M. (2000). *W.I.S.E Up Powerbook*. Silver Spring, MD: The Center for Adoption Support and Education.

Shapiro, V., Shapiro, J., & Paret, I. (2001). International adoption and the formation of new family attachments. *Smith College Studies in Social Work, 71*, 389–418.

Shelley-Sireci, L. M., & Ciano-Boyce, C. (2002). Becoming lesbian adoptive parents: An exploratory study of lesbian adoptive, lesbian birth, and heterosexual adoptive parents. *Adoption Quarterly, 6*, 33–43.

Simon, R., & Alstein, H. (2000). *Adoption across borders*. Lanham, MD: Rowman & Littlefield.

Smith, S., McRoy, R., Freundlich, M., & Kroll, J. (2008). *Finding families for African American children: The role of race and law in adoption from foster care*. Retrieved June 2, 2008 from http://www.adoptioninstitute.org/research/2008_05_mepa.php.

Stacey, J., & Biblarz, T. (2001). (How) does the sexual orientation of parents matter. *American Sociological Review, 66*, 159–183.

Tasker, F., & Golombok, S. (1997). *Growing up in a lesbian family: Effects on child development*. New York: Guilford.

Tyebjee, T. (2003). Attitude, interest, and motivation for adoption and foster care. *Child Welfare, 82*, 685–706.

van Balen, F. (2005). Late parenthood among subfertile and fertile couples: Motivations and educational goals. *Patient Education & Counseling, 59*, 276–282.

van Korff, L., Grotevant, H. D., & McRoy, R. G. (2006). Openness arrangements and psychological adjustment in adolescent adoptees. *Journal of Family Psychology, 20*, 531–534.

Vonk, M. E. (2001). Cultural competence for transracial adoptive parents. *Social Work, 46*, 246–255.

Weston, K. (1991). *Families we choose: Lesbians, gays, kinship*. New York: Columbia University Press.

11

Adoption by Lesbians and Gay Men

What We Know, Need to Know, and Ought to Do

DAVID M. BRODZINSKY, ROBERT-JAY GREEN,
AND KATIE KATUZNY ■

Although lesbians and gay men have always raised children, it is only recently that they have done so while being open about their sexual orientations. Part of the reason for the greater visibility of such parents is their growing public acceptance (ABC News, 2002; Miall & March, 2005; Pertman and Howard, this volume; Schwartz, 2010), as well as the greater opportunities to become mothers and fathers through adoption and new reproductive technologies.

In their analysis of several nationally representative datasets, Gates, Badgett, Macomber, and Chambers (2007) noted that approximately 65,000 adopted children are living with a lesbian or gay parent—representing approximately 4 percent of all adopted children in the United States. Their analysis found that lesbians and bisexual women showed relatively greater interest in adopting children than did heterosexual women (46.2 percent versus 32.1 percent) and more often took steps toward adopting a child (5.7 percent versus 3.3 percent).[1] Moreover, there is evidence that even greater numbers of lesbian, gay, and bisexual people may adopt children in the future, and that they will meet with even greater societal acceptance of their efforts to raise children. In a study of urban and suburban sexual minority youth aged 16–22 years, D'Augelli, Grossman, and Rendina (2006/2007) found that 66 percent of the females and 52 percent of the males said it was "very" or "extremely" likely they would be raising children in the future. Furthermore, between 2003 and 2010, three national public opinion surveys conducted by a team of researchers at Indiana University showed a significant trend toward considering same-sex couples with children as "family"—from 54 percent of respondents in 2003 to 68 percent in 2010 (Associated Press, 2010; Powell, Bolzendahl, Geist, & Steelman, 2010). Given these realities, this book seems especially timely.

In this final chapter, we summarize the main points made by our fellow authors and highlight important research and social casework issues that remain to be addressed, as well as best practices for facilitating successful adoptions by lesbian and gay parents.[2]

WHAT WE KNOW ABOUT LESBIAN AND GAY ADOPTION

Although adoption by sexual minority people may not be new, it is certainly becoming increasingly visible, as well as more supported by laws, by professionals in a wide range of disciplines (e.g., medicine, psychiatry, psychology, and child welfare), and by the public (Schwartz, 2010). As Russett (this volume) and Pertman and Howard (this volume) note in their historical analyses, adoption by lesbians and gays is part of the growing diversity and complexity in adoption practice and adoptive family life that have emerged over the past 25 years in most Western countries. This change in adoption stems from the recognition that previous notions of what constituted a healthy family for children—including those boys and girls who needed new homes—were much too restrictive. As a result, previous barriers to adoption by foster parents, fertile individuals, unmarried adults, older adults, low-income individuals, etc. began to fall by the wayside. Moreover, it was in this context of emerging family diversity that many of the barriers for placing children with sexual minority individuals also began to be questioned and slowly set aside. Yet Pertman and Howard (this volume), as well as Appell (this volume), acknowledge that, even today, many legal roadblocks to adoption by lesbians and gays continue to exist. For example, Mississippi prohibits adoption by same-sex couples, although it leaves open the question of adoption by lesbian and gay individuals, whereas Utah and Arkansas[3] prohibit adoption by all unmarried individuals living with a sexual partner, regardless of their sexual orientation.[4] In addition, Appell highlights the statutory barriers to joint and second-parent adoptions that remain the reality in many states today. Furthermore, the authors of several chapters point out that even when states are silent on the issue of the legality of adoption by sexual minority individuals, stereotypes, misconceptions, and prejudicial attitudes by local judiciary and individual adoption caseworkers often undermine the efforts of lesbians and gays to adopt children.

Despite these pockets of lingering resistance to adoption by lesbians and gay men, recent history has witnessed a definite shift toward greater acceptance of these individuals as prospective adoptive parents. For example, as already noted, Gates et al. (2007) report that lesbians and gays not only are expressing considerable interest in adopting children, but are also stepping forward in significant numbers to actually do so.

At the same time, significant numbers of adoption agencies are expressing their willingness–and desire–to work with these individuals. Research by Brodzinsky and his colleagues (Brodzinsky, this volume; Brodzinsky, 2003; Brodzinsky, Patterson, & Vaziri, 2002) has shown that approximately two-thirds of adoption agencies in the United States accept applications from lesbians and gays, although only about a third of the agencies had actually made any such placements in the time periods studied, and still fewer agencies (16–19 percent) had made efforts to reach out to the lesbian, gay, bisexual, and transgender (LGBT) community as parenting resources for children waiting to be adopted. These results were replicated in two studies covering different time periods (1995–1996 and 1999–2000), thereby adding to the reliability and validity of the findings. The increasing breadth and success of the Human Rights Campaign program "All Children–All Families" also clearly attest to growing interest by adoption agencies to work with gay and lesbian clients (Human Rights Campaign, 2009).

However, not all agencies are equally supportive of this type of adoption practice. The results of Brodzinsky's two studies showed that agencies focusing primarily on the placement of older children and those with special needs were much more supportive of working with lesbian and gay prospective adoptive parents than were those that primarily placed infants for adoption; agencies focusing on international adoption and those with more mixed adoption programs fell in between the other two types of agencies. Furthermore, agencies with a religious affiliation were less likely to place children with lesbian and gay prospective parents than were secular agencies—the exceptions being those affiliated with Judaism and the Lutheran church, which were quite supportive of such placements. Significantly, nearly half of respondents also indicated that their agencies would be interested in receiving training related to adoption by lesbians and gays.

The growing interest by agencies in working with lesbian and gay prospective parents—along with the almost unanimous support for this type of adoption among the medical, mental health, legal, and child welfare professional communities—is supported by findings from nearly 25 years of research on gay and lesbian parents and their children. In their respective chapters, Patterson and Wainright (this volume) and Gartrell, Peyser, and Bos (this volume) review this literature, including their own longitudinal research on the topic. Both groups of professionals reach the same conclusion—namely, that the data are unequivocal in showing that lesbian and gay parents are just as well-adjusted and possess the same level of nurturance and parenting competence as their heterosexual counterparts. Furthermore, children raised in lesbian- and gay-headed households show patterns of psychological, social, and academic adjustment similar to their peers raised by straight parents. As Stacey and Biblarz (2001) noted in a previous review of this literature, to the extent that there are small differences between these groups of parents and children in personal characteristics, behavior, and/or adjustment outcomes, they are of no discernible social importance, especially in relation to adoption policy and practice (see also Goldberg, 2010). In addition, although there are only a few studies examining adoptive families headed by sexual minority individuals compared to heterosexual individuals, the results are consistent with the findings of previous research; lesbian and gay adoptive parents and their children show patterns of adjustment similar to those of heterosexual adoptive parents and their children (Erich, Kanenberg, Case, Allen, & Bogdanos, 2009; Erich, Leung, & Kindle, 2005; Erich, Leung, Kindle, & Carter, 2005; Farr, Forssell, & Patterson, 2010a, 2010b; Goldberg & Smith, 2009).

With the growing awareness and acceptance of adoption by sexual minority individuals, many scholars and practitioners in the field have begun to examine the unique strengths and vulnerabilities of these families, as well as their needs both during the homestudy process and in the postadoption period. This volume contains chapters by Mallon, Brooks, Kim, and Wind, Ryan and Brown, and Goldberg and Gianino, each of which delves into one or more of these issues.

Like all other adoption applicants, lesbians and gay men must go through a homestudy process, which typically includes individual interviews, as well as group preparation and education classes. In his chapter, Mallon points out that adoption caseworkers need to recognize that many gays and lesbians may not voluntarily acknowledge their sexual orientation in the initial interview process. Furthermore, even if they do, they may not be "out" to various people in their lives (e.g., extended family, co-workers, and neighbors).

Before caseworkers can expect applicants to acknowledge their sexual orienta- tion and discuss its implications for adoptive family life, the professionals must create an environment in which their lesbian and gay clients will feel safe and sup- ported. Yet Mallon argues that, too often, the caseworkers' discomfort in discuss- ing issues related to sexual orientation and sexuality, as well as their homophobic beliefs and attitudes, creates an atmosphere of tension, confrontation, and con- flict, leaving sexual minority individuals feeling isolated, vulnerable, and unsup- ported. This can be especially true in group preparation sessions that include straight applicants who may also be homophobic. Mallon further notes that there is a great deal of inconsistency from agency to agency regarding how the issue of the clients' sexual orientation is dealt with in the homestudy process; some case- workers ignore the issue completely, both in discussions with their clients and in their written reports, whereas others deal with the issue in a straightforward manner and encourage the prospective parents to be completely forthcoming in their self-descriptions. In between these two extremes are a range of strategies used by caseworkers. Mallon concludes that children's interests are best served when adoption workers can help their clients feel comfortable in discussing their sexual orientations openly, including their own histories with discrimination and the implications of these issues for parenting children. He also cautions adoption professionals not to expect or require gay and lesbian individuals to go above and beyond the requirements of heterosexual individuals to prove themselves worthy of being adoptive parents.

Concerns about the availability and utilization of supports for gay and lesbian adoptive parents are also common among professionals in the field. These concerns derive, in part, from the homophobia and heterosexism that continue to exist in society, especially related to parenting by lesbians and gays. They also stem, however, from the fact that sexual minority individuals often adopt children who have developmental or mental health issues or who are of a different race or eth- nicity (Brodzinsky, this volume; Brooks et al., this volume; Farr & Patterson, 2009; Gates et al., 2007; Goldberg, 2010; Ryan & Brown, this volume). These types of adoptions are known to create additional challenges and stresses for families, whether they are headed by lesbians, gay men, or heterosexual individuals.

In their respective chapters, Brooks and his colleagues and Ryan and Brown focus on these issues and present data addressing them. Importantly, Ryan and Brown point out that gay and lesbian adoptive families generally present with considerable strengths, which allow them to cope effectively with the challenges of raising children, especially those with special needs (see also Goldberg, 2010). This finding is consistent with other research showing that sexual minority individuals typically are well-adjusted psychologically and provide high-quality parenting to their children (see Patterson & Wainright, this volume; Gartrell et al., this volume). In addition, Ryan and Brown, as well as Brooks and his colleagues, note that gay and lesbian adoptive parents typically have access to and utilize a wide range of preadoption and postadoption supports and services. There are some differences, however, between lesbian- and gay-led families and those headed by their straight peers in relation to their adoption and parenting needs. Brooks and his colleagues report that sexual minority parents are more desirous of legal advice in relation to adoption than are straight parents, which is consistent with the ambiguities and complexities of law that regulate adoption by lesbians and gays in many states.

For example, when state law allows only one of two partners to adopt a child, the question of how to protect the child's relationship with the nonlegal parent usually is of considerable importance to the preadoptive couple (see Appell, this volume). Thus, referring a preadoptive lesbian or gay couple for legal advice about this issue is likely to be perceived as extremely helpful. Brooks et al. also report that sexual minority parents are more likely to want educational programs related to transracial adoption, as well as preadoptive counseling for their children. These findings are consistent with research suggesting that lesbians and gays are more willing to adopt across racial lines (Farr & Patterson, 2009; Gates et al., 2007; Goldberg, 2009, 2010; Goldberg & Smith, 2009), as well as children with more challenging developmental and mental health needs (Brooks & Goldberg, 2001; Matthews & Cramer, 2006). The desire for preadoptive counseling for their children also is consistent with the belief that gay and lesbian adoptive parents are cognizant of the need for preparation of children coming into a home headed by sexual minority individuals (Mallon, 2006; Ryan, 2000). On the other hand, lesbian and gay prospective adoptive parents have reported less of a need for support or counseling groups for themselves. As Brooks et al. point out, this may have to do with different motivations for adoption (i.e., fewer infertility issues), as well as a reluctance to be "out" to other support group members, the majority of whom probably will be straight. Sexual minority preadoptive parents may also feel a sense of isolation and marginalization from other group members, who sometimes are perceived to be unsupportive of their efforts to adopt children.

Like families headed by heterosexuals, those with lesbian or gay parents at times will find themselves and their children in need of mental health services. This is especially true given the higher rates of adoption of children with special needs by sexual minority individuals. Unfortunately, many mental health professionals are inadequately trained about either adoption or LGBT issues. In their chapter, Goldberg and Gianino (this volume) explore some of the important issues in working clinically with lesbian and gay adoptive families, including helping clients confront their own internalized homophobia and their motivations for parenting and adoption. Both of these issues can be roadblocks for couples who are having difficulties deciding whether to adopt. Once a decision has been made to proceed, clinicians can help to guide their clients toward specific types of adoption or specific agencies.

For example, Goldberg and Gianino note that individuals or couples who strongly value openness and honesty in relation to being "out" with others may not be good candidates for international adoption because the policies and cultural traditions of most "sending" countries do not support the placement of children with nonheterosexual parents. On the other hand, these same individuals may be excellent candidates for open adoption placements because of their emphasis on openness and honesty in relation to their own sexual orientation.

Because sexual minority individuals often adopt children with special needs, including children with academic and psychological problems, clinicians can also be helpful in explaining the nature of the children's issues to parents; they can also offer support in developing specialized parenting skills (e.g., behavior management strategies and attachment facilitating child care strategies) that will allow the parents to address the challenges presented by their children. In addition, clinicians can be helpful in fostering appropriate racial socialization skills in lesbian and gay adoptive parents (Brodzinsky, 2008), which can be particularly beneficial as they are more likely to adopt across racial lines. And clinicians can be invaluable in supporting lesbian and gay adoptive parents during periods in which they are trying to help their children understand adoption and their parents' sexual orientation, as well as to cope with the homophobic reactions of others.

In summary, as the authors in this book point out, much has been learned about parenting and adoption by sexual minority individuals and couples over the past few decades. We know that lesbians and gay men are interested in parenting and often turn to adoption as a means of achieving their goal. We know this is happening more and more across the country (as well as in other Western countries), supported by most state laws and the willingness of the majority of adoption agencies to work with this group of individuals. In addition, we know that lesbians and gay men are just as nurturing and competent as their heterosexual peers and that their children show patterns of adjustment similar to the children of straight parents. Despite the support of most agencies for placing children with lesbians and gay men, we also know that there continues to be resistance among some adoption workers regarding this type of placement. Furthermore, even those who are supportive in principle often lack the sensitivity and competence to create a climate that is welcoming to sexual minority clients, thereby leading to a more difficult adoption process. Finally, we are beginning to understand some of the unique needs of lesbian and gay prospective adoptive parents in relation to the homestudy and adoption preparation process, as well as the types of supports they are likely to find most helpful after adopting. Nevertheless, we have a long way to go before we can comfortably say that best practices in this area are grounded in sufficient research on social casework and clinical practice.

WHAT WE STILL NEED TO KNOW ABOUT ADOPTION BY LESBIANS AND GAY MEN

There are many areas related to adoption by sexual minority individuals and couples about which we still have limited knowledge. To better serve the needs of these adoptive parents and their children, it is imperative that we continue to explore these issues, both in research and social casework practice, as well as through the legal and political processes.

Legal Issues

As several authors in this volume have reported, considerable legal roadblocks to adoption by lesbians and gays continue to exist in many states. Future efforts must be directed toward overcoming these impediments, not only in states such as Mississippi and Utah where there are prohibitions against adoption by same-sex or unmarried couples, but also in all those states that do not allow either joint or second-parent adoptions. Children who cannot be adopted by one of their same-sex parents are prevented from enjoying certain legal rights and protections that are connected to that adult, such as health insurance, Social Security benefits, and inheritance. More importantly, should the same-sex couple separate or divorce, their adopted children are not guaranteed access time with the nonadoptive (non-legal) parent, nor is the nonadoptive parent guaranteed the right of guardianship of the children should the legal parent die.

As Appell (this volume) has emphasized, the law governing adoption, including adoption by lesbians and gay men, is highly malleable and has been influenced by a wide range of forces in the past few decades. Although considerable success has been achieved in some states related to adoption by sexual minority individuals and couples (e.g., the recent overturning of the ban on such adoptions in Florida), there have also been setbacks such as in Arkansas, where voters passed a referendum banning adoption by unmarried couples—with lesbians and gay men clearly being the targets of the referendum. As previously noted, the ban on adoption by lesbians and gays recently was declared unconstitutional by state's supreme court.

Although significant efforts are being made to ensure that *all* suitable adults, including sexual minority individuals and couples, are able to adopt children (Howard & Freundlich, 2008), the best strategies for achieving this goal remain unclear. At the very least, legislators, judges, guardian *ad litems*, and adoption professionals need to be educated about the emerging research that is relevant to the subject. Hopefully, the data showing generally positive psychological adjustment of lesbian and gay parents and their children (see Patterson & Wainright, this volume; Gartrell et al., this volume)—comparable to that of heterosexual parents and their children—will be helpful in countering the lingering misconceptions and stereotypes that exist about sexual minority families. Furthermore, in light of the data reported by Brodzinsky et al. (2002) and Brodzinsky (this volume) showing that a significant minority of adoption workers either were wrong or unsure about the legal status of adoption by lesbians and gays in their respective states, it is imperative that such professionals receive ongoing, accurate information. This information also needs to be disseminated to the gay and lesbian communities so that they are better informed about legal changes in their states that could influence their efforts to adopt, including the adopted or biological children of their partners.

The value of clear, articulate, and rational analysis of social science data can be seen in the 2008 ruling by a Florida trial court declaring the state's adoption statute, which barred lesbian and gay adoption, to be unconstitutional. In affirming the lower court's decision, the Third District Court of Appeal cited the following conclusion of the trial judge: "the quality and breadth of research available, as well as the results of the studies performed about gay parenting and children of gay parents, is robust and has provided the basis for a consensus in the field. Many well renowned, regarded and respected professionals have [produced] methodologically sound longitudinal and cross-sectional studies into hundreds of reports. ... The studies and reports are published in many well respected peer reviewed journals... Each of the studies and hundreds of reports also withstood the rigorous peer review process and were tested statistically, rationally and methodologically by seasoned professionals prior to publication. In addition to the volume, the body of research is broad; comparing children raised by lesbian couples to children raised by married heterosexual couples; children raised by lesbian parents from birth to children raised by heterosexual married couples from birth; children raised by single homosexuals to children raised by single heterosexuals; and children adopted by homosexual parents to those raised by homosexual biological parents, to name a few. **These reports and studies find that there are no differences in the parenting of homosexuals or the adjustment of their children.** These conclusions have been accepted, adopted and ratified by the American Psychological Association, the American Psychiatry Association, the American Pediatric Association, the American Academy of Pediatrics, the Child Welfare League of America and the National Association of Social Workers. As a result, based on the robust nature of the evidence available in the field, **this Court is satisfied that the issue is so far beyond dispute that it would be irrational to hold otherwise;** the best interests of children are not preserved by prohibiting homosexual adoption." (Emphasis is in the original opinion; the full written opinion of the appellate court is available at www.3dca.flcourts.org/opinions/3D08-3044.pdf.)

Despite the persuasive value of social science data in the Florida ruling, it is clear that solid research findings alone will not be sufficient to bring about necessary changes in law and practice to remove the barriers to adoption by lesbians and gays. Appell (this volume) emphasizes that the law reflects, in part, the values of a community. Moreover, decision making by judges, guardian *ad litems*, and adoption caseworkers is also value driven. Given this reality, rational arguments, based upon social science information, are unlikely to be sufficiently persuasive for many people. One alternative approach, of course, is to emphasize fundamental values of American democracy, especially the concepts of fairness and equality.

Adoption is not a right, but a privilege. Heterosexual applicants are allowed to adopt children to the extent that they are judged suitable by the proper authorities. Along the same line, it is not that lesbians and gays should have a right to adopt, but rather a right to be assessed in the same way as heterosexual applicants. If found suitable using the same criteria, then it is only *fair* and *equitable* that they, too, be allowed to adopt.

It is most important to emphasize the "needs" of children rather than the "rights" of adults. As Howard and Freundlich (2008) point out, over 100,000 boys and girls in our country are legally free to be adopted, but continue to linger in foster care. Many of these children have significant medical, educational, and mental health needs—and more of them are waiting for permanent homes than there are applicants seeking to adopt them. These authors persuasively argue that by providing lesbians and gays with the same opportunity to adopt as their heterosexual peers, the number of waiting children entering into permanent placements will increase, and their emotional well-being and future prospects will be improved significantly.

Still another argument in favor of adoption by sexual minority individuals is offered by Gates et al. (2007). In assessing the relative costs of maintaining children in foster care versus placing them in permanent adoptive families, they note that states that do not support adoption by sexual minority families—such as Mississippi and Utah—incur higher foster care expenditures each year because of the need to recruit and train other foster parents who would be eligible to adopt the waiting children, as well as because some of these children will likely end up in group or institutional care, both of which are much more costly than family foster care.

In short, continued efforts are needed to remove the legal barriers to adoption by lesbians and gay men. Although reliance on social science data to settle arguments in support of this goal will be helpful, and ought to be determinative, advocates of this type of adoption will need to find additional ways of countering the values-based arguments of those who oppose it.

Psychological Research

To date, most research on sexual minority family life has compared the psychological adjustment of children raised by lesbians and gay men to those youngsters raised by heterosexual parents; it also has compared the parenting skills and relationship qualities of sexual minority individuals to their heterosexual counterparts. As noted previously, few differences have been found between these groups (Gartrell et al., this volume; Goldberg, 2010; Patterson & Wainright, this volume; Stacey & Biblarz, 2001). This has been true for both nonadoptive and adoptive families, although there are fewer outcome studies involving families headed by lesbian and gay adoptive parents.

To deepen our knowledge in this area, there is a need for more research on adoption by sexual minority individuals, including bisexual and transgender parents. However, future research should focus less on comparing LGBT adoptive families to heterosexual families and more on examining individual differences in the parent–child relationships and adjustment of children placed in sexual minority households. As with heterosexual adoptive families, individuals in sexual minority families show a wide range of adjustment patterns. Most children and parents do very well; however, there will always be a minority of family members who display adjustment difficulties and who require various types of professional intervention. To better serve these families, it is important to understand what individual, relational, familial, and contextual factors influence their short- and long-term adjustment. The development of longitudinal research with this group of adoptive families, as well as the use of large-scale national database samples, will be important in exploring these issues. Some of the more interesting questions that researchers might pursue include the following:

- Do differences in adoption motivation among sexual minority clients have an impact on parenting expectations, parenting practices, placement stability, and children's psychological and social outcomes?
- How do adoption motivation and parenting expectations have an impact on the transition to parenthood for lesbian and gay individuals?
- When and how do parents talk to their children about issues related to sexual orientation, and how does this process have an impact on children's adjustment?
- What individual, relational and contextual factors influence the way in which families discuss sexual orientation with their children?
- Does openness in communication about sexual orientation facilitate better adjustment in adopted children?
- Are parents who are more open in their communication about adoption also more open in their communication about sexual orientation?
- How do parents help their children develop appropriate coping strategies for managing homophobic teasing by peers and others?
- What contextual factors in extended families, communities, educational systems, religious groups, healthcare systems, and other social systems, beyond the immediate family, influence the adjustment of children adopted by lesbians and gay men?
- To what extent does adoptive parents' sexual orientation impact the creation and maintenance of open adoption arrangements with birth families?
- What adoption agency and caseworker practices support placement, adoptive parent functioning, and better child functioning over time in families of sexual minorities?

As research in this area expands, our ability to provide better preparation, education, and support services for this group of adoptive families will be enhanced, which undoubtedly will lead to greater placement success and improve the emotional well-being of all family members.

Social Casework Practice

There are many areas of social casework practice related to working with sexual minority adoption applicants that require additional scrutiny and research. As Brodzinsky (this volume) notes, even though approximately 60 percent of adoption agencies are willing to place children with lesbians and gay men, relatively few of these organizations specifically recruit sexual minority individuals as parenting resources for children. Future research needs to clarify the reasons for the low recruitment rate and determine the best methods for reaching out to these potential adoption applicants.

Mallon (2006, and this volume) also points out that agencies are highly variable in the ways they acknowledge the applicants' sexual orientation in the homestudy process, with some adoption workers ignoring the issue completely (i.e., utilizing a "don't ask, don't tell" approach) and, at the other extreme, others directly addressing the issue and encouraging their clients to be completely open in their self-descriptions. The short-term and long-term implications of these varying social casework practices are unclear, however. At the very least, failure to deal openly with the clients' sexual orientation could very well preclude the possibility of providing them with appropriate preadoptive preparation and education. For example, if social workers do not know that their clients are lesbian or gay, or choose to ignore this fact because of agency (or country of origin) policies prohibiting working with such individuals, it is unlikely that the prospective parents will receive the necessary guidance and training about how to handle some of the adoption and/or parenting issues that are unique to this group of individuals (e.g., talking with their children about the parents' sexual orientation, supporting children in response to the homophobic reactions of others, and helping older-placed children explore their own feelings and reactions to their parents' sexual orientation). Given that preadoption and postadoption preparation, education, and support are linked to adoption stability and adjustment for all family members (Brodzinsky, 2008), imore research and specific guidelines are needed regarding the way in which sexual orientation is handled in the adoption application and homestudy process.

Another area of social casework practice in need of further clarification is working with older children who are adopted by lesbian or gay parents. There is little written about the best ways to prepare them for such placements. In fact, we know of no published studies focusing on children's understanding of sexual orientation that could guide the preparation process. When considering placing older children with lesbian or gay parents, social workers need to consider what these boys and girls understand about sexual orientation, their attitudes about lesbians and gays, their experiences with homophobia, and their desire or willingness to grow up in such families. When resistance to such a placement is experienced, caseworkers also need to understand the best ways of addressing it. Answering these questions will require new research and further consideration of these social casework issues.

Although there are numerous studies on lesbian and gay parenting and adoption, as well as social casework literature focusing on working with these groups during and after placement, much less is known about the family lives of individuals who self-identify as bisexual or transgender (Biblarz & Savci, 2010). In fact, it is the latter group of individuals—those who are transgender—who appear to elicit the greatest confusion and discomfort from the non-LGBT community, including adoption professionals (Human Rights Campaign, 2009). Many transgender adults already have children in the context of previous heterosexual marriages; yet there is very little research on such families, and none of it is on transgender adoptive parents. Given the growing tendency of transgender people to be "out," it is very important that the professional community develop a better understanding of them and receive appropriate training to work with those who seek to adopt. This goal will require more research, including explorations of the special challenges facing such parents.

More research and clearer guidance are also needed regarding the postadoption needs of sexual minority adoptive families. As already noted, lesbian and gay individuals are more likely to adopt children across racial and ethnic lines, as well as children with special needs, than are heterosexual individuals (Brodzinsky, this volume; Brooks et al., this volume; Farr & Patterson, 2009; Gates et al., 2007; Goldberg, 2010; Ryan & Brown, this volume). Both types of adoption require a wide range of supports and services to ensure placement success and children's long-term emotional well-being. Future research needs to focus on the best ways of providing such supports to lesbian and gay adoptive families, as well as on ways of maximizing the strengths of these families to support children's adjustment (see Smith, 2010 for a general discussion of the importance of postadoption services for all families).

Of course, the provision of appropriate postadoption services is only as good as the competence and sensitivity of those providing it. As numerous authors in this volume have noted, many adoption professionals and mental health professionals lack the necessary training, including self-assessment regarding homophobic and heterosexist attitudes, upon which knowledgeable, respectful, and LGBT-affirmative services rest. Future research needs to assess the training requirements of preadoption and postadoption professionals who work with sexual minority adoptive families, and appropriate training models must be developed to help them become "culturally competent" to work with this group of parents and children. As a starting point, the reader is referred to the training materials offered by the Human Rights Campaign (www.hrc.org/acaf).

In sum, although sexual minority individuals are increasingly seeking to adopt children, and more and more agencies are amenable to working with them, important areas of social casework practice remain about which we know too little from a scientific standpoint. Future research and social casework literature must address these and other relevant issues.

CREATING LGBT-AFFIRMATIVE ADOPTION
SERVICES: WHAT WE OUGHT TO DO

In this final section, we review what we consider to be "best practices" for adoption and foster care agencies working with LGBT parents.[5] The guidelines below draw heavily on the careful research and comprehensive description of "best practices" developed by the Human Rights Campaign (2009) and on previous policy analyses and research conducted by the Evan B. Donaldson Adoption Institute in New York City, with which the co-editors of the current volume are associated (Brodzinsky, 2003; Howard, 2006; Howard & Freundlich, 2008), as well as the analyses and recommendations of Mallon (2006). We strongly recommend that adoption professionals consult these primary sources for more detailed descriptions of best practices.

Legal Advocacy

Adoption agency policies and practices derive, in part, from the legal standards of the states in which they operate and, in the case of international adoption, from the laws and regulations of the adopted children's birth countries, as well as U.S. federal law and an international treaty (the Hague Convention on Intercountry Adoption). As noted previously, in the United States and many other nations, there remain significant barriers to adoption by lesbian and gay couples, such as those in Mississippi and Utah. Furthermore, numerous states continue to prohibit joint and/or second-parent adoptions (see Appell, this volume). When a lesbian or gay parent cannot legally adopt a partner's child, not only is the child deprived of various rights related to the nonadoptive parent (e.g., Social Security benefits insurance, and healthcare), but the parent–child relationship itself can be jeopardized if the couple decides to divorce or separate. To support the integrity of sexual minority adoptive families, including the emotional well-being of their children, we must do everything possible to ensure that all legal barriers to adoption by LGBT individuals and couples are removed. We also must begin to educate the authorities in other countries about lesbian and gay parenting and family life—including the strengths that sexual minority individuals and couples bring to the task of raising children—in an effort to make progress in shaping LGBT-affirmative laws, regulations, and policies related to adoption.

LGBT-Affirmative Leadership and Agency Policies

Adoption agencies and organizations that hope to provide a welcoming atmosphere for potential LGBT parents should have specific policies in place that delineate a standard of service to this community. Although social workers have the most direct contact with clients, all staff members need to support the agency's mission to provide services to diverse parents.

The creation of a welcoming atmosphere begins with the agency's Board of Directors, which delineates the organization's mission, sets the tone for affirmative policies, and provides broad guidance to the Executive Director and the staff about the execution of the agency's mission. It is the Executive Director, however, along with supporting personnel who have the immediate responsibility of translating the agency's mission into actionable policies and practices. This process begins with ensuring that all directors and staff members are knowledgeable about relevant research regarding adoption by sexual minority individuals and couples. Moreover, it is the responsibility of the managing directors and supervisors to ensure that all staff members working directly with prospective LGBT adoptive parents are competent in this area. Recruiting appropriate individuals from the LGBT community to serve on the Board of Directors, as well as on staff, not only provides an "in-house" voice for the community that the agency serves, but also increases the likelihood of creating a welcoming and supportive atmosphere for prospective sexual minority adoption applicants.

In addition to the presence of competent personnel, the policies of an adoption organization need to explicitly state that LGBT parents are welcomed and will be treated fairly. Agency mission statements should include language about providing services and placements to families regardless of marital status, sexual orientation, gender identity, or gender expression. The same language should appear in nondiscrimination policies as well. These policies should avoid vague language and should use only appropriate terms to refer to specific populations. When members of the LGBT community are not mentioned specifically in mission statements and organizational policies, such clients may assume they will not be welcome.

Recruitment and Hiring of LGBT-Affirmative Staff

Agencies that hope to recruit LGBT families should expect to hire LGBT and LGBT-affirmative staff members who have knowledge of the community and can make prospective parents feel more comfortable throughout the adoption or foster care process. Equal benefit plans, such as health insurance for domestic partners, should be available for all staff members irrespective of their sexual orientation. Also, Equal Employment Opportunity Policies should state that all employees, regardless of gender identity, gender expression, or sexual orientation, will be treated equally. Agencies or organizations that expect to provide services to LGBT families should have staff members who reflect the community. A staff that consists solely of heterosexuals could be threatening—or at least not welcoming—to LGBT individuals who are anxious about starting the adoption process and/or are unaware of their own rights.

It should not be expected that all potential LGBT parents should or would prefer to work with gay or lesbian staff members. Therefore, it is the responsibility of the organization to provide training to and ensure the competence of all staff members who work with such parents. There should also be a process for gay and lesbian prospective parents to provide feedback on staff members' actions, as well as on agency policies and practices before, during, and after adoption so that the organization can learn what does and does not work well, and thereby obtain the information necessary for providing a higher quality of service.

Staff Education and Training

Staff training is essential in the process of creating an LGBT-affirmative organization. All personnel, regardless of the amount of time they have been on the job, must be competent in providing services to every client; therefore, every agency should develop a training curriculum that reflects its policies and any state laws that are relevant to the LGBT community. In addition, trainings should focus on utilizing appropriate language and terms that are preferred by clients, teaching personnel how to evaluate their own biases, and dispelling myths they may hold about the suitability of LGBT individuals to become parents.

An overarching goal of the trainings should be to end the too-frequent assumption that potential parents will (or should) be heterosexual. Such a "climate change" within the agency should begin with receptionists who take initial calls and continue throughout each department of the organization. Staff members should be exposed to the latest research relevant to LGBT parents and learn basic skills to provide affirmative services. Core changes, such as updating intake forms to say "parent one" and "parent two," instead of father and mother, are a major step toward a new, affirmative atmosphere. Staff members should also understand how the world reacts to LGBT families and learn how to explain relevant issues to children in an age-appropriate manner. Once again, the reader is referred to the Human Rights Campaign's training program at www.hrc.org/acaf.

Recruitment of Adoptive Parents

To recruit LGBT adoptive parents, agencies should work with their community and build relationships with germane organizations. Before an agency creates an outreach program, it should assess the adequacy of the staff and resources to work effectively with LGBT groups. This is another way in which having gay and lesbian personnel can be extremely helpful during the recruitment process. Agencies can also reach the sexual minority community through LGBT Pride events, as well as listservs, publications, and websites. LGBT individuals will be much more likely to work with agencies that actively recruit them and show that they have the competence to work with their families. Some individuals may even be surprised that they have the option to adopt if they were unaware of the realities of their state laws.

Organizations should seek help and input from the LGBT community to ensure that their recruitment methods are appropriate and acceptable within the community. To do so, agencies can form alliances with LGBT organizations that have already gained the trust of their communities. Once these individuals come to the agency, it is important to work collaboratively and build upon individual relationships as well. By continuing to support LGBT families even after adoptions are finalized, agencies can increase the likelihood that they will express their satisfaction to other members of their community, thereby creating more referrals.

Creating a Welcoming Agency Atmosphere

Agencies that want to demonstrate that they are welcoming to LGBT applicants should illustrate that fact in brochures, advertisements, and other media released to the public. Internally, paperwork, pictures in the workplace and waiting room, and other office items should reflect the diversity of families served, including those headed by sexual minority individuals. LGBT parents can be sensitive to signs that they are not welcome, so extra efforts should be taken to make them feel valued and respected. Relevant laws and policies regarding LGBT parents and families should be easily accessible through agency websites and other materials. LGBT representation in agencies can provide potential parents with a model to which they can relate. It is also necessary to realize that LGB competency does not equate to transgender competency. Therefore, agencies that work with transgender people should ensure that all their staff members receive the appropriate training to do so.

LGBT prospective adoptive parents, like their straight counterparts, generally are required to attend multiple classes and seminars during the preadoption process—and are encouraged to do so after adoption as well. Professionals speaking at these sessions, especially if they are consultants and not staff members, should be aware of the agency's policies and practices related to adoption by sexual minority people, and should have the competence to address specific LGBT concerns and issues. The majority of people who attend these educational sessions are heterosexual, so LGBT individuals may feel excluded and devalued if they remain invisible and their unique circumstances go unmentioned. Training sessions that are hosted by agencies should be consciously structured to be inclusive of LGBT parents and introduce issues that are relevant to their families.

Conducting the Homestudy and Family Assessment

Staff members who conduct homestudies should be aware of appropriate LGBT language, respectful of all kinds of families, and knowledgeable about applicable local, state, and federal laws, as well as local school systems' attitudes and policies. Professionals who conduct homestudies should be prepared to ask potential LGBT parents only questions that are relevant to the placement of a child; questions about various aspects of the parents' sexual orientation should not be predominant, nor should such questions be avoided altogether if they seem relevant to a placement decision (see Mallon, this volume; Mallon, 2006). In any case, potential parents deserve to know the types and purposes of the questions they will be asked related to sexual orientation during the homestudy phase of the adoption process.

Potential LGBT parents should be asked about where they are in the coming out process, the level of their families' acceptance, how they plan to deal with homophobia and discrimination, and relevant legal issues that they must address. Questions about dating and relationships should not be any different than those asked of heterosexual clients. In states in which only one unmarried person can adopt, the prospective parents should still be treated and evaluated as a couple, and not as simply roommates. Social workers should inform potential parents about all of the involved parties who may play a role in the final adoption decision and be prepared to help potential parents—gay or straight—deal with the possibility of rejection.

Placement Decisions

Agencies have the responsibility to provide services and support to all families throughout the placement process. Many potential LGBT parents do not realize that an adoption can take a year or longer to complete. Staff members should communicate with these families regularly to remind them that they are still working to find them a placement.

As placements are made, agency staff should evaluate the variety of children who are adopted by LGBT parents. Research suggests that a larger proportion of more challenging children is placed in LGBT households as compared to heterosexual households (Brodzinsky, this volume; Brooks et al., this volume; Brooks & Goldberg, 2001; Matthews & Cramer, 2006; Ryan & Brown, this volume). Agencies need to ensure that this pattern does not reflect a bias on the part of staff about matching sexual minority individuals with "harder to place" children (Kenyon, Chong, Enkoff-Sage, Hill, Mays, & Rochelle, 2003). One way of preventing this from occurring is to ensure that placement decisions are never made by a single individual, but are reviewed by the caseworker's supervisor and others.

Before a placement is finalized, staff members should discuss LGBT issues with the preadoptive child in an age-appropriate manner. Older children who are part of the placement decision should receive information about possible LGBT families. In the same way, birth parents should be informed about all possible options for their children. Placement decisions should always be made in the child's best interest, and staff members should be prepared to support LGBT foster parents if and when birth parents challenge such placements.

Agencies also have the responsibility to alert prospective parents about who they will share their personal information with throughout the adoption process. That is necessary because some of these individuals may be selectively closeted in aspects of their lives in which they feel it is unsafe to reveal their sexual orientation. In cases in which problems arise, LGBT parents need to be informed in advance about who in the agency handles grievances.

Adoption Finalization

Before an adoption is finalized, agencies should review all of the previous steps, acknowledge existing laws, and work with LGBT families to complete the process. Although it should be common knowledge from the beginning, all parties involved need to know before the final stages if the adoption will be completed by one or both parents. Social workers also need to ensure that any resistance on the part of an older child about placement in an LGBT family has been resolved prior to appearing before the judge for adoption finalization.

Postadoption Services and Support

Because adoption is a lifelong experience (Brodzinsky, Schechter, & Henig, 1992), LGBT adoptive families, like those headed by heterosexual parents, will periodically require support in the years following the finalization of the adoption (see Goldberg, 2010; Goldberg & Gianino, this volume). Agencies and other professionals who facilitate adoptive placements have an ethical responsibility to ensure that they continue to support those placements in the postadoption period (Brodzinsky, 2008). When they cannot provide those services themselves—because of insufficient staff and resources or limited expertise—they have the responsibility to ensure that their clients are aware of appropriate and available postadoption resources in the community. For families headed by sexual minority parents, this means working with professionals who are aware not only of adoption issues (e.g., talking with children about adoption) but also of LGBT issues (e.g., talking with children about parental sexual orientation and helping them cope with the homophobic comments of others).

Because many families never return to their original adoption agency for post-adoption counseling and support, adoption agencies need to ensure that their staff members are aware of appropriate adoption and LBGT-affirmative referral sources in the community, and provide information about them to their clients prior to the finalization of the adoption. When agencies partner with existing LGBT family-oriented organizations, they are much more likely to be aware of community professional resources that other LGBT families have used and found helpful. This knowledge will result in more effective referrals for their LGBT clients.

CONCLUSIONS

As sexual minority individuals have come out of the closet and more openly assumed parenting roles—both biological and adoptive—the professional research and social service communities have sought to better understand their needs and provide the services and supports to meet them. Tremendous changes in LGBT family life have occurred during the past few decades, including huge growth in the use of adoption as a means by which sexual minority individuals have sought to become parents (Gates et al., 2007). Moreover, research suggests that they are doing so in escalating numbers, supported by changes in law and the affirmative findings of social science research, as well as by the supportive endorsements of almost every major professional organization in medicine, psychiatry, psychology, law, and social work. In the end, of course, it is the children who benefit from this enlightened evolution in family life, as they are the recipients of the stability, commitment, love, and nurturance provided by their parents. Ultimately, this is what adoption is all about: ensuring that all girls and boys who need new families will find ones in which they can thrive and grow up happy and healthy. When sexual minority parents join their heterosexual counterparts in providing those families, children reap the benefits—as does all of society.

Notes

1. Comparable data and comparisons were not available for gay and heterosexual men.
2. Although sexual minority individuals also include those who are bisexual and transgender, there is very little research on parenting by these individuals or on how adoption agencies work with them.
3. On April 7, 2011, the Arkansas supreme court declared the state's law banning adoption by lesbians and gays to be unconstitutional.
4. Until recently, Florida had a ban on all adoptions by lesbians and gay men. The ban was declared unconstitutional in a trial court decision in 2008 and the Third District Court of Appeal upheld the ruling (*FL. Department of Children and Families v. In the Matter of Adoption of X.X.G. and N.R.G.*, 2010, No. 3D08–3044, 2010 WL 3655782). At this time, the Attorney General of Florida has declined to challenge the appellate court ruling.
5. Although there is little research, or even social casework literature, on bisexual and transgender parents, we include them here because of the importance of developing "best practices" for all sexual minority individuals and couples; see the Human Rights Campaign (2009) for important first steps in this area.

References

ABC News (2002). *More Americans support gay adoption*. ABCNews.com telephone survey, March 27–31, 2002. Available from www.abcnews.go.com/sections/us/dailynews/gayadopt_poll020402.html.

Associated Press/David Crary. (September 14, 2010). Who's a family? New study tracks shifting US views [retrieved 09.15.10 from http://www.google.com/hostednews/ap/article/ALeqM5j96YLum-LHJDA5DT1skwQ8CR2zngD9I84AAO1].

Biblarz, T. J., & Savci, E. (2010). Lesbian, gay, bisexual, and transgender families. *Journal of Marriage and Family, 72*, 480–497.

Brodzinsky, D. (2003). *Adoption by gays and lesbians: A national survey of agency policies, practices and attitudes*. New York: Evan B. Donaldson Adoption Institute. Available online at www.adoptioninstitute.org.

Brodzinsky, D. (2008). *Adoptive Parent Preparation Project. Phase 1: Meeting the mental health and developmental needs of adopted children. Final policy and practice report.* New York: Evan B. Donaldson Adoption Institute. Available online at www. adoptioninstitute. org.

Brodzinsky, D., Patterson, C., & Vaziri, M. (2002). Adoption agency perspectives on lesbian and gay prospective parents: A national study. *Adoption Quarterly, 5,* 5–23.

Brodzinsky, D. M., Schechter, M. D., & Henig, R. M. (1992). *Being adopted: The lifelong search for self.* New York: Doubleday.

Brooks, D., & Goldberg, S. (2001). Gay and lesbian adoptive and foster care placements: Can they meet the needs of waiting children? *Social Work, 46,* 147–158.

D'Augelli, A. R., Grossman, A. H., & Rendina, J. (May 23, 2006). *Lesbian, gay, and bisexual youth: Marriage and child-rearing aspirations.* Paper presented at the Family Pride Academic Symposium, University of Pennsylvania, Philadelphia.

D'Augelli, A. R., Rendina, H. J., Sinclair, K. O., & Grossman, A. H. (2006/2007). Lesbian and gay youths' aspirations for marriage and raising children. *Journal of LGBT Issues in Counseling, 1,* 77–98.

Erich, S., Kanenberg, H., Case, K., Allen, T., & Bogdanes, T. (2009). An empirical analysis of factors affecting adolescent attachment in adoptive families with homosexual and straight parents. *Children and Youth Services Review, 31,* 398–404.

Erich, S., Leung, P., & Kindle, P. (2005). A comparative analysis of adoptive family functioning with gay, lesbian, and heterosexual parents and their children. *Journal of GLBT Family Studies, 1,* 43–60.

Erich, S., Leung, P., Kindle, P., & Carter, S. (2005). Gay and lesbian adoptive families: An exploratory study of family functioning, adoptive child's behavior, and familial support networks. *Journal of Family Social Work, 9,* 17–32.

Farr, R. H., Forssell, S. L., & Patterson, C. J. (2010a). Parenting and child development in adoptive families: Does parental sexual orientation matter? *Applied Developmental Science, 14,* 164–178.

Farr, R. H., Forssell, S. L., & Patterson, C. J. (2010b). Gay, lesbian, and heterosexual adoptive parents: Couple and relationship issues. *Journal of GLBT Family Studies, 6,* 199–213.

Farr, R. H., & Patterson, C. J. (2009). Transracial adoption by lesbian, gay, and heterosexual couples: Who completes transracial adoptions and with what results? *Adoption Quarterly, 12,* 187–204.

Florida Department of Children and Families v. In the Matter of Adoption of X.X.G. and N.R.G., No. 3D08–3044, 2010 WL 3655782 (Fla. Dist. Ct. App., Sept 22, 2010).

Gates, G. J., Badgett, M. V., Macomber, J. E., & Chambers, K. (2007). Adoption and foster care by gay and lesbian parents in the United States. Technical report issued jointly by the Williams Institute (Los Angeles, CA) and the Urban Institute (Washington, D.C.).

Goldberg, A. E. (2009). Lesbian and heterosexual preadoptive couples' openness to transracial adoption. *American Journal of Orthopsychiatry, 79,* 103–117.

Goldberg, A. E. (2010). *Lesbian and gay parents and their children: Research on the family life cycle.* Washington, D.C.: American Psychological Association.

Goldberg, A. E., & Smith, J. (2009). Perceived parenting skill across the transition to adoptive parenthood among lesbian, gay, and heterosexual couples. *Journal of Family Psychology, 23,* 861–870.

Howard, J. (2006). *Expanding resources for children: Is adoption by gays and lesbians part of the answer for boys and girls who need homes?* New York: Evan B. Donaldson Adoption Institute. Available online at www.adoptioninstitute.org.

Howard, J., & Freundlich, M. (2008). *Expanding resources for waiting children II: Eliminating legal and practice barriers to gay and lesbian adoption from foster care.* New York: Evan B. Donaldson Adoption Institute. Available at www. adoptioninstitute.org.

Human Rights Campaign. (2009). *Promising practices in adoption and foster care: A comprehensive guide to policies and practices that welcome, affirm, and support lesbian, gay, bisexual and transgender foster and adoptive parents.* Washington, D.C.: Human Rights Campaign All Children–All Families Initiative.

Kenyon, G. L., Chong, K., Enkoff-Sage, M., Hill, C., Mays, C., & Rochelle, L. (2003). Public adoptions by gay and lesbian parents in North Carolina: Policy and practice. *Families in Society, 84,* 571–575.

Mallon, G. P. (2006). *Lesbian and gay foster and adoptive parents: Recruiting, assessing, and supporting an untapped resource for children and youth.* Washington, D.C.: Child Welfare League of America.

Matthews, J. D., & Cramer, E. P. (2006). Envisaging the adoption process to strengthen gay- and lesbian-headed families: Recommendations for adoption professionals. *Child Welfare, LXXXV,* 317–340.

Miall, C. E., & March, K. (2005). Social support for changes in adoption practice: Gay adoption, open adoption, birth reunions, and the release of confidential identifying information. *Families in Society: The Journal of Contemporary Social Services, 86,* 83–92.

Powell, B., Bolzendahl, C., Geist, C., & Steelman, L. C. (2010). *Counted out: Same-sex relations and Americans' definitions of family.* New York: Russell Sage Foundation.

Ryan, S. D. (2000). Examining social workers' placement recommendations of children with gay and lesbian adoptive parents. *Families in Society, 81,* 517–528.

Schwartz, J. (2010). Investigating differences in public support for gay rights issues. *Journal of Homosexuality, 57,* 748–759.

Smith, S. (2010). *Keeping the promise: The critical need for post-adoption services to enable children and their families to succeed.* New York: Evan B. Donaldson Adoption Institute. Available online at www.adoptioninstitute.org.

Stacey, J., & Biblarz, T. (2001). (How) does the sexual orientation of parents matter? *American Sociological Review, 66,* 159–183.

and mother-child bonding, 117–118
motives for adopting, 36, 64, 107,
    206–209
outcomes for children, 15–16, 25–28,
    64, 85–108, 112–113, 119–125,
    141–142, 151, 154, 205–206, 235,
    240–241
professional organizations position
    statements about, 87, 112, 184
relationship characteristics and
    stability related to, 118–119,
    122–123, 139–140, 176
and semen donor selection, 115–116
societal attitudes about, 205, 233
statistics related to, 63–64, 113,
    205, 233
support from family and others,
    116–117, 138, 154, 176, 206, 211
related to talking with children
    about sexual orientation, 81, 140,
    238, 243
use of physical punishment, 123
values related to, 115, 124
Gender roles and gay/lesbians, 15,
    115–116, 121

Heterosexism
    impact on family experiences, 205,
    221
    and internalized homophobia, 205
Homestudy, 76, 80, 130–144, 215, 243,
    248–249
    anticipating concerns and problems,
    142
    related to client comfort with sexual
        orientation, 137–139
    decision making, 143–144
    first contact with gay/lesbian clients,
        132–133
    issues to address in, 137–144
    mistakes to avoid, 142–143
    motives for adopting, 140–141,
        237–238
    preparing children for prejudice,
        141–142, 243
    related to sexual orientation issues,
        76, 131–144, 236–237, 243–244,
        248–249

with same-gender couples,
    135–137, 236
with single gay/lesbian clients,
    134–135, 140
social worker attitudes about
    sexuality and sexual orientation,
    131–132, 137, 139, 142, 144, 236,
    243
types of, 134–137
use of training groups, 133
Homophobia, 63, 80, 120–122, 125,
    133, 138, 154, 187, 236
children's reactions to, 120–122,
    124, 243
internalized homophobia in LGBT
    individuals, 124, 238
preparing children for, 120–121, 220,
    238, 243
Homosexual agenda, 22–23
Homosexuality
    decriminalization of, 22–23, 87
    professional attitudes and biases
        about, 31
    related to removal from list of
        mental disorders, 82, 87
    society attitudes about, 14
Human Rights Campaign, 31, 77,
    79, 82, 108, 146, 228, 235,
    244–245, 251

Illegitimacy, stigma related to, 21–22
Independent adoption, 77, 80, 160
Infertility, 214, 237
    impact on adoption issues, 207
Institutional care, 4–6, 224
    impact on children, 5, 30,
        154, 224
Intercountry adoption (see
    international adoption)
Internalized homophobia, 124, 205–206
International adoption, 11
    by gay/lesbian individuals, 33, 71, 73,
        75, 78, 160, 209–210, 216, 235, 238
    opponents of, 11
    and second parent adoption, 209

Justice Action Center, New York Law
    School, viii